Critical Essays on
Lillian Hellman

Critical Essays on
Lillian Hellman

Mark W. Estrin

G. K. Hall & Co. ● Boston, Massachusetts

Library of Congress Cataloging-in-Publication Data

Critical essays on Lillian Hellman / [edited by] Mark W. Estrin.
    p.   cm.—(Critical essays on American literature)
  Includes index.
  ISBN 0-8161-8890-4 (alk. paper)
  1. Hellman, Lillian, 1905–1984—Criticism and interpretation.
I. Estrin, Mark W. II. Series.
  PS3515.E343Z628 1989
  812′.52—dc19

89-30985
CIP

This publication is printed on permanent/durable acid-free paper
MANUFACTURED IN THE UNITED STATES OF AMERICA

61881

CRITICAL ESSAYS ON AMERICAN LITERATURE

This series seeks to anthologize the most important criticism on a wide variety of topics and writers in American literature. Our readers will find in various volumes not only a generous selection of reprinted articles and reviews but original essays, bibliographies, manuscript sections, and other materials brought to public attention for the first time. *Critical Essays on Lillian Hellman* contains the most comprehensive collection of scholarship ever assembled on this controversial and important writer. The volume contains twenty-three essays that explore the "Hellman persona" as well as her plays and memoirs. Among the authors of reprinted articles are John Hersey, Pauline Kael, Robert Brustein, Martha Gellhorn, Alfred Kazin, and Linda Wagner-Martin. In addition to an extensive introduction by Mark W. Estrin that surveys both Hellman's career and critical reactions to it, there are also, commissioned specifically for this volume, five new studies by Jacob H. Adler, Doris Fleischer and Leonard Fleischer, Timothy J. Wiles, Pamela S. Bromberg, and Timothy Dow Adams. We are confident that this book will make a permanent and significant contribution to American literary study.

JAMES NAGEL, GENERAL EDITOR

Northeastern University

Once more, to Barbara and Robin
and to my parents
Clara and Abe Estrin

CONTENTS

Contents

INTRODUCTION

For much of her life, Lillian Hellman's prominence as a controversial figure in American letters (and, not inconsequentially, an American *woman* of letters at that) threatened to overwhelm her public's ability to respond objectively to her diverse gifts as a writer. By the time she died at age seventy-nine on 30 June 1984, exactly fifty years after her first encounter with notoriety and following numerous swings of the critical pendulum, her life and art appeared to have merged completely. Hellman seemed to many to have become the heroine—or, persuasively, to others, the villain—of her own story through a process now implicitly demanding that the woman and her writing be attacked or defended as one.

On the assumption that the woman and her writing should be judged apart, *Critical Essays on Lillian Hellman* seeks to reseparate the two, even as a portion of its contents must acknowledge that the Hellman persona invited controversy, which, by the last decade of her life, alternated between such extremes of praise and vituperation that virtually everything printed about her work led to a discussion of Hellman herself as well.[1] Even for a society that enjoys first mythologizing, then devouring its larger than life public figures, the personalization of Hellman criticism in (and beyond) the last years of her life is perhaps unrivaled for an American writer in recent memory.[2]

Hellman frequently maintained that she grew to detest the theater, enjoyed only the solitary writing of a play, and functioned badly in pre-Broadway opening atmospheres of collaboration, revision, and perpetual crisis.[3] Her diverse writing interests were evident throughout her theater and Hollywood screenwriting period in the newspaper and magazine reports she published on a broad range of social and political issues, including articles on the Spanish Civil War[4] and the Soviet army in wartime.[5] In the prememoir years she edited and wrote introductions for *The Selected Letters of Anton Chekhov* (1955)[6] and *The Big Knockover: Selected Stories and Short Novels by Dashiell Hammett* (1966).[7] Before her first play, *The Children's Hour,* opened on Broadway, she reviewed for the *New York Herald Tribune* and published two short stories, "I Call Her Mama Now" and "Perberty [sic] in Los Angeles."[8]

But for thirty-two years Lillian Hellman was associated essentially with dramatic writing and it is upon that writing that her reputation originally and deservedly rests. In addition to eight original plays and four adaptations for Broadway (1934–63), she wrote seven screenplays (1935–46), resuming briefly with an eighth and final film, *The Chase*, in 1966.[9] She directed three Broadway productions of her work (*Another Part of the Forest, Montserrat* and the 1952 Broadway revival of *The Children's Hour*), and in her plays and memoirs she provided the source material for another five films and an opera adapted by others.[10]

With the publication of *An Unfinished Woman* in 1969, Hellman shifted her writing mode entirely, initiating a series of memoirs that brought the renewed acclaim and renewed controversy that kept her in the public eye until her death fifteen years later. Remarkably, she never returned to dramatic writing and, despite continuing revival of her plays, it is startling to discover that among younger generations of readers she is known almost exclusively as a writer of autobiography. In England, where her memoirs are readily available in Penguin paperbacks, her plays are at this writing out of print.

THE PLAYS

A review of the half century of Hellman criticism reveals that from the beginning the focus of attention was often directed away from the text, toward extradramatic discord. Initial coverage of *The Children's Hour* centered on Hellman's introduction of the taboo (for 1934) subject of lesbianism, and on censorship attempts preceding and following the Broadway opening.[11] Stories concerning the play's later failure to win the Pulitzer Prize for American drama[12] blamed (no doubt accurately) its alleged sexual content, without ever suggesting that lesbianism functions only as a diversionary plot device to dramatize *The Children's Hour*'s real subject: the incalculably destructive power of gossip. A brief outcry claimed, moreover, that Hellman had failed to extend sufficient credit to the play's plot source: a Scottish scandal known as "The Great Drumsheugh Case," reported by William Roughhead in a book entitled *Bad Companions*.[13] More damaging and explicit charges of dishonesty regarding sections of Hellman's memoirs would erupt near the end of her life and linger after her death.

The controversies surrounding *The Children's Hour* thus deflected much of the critical attention that more properly should have been addressed to the play itself, one of the most compelling works to emerge from the serious American theater before Blanche DuBois and Willy Loman arrived on Broadway in the late 1940s. The fact that the playwright was a woman, one who would clearly not be content with the dramatic fluff of, say, a Rachel Crothers, also became appropriate theatrical grist for the critical mill (though it must be acknowledged that the hoopla surrounding her Broadway debut almost certainly contributed to the play's financial success and to Hellman's instant appeal at age twenty-nine as good newspaper copy).

By 1941 the powerful critic George Jean Nathan (who had earlier praised *The Children's Hour*) could no longer disguise his resentment of Hellman's gender. In an essay entitled "Playwrights in Petticoats," he wrote that Hellman's "latest play, *Watch on the Rhine*, proves two things. It proves again that Lillian Hellman is the best of our American woman playwrights and it proves that even the best of our American woman playwrights falls immeasurably short of the mark of our best masculine."[14] Throughout her career as a dramatist, Hellman bristled at the "woman playwright" label and, much later, often to the chagrin of those who so embraced them, she would vehemently deny that her memoirs certified her as a feminist. ("I don't like labels and isms," she told John Phillips and Anne Hollander in a 1964 *Paris Review* interview reprinted in this volume. "They are for people who raise or lower skirts because that's the thing you do for this year."[15])

In other central respects Lillian Hellman's critical reputation is curious. Her fame rests originally upon her eight original plays, written along with four dramatic adaptations between 1934 and 1963. Yet, although those works include two of the most enduring plays in the American theater (*The Little Foxes* and *The Children's Hour*), her drama with rare exception has failed to attract the kind of detailed, scholarly analysis that it deserves. The "woman playwright" and "feminist" labels to which I have already alluded were matched over the years with equally biased simplifications of her dramaturgical methods as excessively "well-made" and "melodramatic" or, contradictorily, as not "well-made" or "melodramatic" enough when (as in *The Autumn Garden, Toys in the Attic*, and all four of her adaptations) she experimented with dramatic form.

The essays that comprise the "Plays" section of this volume seek to reinterpret the dramatic canon in response to glib canards perpetuated by critics who misread Hellman's thematic interests, dramatic sources and methods, and true generic home in the theater. She arrived on the American stage two decades before absurdist playwrights began effectively and for all time to render unfashionable the taut dramatic structures American playwrights had inherited from the well-made tradition, one with which Hellman was immediately (and uncritically) identified.

In certain respects Hellman does, in fact, depend upon conventions of the well-made play. But few critics bother to notice how frequently she stands them on their collective head, or uses them to lure the audience into confrontation with unpleasant truths. Hellman developed a craft of playwriting to tell rattling good stories suspensefully, initially in the manner of Ibsenite social realism, where plot functions as the diversionary avenue by which the dramatist attacks particular contemporary issues. As she freely acknowledges in the important *Paris Review* interview, Hellman often relies upon what she calls "tricks" of the theatre—strong curtains, overheard conversations, the employment of blackmail and such props as Horace's bottle of medicine and safety deposit box in *The Little Foxes*—to propel dramatic action. These devices and other dramatic coincidences (for example, the convenient proximity of Teck de Brancovis to the Farrelly home in *Watch on the Rhine*) do periodically test credulity on the printed page, though much less obviously in a well-directed production.

In "The Dramaturgy of Blackmail in the Ibsenite Hellman," one of three original essays in the "Plays" section of this volume, Jacob H. Adler isolates one of those theatrical "tricks" to illustrate Hellman's debt to Ibsen. But by examining Hellman's uses of blackmail in philosophical, thematic, and structural terms, Adler shows how she also departs from Ibsen by linking blackmail to notions of money and power that define her major theatrical preoccupations. Adler's companion piece, "Miss Hellman's Two Sisters," identifies the explicitly Chekhovian, anti-well-made source in *Toys in the Attic* (1960), an influence that first appeared to take center stage in Hellman's work in *The Autumn Garden* (1951). (See also Marvin Felheim's "*The Autumn Garden*: Mechanics and Dialectics," reprinted in this volume.)

Often perceived as conflicting or sequential influences in Hellman's plays, the Ibsenite and Chekhovian strains were always complementary to her work and coexist much earlier than most critics have perceived. The automatic equation of Ibsenite dramaturgy with well-made rigidity makes no more sense than the glib association of Chekhovian playwriting with a totally unstructured dramatic style. Yet critics repeatedly fall prey to such distinctions in their evaluation of Hellman's drama.[16] *The Autumn Garden*'s multiple character analysis and novelistic structure in fact pinpoint Chekhovian antecedents evident in *Watch on the Rhine* (1941), *The Searching Wind* (1944), and *Another Part of the Forest* (1946), where leisurely discursiveness resembling Jamesian (*Watch on the Rhine*) or Jonsonian (*Forest*) comedies of manners alternates with tight dramaturgy. The leap from Ibsen to Chekhov discerned by *Autumn Garden* commentators was merely a slight jump.

Consider, too, some of the ways in which what actually happens in Hellman's plays frequently contradicts the claim that she is bound by the rigid plot demands of the well-made play. In a well-made play, every dramatic hair is combed into place; every character's fate accounted for; every "casual" reference in act 1 integrated importantly into plot developments by act 3. In a well-made play, even a minor character who departs the stage muttering "See you later" almost certainly means it and will reappear for vital purpose by play's end. While her memoirs were later to draw critical praise for their generic ambiguity and stylistic elusiveness, critics persisted in categorizing Hellman's pre–*Autumn Garden* plays as taut exercises in well-made technique, failing to perceive that even her more contrived work anticipates the memoirs' narrative ambiguity through deliberately imposed informational gaps.

Hellman is quite casual, for example, about the comings and goings of her characters. Mr. Marshall, who catalyzes virtually the entire action of *The*

Little Foxes (1939) by bringing his cotton mill to the Hubbards' town and by becoming the object of Regina's enduring sexual fantasy (which, in turn, contributes to her murdering her husband), disappears from the stage early in act 1, never to reappear. Cyrus Warkins, one of the most important characters in *Toys in the Attic* (a play commonly and mistakenly understood by critics to rely more on Ibsen than on Chekhov), never appears in the play at all. The dreadful child Mary Tilford, in *The Children's Hour* (1934), disappears from view after the second act, never to reemerge for the antici- pated confrontation of the third, which well-made dramaturgy would de- mand. Like Iago, who never will "speak word" in his own defense, Mary can offer no rational explanation for her behavior because there is none, or because she has so many private excuses that they collectively collapse.[17] Moreover, this play, which appears to concern itself with the destructive power of gossip, suddenly shifts thematic gears in the final act to convert Mary's lie into partial truth when Martha Dobie declares her love for Karen Wright.

Like most of her other plays, *The Children's Hour* and *The Little Foxes*, her two most famous, deny their audience the sop of poetic justice that well- made playwrights typically provide. In Hellman's world goodness invariably suffers at the hands of the wicked, with little prospect dangled for any future reordering of the balance. Both plays conclude with deliberately loose strands, in marked contrast to well-made denouements that leave no plot element unsettled. In *The Little Foxes*, the vague threat that Ben Hubbard will eventually prove his sister's responsibility for her husband's death pre- pares the audience for the trilogy Hellman intended to write. But she deals in the second play (*Another Part of the Forest*) only with the family's past, dropping plans for the third play, which was to have examined its grotesque future. And the end of *Forest* makes genuine sense only to an audience that knows *The Little Foxes*, which it precedes (in marked contrast to most se- quels) in time. *The Children's Hour* for its part rings down the third act curtain following an ambiguous conversation between the surviving teacher and Amelia Tilford, both of whose futures (like the now unseen Mary's) remain bleakly uncertain.

Her adaptations reveal even further Hellman's flexibility and willing- ness to experiment with dramatic form. This collection includes two discus- sions of those rarely considered plays: Leonard and Doris Fleischer's "The Dramatic Adaptations of Lillian Hellman," commissioned for this volume; and Henry Knepler's detailed comparison of Hellman's *The Lark* and Christo- pher Fry's adaptation of Jean Anouilh's *L'Alouette*. The four adaptations (*Montserrat*, 1949; *The Lark*, 1955; *Candide*, 1956; *My Mother, My Father and Me*, 1963) share with Hellman's original drama a universe propelled by money and cynicism, populated by well-meaning, basically good people forced into futile confrontations against malevolent antagonists or shattering sociopolitical forces by which they are invariably trounced.

Scoundrels tend to prevail in Hellman's plays because she detests sentimentality and therefore avoids the last-minute conversions of villains so dear to the hearts of genuinely well-made dramatists. The battles that provide the most fun in her plays (especially the two Hubbard plays) are fought between one scoundrel (or set of scoundrels) and another. In this regard certain critics have proposed that the ineffectuality of Hellman's victims renders them undeserving of audience sympathy. In "Bohemia Bumps into Calvin: The Deception of Passivity in Lillian Hellman's Drama," Mary Lynn Broe rejects such notions and argues for a new reading of these beleaguered figures, which sees them as catalysts "for truth-telling, deception, and most importantly, self-deception." For Broe, the "socially negligible become the dramatically invaluable" characters who clarify important, recurring themes in Hellman's plays.

In its rejection of sentimentally tidy endings, its Marxist treatment of wealth, its apparent conviction that the meek are destined to disinherit the earth, in, above all, its barely veiled anger, Hellman's universe resembles Brecht's.[18] In an extended analysis of Hellman's plays written especially for this volume, Timothy J. Wiles examines her links to Brecht and to the entire dramatic tradition of depression America. "Lillian Hellman's American Political Theater: The Thirties and Beyond" articulates Hellman's true lineage in the American drama as it has rarely been articulated before. Her best plays, suggests Wiles, "demonstrate that political art is both a product of its age and a force of innovation, one which can lead to wider speculations about the genre (including her kinship with Brecht) and toward a more substantial evaluation of her current reputation as a feminist precursor." Maintaining that Hellman is finally comparable only to Arthur Miller among American playwrights in the length of her career, the coherence of her politics, and her willingness to experiment with form and fable, Wiles moves on to a reading of Hellman's women startling in its implications for, especially, Regina Hubbard Giddens as a figure approaching tragic complexity.

Since so many characters in Hellman's plays commit atrocious acts, and since would-be villains require would-be victims, early critics alleged (in charges destined to be repeated throughout her playwriting career) that Hellman's dramatis personae represented melodramatic extremes. While in isolated instances the observation is valid, Hellman's characterizations—as essays in this collection attest—are frequently deceptive, complicated beyond their surface impression by her ironic recognition (especially in the Hubbard plays, *The Children's Hour*, *Watch on the Rhine*, and *Toys in the Attic*) that skullduggery can be entertaining, actually funny, even while it is being exposed to ethical condemnation. Modeled on Hellman's mother's family, the rapacious Hubbards were intended, for example, as a composite portrait of the comic and evil elements inherent in greed and cheating. But critics mistook the satiric elements of *The Little Foxes* and the funny, outrageous sections of *Another Part of the Forest* for what Hellman was later to call "straight stuff."[19]

In fact, the comic aspects of Hellman's drama, especially the presence of unrelieved villainy pushed toward Jacobean or Dickensian excess, simultaneously heighten moral outrage (hers and ours) and mute potential tendentiousness by inhibiting through laughter the audience's full condemnation of the diabolical behavior it witnesses. For connected to that laughter is grudging admiration at the gall, and periodic success, of such clever Hellman rascals as Marcus, Ben, and Regina Hubbard, and (even though she is rarely portrayed this way in actual performance) Mary Tilford in *The Children's Hour*, whose victory in the last scene of the second act is one the audience is manipulated into desiring. Like Shakespeare's Richard III and Iago, these figures delight in their capacity for evil and enrich Hellman's plays with a macabre comic sense that eludes many of her critics. The Hubbards are as capable of self-directed irony as some of Hellman's more sympathetic sharp-tongued characters like Fanny Farrelly (*Watch on the Rhine*) and Ned Crossman (*The Autumn Garden*), whose sardonic observations on human behavior lead to moral recognitions thematically central to the plays in which they appear. Hellman's particular gift for tough-minded, caustically funny dialogue is displayed through such characters' ironic intelligence, which, like the Hubbards', can be turned inward when necessary—but Fanny and Ned, like other Hellman figures, exist without an inclination toward evil because their dramatic contexts demand that they function as *raisonneurs*.

Numerous Hellman adults behave like children. Masters of rationalization, they naively appease the Nazi menace in *The Searching Wind* and *Watch on the Rhine;* deny their complicity in lives of middle-aged mediocrity in *The Autumn Garden;* cling to incestuous desires in *Toys in the Attic*. The astringent tone of *The Autumn Garden*, her most reflective, probing play, and *Toys in the Attic*, her most Freudian and mordant, illuminates the injuries that people, with time's help, inflict upon each other in the name of security and love.

Like the characters who inhabit them, Hellman's plays are flawed but their flaws often derive from their misunderstood strengths. Hellman's theatrical excesses, which her critics often belittle as the devices of melodrama, function as the deliberate dramaturgical equivalents to the moral outrage that permeates her work and goads her audience into sharing her anger. But her dark view of human nature subtly implicates that same audience in the onstage crimes to which its laughter bears guilty witness. While few of us possess the literal capacity to duplicate the actions of a Mary Tilford or Regina Giddens, we certainly do harbor the potential to contribute to their triumph—through financial self-interest or fear of involvement, through a misguided code of silence or an inclination to accept unchallenged lies as truth. Hellman's eaters of the earth might be denied some of the fruits of their labors were there not so many "people who stand around and watch them eat it."[20]

Like Brecht, Hellman expects her audience to be enraged enough by the injustice she dramatizes to leave the theatre and take social action. But, also like Brecht, she has scant faith in that audience's own capacity for moral commitment. Thus, while prodding the audience toward political action to correct social ills, she simultaneously indicts it for complicity in their perpetuation. Such attitudes account for John Gassner's charge that Hellman is the "hanging judge of the American theater,"[21] that her plays extend insufficient compassion to flawed characters like Amelia Tilford, the gullible grandmother of *The Children's Hour* who discovers her error and seeks forgiveness that is denied to her. Philip M. Armato's essay " 'Good and Evil' in Lillian Hellman's *The Children's Hour*," reprinted in this collection, argues forcefully that Hellman seeks to restore compassion to the world of the play, that the final confrontation between Mrs. Tilford and Karen Wright reaffirms the dramatist's central concern with "the dichotomy between primitive justice and mercy."

Arguably the most important American playwright next to O'Neill in the first half of this century, Hellman has been the subject of an astonishingly small number of book-length studies devoted exclusively to her work. That major symptom of critical condescension and neglect began to change significantly following the publication of her memoirs, by which time, however, primary attention was being addressed to the life-writing, not to the life in the theater. Hellman's plays deserve the sustained scholarly analysis that will extend the revisionist view initiated in this volume and restore her to her proper place in the American dramatic canon. A number of longer studies, most of them published within the past decade, do suggest that the balance is finally being redressed.

Prior to the late seventies only four long studies had appeared in print. Manfred Triesch catalogues play manuscripts, notebooks, and letters in *The Lillian Hellman Collection at the University of Texas* (1966).[22] That collection is at this writing open only to Hellman's official biographer, William Abrahams; presumably, when accessible to all scholars, an updated listing of holdings will be published. Jacob Adler's monograph, *Lillian Hellman* (1969),[23] offers the first extended view of the plays and places Hellman as the single most important American playwright in the Ibsenite tradition outside of Arthur Miller. Richard Moody's *Lillian Hellman, Playwright* (1972)[24] explores her rewriting methods and provides considerable theatrical and biographical lore, but depends excessively on information already available in *An Unfinished Woman* and the *Paris Review* interview. Moody's tone is unfailingly adulatory. Lorena Ross Holmin, in *The Dramatic Works of Lillian Hellman* (1973),[25] examines the original plays excluding *Days to Come*, but relies too heavily on plot synopsis in place of sustained analysis.

Hellman is the subject of three annotated bibliographies: Steven Bills's *Lillian Hellman: An Annotated Bibliography* (1979);[26] Mary Marguerite Riordan's *Lillian Hellman, A Bibliography: 1926–1978* (1980);[27] and my own reference guide, *Lillian Hellman: Plays, Films, Memoirs* (1980).[28]

Two introductory studies of Hellman's life and work by Doris Falk (1978)[29] and Katherine Lederer (1979)[30] include contrasting overviews of the plays. More reliable on the memoirs than on the plays, Falk insists on perpetuating the notion that Hellman is strictly a well-made, realistic playwright. She much too tidily divides the eight original dramas into misleading categories depicting, on the one hand, "despoilers" who exploit or destroy other figures for selfish ends, and, on the other, "bystanders" who behave as passive victims in a group of lower-keyed, more discursive plays. Neither Falk nor Lederer discusses Hellman's four adaptations, but Lederer is on firm ground in her analysis of Hellman's novelistic dramatic techniques and pungently ironic dialogue. Lederer sensibly debunks the "automatic genre labeling" of the plays, which is precisely the sort of distortion evident in Falk's reading. Neither study speculates on Hellman's possible influence on such contemporary forces in the American theater as David Rabe or Sam Shepard, an area still ripe for critical consideration.

In *Hellman in Hollywood* (1982),[31] Bernard Dick insightfully analyzes the film adaptations of the plays and the films Hellman adapted for the screen from other sources. He includes a discussion of the film adaptation of the "Julia" section of *Pentimento* and provocative speculation on the "Julia" figure in Hellman's other work, along with a rebuttal to the early questioning of the story's veracity. *Conversations with Lillian Hellman* (1986),[32] an array of interviews collected by Jackson Bryer, sheds considerable light on the life and work, all of course articulated from Hellman's point of view.

Two unauthorized biographies and a memoir complete the list of books on Hellman published to date. William Wright's *Lillian Hellman: The Image, the Woman* (1986)[33] is most telling on details of Hellman's life, including her attempts to impede the book's publication. In the relatively brief space he allots to the plays themselves, Wright maintains an admirable objectivity, suggesting for example (even while alleging that Hellman almost certainly lied or plagiarized or both) that such allegations against *The Children's Hour* disregard the fact that she utterly transformed her Scottish source into an entirely original work.

Carl Rollyson's similarly titled *Lillian Hellman: Her Legend and Her Legacy* (1988) perhaps understandably overstates the case by suggesting that all her plays are as "polemical" as her life. Rollyson's biography, like Wright's, is most interesting for its anecdotal reportage and extensive interviews with Hellman acquaintances. Judgments on the plays are at times curious, and scholarly sources are cited with little discrimination. But Rollyson's search for links between the plays and the life occasionally yield fresh fruit as in his suggestion that Hellman's unproduced "Dear Queen" foreshadows the material of *My Mother, My Father and Me;* or when he connects the fascination with violence evident late in her dramatic career (in *Toys in the Attic* and the screenplay for *The Chase*) to her friendship with Norman Mailer. Like Wright's, this biography is most useful, finally, for its revelation of new facts, including the discovery that Hellman had in truth been a member of the Communist party, despite her denials. It should be consulted alongside *Lilly: Reminiscences of Lillian Hellman* (1988), Peter

Feibleman's startling memoir of their long friendship and love affair.[34] All three books are welcome additions to the growing Hellman literature but the definitive biographical portrait remains to be written.

Overwhelmingly, the criticism of individual Hellman plays, also until quite recently, has been limited to capsule reviews in daily newspapers or weekly and monthly magazines, and passing comments, rarely supported by sustained analysis, in surveys of American drama. A happy exception in the latter instance is C. W. E. Bigsby's careful, compact, and unpatronizing Hellman chapter in his survey of twentieth-century American drama.[35]

Certain reviews, however, reveal key responses that contribute to the development of standard interpretations and, often, to misapprehension of Hellman's proper place in the American theater. To examine the responses of reviewers over the years is to discover inordinate contradictions among them. Hellman is praised for her taut dramatic construction but also attacked for alleged dependence on well-made technique, upon which taut dramatic construction must ordinarily rely. She is considered a staunch moralist who attacks society's evils but is often criticized for denoting her universe in exaggeratedly moralistic terms. It is commonly—and often erroneously—assumed that she employs the devices of melodrama to achieve her ends but the melodramatist's label is attached both to applaud and to condemn her dramaturgical style.

The Children's Hour (1934), the play that made her an overnight sensation, won initial strong praise for its tight craftsmanship and unusual theme. But tight craftsmanship became immediately associated with the idea that she was essentially a melodramatist, a term that stuck throughout her playwriting career, despite the fact that *The Children's Hour*'s tragic aims were repeatedly observed by the more astute critics in their original reviews of the play. Robert Benchley objected not to Hellman's use of melodrama but to her departure from it in favor of O'Neillian tragedy in the last act of the play.[36] Other critics, including Brooks Atkinson, Joseph Wood Krutch, and George Jean Nathan, agreed that the third act subverted the apparent aims of the first two.[37] Atkinson, however, tacitly combining the critical vocabulary of tragedy and melodrama, considered the work "venomously tragic," and repeated Benchley's criticism of the last act, but on precisely the opposite ground, maintaining that within it Hellman lapsed into excessively melodramatic—not tragic—conventions.

Among others noting the play's tragic characterizations were Percy Hammond and the anonymous *Literary Digest* reviewer.[38] In their insightful reviews of *These Three*, the first film adaptation of *The Children's Hour*, Alistair Cooke praised the adaptation for its "Aristotelian"[39] effects and novelist Graham Greene, writing in *Spectator*, spoke of its realistic representation of "nothing less than life,"[40] astonishing indications of the play's inherent power since censorship demands resulted in the film's total elimination of lesbian plot implications and introduction of a quasi-happy ending. Perhaps the most negative but incisive targeting of the play's structural problem was articulated in Eric Bentley's review of the 1952 Broadway revival, directed by Hellman and intended to convey a parallel between the play's thematic implications and the McCarthy era's power to destroy reputations. Hellman, suggested Bentley, tries to tell two conflicting stories at once: "The first is a story of heterosexual teachers accused of lesbianism; the enemy is a society which punishes the innocent. The second is a story of lesbian teachers accused of lesbianism; the enemy is a society which punishes lesbians."[41]

Days to Come (1936), Hellman's second play and one critical failure, was essentially attacked for its divergence from well-made structure, another early example that glib assumptions concerning her dependence upon such dramaturgy have been grossly exaggerated. As Timothy J. Wiles's essay in this volume and several reviews of a 1978 New York revival suggest, the play deserves reconsideration as "one of those crucial transitional works."[42] While Stark Young's review of the original Broadway production was representative of the general dismissal of *Days to Come,* Joseph Wood Krutch and Alexander Taylor were among the few who praised Hellman's attempt to expand her dramatic canvas.[43] Also one of the few ever to perceive the kinship, Krutch recognized the Hellman of *Days to Come* as an heir to the playwright August Strindberg.

A group of reviews and occasional articles on the two Hubbard plays, *The Little Foxes* (1939) and *Another Part of the Forest* (1946), convey that same curious admixture of reputation-making and misunderstanding so apparent in the early Hellman criticism. The anonymous *Time* reviewer wrote the characteristic *Little Foxes* review, praising Hellman as a "moralist" and the creator of powerful, exciting "melodrama."[44] Richard Watts, Jr., claiming it surpassed even *The Children's Hour,* considered it a bitter, merciless study of "the relentless emergence of a new industrialism from the ashes of a sentimental past."[45] Another critic suggested that *Little Foxes* deliberately "denies us all sense of tragedy," sending the audience from the theater "not purged, not released, but still aroused and indignant."[46]

While establishing Hellman as a major force on the Broadway stage, such reviews and those of *Another Part of the Forest* seven years later tended to take the works too seriously, categorizing them as melodramas of social protest, failing to grasp their genuinely satiric base. Infrequently, though appropriately, these two plays have been identified (in Martin Knelman's phrase) as comedies of greed.[47] Louis Kronenberger compared *Forest* to those "sombre Elizabethan 'comedies' swarming with cheats and knaves and evildoers."[48] Joseph Wood Krutch cleverly suggested that *Forest*'s tale of "four scoundrels, two half-wits, one insane woman, and a whore" begins to seem "funny when exhibited for too long."[49] But Krutch's remarks fail to account for Hellman's intentional utilization of Jacobean grotesquerie, a presence also missed by the *New York Times* critic who rather naively called *Forest* a "witches' brew of blackmail, insanity, cruelty, theft, torture, insult, [and] drunkenness, with a trace of incest thrown in for good measure."[50] John Mason Brown, correctly identifying those same ingredients as the source of the audience's delight, concluded, however, that the "guignol" of *Forest* prevents one from taking the play seriously.[51] Determined to connect Hellman's style with the social realism that launched her career, critics like Brown and Brooks Atkinson, though often highly laudatory of Hellman's work, continued to remain uncomfortable with her forays into other dramatic structures.

Both the play's durability and the diverse critical response to *The Little Foxes* are exhibited further over the years by reactions to major New York revivals, usually produced as star vehicles. An exchange in the *New York Review of Books,* prompted by a 1967 Lincoln Center revival, was triggered by Elizabeth Hardwick's claim that the play lacks tragic conflict, displays a false view of the Old South, and turns on an awkward dramatic construction. Defenses of the play in a subsequent issue,[52] and a separate piece by Edmund Wilson praising his friend Hellman, comprise a lively interchange.[53] In a *Players* essay James Eatman analyzes the play's semidocumentary tone of authenticity.[54] Frank Rich, in a *New York Times* review of the 1981 Broadway revival, which starred Elizabeth Taylor, incisively acknowledged the play's staying power.[55] *The Little Foxes* does, in fact, remain Hellman's most popular play, and one of the most frequently revived in the American theater.

Very much a play of a particular time and place in American political history, *Watch on the Rhine* (1941), arguing against American isolationism, fortuitously opened on Broadway just eight months before the bombing of Pearl Harbor and the United States entry into World War II. Much in the play resists the erosion of time, including the presence of one of Hellman's memorably sharp-tongued figures in the person of Fanny Farrelly, and the recurrent tone and dialogue of a Jamesian comedy of manners unappreciated when the play became such a topical hit. The context of its time and the urgency of its message, however, possibly led critics to overpraise *Watch on the Rhine* as Hellman's best play.[56] Even demanding *New Republic* critic Stark Young, while noting that hero Kurt Müller's farewell to his children at play's end needed tightening, suggested that the scene (in fact, one of the few sentimental moments in Hellman's entire dramatic canon) might be compared to the "high tradition" of Sophocles, who gave Oedipus "thirty-four full lines of this same farewell."[57] The British response to the 1942 London production not surprisingly corroborated Hellman's message as a movingly appropriate "framework for the European tragedy."[58] A New York revival in 1979 prompted Mel Gussow to point out that the play is more durable than most antiwar dramas and that the character of Sara Müller is "a fictional representative of the author's friend, Julia."[59]

The Searching Wind (1944), Hellman's talkiest and, along with *Days to Come,* most commonly neglected play, reflects her continued involvement with timely world politics, in this case the folly of appeasement. Typical reviews were mixed, but Barrett Clark in the first academically oriented study of the plays praised it for rejecting the melodrama of her earlier work and for focusing on character instead of plot.[60] More typical reviews were represented in the criticisms of Margaret Marshall, George Jean Nathan, and Stark Young.[61]

The Autumn Garden (1951), usually cited as Hellman's most mature play, once again revealed critics' inability to agree on generic categories for her work. Most were intent on calling the play a Chekhovian comedy or a Chekhovian tragedy or a near tragedy derailed by too many central characters.[62] Many praised the multiple character technique, again citing Chekhov as Hellman's "new" source, when, in fact, the reflective, rueful voice of the play has its structural roots not in Chekhov, but in the discursive elements within *Watch on the Rhine, The Searching Wind,* and *Another Part of the Forest.* "Diffuse and somnambulistic," charged George Jean Nathan, objecting to the divergence from tight dramaturgy. Still others lamented Hellman's alleged lack of compassion for her characters.[63]

Toys in the Attic (1960), her last original play, reflects the influence of Tennessee Williams's psychosexual dramatic terrain. Robert Brustein suggested that in *Toys* Hellman seems much more at home with her favorite topic—the effects of money on human behavior—than with her "new flirtation with Freudianism," but he regarded the play highly.[64] *Toys* is commonly and accurately considered among Hellman's most trenchant dramas, as Alan Downer, John Gassner, and Marya Mannes maintained.[65]

As the essays in this collection reveal, Hellman's four adaptations for Broadway contain appropriate Hellmanesque themes. *Montserrat* (1949), her first, unfortunately opened on Broadway only two evenings before the premiere of *Regina,* Marc Blitzstein's opera adaptation of *The Little Foxes.* Most weekly and monthly journals reviewed the two works together, and critics, thus freshly reminded of the crackling *Little Foxes,* seemed especially eager to find the new and very different *Montserrat* dramatically inadequate. John Gassner, expressing a typical response, attacked the play for its excessive reliance on well-made dramatic structure—just one year before certain critics were to attack *The Autumn Garden* for daring to depart from it.[66]

Hellman's most successful adaptation, *The Lark* (1955), usually evokes responses primarily for its treatment of Joan of Arc, especially as compared to the Joans created by George Bernard Shaw and Jean Anouilh (on whose *L'Alouette* Hellman based her version of the story).[67] Representing opposing views of the play were Walter Kerr, who praised *The Lark* for its "tough-minded" Joan, and Eric Bentley, who criticized the characterization as too much that of the "good girl."[68]

Hellman's libretto for *Candide* (1956), a collaboration by some of the most famous names in American music and letters, wavers in the judgment of critics like Henry Hewes and Richard Hayes, who object to her astringent tone, which seems to them excessively to favor the position of Voltaire's pessimist Martin.[69] Among *Candide*'s harshest critics—in an especially interesting review in light of the later, public hostilities between the two women—was Mary McCarthy, who considered the adaptation "bowdlerized"

Voltaire, and a "sad fizzle which is more like a high school pageant than a social satire."[70] On the other hand, in a key review of a work destined to become a classic primarily for its Leonard Bernstein score, Brooks Atkinson hailed the production as a "brilliant musical satire."[71]

My Mother, My Father and Me (1963), Hellman's last adaptation and last play, is her most sardonic, anarchic work. Its structure and content are outrageously unified with theater of the absurd joining forces with theater of cruelty. Most critics were offended by Hellman's radical departure from well-made form even though they had previously so often attacked her for its rigid employment. Considerably ahead of its time, the play was nevertheless derided even by Hellman stalwarts, though the *Time* reviewer genuinely praised the daring new form.[72]

In addition to the articles reprinted in this collection, several miscellaneous essays and reviews prompted by publication of *The Collected Plays* in 1972 accentuate the divergent critical terrain. Along with Barrett Clark,[73] Edith Isaccs was among the early critics to treat several dramatic displays of Hellman's social anger as a subject for serious analysis.[74] A strongly disparaging review of *The Collected Plays* by Charles Thomas Samuels triggered an angry response in the pages of the *New York Times Books Review* from Renata Adler; both views illustrate the ongoing nature of the polar reactions so often elicited by Hellman's work.[75] In a highly favorable treatment of *The Collected Plays*, Alex Szogyi provocatively pinpoints Hellman's major themes, suggesting that *Toys* is her most poetically written play and that her true purpose in the theater has been "to ferret out truth in lives frittered away by aberrant lying obsessions."[76] The role of money and its force in family and world politics in Hellman's plays is cogently analyzed in essays on *The Little Foxes* by Robert Heilman and on *The Collected Plays* by Ellen Moers, who contends that family and capital are the "two consuming obsessions" of Hellman's world.[77] Included among a number of overviews surveying her work is my own essay "Lillian Hellman," in *Contemporary Dramatists*.[78] Pieces by Nancy M. Tischler and W. Kenneth Holditch specifically consider her importance as a "southern" artist, an aspect of her writing more commonly considered in the context of Hellman's memoirs.[79] An important essay in setting the Hellman dramatic record straight is Mary Lynn Broe's reevaluation, reprinted in this volume.[80]

THE MEMOIRS

An Unfinished Woman (1969) initiated a series of four memoirs that returned Hellman, already in her mid-sixties, to a prominent place before the American public. The memoirs introduced her to new generations of readers and earned her (in marked contrast to the dark days of Senator Joseph McCarthy and the House Committee on Un-American Activities recorded in *Scoundrel Time*) widespread praise as prose stylist and, for many, political heroine. Even *Time* magazine, which in 1952 treated Hellman's position before the HCUA[81] with snide, red-baiting innuendo, by 1976 was heaping praise on *Scoundrel Time,* published just two years after Richard Nixon's resignation from the presidency and detailing the scoundrelism that led, in Hellman's view, to his election and near impeachment.[82] In the mid-1970s it had become far more fashionable, if belatedly appropriate, to embrace the resistance of, especially, a woman to the McCarthy pack than had been the case in 1952.

An Unfinished Woman and *Pentimento* (1973), the first two memoirs, won critical acclaim and numerous awards, and brought Hellman an impressive following of new readers. Though she maintained that she had never been a feminist (and would continue to reject that label as she rejected all labels), her memoirs were embraced as illustrative of the independence and moral determination espoused by the women's movement. ("I believe in women's liberation," she told Bill Moyers in 1974. "I think some of its cries are rather empty cries because I think it all comes down to whether or not you can support yourself as well as a man can support himself and whether there's enough money to make certain decisions for yourself rather than dependence."[83])

As the seventies began, Hellman was being praised, in the words of one critic, as a "super-literate Humphrey Bogart";[84] as the decade closed, though she retained her ardent defenders, she was being attacked in a backlash by those resentful of what another critic identified as the inevitable reaction to "the gradual canonization of Saint Lillian."[85] *Scoundrel Time* (1976) unleashed a barrage of controversy in response to Hellman's version of events leading up to and following her stand before the HCUA in 1952. The book reopened old wounds among American intellectuals who objected to charges directed by Hellman at the "anti-Communist writers and intellectuals of those times."[86] She defended her position in *Three* (1979), the collected edition of her first three memoirs, which in turn triggered further charges and countercharges that spread to attacks in the early eighties, not only on her version of events in *Scoundrel Time,* but now directed at the veracity of self-portraits in *An Unfinished Woman* and *Pentimento* (particularly the "Julia" section).

In the context of those charges, *Maybe* (1980), her last memoir (which she calls "A Story" and which therefore may not be a memoir at all), takes on particular significance. Pamela S. Bromberg's "Establishing the Woman and Constructing a Narrative in Lillian Hellman's Memoirs," one of two original essays commissioned for the "Memoirs" section of this collection, connects *Maybe* to the earlier volumes and argues that here Hellman portrays herself more honestly than ever before. *Maybe*'s elliptical stance, especially its deliberate denial of narrative closure, is for Bromberg a reflection of Hellman's "crisis of despair," as she metaphorically confronts the terrors of her final years of life, admitting more openly than in any other memoir to her "neurotic fear of her own body and sexuality." The variety within the memoirs' narrative methods is traced by Linda Wagner-Martin in "Lillian Hellman:

Autobiography and Truth" (reprinted here from the *Southern Review*) to reveal Hellman's willingness (unusual for women writers, argues Wagner-Martin) "to confront the labyrinth of autobiography/memoir/story."

The story of the *Scoundrel Time* controversy is complicated and confusing. Several representative essays both defending (by Richard Falk and, guardedly, by Murray Kempton) and attacking (by, respectively, Sidney Hook and Alfred Kazin) that book are included here. Two essays extend allegations concerning Hellman's memoirs to *An Unfinished Woman* and *Pentimento:* Martha Gellhorn's scathing indictment of Hellman, "Close Encounters of the Apocryphal Kind," reprinted from the *Paris Review;* and Alexander Cockburn's speculations on "Who Was Julia?" originally published in the *Nation*.

Concluding the "Memoirs" section is Timothy Dow Adams's innovative essay, " 'Lies Like Truth': Lillian Hellman's Autobiographies." As Adams notes, further light is likely to be shed on, for example, the identity of Julia (if, indeed, an actual Julia ever existed) by future biographers, including William Abrahams, Hellman's literary executor who is preparing the official life story.[87] Approaching the memoirs as literary documents, Adams codifies the numerous allegations raised against Hellman's version of her life through the methodology of contemporary autobiographical theory. In the process he links the mysteries that Hellman so adamantly refused to clarify before her death to notions of genre and tone.

A number of books already cited in the "Plays" section of this introduction also prove extremely useful in sorting out the issues of the memoirs, especially the tangled political context of *Scoundrel Time*. The three annotated bibliographies collectively provide extensive material on the memoirs and the critical reaction up to 1979, by which time Hellman had published all of them except *Maybe*.[88] Doris Falk's survey conveys a solid sense of Hellman's moral concerns and the persona that emerges from the memoirs. She makes a number of intelligent connections between the memoirs and the plays, though her attempts to relate Hellman to other American writers are strained. Falk is particularly adroit, however, at clarifying the confusing charges and countercharges surrounding *Scoundrel Time*.[89] Katherine Lederer devotes eight pages to an analysis of Hellman's early nondramatic writing, emphasizing the "steady development" toward the persona of the memoirs evident in these newspaper and magazine pieces, but on the memoirs themselves she disappoints, in contrast to her strong readings of the plays. She simplifies the complexities surrounding the *Scoundrel Time* controversy and fails to make appropriate distinctions among the political alliances of Hellman's critics.[90] More than half the interviews in *Conversations with Lillian Hellman* are relevant to the memoirs, especially the transcript of Marilyn Berger's 1979 television profile.[91] Hellman's biographers[92] devote considerable attention to the memoirs, but attempts to deal with allegations against her veracity tend to overwhelm tentative efforts at genuine literary analysis. Carl Rollyson's book makes the stronger attempt to distinguish between gossip and the inherent literary value of the memoirs, but both biographers shed new light on the ongoing controversy of Hellman's life. It is clear, however, that the story will continue to unfold for many years to come.

Among shorter pieces, insightful comments regarding *An Unfinished Woman* appear in articles by Robert Kotlowitz, Edward Weeks, and Dorothy Rabinowitz. Patricia Meyer Spacks was among the first academics to accord Hellman's memoirs appropriate attention. Martha Gellhorn alleges in her attack on the book that, from the first, Hellman's self-portrait in the memoirs was virtually fictional.[93]

The varied portraits in *Pentimento* attracted a number of highly laudatory responses along with initial flashes of the negativism that would erupt over the book much later, especially those centered on its "Julia" segment. Richard Poirier's *Washington Post* review and, later, his introduction to the collected memoirs, *Three*, epitomize Hellman's memoir criticism at its most literary and most lucid. Other important essays contributing to the various, usually positive positions on the literary merits of *Pentimento* include pieces by Eliot Fremont-Smith, Mark Schorer, John Simon, Paul Theroux, the anonymous critics for *TLS* and the *Economist*, and a penetrating discussion by Marsha McCreadie on the film adaptation of "Julia."[94] Samuel McCracken's " 'Julia' and Other Fictions by Lillian Hellman" articulated a major argument in the anti-Hellman literature of the eighties, alleging that she manipulated other sources for the fabrication of her own image in the "Julia" segment of *Pentimento*.[95]

The complex political context and shrill publication aftermath of *Scoundrel Time* are best sorted out through comparing the essays in this collection by Murray Kempton, Sidney Hook, Richard A. Falk, Alfred Kazin and, especially, Timothy Dow Adams,[96] along with appropriate sections of books already mentioned that consider Hellman's memoirs.[97]

Additionally, certain key reviews and articles reveal how deep political wounds of the past were reopened among American intellectuals by Hellman's third memoir. After being hailed for the first two, which appeared to cast her in the most positive public light, *Scoundrel Time*'s publication triggered what in retrospect was almost certainly the beginning of the attack on Hellman's integrity that persists to this day. *Scoundrel Time* did, however, receive numerous reviews that were glowing in nature, including a front-page tribute in the *New York Times Book Review* as a compelling and "beautiful work of self-definition."[98] Reviews by Robert Sherrill, Saul Maloff, Vivian Gornick, and Paul Gray represent positions strongly favoring Hellman's portrayal of her role during the grim McCarthy years.[99] But *Scoundrel Time* and its introduction by Garry Wills[100] infuriated many, who assailed, in the words of Irving Howe, Hellman's insistence on clinging to "old dogmas that, at other and more lucid moments, she knows she should have given up long ago."[101]

Other attacks that became central to the debate included those of Nathan

Glazer, Hilton Kramer, William Phillips, William Buckley, and Walter Goodman.[102] Philip French used *Scoundrel Time*'s publication to suggest that in her memoirs Hellman recreated Hammett and herself as figures in history—"as Lilly and Dash, the exemplary heroic couple of committed Thirties seriousness to match the now unfashionable Zelda and Scott, the representatives of disengaged Twenties frivolousness."[103] Also of interest to the *Scoundrel Time* story are portions of Diana Trilling's *We Must March My Darlings*, and several opposing considerations of the Hellman-Trilling contretemps.[104]

The contrastingly tame response to *Maybe* is reflected in reviews by Vivian Gornick, Robert Towers, Walter Clemons, Maureen Howard, Anne Duchene, and Maggie Scarf.[105] But as this introduction and several essays in the collection suggest, *Maybe* has assumed additional resonance, both as Hellman's final memoir and for its possible implications in the context of subsequent charges of distortion leveled against her.

Four miscellaneous articles also focus on the memoirs: Marcus K. Billson and Sidonie A. Smith's "Lillian Hellman and the Strategy of the Other," an influential discussion cited by several essayists in this volume; Bonnie Lyons's "Lillian Hellman: The First Jewish Nun on Prytania Street," which praises the memoirs but attacks the plays; Maurice F. Brown's friendly *Biography* essay; and Anita Susan Grossman's *Clio* article, which is critical of Hellman and "Hellman apologists."[106]

THE HELLMAN PERSONA

Throughout her life Lillian Hellman was drawn into—some would say she courted—occasionally nasty public debate. In certain instances, notably her appearance before the HCUA in 1952 and subsequent blacklisting, the stakes became considerably higher than she perhaps anticipated, though no stake seems higher now than the Hellman reputation itself, which has been challenged by those who maintain that segments of her memoirs are fictional figments of her imagination.

My conscious attempt to detach objective analyses of her work from the personalized celebrations or diatribes that frequently creep into its assessment has been more easily fulfilled in the "Plays" section of this collection, where original and reprinted essays are restricted to consideration of Hellman as dramatist. While the major critical essays in the "Memoirs" section are careful to separate the literature from the life and to approach those memoirs as literary documents, the shift in genre to autobiography invites comparison to the life there recorded in a way that the plays do not. Any group of essays seeking to convey a representative evaluation of the memoirs must account for political reaction against *Scoundrel Time* and more recent claims against episodes of *An Unfinished Woman* and *Pentimento*. The "Memoirs" section of *Critical Essays on Lillian Hellman* therefore includes pieces that cross the boundary between objective criticism and personal evaluation.

The essays in the "Persona" section collectively contribute to an understanding of what came to be viewed (variously with admiration or with rancor) as the legend of Lillian Hellman. She was thrust into the public spotlight very early—because she was young, because she was a woman, because she aimed to be a "serious" playwright, and because, too, she was a cantankerously outspoken political leftist. She remained there for most of the rest of her life, feuding publicly with actors, politicians, and other literary figures, and with friends who toward the end of her life joked that it was impossible any longer to keep track of which "friend" had bounced onto her growing list of enemies. Her image became so ingrained in her critical reception that (though one may wish it were otherwise) the Hellman persona must to some extent be considered in any collection aiming to present the most important commentary on her work.

"Miss Lily of New Orleans," Margaret Case Harriman's early profile, conveys in its breezy *New Yorker* style elements of the persona Hellman clearly enjoyed encouraging and which would reemerge in numerous public portraits later in her life (including her own memoirs): the Southern background; her detestation of the "woman playwright" label; an abysmal sense of geographical direction; her witty literary set; her left-wing—many said Communist—politics (the only thing, Harriman reports, about which "she has a regrettable tendency to be coy");[107] her quarrels; the guarded reference to Dashiell Hammett as "an old and solicitous friend." Even "rage" and "indignation," words that would become Hellman hallmarks, appear prominently in Harriman's perceptive profile.

The most important and revealing interview Hellman ever gave regarding her work and the life that affected it occurred in 1964. The date of that *Paris Review* interview turns out to be a significant one in Hellman's transition as a writer, coming three years after the death of Hammett and just one after the failed production of what was to be her final play; publication of *An Unfinished Woman* was only five years away. Hammett's influence on her life and writing emerges much more explicitly here than in the Harriman profile, but their sexual relationship still remains inferential. Considerable light is shed on her habits and interests as a playwright (more, in fact, than she will reveal in the memoirs), and on what she calls the "botching" of certain plays. She assesses the work of contemporaries, including longtime (even in 1964) foe Mary McCarthy, whom she dismisses as a "lady magazine writer." In a preface, the interviewers apologize for the tone of their "too eagerly 'literary' questions," but the conversation strikes an excellent balance between conveying a picture of Hellman the artist and Hellman the public woman. Note, particularly, the occasional resemblance in the narrative voice of Hellman's responses to the clipped, tough-guy prose she will employ in the memoirs.

Included in this section as well are two tributes to Hellman: a witty homage by the writer John Hersey, delivered on the occasion of her receiving the Edward MacDowell Medal in 1976, and "Epilogue to Anger," Robert

Brustein's characteristically astute, moving evaluation of her final years (keeping death "at bay through blind fury") and her permanent place in the American theater.

Chronologically arranged, the selections in the "Persona" section reflect forty-three years in the presentation of the Hellman image. A surprising number of elements revealed in these essays from Harriman (1941) through Brustein (1984) remain constant, including (as early as the Harriman profile) the manner in which the Hellman mystique often seemed to have become more interesting to the essayist (and therefore to the reader) than her work. By the time the film adaptation of *Pentimento*'s "Julia" section was released in 1977, still a number of years before publication of pieces attacking the story's veracity, discussion of the Hellman persona in fact dominated reviews of the picture. Two contrasting examples by Pauline Kael (who compares the "national monument" called Lillian Hellman to the character played by Jane Fonda in the film) and Martin Knelman (who maintains that "the most unforgettable character Lillian Hellman has ever created is Lillian Hellman") are reprinted here to suggest how the Hellman personality dominates the critical response even to a work twice removed from her writing.[108]

Lillian Hellman's own life often does in summation seem more dramatic than that of any character she created. She left numerous mysteries about that life when she died, which future biographers have an obligation to explore. The famous anger, said novelist John Hersey in a graveside eulogy, "was immensely important and valuable to our time. It electrified a mood of protest. The protest was that of every great writer: 'Life ought to be better than this!' "[109]

Though not everyone portrayed it in as favorable a light, that anger informed Hellman's writing, made her dialogue and, later, her prose vibrate. Her plays have stood the test of time and deserve ongoing revival, to be judged apart from the life. The memoirs continue to enjoy critical and popular esteem but, as essays in this volume variously suggest, their future representation is certain to be linked both to further revelations concerning their veracity and to their contrasting placement within the vanguard of a new genre that erases the boundaries between life-writing and fiction.

Much of the memoir-related material already cited also discusses the Hellman persona. Additionally, items published in the popular press following her death—obituaries,[110] tributes,[111] varied assessments[112]—contribute further to the composite portrait of Hellman the public woman. In 1986 a dramatization of her memoirs by William Luce opened on Broadway and in major U.S. cities; reviews were almost invariably influenced by critics' attitudes toward Hellman.[113] Characteristically, when later that year a production was mounted in London, a row erupted in the pages of the *Observer*, variously berating and defending the Hellman image.[114] More than two years after her death even a dramatization of portions of her life, conceived as an actress's tour de force in a one-woman play, had become embroiled in dispute.

I am grateful to the many friends and colleagues who in a wide variety of ways contributed to the completion of *Critical Essays on Lillian Hellman*. My thanks, most especially, to my wife, Barbara Lieben Estrin, for her invaluable editorial judgment and encouragement throughout the project, and to Natalie DiRissio for her consummate professional skill and ongoing perfectionism. I also want to thank all essayists represented in this collection, particularly Timothy Dow Adams, Jacob H. Adler, Pamela S. Bromberg, Robert Brustein, Doris Fleischer, Leonard Fleischer, and Timothy J. Wiles; the Rhode Island College Faculty Research Committee and the college's Adams Library staff; Jackson Bryer, Joan Dagle, Robin Estrin, Robert Hogan, Michelle Martineau, Mary McGann, Arlene Robertson, and Nancy Sullivan. To Joseph Plut and to Tess and Charles Hoffmann, a note of special appreciation for their continuing support and friendship.

MARK W. ESTRIN

Rhode Island College

Notes

1. See, especially, the "Memoirs" section of this volume, where, for example, Murray Kempton, writing in praise of *Scoundrel Time*, notes that "although it is never gracious to say such things . . . Miss Hellman's voice in these discourses does not fall upon my ear as coming from someone I should want overmuch as a comrade" ("Witnesses," *New York Review of Books*, 10 June 1976, 22–25, reprinted in this volume).

2. Hemingway, whose style Hellman is occasionally accused of imitating in the memoirs, also comes to mind in this regard. Although he was only six years older than Hellman, Hemingway died twenty-three years before her, and during that period Hellman forged a second writing career with her four memoirs. See, on the Hellman-Hemingway relationship, *An Unfinished Woman* (Boston: Little, Brown & Co., 1969) and, in contradiction of Hellman, Martha Gellhorn, "On Apocryphism," *Paris Review* 23 (Spring 1981):280–301, reprinted in abridged form in this volume.

3. See, for example, the chapter entitled "Theatre" in her memoir *Pentimento* (Boston: Little, Brown & Co., 1973).

4. "Day in Spain," *New Republic*, 13 April 1938, 297–98.

5. "I Meet the Front-Line Russians," *Collier's*, 31 March 1945, 11, 68, 71.

6. New York: Farrar, Straus & Cudahy, 1955.

7. New York: Random House, 1966.

8. Published, respectively, in *American Spectator* 1 (September 1933):2, and *American Spectator* 2 (January 1934):4.

9. In addition to *The Chase*, Hellman wrote screenplays for the following films: *The Dark Angel* (1935), *These Three* (the first film version of *The Children's Hour*, 1936), *Dead End* (1937), *The Spanish Earth* (with Ernest Hemingway, John Dos Passos, and Archibald MacLeish, 1937), *The Little Foxes* (1941), *The North Star* (1943), and *The Searching Wind* (1946).

10. Films: *Watch on the Rhine* (screenplay by Dashiell Hammett, 1943), *Another Part of the Forest* (screenplay by Vladimir Pozner, 1948), *The Children's Hour* (second film version; released in England as *The Loudest Whisper*; screenplay by John Michael Hayes, 1962), *Toys in*

the Attic (screenplay by James Poe, 1963), *Julia* (screenplay by Alvin Sargent, 1977). Opera: *Regina* (adapted from *The Little Foxes* by Marc Blitzstein, 1949).

11. See, for example, two anonymous articles: *"Children's Hour* Banned in Boston," *New York Times*, 15 December 1935, 42, and "Censorship Conflict in Theater," *Literary Digest*, 28 December 1935, 20.

12. See Joseph Wood Krutch, "Drama: 'Best Play,' " *Nation*, 22 May 1935, 610.

13. New York: Duffield and Green, 1931. See Earle Walbridge, " 'Closed Doors,' " *Saturday Review of Literature*, 16 March 1935, 548, and William Wright, *Lillian Hellman: The Image, the Woman* (New York: Simon & Schuster, 1986), 85–92.

14. *American Mercury* 54 (June 1941):750–55.

15. "The Art of the Theater: Lillian Hellman, An Interview," *Paris Review* 33 (Winter-Spring 1965):64–95, reprinted in *Writers at Work: The Paris Review Interviews*, third series, ed. George Plimpton (New York: Viking, 1967). Reprinted in this volume.

16. As characteristic examples of such assessments of Hellman's playwriting technique, see Joseph Wood Krutch, "Unpleasant Play," *Nation*, 25 February 1939, 244–45; John Mason Brown, "Seeing Things: A New Miss Hellman," *Saturday Review*, 31 March 1951, 27–29; and Charles Thomas Samuels, review of *The Collected Plays, New York Times Book Review*, 18 June 1972, 2–3, 16, 18.

17. Mary's disappearance in the final act of *The Children's Hour* is a central point of critical contention over the play. See, among the more astute commentaries on the matter, Brooks Atkinson, "The Play," *New York Times*, 21 November 1934, 23; Joseph Wood Krutch, "Drama: The Heart of a Child," *Nation*, 5 December 1934, 656–57; anonymous review, *New Statesman and Nation*, 21 November 1936, 810; and Eric Bentley, "Hellman's Indignation," *New Republic*, 5 January 1953, 30–31. Hellman herself remained dissatisfied with the play's ending, primarily with Mrs. Tilford's reappearance in the final scene. See Fred Gardner, "An Interview with Lillian Hellman," in *Conversations with Lillian Hellman*, ed. Jackson R. Bryer (Jackson: University Press of Mississippi, 1986), 110–11.

18. Most critics, unaware of explicit Brecht parallels, identified in Hellman what in fact were Brechtian structures. See, for example, Louis Kronenberger, "Greed," *Stage* 16 (1 April 1939):36–37, 55; Joseph Wood Krutch, *American Drama Since 1918* (New York: Random House, 1939), 130–33; and Clarke Robinson, "Silhouettes of Celebrities," *World Digest* 15 (January 1942):78–83.

19. *Pentimento*, 197. See also Hellman's *Paris Review* interview, reprinted in this volume.

20. *The Little Foxes*, in Lillian Hellman, *The Collected Plays* (Boston: Little, Brown & Co., 1972), 182.

21. John Gassner, "Entropy in the Drama," *Theatre Arts* 35 (September 1951):16–17, 73.

22. Manfred Triesch, *The Lillian Hellman Collection at the University of Texas* (Austin: Humanities Research Center, University of Texas at Austin, 1966).

23. Jacob Adler, *Lillian Hellman* (Austin, Texas: Steck-Vaughn, 1969).

24. Richard Moody, *Lillian Hellman, Playwright* (New York: Pegasus/Bobbs Merrill, 1972).

25. Lorena Ross Holmin, *The Dramatic Works of Lillian Hellman* (Uppsala, Sweden: Almqvist and Wiksell, 1973). Ph.D. diss., Uppsala University, published in Uppsala University's English Studies series.

26. Steven Bills, *Lillian Hellman: An Annotated Bibliography* (New York: Garland, 1979).

27. Mary Marguerite Riordan, *Lillian Hellman, A Bibliography: 1926–1978* (Metuchen, N.J.: Scarecrow Press, 1980).

28. Mark W. Estrin, *Lillian Hellman: Plays, Films, Memoirs* (Boston: G.K. Hall, 1980). Includes a detailed critical introduction.

29. Doris Falk, *Lillian Hellman* (New York: Ungar, 1978).

30. Katherine Lederer, *Lillian Hellman* (Boston: Twayne Publishers, 1979).

31. Bernard F. Dick, *Hellman in Hollywood* (Rutherford, Madison, and Teaneck, N.J.: Fairleigh Dickinson University Press, 1982).

32. Bryer, *Conversations with Lillian Hellman*.

33. William Wright, *Lillian Hellman: The Image, the Woman* (New York: Simon and Schuster, 1986).

34. Carl Rollyson, *Lillian Hellman: Her Legend and Her Legacy* (New York: St. Martin's Press, 1988); Peter Feibleman, *Lilly: Reminiscences of Lillian Hellman* (New York: William Morrow & Co., 1988).

35. C. W. E. Bigsby, *Twentieth-Century American Drama. Volume I: 1900–1946.* (Cambridge: Cambridge University Press, 1982).

36. Robert Benchley, "Good News," *New Yorker*, 1 December 1934, 34, 36, 38.

37. Atkinson, "The Play," 23; Krutch, "Drama: The Heart of a Child," 656–57; George Jean Nathan, review of *The Children's Hour, Vanity Fair* 43 (February 1935):37.

38. Percy Hammond, "The Theaters," *New York Herald Tribune*, 23 November 1934, 16; "The Thunderbolt of Broadway," *Literary Digest*, 1 December 1934, 20.

39. Alistair Cooke, review of *These Three, Sight and Sound* 5 (Summer 1936):22–25.

40. Graham Greene, review of *These Three, Spectator*, 1 May 1936, 791.

41. Eric Bentley, "Hellman's Indignation," *New Republic*, 5 January 1953, 30–31. For a contrasting assessment, see Philip M. Armato, " 'Good and Evil' in Lillian Hellman's *The Children's Hour*," *Educational Theatre Journal* 25 (December 1973):443–47, reprinted in this volume.

42. Terry Curtis Fox, "Early Work," *Village Voice*, 21 August 1978, 127, 129. Also see Harold Clurman, review of *Days to Come* revival, *Nation*, 25 November 1978, 587–88.

43. Stark Young, review of *Days to Come, New Republic*, 30 December 1936, 274; Joseph Wood Krutch, "Plays Pleasant and Unpleasant," *Nation*, 26 December 1936, 769–70; Alexander Taylor, "Sights and Sounds," *New Masses*, 29 December 1936, 27.

44. *Time*, 27 February 1939, 38, 40.

45. Richard Watts, Jr., "The Theaters," *New York Herald Tribune*, 16 February 1939, 14.

46. Louis Kronenberger, "Greed," *Stage*, 1 April 1939, 36–37, 55.

47. Martin Knelman, "Starring . . . the Writer," *Atlantic Monthly* 240 (November 1977):96–98, reprinted in this volume.

48. Kronenberger, "Greed," 36–37, 55.

49. Joseph Wood Krutch, review of *Another Part of the Forest, Nation*, 7 December 1946, 671–72.

50. Brooks Atkinson, "The Play in Review," *New York Times*, 21 November 1946, 42.

51. John Mason Brown, "Seeing Things," *Saturday Review*, 14 December 1946, 20–23.

52. See Elizabeth Hardwick, "The Little Foxes Revived," *New York Review of Books*, 21 December 1967, 4–5, and letters of response by Richard Poirier and others (18 January 1968, 32) and by Penelope Gilliatt and Hardwick (1 February 1968, 30).

53. Edmund Wilson, "An Open Letter to Mike Nichols," *New York Review of Books*, 4 January 1968, 5–6, 8. This production, directed by Mike Nichols, starred Anne Bancroft as Regina.

54. James Eatman, "The Image of American Destiny: *The Little Foxes*," *Players* 48 (1973):70–73.

55. Frank Rich, review of *The Little Foxes* revival, *New York Times*, 8 May 1981, sec. C, p. 3. The popular press both reveled in and pilloried the Elizabeth Taylor presence in this production. A Sunday piece reporting on Hellman's attendance at a pre-Broadway, Washington, D.C.,

performance, notes that "everyone except Miss Taylor is afraid of her." See Leslie Garis, "Elizabeth Taylor: She Has Conquered Everything But Broadway and Now . . . ," *New York Times*, 31 May 1981, sec. 2, pp. 1, 6.

56. Brooks Atkinson, "Hellman's *Watch on the Rhine*," *New York Times*, 13 April 1941, sec. 9, p. 1.

57. Stark Young, review of *Watch on the Rhine*, *New Republic*, 14 April 1941, 498–99.

58. Basil Wright, review of *Watch on the Rhine* (London production), *Spectator*, 1 May 1942, 419. The play was successfully revived in the early eighties at London's National Theatre, starring Dame Peggy Ashcroft as Fanny Farrelly.

59. Mel Gussow, "*Watch on the Rhine* Revived," *New York Times*, 16 October 1979, sec. C, p. 20. More commonly, it is Sara's husband Kurt who is thought to resemble Julia. Gussow's suggestion is among the first to connect the figure of Julia to a character in a Hellman play.

60. Barrett Clark, "Lillian Hellman," *College English* 6 (December 1944):127–33.

61. Margaret Marshall, "Drama," *Nation*, 22 April 1944, 494–95; George Jean Nathan, review of *The Searching Wind*, in his *The Theatre Book of the Year, 1943–44* (New York: Knopf, 1944), 295–99; Stark Young, "Behind the Beyond," *New Republic*, 1 May 1944, 604.

62. See, for example, John Chapman, ed., *The Best Plays of 1950–51* (New York: Dodd, Mead, 1951); Walter Kerr, "The Stage: *The Autumn Garden*," *Commonweal*, 6 April 1951, 645; John Mason Brown, "Seeing Things: A New Miss Hellman," 27–29; and review of *The Autumn Garden*, *Time*, 19 March 1951, 51–52.

63. George Jean Nathan, *The Theatre Book of the Year, 1950–51* (New York: Knopf, 1951), 241–44. Also see Harold Clurman, "Lillian Hellman's Garden," *New Republic*, 26 March 1951, 21–22.

64. Robert Brustein, "The Play and the Unplay," *New Republic*, 14 March 1960, 22–23.

65. Alan Downer, *Recent American Drama* (Minneapolis: University of Minnesota Press, 1961), 41–42; John Gassner, "Broadway in Review," *Educational Theatre Journal* 12 (May 1960):113–31 passim; Marya Mannes, "Miss Hellman's 'Electra,' " *Reporter*, 31 March 1960, 43. Also see Jacob Adler, "Miss Hellman's Two Sisters," *Educational Theatre Journal* 15 (May 1963):112–17, reprinted in this volume.

66. John Gassner, "The Theatre Arts," *Forum* 112 (December 1949):337–40. Also see Howard Barnes, "Brilliant Adaptation," *New York Herald Tribune*, 31 October 1949, 10; Kappo Phelan, "The Stage and Screen: *Montserrat*," *Commonweal*, 18 November 1949, 179–80; John Mason Brown, "With and without Music," *Saturday Review*, 19 November 1949, 52–55; "The State of the Theatre: The Strindberg Heritage," *School and Society*, 14 January 1950, 23–28; and Harold Clurman, "Theatre: Roblès, Hellman, Blitzstein," *New Republic*, 5 December 1949, 21–22.

67. See Henry Knepler, "*The Lark*, Translation vs. Adaptation: A Case History," *Modern Drama* 1 (May 1958):15–28, and Leonard Fleischer and Doris Fleischer, "The Dramatic Adaptations of Lillian Hellman." Both essays are included in this volume.

68. Walter Kerr, "Theater: A Brisk New Joan," *New York Herald Tribune*, 17 November 1955, sec. 4, pp. 1, 3; Eric Bentley, "Theatre," *New Republic*, 5 December 1955, 21. Also see Frank O'Connor, "Saint Joans, from Arc to Lark," *Holiday* 19 (March 1956):77, 88–89; Alan Hewitt, "*The Lark*: Theatrical Bird of Passage," *Theatre Arts* 40 (March 1956):63–64, 96; and Vincent O'Flaherty, "St. Joan Wouldn't Know Herself," *America*, 28 April 1956, 109–10.

69. Henry Hewes, review of *Candide*, *Saturday Review*, 22 December 1956, 34–35; Richard Hayes, "The Stage: Mr. Bernstein Cultivates His Garden," *Commonweal*, 28 December 1956, 133–34.

70. Mary McCarthy, "Theatre: The Reform of Dr. Pangloss," *New Republic*, 17 December 1956, 30–31.

71. Brooks Atkinson, "The Theatre: *Candide*," *New York Times*, 3 December 1956, 40.

72. See "Family of Gargoyles," *Time*, 8 April 1963, 85; Marya Mannes, "The Half-World of American Drama," *Reporter*, 25 April 1963, 48–50; and, especially, *New York Theatre Critics' Reviews, 1963*, vol. 24 (New York: Critics' Theatre Reviews, 1963), 302–5, a special issue containing reviews of *My Mother, My Father and Me* not published by New York dailies because of a newspaper strike when the play opened. Also see the original essays by Timothy J. Wiles and by Leonard Fleischer and Doris Fleischer in this volume.

73. Clark, "Lillian Hellman," 127–33.

74. Edith Isaacs, "Lillian Hellman, A Playwright on the March," *Theatre Arts* 28 (January 1944):19–24.

75. Charles Thomas Samuels, review of *The Collected Plays*, 2–3, 16, 18; Renata Adler, "A Review Reviewed," *New York Times Book Review*, 9 July 1972, 39.

76. Alex Szogyi, "*The Collected Plays* by Lillian Hellman," *Saturday Review*, 12 August 1972, 51–52.

77. Robert Heilman, *The Iceman, The Arsonist and the Troubled Agent: Tragedy and Melodrama on the Modern Stage* (Seattle: University of Washington Press, 1973), 301–2; Ellen Moers, "Family Theatre," *Commentary* 54 (September 1972):96–99. Also see Brustein, "The Play and the Unplay," 22–23; and Estrin, *Lillian Hellman: Plays, Films, Memoirs*, 11.

78. Mark W. Estrin, "Lillian Hellman," in *Contemporary Dramatists*, 3d ed., ed. James Vinson (London: St. James Press, New York: St. Martin's Press, 1982), 374–78.

79. Nancy M. Tischler, "The South Stage Center: Hellman and Williams," in *The American South: Portrait of a Culture*, ed. Louis D. Rubin, Jr. (Baton Rouge: Louisiana State University Press, 1980), 323–33; W. Kenneth Holditch, "Another Part of the Country: Lillian Hellman as Southern Playwright," *Southern Quarterly* 25 (Spring 1987):11–35.

80. Mary Lynn Broe, "Bohemia Bumps into Calvin: The Deception of Passivity in Lillian Hellman's Drama," *Southern Quarterly* 19 (Winter 1981):26–41.

81. Although (as in certain essays included in this volume) the HUAC acronym is frequently employed to designate the House Committee on Un-American Activities, I prefer the more appropriate HCUA abbreviation.

82. See, respectively, "Meeting-Goer," *Time*, 2 June 1952, 74, and Paul Gray, review of *An Unfinished Woman*, *Time*, 10 May 1976, 83.

83. Bill Moyers, "Lillian Hellman: The Great Playwright Reflects on a Long, Rich Life," in Bryer, *Conversations with Lillian Hellman*, 149.

84. Joseph Epstein, "No Punches Pulled," *New Republic*, 26 July 1969, 27–29.

85. Stephen Schiff, "In Defense of *Julia*," *Boston Phoenix*, 18 October 1977, sec. 3, pp. 5, 8, 10.

86. *Scoundrel Time* (Boston: Little, Brown & Co., 1976), 154.

87. See also two unauthorized biographies (William Wright, *Lillian Hellman: The Image, the Woman*, and Carl Rollyson, *Lillian Hellman: Her Legend and Her Legacy*) for discussions of Hellman's long feud with writer Mary McCarthy, who in 1980 declared in a television interview that Hellman was a dishonest writer whose "every word . . . is a lie, including 'and' and 'the.' " Hellman brought a much publicized lawsuit against McCarthy, which in turn triggered additional charges against Hellman in support of McCarthy. Also see in this regard Norman Mailer, "An Appeal to Lillian Hellman and Mary McCarthy," *New York Times Book Review*, 11 May 1980, 3; John Simon, "Literary Lionesses," *National Review*, 16 May 1980, 614–16; and Peter Feiblemen, *Lilly: Reminiscences of Lillian Hellman*.

88. Bills, *Lillian Hellman: An Annotated Bibliography*; Riordan, *Lillian Hellman: A Bibliography: 1926–1978*; Estrin, *Lillian Hellman: Plays, Films, Memoirs*. See, for example, Estrin, 20–23.

89. Falk, *Lillian Hellman*, 95–157.

90. Lederer, *Lillian Hellman*, 104–36. Lederer appears, for example, to lump together all

Scoundrel Time critics—including Sidney Hook, Alfred Kazin, Murry Kempton and William Buckley—as the "political Right" (135).

91. Marilyn Berger, "Profile: Lillian Hellman," in Bryer, *Conversations with Lillian Hellman*, 232–73.

92. William Wright, *Lillian Hellman: The Image, the Woman;* Carl Rollyson, *Lillian Hellman: Her Legend and Her Legacy.*

93. Robert Kotlowitz, "The Rebel as Writer," *Harper's* 238 (June 1969):87–88, 90–92; Edward Weeks, review of *An Unfinished Woman, Atlantic* 224 (July 1969):106; Dorothy Rabinowitz, "Experience as Drama," *Commentary* 48 (December 1969):95–98; Patricia Meyer Spacks, *The Female Imagination* (New York: Knopf, 1975); Martha Gellhorn, "On Apocryphism," *Paris Review* 79 (Spring 1981):280–301, reprinted in abridged form in this volume.

94. Richard Poirier, review of *Pentimento, Washington Post Book World,* 16 September 1973, 1, 4–5; Richard Poirier, introduction to *Three* (Boston: Little Brown, & Co., 1979), vii–xxv; Eliot Fremont-Smith, "Lillian Hellman: Portrait of a Lady," *New York,* 17 September 1973, 82–83; Mark Schorer, review of *Pentimento, New York Times Book Review,* 23 September 1973, 1–2; John Simon, "Pentimental Journey," *Hudson Review* 27 (Winter 1973–74):743–52; Paul Theroux, "Dowager Empress," *New Statesman,* 26 April 1974, 587–88; "Painted Over," *TLS,* 26 April 1974, 440; "Flashback," *Economist,* 25 May 1974, 143–44; Marsha McCreadie, "*Julia:* Memory in *Pentimento* and On Film," *Literature/Film Quarterly* 7, no. 4 (1979):260–69.

95. Samuel McCracken, "Julia and Other Fictions by Lillian Hellman," *Commentary* 77 (June 1984):35–43. See Timothy Dow Adams, " 'Lies Like Truth': Lillian Hellman's Autobiographies," in this volume.

96. Murray Kempton, "Witnesses," 22–25; Sidney Hook, "Lillian Hellman's *Scoundrel Time,*" *Encounter* 48 (February 1977):82–91; Richard A. Falk, "*Scoundrel Time:* Mobilizing the American Intelligentsia for the Cold War," *Performing Arts Journal* 1 (Winter 1977):97–102; Alfred Kazin, "The Legend of Lillian Hellman," *Esquire* 88 (August 1977):28, 30, 34; and Timothy Dow Adams, " 'Lies Like Truth': Lillian Hellman's Autobiographies," all included in this collection.

97. See, among others cited earlier, Estrin, *Lillian Hellman: Plays, Films, Memoirs,* 20–23; Falk, *Lillian Hellman,* 147–57; Wright, *Lillian Hellman: The Image, the Woman;* and Rollyson, *Lillian Hellman, Her Legend and Her Legacy.*

98. Maureen Howard, review of *Scoundrel Time, New York Times Book Review,* 25 April 1976, 1–2.

99. Robert Sherrill, "Wisdom and Its Price," *Nation,* 19 June 1976, 757–58; Saul Maloff, "Jewel without Price," *Commonweal,* 1 July 1976, 438–42; Vivian Gornick, "Neither Forgotten Nor Forgiven," *Ms.* 5 (August 1976):46–47; Paul Gray "An Unfinished Woman," *Time,* 10 May 1976, 83.

100. Garry Wills, introduction to *Scoundrel Time,* 3–34.

101. Irving Howe, "Lillian Hellman and the McCarthy Years," *Dissent* 23 (Fall 1976):378–82.

102. Nathan Glazer, "An Answer to Lillian Hellman," *Commentary* 61 (June 1976):36–39; Hilton Kramer, "The Blacklist and the Cold War," *New York Times,* 3 October 1976, sec. 2, pp. 16–17, and "The Life and Death of Lillian Hellman," *New Criterion* 3 (October 1984):1–6; William Phillips, "What Happened in the Fifties," *Partisan Review* 43, no. 3 (1976):337–40; William F. Buckley, "*Scoundrel Time:* And Who Is the Ugliest of Them All?" *National Review,* 21 January 1977, 101–6, and "Night of the Cuckoo," *National Review,* 29 April 1977, 513; Walter Goodman, "Fair Game," *New Leader,* 24 May 1976, 10–11.

103. Philip French, "I Puritani," *New Statesman,* 5 November 1976, 635–36.

104. Diana Trilling, "Liberal Anti-Communism Re-Visited," in her *We Must March My Darlings* (New York: Harcourt Brace Jovanovich, 1977), 41–66. Also see Robert D. McFadden, "Diana Trilling Book Is Canceled; Reply to Lillian Hellman Is Cited," *New York Times,* 28

September 1976, 1, 46; Judy Klemesrud, "Lillian Hellman Denies Role in Book Rejection," *New York Times*, 29 September 1976, sec. C, p. 28; Thomas R. Edwards, review of *We Must March My Darlings*, *New York Times Book Review*, 29 May 1977, 1, 17; and Irving Howe, review of *We Must March My Darlings*, *New Republic*, 20 and 27 August 1977, 31–33.

105. Vivian Gornick, "Rhetoric of Things Past," *Village Voice*, 19 May 1980, 45–46; Robert Towers, "A Foray into the Self," *New York Times Book Review*, 1 June 1980, 3, 36; Walter Clemons, "Memory's Tricks," *Newsweek*, 2 June 1980, 76–77; Maureen Howard, "Lillian Hellman Remembers," *Washington Post Book World*, 8 June 1980, 3; Anne Duchene, "An Inattentive Pythia," *TLS*, 18 July 1980, 799; and Maggie Scarf, review of *Maybe*, *New Republic*, 2 and 9 August 1980, 36–38.

106. Marcus K. Billson and Sidonie A. Smith, "Lillian Hellman and the Strategy of the Other," in *Women's Autobiography: Essays in Criticism*, ed. Estelle C. Jelinek (Bloomington: Indiana University Press, 1980), 163–79; Bonnie Lyons, "Lillian Hellman: The First Jewish Nun on Prytania Street," in *From Hester Street to Hollywood: The Jewish-American Stage and Screen*, ed. Sarah Blacher Cohen (Bloomington: Indiana University Press, 1983), 106–22; Maurice F. Brown, "Autobiography and Memoir: The Case of Lillian Hellman," *Biography* 8 (Winter 1983):1–11; Anita Susan Grossman, "Art Versus Truth in Autobiography: The Case of Lillian Hellman," *Clio* 14 (Spring 1985):289–308.

107. Carl Rollyson, in *Lillian Hellman: Her Legend and Her Legacy*, reveals that Hellman had in fact been a member of the Communist party from 1938 to 1940 (320).

108. The *Julia* screenplay was written by Alvin Sargent, not by Hellman. Reviews of *Julia* are annotated in Estrin, *Lillian Hellman: Plays, Films, Memoirs*. Also see Riordan, *Lillian Hellman, A Bibliography: 1926–1978*.

109. One of nine eulogies to Hellman, published in the [Martha's] *Vineyard Gazette*, 6 July 1984, 10.

110. See, for example, "Lillian Hellman, Playwright, Author and Rebel, Dies at 77," *New York Times*, 1 July 1984, 1, 22; and Henry Beetle Hough, "Lillian Hellman is Burried Here Today on Beloved Island," [Martha's] *Vineyard Gazette*, 3 July 1984, 1, 11.

111. See Kevin Kelly, "Appreciation," *Boston Sunday Globe*, 1 July 1984, 16; unsigned tribute by Sheridan Morley, "Lillian Hellman," *The Times* (London), 2 July 1984, 14 (a slightly longer version appears in *Plays and Players* 44 [September 1984]:140); "Friends Offer Tributes to Lillian Hellman at a Service," *New York Times*, 4 July 1984, sec. D, p. 15; and, especially, texts of eulogies by John Hersey, William Styron, Patricia Neal, Jules Feiffer, Jerome Weisner, Annabel Nichols, Peter Feibleman, Robert Brustein, and Jack Koontz, [Martha's] *Vineyard Gazette*, 6 July 1984, 10–12. Also see Peter Feibleman, *Lilly: Reminiscences of Lillian Hellman*.

112. See, for example, David Ansen, "An Unmellowed Woman," *Newsweek*, 9 July 1984, 73; Marsha Norman, "Lillian Hellman's Gift to a Young Playwright," *New York Times*, 26 August 1984, sec. 2, pp. 1, 7; Sam A. Portaro, Jr., "Lillian Hellman and Truman Capote: An Appreciation," *Christian Century*, 15 May 1985, 494–97; and Jennifer Phillips, "Fishing with Lillian, or The Old Woman and the Sea," *Boston Sunday Globe*, 16 August 1987, sec. A, pp. 15, 18.

113. See Helen Dudar, "Shaping a Portrait of a Playwright," *New York Times*, 12 January 1986, sec. 2, pp. 1, 5; and Frank Rich, review of *Lillian*, *New York Times*, 17 January 1986, sec. C, p. 3. Also see Rollyson, *Lillian Hellman: Her Legend and Her Legacy*, 534–36, which describes William Luce's relationship with Hellman during his preparation of the play. The role of Hellman was originally performed by Zoe Caldwell, who is also quoted by Rollyson (7, 8, 20).

114. See three related articles in *The Observer* (London): Michael Davie, "The Life and Lies of Lillian Hellman," 26 October 1986, 64; Vanessa Redgrave, "When the Little Foxes Come Out of Their Lair," 2 November 1986, 12; and Michael Davie, "Lillian Hellman: Life as Fiction," 9 November 1986, 60. In the London production, Hellman was impersonated by Frances de la Tour. See Carole Woddis, review of *Lillian*, *Plays and Players*, no. 399 (December 1986):28–29.

THE PLAYS

The Ibsenite Hellman

The Dramaturgy of Blackmail in the Ibsenite Hellman

Jacob H. Adler*

As a dramatist Lillian Hellman relied heavily on blackmail. In one immediate sense it seems a dramatic convention indispensable to her work since among her six most effective out of her eight original plays (the remaining two being *Days to Come* and *The Searching Wind*), five contain clearcut instances of blackmail and the sixth, *Toys in the Attic*, employs a very near relative, coercion to obtain money through the use of a secret, but in another way rather than the threat to reveal it. Blackmail in this essay refers to *coercion by the threat to reveal a secret*.[1]

Blackmail is infrequent enough in real life, at least one must so assume, as to be a surprising feature in so many plays by a dramatist of Hellman's integrity. Few prominent dramatists use it so frequently. Very few use it at all. There is none, for example, in Chekhov; none in any of the major disciples of Ibsen other than Hellman—none in Shaw, O'Casey, Miller; one minor instance each in Strindberg's two major American heirs, O'Neill and Williams. Blackmail occurs with some frequency in the well-made play, a tradition from which Hellman sometimes borrows. In *The Rise and Fall of the Well-Made Play*[2] John Russell Taylor outlines several plots that involve blackmail, including plays by Wilde and Galsworthy, but he also details a great many plots that do not. There is no suggestion that blackmail was so frequent in any dramatist in the heyday of the well-made play as it is with Hellman.

Yet Ibsen himself—Hellman's principal master—used blackmail at least three times,[3] and it is instructive to compare the dramaturgical and philosophical purposes and effects of blackmail in the plays of these two playwrights.

In *A Doll House*, for example, Krogstad blackmails Nora Helmer for having forged her father's name in order to get money to save her husband's life. She innocently failed to realize the legal gravity of her act, and the blackmailer is himself a man more desperate than evil. By play's end the blackmailer is redeemed and Nora confronts the extent of her ignorance,

*This essay was written specifically for this volume and is published here for the first time by permission of the author.

naiveté, and false idealism. The play's structure demands that there be a blackmailer so he may reveal the truth to Nora's husband, with the threat to reveal it more widely. The blackmailer must be redeemable so that he will presently withdraw the threat. And this must be the pattern so that Nora may first see her husband's reaction to the threat and then his reaction to the threat withdrawn.[4] It is true that Mrs. Linde could have told Helmer the truth because of her belief that marriage should be open; or in some way Helmer could have been made to find it out for himself. But neither of these alternatives could have resulted in the necessary double pattern. Blackmail is indispensable to the plot of A Doll House. One may wish it were not—wish that Ibsen had found some less melodramatic, less well-made and nineteenth-century-villainish device for achieving his purpose, but no reasonable alternative seems possible.

In Ghosts the blackmail is much less prominent and central. Engstrand, the plausible rascal, convinces his dupe Manders that Manders's carelessness was responsible for the fire that destroyed the orphanage; and by promising to keep the "secret," or even to take the blame himself, he coerces Manders (who scarcely realizes he is being coerced) into providing financial and moral backing for his proposed "sailors' rest home," which will actually be a brothel. The transaction has ironic, almost tragic significance in relation to the Alving heritage;[5] but occurring as it does near the end of a play in which Manders may be viewed as partly comic in his credulousness and Engstrand as partly comic in his hypocrisy, the blackmail is of itself partly laughable: two characters who closely resemble traditional comic types perform an action that would be far more at home in comedy than in tragedy. And such generic confusion leads to another irony: the Alving heritage not only ends in a brothel, it arrives there in a traditionally comic way. Because it is a side issue, as it is in A Doll House, the blackmail is certainly not as essential to the plot, and given Manders's credulity, one would think that Engstrand could have duped him—though not as swiftly—with some other kind of chicanery. Blackmail thus functions in Ghosts as a subtle example of generic irony and, more obviously, as one of dramatic literature's frequent timesaving devices to speed an action to its inevitable conclusion.

In Hedda Gabler the blackmail is once more central and serious: the victim, Hedda, is driven to suicide (as Nora had once threatened suicide). But here the blackmail comes more naturally than in A Doll House in that the blackmailer, Judge Brack, is scarcely aware that what he is doing is blackmail. It is for him a variety of seduction, and he does not remotely expect his gambit to be declined, much less avoided through suicide. It is of course wonderfully ironic that having made Lovborg her victim by attempting to drive him to suicide, Hedda makes herself another man's victim and is driven to suicide in turn. What happens is thoroughly in character for both Hedda and Brack. The blackmail is in this sense a credible result of what has occurred, neither intrusive nor forced, and it is difficult to envision any alternative. For Ibsen's purposes it is almost the ideal device. If there is a hint of bad nineteenth-century melodrama with Brack as the mustachioed villain whispering threats to a helpless woman, it is unavoidable but singularly appropriate: Hedda, who creates melodrama, rings down the fourth act curtain, herself both victim and perpetrator of the most blatantly melodramatic kind of action.

Yet in another sense the blackmail in *Hedda Gabler* is less organic and essential than that in *A Doll House*. The more natural outcome for the neurotic Hedda Gabler type is, as Shaw said,[6] to live out a long life, forever bored, forever poisoning everything she touches. Ibsen desired a theatrical ending and achieved a marvelous one, endowing Hedda with characteristics that make the suicide highly probable. Skepticism arises not over the suicide but over its immediate circumstances—the detective story premise by which precisely the wrong person learns the damning facts of Lovborg's death and possesses the power to use them. What the audience is entitled to know, but what *Hedda Gabler* cannot tell, is what would have happened to Hedda if everything occurred as written *except* Judge Brack's discovery of his fatal knowledge. In this sense, the blackmail is an intrusion, perhaps even a mistake. Its best defense is probably that the sort of alternative Shaw suggested would be generically more appropriate to a novel than to a play.

Ibsen shows blackmail to be a danger to the naive, for Hedda is in her own way as naive as Nora and Manders. And Ibsen shows attempts made to exploit or to coerce the naive in other ways, in such cases as Dr. Stockmann (*An Enemy of the People*), Hedvig (*The Wild Duck*), and Rosmer (*Rosmersholm*), with Stockmann, like Nora, learning from the process, and the other two, like Hedda, committing suicide. Ibsen's blackmailers have a variety of purposes, not just extortion of money: to recover a job (*A Doll House*), to gain respectability for a nefarious project through the support of a minister (*Ghosts*), to gain a woman's bed (*Hedda Gabler*).

Similarly, his blackmailers vary in the degree of their villainy: Engstrand is an amoral rascal, Brack a rake, Krogstad a man desperately trying to recover from past error, a man capable of conversion to good. At least two of his cases smack of nineteenth-century melodrama; the third recalls traditional dramatic types. The blackmailers transcend these limitations in varying degrees. Krogstad, the most fully drawn of the three, is a credible if limited picture of a man both sinned against and sinning. Brack is little more than a womanizer, Engstrand little more than a hypocritical scoundrel. In other words, Krogstad is relatively round, the others flat. The causes of their villainy are not probed, as are those of Krogstad.[7]

Along the same line, in realistic literature a blackmailer, like a murderer, requires credible motive and credible opportunity. All three motives are credible; opportunity is more complicated. Krogstad's discovery of Nora's clumsy forgery is natural enough, though the occasion for him to use the knowledge (his being dismissed and Mrs. Linde given his job) involves considerable coincidence. In *Ghosts,* the opportunity depended on the fire, and the fire itself is a contrivance whose effectiveness is argued by critics,[8] one that Ibsen imposed upon the play, perhaps justifiably, perhaps not. Beyond this, the fire had to occur when Manders was available (which was seldom), and he and Engstrand had to be at the orphanage at a time just preceding it: a combination of circumstances almost as unlikely as the fire itself, though the occasion, the night before the dedication of the orphanage, lends some likelihood. In *Hedda Gabler* it is not unnatural that a man in Brack's position should learn about the pistol; what might be unnatural is that the Tesmans' one close friend should be the man in a position to derive that information.

The blackmail has differing degrees of relationship to Ibsen's structure. In *A Doll House* it is apparently essential to the outcome. In *Ghosts* the structural, as opposed to the symbolic, involvement is minimal. In *Hedda Gabler* the blackmail is essential to the ending Ibsen chose, though one might question whether it is the right ending. All three instances involve irony: the irony of Torvald Helmer's double shift in attitude, behavior at least as morally ambiguous as the blackmailer's; the irony of a minister duped into supporting immorality, and the Alving heritage ending in a brothel; the ironies already described in *Hedda Gabler*, plus the irony of Tesman's being far better off after his wife dies. In all three cases the irony is successful, though it naturally has more significance in the two plays where the blackmail is structurally necessary.

Blackmail occurs in at least three out of a series of seven Ibsen plays (from *A Doll House* to *Hedda Gabler*), surely more often than one might "realistically" expect from the father of modern dramatic realism. But in three of the last four of this series suicide occurs even more frequently—at least six times, with the threat of a seventh: one in *The Wild Duck* with the threat of another, three in *Rosmersholm*, two in *Hedda Gabler*.

If Hellman uses blackmail more often than Ibsen, she uses suicide less—only once, and that in her first play, *The Children's Hour*. On the one hand, there is one murder in each of her next three plays (*Days to Come*, *The Little Foxes*, *Watch on the Rhine*); there are no murders in Ibsen. Thereafter she does a better job than Ibsen in eliminating physical violence. It occurs again significantly (but not to the extent of death) only in her last original play, *Toys in the Attic*. She cuts down, then, on the violence but increases the psychic violence of blackmail.

The blackmail is in some respects at least as various as in Ibsen. In *The Children's Hour* Mary Tilford intimidates one of her schoolmates into supporting her vicious, destructive lie by threatening to reveal the other child's petty thievery if she does not. In *The Little Foxes* Regina extorts far more than her legitimate share of the profits in a family enterprise by threatening to reveal that her brothers have stolen her dead husband's bonds. In *Watch on the Rhine* a penniless Roumanian count warns that he will reveal to the German Embassy (in the summer of 1941) the identity of the son-in-law of a wealthy Washington family as that of a prominent member of the anti-Nazi underground unless he is given a large sum of money; and while the family agrees to pay it, the son-in-law, who does not trust the count and who knows that the count's information endangers not only his own life but that of many of his friends, murders the count in what he considers a legitimate act of war.

In *Another Part of the Forest* Ben Hubbard forces his father to relinquish to him his entire estate by threatening to reveal an episode from his past that he has just discovered, which, if publicized, would probably result in the father's lynching. In *The Autumn Garden* a seventeen-year-old girl insists upon blackmailing a wealthy woman for money (by threatening to exaggerate a very minor scandal about the woman's husband), when the woman would be quite willing to aid her financially simply as an act of generosity. And in *Toys in the Attic* in a plot that keeps flirting with blackmail, if never quite crossing its literal line, Julian Berniers acquires $100,000 by learning the truth about the value of a piece of apparently worthless property that a wealthy man will need to own, buying the property, and gouging the man.

Within this seeming variety, however, two significant elements emerge: first, the similarity of the blackmail in *The Little Foxes* and *Another Part of the Forest;* second, the fact that Hellman's blackmail is unlike Ibsen's in that all but one instance (and that the first, *The Children's Hour*) has money as its motive. It is both appropriate and ironic that the instance of blackmail in the two Hubbard plays should be virtually identical, since Ben Hubbard treats his father in the second play precisely as he in turn will be treated by his sister Regina twenty years later in the first one. Blackmail runs in the family, and Ben gets what he has given. But blackmail is only one aspect of the evil of these people who are equally prepared to commit theft and murder, and who are capable of blatant acts of cruelty and oppression. Blackmail is simply part of the pattern, a part that works best on your own family, if only because they are scoundrels and because it is less likely that you will know anyone else well enough to blackmail. In *The Little Foxes,* indeed, it is almost cozy. And no one can really be called a victim since the blackmailed would readily become the blackmailer should the opportunity present itself. To the Hubbards blackmail is a natural business tactic.

Blackmail is an essential device to bring the plots of both plays to neat and satisfying conclusions wherein the tables are turned. One has trouble imagining anything else that would enable Ben to defeat his father or Regina her brothers. On the other hand, one may feel, as one does with Ibsen, that the device in these cases reflects the worst aspects of nineteenth-century melodrama and the well-made play. And in *Another Part of the Forest* the sequence of events leading to Ben's victory is overmanipulated, too coincidental and cliff-hanging, on sober thought if not in the viewing, to retain credibility.[9] But if one can accept the Hubbards at all—and some critics and audiences have found them too unrelievedly evil to believe—then one can easily accept them as seizing willingly upon blackmail when it comes to hand, and as having committed acts that would have made them vulnerable to it in the first place.

At the other extreme are the cases in *Watch on the Rhine* and *The Autumn Garden* where the victims of blackmail are guilty of nothing, are indeed more (in *Rhine*) or less (in *Garden*) admirable in their willingness to behave in such a way as to protect others. And the blackmailers, too, differ from the Hubbards. The count in *Watch on the Rhine*—an opportunist, thief, petty power seeker—would like to be a Hubbard but can't, partly because (like that lesser Hubbard, Oscar) he lacks the brains, partly because he has the glimmerings of a conscience and the ability to recognize good when he sees it and differentiate it from evil. Sophie in *The Autumn Garden* commits blackmail only to avoid being patronized, surely a motive very close to unique; unlike the count and the Hubbards she is in no sense evil at all.

Yet blackmail is apparently essential to *Watch on the Rhine*, though, in contrast to the Hubbard plays, more for the sake of theme than plot. One can imagine in the circumstances almost nothing else that would drive Kurt to murder, and it is essential to Hellman's philosophic purpose to show that war and oppression can drive to violence the most philosophically and temperamentally nonviolent of men; to show that not even a wealthy and cultured family on a country estate in a noncombatant country three thousand miles from war is safe from war's violence; and to show the heroism of the anti-Nazi underground. (Except that the murder sends Kurt back to Europe sooner and more dangerously, the blackmail is necessary to plot in *Watch on the Rhine* only to the extent that it results in the murder of the count, leaving his wife free to marry the son of the household: a subplot that is something of an excrescence on the play.) It is true that the count might have been a real Nazi who planned to report to the embassy simply out of a sense of duty, without attempting blackmail, but Kurt had a much less ostensible choice, and the necessary point that he chose murder when there seemed to be, from his wife's family's point of view, a viable alternative, would have been lost.

In *The Autumn Garden,* in contrast, the blackmail seems almost wholly gratuitous, as though Hellman could scarcely let go of a play without it. True, she wants to show Nick's wife paying cash to extricate Nick from another folly, as she has had to do, humiliatingly, time and again, and she wants to get Sophie the money to return to France where she belongs (not in her American aunt's household). Blackmail increases Nina's humiliation and emphasizes Sophie's sense of independence. It throws light on the characters of both, though the light is merely additional, not new. But in real life, one imagines, Sophie would either ask for and accept the money as a gift—at some cost to her self-respect—and go, or refuse it and stay. Blackmail is surely not so obvious an option. Indeed, by using it Sophie saves her self-respect at the cost of a rather acrobatic rationalization.

In *The Children's Hour* Rosalie Wells is a pathetic child who in the play is little more than an instrument, a tool of the plot, since without some sort of corroboration Mary's slander would not have the necessary effect. The blackmail is another example of Mary's destructive, psychotic evil, her urge to tyrannize, but its primary purpose is as a plot necessity, to be defended only on the assumption that in a girls' school there is almost certain to be some misbehavior open to blackmail, and that if there is, Mary is the type who will almost surely discover it. To be sure, a child who simply hates the schoolmistresses as much as Mary does might serve as an accomplice instead of a victim, but it is difficult to imagine Mary with an accomplice—she is a loner—and an accomplice would keep Mary's specific evil from standing out in such bold relief.

In *Toys in the Attic* Cyrus Warkins, the unseen victim, is apparently a powerful and sinister figure, a latter-day Hubbard who quite probably gets what he deserves. But the man who victimizes him is not evil, merely weak—and a part of his purpose may even seem admirable since he wants to help other people, including his own wife and sisters and the wife of his victim. The coercion-for-money in *Toys* is, first, a device for getting the plot started—a device for supplying Julian with the cash with which he unintentionally and devastatingly disillusions his sisters—and, second, a device for bringing the plot to a circular conclusion, since the victim—and he must be someone capable of doing it—turns the tables, recovers his money, and almost destroys Julian. In a number of ways, coercion-for-money is used differently. This is the only play except *Rhine* in which coercion-for-money motivates an action beyond merely bringing the plot to its conclusion; in *Toys* its use as motivation occurs much earlier. It is the only play except *Rhine* in which the victim turns the tables. But as in most of the other plays, the coercion-for-money is essential. The only other ways for Julian to have secured the money are by stealing it or by real blackmail (either of which actions would make him worse than he is), or by winning it, which would have its own irony but which would make the ending (and his wife's and his sister Carrie's involvement in the ending) virtually impossible to achieve.

Hellman uses blackmail for different dramatic and moralistic purposes than does Ibsen. In Ibsen it is the naive who are blackmailed. In Hellman it is the naive only in *Children's Hour* and *Rhine,* and even these are very special cases, since in the first the situation demands a naive child—that is, a person who is almost by definition naive—and in the second the victims, sophisticated and worldly-wise, are naive only in one very special way. In general Hellman's naive characters—Lavinia Hubbard, Birdie Hubbard, Constance Tuckerman in *Garden,* the sisters in *Toys*—are not blackmailed, partly no doubt because this dramatist presents blackmail as almost always motivated by money, and such characters in Hellman rarely have any. (In Ibsen, interestingly, while the rich may have blackmailable secrets, they are not blackmailed: for example, Bernick in *Pillars of Society,* Mrs. Alving in *Ghosts,* Old Werle in *The Wild Duck.*)

Thus, as suggested earlier, the motive for blackmail is much less various than in Ibsen: it is for money in five out of the six plays. Money in Hellman's plays is the normal symbol of power.[10] This does not mean that the penniless are necessarily naive—witness Kurt in *Rhine*—or that they may not have a kind of power of their own; nor does it mean that the wealthy, such as the Farrellys in *Rhine*, are necessarily evil. It does mean that in Hellman, again unlike in Ibsen, what the blackmailer generally seeks—and this includes Mary Tilford—is power. The count in *Rhine* wants once again to throw his weight around in Europe. Ben in *Forest* has almost literally no use for his father's money except in terms of the power it gives him; he is not interested in culture, in recreation, in travel, in sex. Regina in *Foxes* wants to move to Chicago, but her motive is to be a power in a society she views as glamorous— and in any case a large part of her satisfaction in blackmail is in getting the better of her brothers. Even in *Garden* Sophie is seeking the power not to be patronized or supported. Only in *Toys* is "power" not a very suitable term for what is being sought, though even there the ability to give away money, and hence make people take certain actions, provides Julian with a certain enjoyment of power, even if he doesn't realize it.

As in Ibsen, the perpetrators vary widely in their villainy, from Mary Tilford and the Hubbards who vastly relish their wicked machinations; to the count whose machinations are amateurish and immoral rather than amoral; to Sophie whose wrong is limited to making an unhappy woman momentarily still more so; to Julian, who is not a blackmailer and whose wrongdoing is shakily legal and not consciously meant for anything but good.

Except for the Hubbards, the blackmailers are not more melodramatic than in Ibsen, and in one case, Sophie in *Garden*, less so. (Ibsen's victims are naive, and naiveté probably increases the sense of melodrama, as it does in such Dickens characters as Little Nell. Ibsen mitigates this to an extent by showing Nora starting to grow out of her naiveté, by making Manders both exasperating and comical, and by making Hedda partly unsympathetic, someone whose behavior has made her deserve what she gets.) In Ibsen two of the three blackmailers are credible within the limits of dramatic types; the third, while still hinting of melodrama, is rounder, his motives probed, his characterization less limited to type. In Hellman the degree and variety of credibility are greater. People differ, as already stated, in their acceptance of the Hubbards, and while Hellman's probing of their background in *Forest* makes their behavior in *Foxes* more believable in retrospect, the characters in *Foxes* have their being in that play and must be accepted or rejected accordingly. In both plays the blackmailer is unadulteratedly evil and smacks of melodramatic villainy. But Regina and Ben have a greater *variety of existence* than Engstrand or Brack or even Krogstad, and they are much more vivid creations: partly but not wholly because they, unlike Ibsen's blackmailers or the rest of Hellman's, are central characters in their plays. Mary Tilford's psychosis makes her necessarily a flat character, believable within the limits of that psychosis. The relative depth of Hellman's conception of Kurt and Sara in *Rhine* makes the count, in spite of his moral ambivalence, seem contrastingly superficial. Sophie in *Garden* is a believable, though not especially distinctive or interesting, minor character, not a type but not a very distinct individual. Julian is a credible and individualized example of the genus ne'er-do-well, though Hellman strains belief in the degree of his irresponsibility in certain behavior (coming home a day too soon, carrying $100,000 in cash), which is essential to the plot.

In every play but *Garden* the motive is credible—and even there the motive for gaining money is acceptable though the insistence upon blackmail is not. Opportunity, however, is in most cases more badly strained than in Ibsen. It may be defensible in *Children's Hour* although the presence of Mary's dupe when necessary takes some manipulating. But in *Foxes*, it depends upon the device of the stealing of the bonds, an act too clumsy and too dangerous for a Ben Hubbard (something Hellman may herself have recognized: "You're getting old, Ben," she has Regina say; "Your tricks aren't as smart as they used to be"[11]). In *Rhine* the count's availability as a houseguest and Kurt's carelessness with his confidential papers, which makes the count's knowledge possible, stretch credulity.[12] In *Forest* the sequence of Ben's discovery about his father places the greatest strain on belief of anything in all the plays. In *Garden* the opportunity depends on the complex coincidence of Nick's falling asleep dead drunk in one of the public rooms on the sofa that Sophie uses as a bed; on Sophie's permitting him to sleep there all night, while she reports it to no one and stays in the room; and on his being discovered by the one guest in the house who would put the worst construction on what she saw and report it widely. In *Toys* the opportunity and the coercion precede the play and are hence of less importance in it. The opportunity is complex but, insofar as it can be deciphered, believable.

Blackmail is at least as essential structurally as in Ibsen. In the Hubbard plays it is crucial to the turning of the tables. In *Children's Hour* the structure demands that Mary triumph, which she could not do without corroboration, and the corroboration, given Mary's character, demands blackmail. In *Rhine* it is essential thematically and may also be essential in the sense that the play would not have an action without it. It is only incidental in *Garden*. Coercion-for-money motivates the action in *Toys* and is central in that no other method of obtaining the money is appropriate to Julian's character or can lead to the same circular effect.

The irony is less consistent and on the whole less telling than in Ibsen. In *Children's Hour* it is minimal, almost entirely limited to Martha's discovery that Mary's lie is for her, in spirit at least, not a lie at all; and this has no direct connection with the blackmail. In the Hubbard plays there is the irony of the tables turned—the victimizers caught out and made victims—and such subsidiary ironies as Regina's discovery in *Foxes* that what she has done frightens her, or Regina's turning in *Forest* from her father to Ben, the new source of power: ironies that are theatrically very satisfying but probably rather shallow. In *Rhine* they are various and deeper: Kurt and his family, trying to gain respite from Europe's evil, confront it even in their American refuge; Fanny, with all her woman-of-the-world sophistication and genuine wisdom, is naive in the one necessary area; the man of peace must commit murder. Such ironies are useful and biting, and they are remarkably relevant and revealing to a nation literally on the eve of Pearl Harbor. In *Garden*, in a minimal incident, there is slight irony in Nina Denery's rather spurious attempt to play Lady Bountiful being seen through and overturned by a very determined young girl. In *Toys* the irony lies in Julian's unawareness of evil and in the uselessness of the extortion, since money, it turns out, is not what anyone wants: this is an irony as central and as biting as those in *Rhine* and less limited to a particular historical moment in its relevance.

Hellman employs many more instances of blackmail than Ibsen. If criteria for successful use of blackmail in drama are believable characters, structural soundness, credible motive, credible opportunity, and sufficient irony, then in most areas Hellman meets the test as well as Ibsen. In one area, opportunity, neither does very well, though Ibsen does better. In another, irony, Ibsen may again do somewhat better. Both playwrights are melodramatic because to an extent melodrama is inherent in blackmail.

But why is there so much blackmail in either playwright? Why do they write plays in which blackmail is necessary, or even possible? One conceivable answer is that they write plays about secrets. Secrets are a part of the well-made tradition from which both Ibsen and Hellman draw. But another reason that Ibsen writes plays about secrets is that he writes end-plays,[13] plays that depict the very end of a long story in which the revelation of something that occurred earlier to someone previously ignorant of it precipitates action that brings the story to a conclusion. There are secrets in most of the plays from *Pillars of Society* onward, and most of them are end-plays. Where there are secrets there may be blackmail, though there is of course none in those two greatest of end-plays *Oedipus* and *Hamlet,* and Ibsen creates many situations where blackmail would be perfectly possible and does not occur.

Hellman also writes plays about secrets, but only one of her plays containing blackmail is even partially an end-play—*Another Part of the Forest.* Two others, *Rhine* and *Toys,* are not end-plays even though the secret precedes the play. In two others, *Foxes* and *Garden,* the secret making the blackmail possible occurs in the play itself. And in *Children's Hour* there is no genuine secret other than Martha's—a provocative one but unrelated directly to the blackmail and revealed after the fact, almost (as the play is structurally conceived) to a point of irrelevance.

So "end-play" is not an explanation for the blackmail in Hellman, and the existence of secrets isn't either. Many other modern American plays contain major secrets of one kind or another: plays as various as *Anna Christie, Desire Under the Elms, Strange Interlude, The Iceman Cometh, Winterset, A Streetcar Named Desire, Cat on a Hot Tin Roof, All My Sons, Death of a Salesman, Who's Afraid of Virginia Woolf?* And in some instances they are quite blackmailable secrets. Joe Keller in *All My Sons,* for example, is wide open to blackmail for the crime he has committed. In *Streetcar* Stanley has two options for achieving his goal: either to tell Mitch the truth about Blanche or to threaten Blanche with doing so if she does not break with Mitch and leave. He chooses, of course, the former. No other American makes such extensive use of blackmail as Hellman does. It is hard to find other instances at all.

For her, the *why* has probably no simple answer. There is the background of melodrama and the well-made play. There is the background of Ibsen. There is Hellman's constant use, her near obsession, with money as motive.[14] There is her concern with oppression; and while the people who get blackmailed in her plays are, as already shown, not necessarily of the "oppressed" type, neither are the blackmailers necessarily of the "oppressor" type; nevertheless her plays show a wide range of the possibilities of oppression in one of its manifestations, blackmail. Blackmail adds to the scope of the Hubbards' capacity for oppression in *The Little Foxes*. It enables the oppressed (Ben) to rebel and become the oppressor in *Another Part of the Forest*. It is revelatory of Nazi oppression in *Watch on the Rhine*. *The Autumn Garden* shows generosity as a form of oppression that blackmail can counter. In *Toys in the Attic* what Julian does may show that love itself can become a form of oppression. Hellman makes clear that, for her, greed and oppression are among the worst of evils. While her range of blackmail is such that sometimes it represents neither of these evils in its ordinary sense, nevertheless it would be hard to find another human action so neatly capable of representing both.

Notes

1. There are, of course, other kinds of coercion. Thus, for example, in Ibsen's *Pillars of Society* Bernick threatens his foreman with dismissal unless he agrees to direct shoddy repairs on a ship. In Hellman's *Days to Come* Rodman's lawyer is able to force Rodman to bring in strikebreakers because Rodman owes his lawyer a great deal of money. These are instances of coercion, but not blackmail.

2. New York: Hill and Wang, 1967.

3. In two other cases, those of Stockmann (*An Enemy of the People*) and Rosmer (*Rosmersholm*), the means used to coerce come close to attempted blackmail. This is especially true of Mortensgaard's attempt to keep Rosmer from revealing his abandonment of Christianity.

4. "For the catastrophe to be precipitated in the precise form which it takes, Krogstad's destruction of the forged bill is essential" (Brian Downs, *A Study of Six Plays by Ibsen* [Cambridge: Cambridge University Press, 1950], 111).

5. See, for example, Robert Brustein, *The Theater of Revolt* (Boston: Little, Brown & Co., 1964), 69.

6. See, for example, *Quintessence of Ibsenism* (New York: Hill & Wang, 1964), 180–81. See also Richard Gilman, *The Making of Modern Drama* (New York: Farrar, Straus, 1974), 66.

7. But some critics disagree, and one might take the point of view that Ibsen recognized that his plot demanded an improbability, that he attempted to shore it up by examining Krogstad's background, and that the attempt fails. See, for example, Eric Bentley: "When convenient to Ibsen, he [Krogstad] is a blackmailer. When inconvenient, he is converted" (*In*

Search of Theater [New York: Knopf, 1953], 345). See also Downs, *Six Plays,* 111, and John Gassner, *Masters of the Drama,* 3d ed. (New York: Dover Publications, 1954), 370.

8. For example, Bentley, *Search,* 344.

9. For a fuller treatment of this point, see Jacob H. Adler, *Lillian Hellman,* (Austin, Texas: Steck-Vaughn, 1969), 29–30. Here and elsewhere in the present essay I express attitudes similar to those in my earlier studies of Hellman, though for different purposes.

10. See also Jacob H. Adler, "The Rose and the Fox: Notes on the Southern Drama," in *South: Modern Southern Literature in Its Cultural Setting,* ed. Louis D. Rubin, Jr., and Robert D. Jacobs (Garden City, N.Y.: Doubleday, 1970), 369–70.

11. *The Little Foxes,* in *The Collected Plays* (Boston: Little, Brown & Co., 1972), 197.

12. Hellman tried to rationalize this through Kurt: "There seemed no safer place than Sara's home. It was careless of you [Fanny] to have in your house a man who opens baggage and blackmails" (*Watch on the Rhine,* in *Collected Plays,* 247).

13. Cf. Downs, *Six Plays,* 84; Raymond Williams, *Drama from Ibsen to Brecht* (New York: Oxford University Press, 1969), 48. But while "end-plays" help explain the prevalence of secrets in Ibsen, they do little to explain the blackmail. *Ghosts* is an end-play, but the blackmail does not concern that aspect of it. *Hedda Gabler* is not strictly an end-play. Only in *A Doll House* (and in *Rosmersholm,* if Mortensgaard's conversation may be viewed as attempted blackmail) does the blackmail relate to the end-play structure.

14. In value money in her plays is at best neutral. It gives old Mrs. Tilford a power in society the use of which destroys her. It gives old Mrs. Ellis in *Garden* the power to be independent, which is good, but also the power to force other people around, which is not. In the hands of the Hubbards money is evil. In the hands of Kurt, who has collected contributions of $23,000 to help his cause, it is good. The wealthy old Mrs. Farrelly had a very happy marriage. The marriage of her penniless daughter Sara is at least equally happy. Money enables Mrs. Prine in *Toys* to live a life of complete unconventionality, which might be admirable were it not representative of her equally complete lack of concern for anyone other than herself and her lover; and otherwise in that play money is totally destructive. Money is important in Hellman's plays presumably because she finds it important in the world she scrutinizes. But this is true in Ibsen also. Money or the lack of it is a major concern in almost every play from *Pillars of Society* through *Hedda Gabler.*

The Chekhovian Hellman

Miss Hellman's Two Sisters   Jacob H. Adler*

Of *Toys in the Attic*, Lillian Hellman's most recent play, Alan S. Downer has declared that it "achieves that magnitude long ago declared an essential of serious drama."[1] I agree with Downer; and since magnitude is not a quality one would have readily associated with Miss Hellman, it seems worth while to investigate *Toys in the Attic* in some detail to see how it differs from her earlier plays, and just what kind of a play it is.

Critics have spoken frequently of Miss Hellman's debt to Ibsen, and less frequently of her debt to Chekhov. The pattern they have seen, and roughly a correct pattern, is that Miss Hellman was a disciple of Ibsen from *The Children's Hour* to *Another Part of the Forest;* that she turned to Chekhov for her theme and plot technique in *The Autumn Garden;* and that she returned to Ibsen (with perhaps a touch of Tennessee Williams) in *Toys in the Attic*. I have written at considerable length of this pattern in Miss Hellman's work in another place.[2] Here I should like to consider what I there mentioned briefly: that, while Miss Hellman may—possibly—return to Ibsen's technique in *Toys in the Attic*, her basic material comes from Chekhov's *The Three Sisters*.

The broad outlines of the connection are clear enough. In both plays, we find unhappy sisters and a brother who is a failure. In both plays, the family is of genteel origin and the sisters live in the family home, which they all own in common. In both plays, the brother marries, against the wishes of his sisters, a silly woman who increases the family's stock of unhappiness. In both plays, the sisters want, or think they want, to go somewhere else (Moscow; "Europe"), and finally discover that they never will. In both plays, money is blamed for a good deal, but (we discover, whether or not the characters do) does not deserve all the blame. In both plays, an act of violence near the close (the death of the baron in a duel; the beating and robbery of Julian) returns the situation to a state of, more or less, equilibrium.

Of course in the Prozoroff family there are three sisters, in the Berniers family only two. This is mainly evidence that Chekhov is more interested in

*Reprinted from *Educational Theatre Journal* 15 (May 1963):112–17, by permission of the Johns Hopkins University Press.

the changes to be rung on his theme, Miss Hellman in a tight, neat plot. The one left out is the unhappily married sister, who would be an excrescence in Miss Hellman, but who allows Chekhov to demonstrate another kind of frustration, and to show that marriage is no escape from the doom of the helpless aristocrat. (And thus the duel which kills Irina's fiancé at the end of *The Three Sisters* is not unmotivated piling on of suffering, since we have seen enough to guess that Irina will be equally unhappy and long-suffering, married or unmarried.)

But in another sense the third sister is not really missing from *Toys in the Attic*. Personalities dovetail. Anna, the elder Berniers, parallels Olga, the eldest Prozoroff. Olga and Anna are alike comparatively reserved and self-sustaining, though Anna is the more stoic and the more clear-sighted, and Olga (being Russian!) the more openly emotional; and both have frequent headaches which seem to be the result of their self-retraint. Caroline Berniers is like the youngest Prozoroff, Irina, in that she was once pretty and that she still wants to be treated as the baby; and both Carrie and Irina feel a psychological need to work, even though they hate (or pretend to hate, or think they hate) the work they do. But Carrie is like Masha, the middle Prozoroff sister, in that men are a primary source of her misery. Masha is desperately bored by her husband, and by his superior, the director of schools. She is hopelessly in love with another man, who leaves permanently at the play's end. Carrie Berniers bitterly hates her employer and is in love with her brother—who threatens to leave permanently near the play's end. But another important characteristic of Masha is shared by Anna Berniers. Masha, like Anna, has a strong sense of justice. Masha, like Anna, would bring her brother's irresponsibility out into the open. Thus, while Anna primarily parallels Olga, and Carrie parallels Irina, the main characteristics of Masha are shared between the two.

The parallels between Andrei Prozoroff and Julian Berniers are obvious. Both are considered to have promise; neither fulfills it. Both gamble. Both impose heavily on their sisters, who adore them. Prozoroff mortgages his family home and Berniers pays off the mortgage on his, but the results are not very different. If Prozoroff is less obviously a drag on society than Berniers, it is mainly because a not entirely destitute aristocrat still had position and prestige in a provincial Russian town.

The similarities between the girls that the two married are less manifest but still discernible. Both girls at first appearance are childish and uncertain (though Natasha's behavior may be partly pretence). But we see Natasha's development over the years, while we see Lily only on two early, critical, still childish days. Both are at first very much afraid of their sisters-in-law. Natasha's strong will, her lack of imagination and of aristocratic feeling, enable her eventually to get her way about everything. Lily's off-balance emotions and unorthodox unworldliness make prediction difficult. But we do see her going directly after what she wants without the slightest regard for the feelings or opinions of others; and while the Berniers sisters represent more formidable opposition than the Prozoroffs, the outcome once Lily settles into the family home (as Natasha did) is very far from assured. Both girls dress unorthodoxly. Both have neurotic attachments—Lily for her husband, Natasha for her children. Natasha carries on a love affair almost openly; Lily's desire for her husband is expressed with a startling and embarrassing openness.

The other on-stage characters in the two plays offer no discernible parallels. But in both plays there are off-stage characters who have a good deal of life and reality:[3] in *The Three Sisters*, Vershinin's wife and the director of schools; in *Toys in the Attic*, Mr. and Mrs. Cy Warkins. And in each case the man is regarded as a tyrant with some power, and the woman is desperately unhappy in her marriage.

There are other minor but convincing parallels. Olga's second speech is, "It's warm today." Carrie's second speech is (referring to the weather), "Hot."[4] Olga's opening speech is, "Father died just a year ago today." Early in act 1, Anna says, "Papa's been dead twenty-two years." Both sets of sisters talk about cemeteries and family graves. Masha refuses to believe Andrei is in love; Carrie refuses to believe Julian had an affair, and she doesn't like to think of the physical facts of his marriage. Olga says of Andrei, "That's the way he does—he's always leaving us"—which is just Carrie's complaint about Julian. Carrie and Anna practice their French, which they will never have occasion to use; much is made of the fact that the Prozoroff sisters know three or four languages and have no use for them. There are of course important differences, such as the emphasis on the military in Chekhov and on sex in Miss Hellman; and the important character of Lily's mother in *Toys* is like no one in *The Three Sisters*, though in her break from upperclass mores, her dependence on her lover, and her neglect of her child she does somewhat resemble Madame Arkadin in Chekhov's *The Sea Gull*.

The plot technique is of course very different. *The Three Sisters* seems the most casually developed of any of Chekhov's four major productions. The action covers a period of almost four years. *Toys in the Attic* is very tightly plotted and covers less than twenty-four hours—the briefest time, it is worth noting, in any of Miss Hellman's plays. The plot has decided artificialities. It is absolutely necessary that Julian carry his ill-gotten gains (the melodramatic phrase seems highly appropriate) around in cash. It is absolutely necessary that, even though he has been in New Orleans a week completing his "deal" without coming home, he should come home the night before the final step in the "deal" is to be carried out. It is absolutely necessary that Carrie should overhear, and understand, a vital, rather cryptic conversation. It is absolutely necessary that Anna should stay out of the room for a long time—long enough for Carrie to work Lily up to the fatal telephone call. Miss Hellman's play seems too heavily plotted to have the conclusiveness of a Chekhov play in which everything will go on as before because people are as they are; where all actions (like the selling of the cherry orchard or the suicide of Treplev in *The Sea Gull*) have the inevitability of a clock running down. And it lacks the conclusiveness of Ibsen's kind of play because the plot is too artificial. Among Miss Hellman's other plays, only *Another Part of the Forest* depends so very heavily on machinery; and *Another Part of the Forest* is so clearly melodrama (and so good on that level) that it does not matter, whereas *Toys in the Attic* has something of major importance to say, so that it does matter very much what the quality of the vehicle is.

One is left with questions of the wrong kind in *Toys in the Attic*. (There are questions of the right kind: Will Nora and Helmer ever find a true marriage after living in *A Doll's House?* Will her brothers ever turn the tables on Regina after the conclusion of the *The Little Foxes?* But in Chekhov's plays, and in Miss Hellman's *The Autumn Garden*, such questions do not arise at all.) One may grant that Julian is the kind of fool who would carry a hundred and fifty thousand dollars around in his pocket; and Miss Hellman's having him perfume it is a masterly touch to make his behavior convincing. One may grant that he is the kind of fool to leave a deal dangerously unfinished. But what if Carrie had *not* overheard a fatal conversation? What if Anna had *not* stayed out of the room? Would Anna have carried out her apparent determination and sailed for Europe? Would Carrie have stayed at home alone, bereft, and necessarily idle, and followed many another fictional Southern female by losing her mind? In what terms, and how clearly, would Julian have been made to see the havoc his money had wrought? One may say in Miss Hellman's defense that Julian would have lost his money soon in one way or another. But the only reason one can find for his losing it so very rapidly and theatrically is that the more natural gradualness would not do for Miss Hellman's tightly-constructed, unities-rigidly-observed kind of play. For Anna to sail away, for Carrie to face herself alone, for Julian to dissipate his money in New York and come home again (to what, one wonders): these more normal events would require, dramatically, the spaciousness of a *Mourning Becomes Electra*, or the (apparent) casualness of *The Three Sisters*.

It is possible, however, to look at Miss Hellman's performance from another angle. Her play is, in a sense, a development of a comment of Irina's in *The Three Sisters:* "What I wanted so, what I dreamed of, that's exactly what's not there." Chekhov develops this theme in terms of melancholy comedy, of true-to-life, casual reality. Miss Hellman develops it as a fable about money, as startling, as artificial, as theatrical, and as true as *The Pardoner's Tale*. This is not merely an attempt at realism, which fails because of the artificiality. A fable does not have to apologize for artificiality. It is only necessary that it tell an interesting story, and tell it economically; that its characters display genuine human failings; and that the point it makes be universally true. Miss Hellman gives her characters life, but (especially in the case of Lily, Julian, and Albertine) it is exaggerated life. Her plot is so mechanically perfect as to be almost a parody of her own earlier efforts. (And one is reminded again that *Toys in the Attic*, surprising as it may seem, is the first of her plays to observe unity of time.) It is as though she decided after *The Autumn Garden* that she was comfortable only with her own strong-plot methods, and reached the conclusion that if those methods were limited in the service of realism, and of the problem play, then she would try to employ them in the service of something else. In *Toys in the Attic*, then, the genre is not problem play but fable, and the technique is not realism but what might be called realism stylized. Seen from this angle the play reveals far fewer flaws. And seen from this angle there are other interesting parallels and contrasts with *The Three Sisters*.

The basic similarity, and the basic difference, between the characters in *The Three Sisters* and *Toys in the Attic* is that, while in neither play do the characters want what they think they want, or ever get it, in *Toys in the Attic* they come to realize the truth and in *The Three Sisters* they do not. In *The Three Sisters* there is always rationalization. To be sure, Irina says, "We'll never go to Moscow," but one is far from certain that this is more than a piece of hysteria to be forgotten tomorrow; and even if it is a genuine insight, it does not go deep enough to see *why* they will never go to Moscow, or that it would not make any difference if they did—and even if it is a genuine insight it *still* might be forgotten tomorrow. Irina goes from job to job, always convinced that she will like the next one better. Andrei slides from potential professor to Member of the District Board, and convinces himself that it is what he wanted. Masha is convinced that she wants the truth about Andrei's gambling and financial dealings brought into the open, but when Andrei offers to "have it out" Masha exits, and Olga persuades him to postpone it until tomorrow. When Masha tries to confess her love for Vershinin to her sisters, Olga insists that she is not listening. (And occasionally the characters really keep from listening to what it would disturb them to hear.) True, events force Olga to recognize Masha's passion and Andrei to recognize that his marriage is less than happy; but these are partial insights that lead nowhere. The end of the play finds things, really, just where they were, with no change in circumstance and no increase in self-knowledge. If there is any change, it is that any real change is less likely than ever, because will continues to atrophy, circumstances to bind, and self-deception to become ever more habitual.

Until Julian comes home dripping dollars, this is also how things look in *Toys in the Attic*. The trip to Europe, like the trip to Moscow, is definitely postponed without any comprehension of the real reasons. Life is led from day to day, with most unpleasantness unperceived or unspoken. Even after Julian's return, the characters fight self-realization. When Anna tries to find out from Julian what his circumstances are and why he has behaved as he has, Carrie tries to postpone the questioning. When Anna is driven to telling Carrie a very bitter truth, Carrie reacts in almost the same way as Olga's "I'm not listening": "You never said those words. Tell me I never heard those words."

But Julian does come home with the money, and all three must face the unpalatable truth about themselves and each other. The daily round of large duties and tiny pleasures can no longer act as a blind. In *The Three Sisters*, it always acts as a blind, and this is one of the truths in Chekhov, and one of the reasons that his plays have their comic side: no one suffers every minute, there are tasks to be performed, and saint's days to be celebrated, and calls to be paid. It is necessary to both Miss Hellman's purpose and her plot to force people behind the blind of everyday trivia to a view of the truth. In *The Three Sisters* one is not faced with the problem of Prozoroff's winning a hundred and fifty thousand rubles and coming home with tickets to Moscow in his pocket. "Things like that don't happen." But in fables they do, and Miss Hellman has every right to show us the outcome. Chekhov's story is natural, and true. Miss Hellman's (like *The Pardoner's Tale*, or *The Fox and The Grapes*) is unnatural but equally true.

But probe still deeper, and *Toys in the Attic* concludes with exactly the same meaning as *The Three Sisters*. As the moments of partial insight and revelation in *The Three Sisters* were momentary aberrations, so are the moments of complete insight and revelation in *Toys in the Attic*. Carrie is already on the road back to deception in the last few speeches, as she prepares to cook soup and to find herself another job. "So much to do," she says, and she almost purrs it. "Tomorrow's another day." Julian may see (as Andrei never did) that for his type of person, to be beaten once is to be beaten forever. But he isn't going to remember it very long. Even Anna will have to soothe the hurts and try to go on as though nothing had happened— which sooner or later will mean that she *will* go on as though nothing had happened. One is reminded of the conclusion of *The Wild Duck*, and Relling's prediction that in a year the Ekdal family will be happily in the same old rut. The ultimate irony for Prozoroffs, for Ekdals, and for Berniers alike, is that there is nowhere else for them to be.

One may ask, finally, why Miss Hellman chose to model her play, insofar as she did, after Chekhov's. Most of her other plots are highly original; so far as I am aware, only a slight debt of *The Little Foxes* to Becque's *The Vultures* and a debt to nineteenth-century well-made play and melo-drama for certain turns of plot have been mentioned. Critics have suggested, of course properly, that Miss Hellman turned to Chekhov's methods in *The Autumn Garden* as a means of loosening up her plot structure. Yet in *Toys in the Attic* she adapts from what seems to be Chekhov's most loosely plotted full-length play in order to write a play as tightly constructed as any she ever wrote. One must try to determine, therefore, whether *Toys in the Attic* differs in any significant and Chekhovian ways from Miss Hellman's earlier tightly constructed plays. And it does. As in *The Autumn Garden*, as in *The Three Sisters*, as in all of Chekhov's plays, there is no villain. And as in *The Autumn Garden*, *The Three Sisters*, and all of Chekhov's plays, Miss Hell-man has no fish to fry, takes no sides, urges no action or attitudes. Like Chekhov, she displays compassion and detachment in the process of reveal-ing character and demonstrating universal uncontroversial truth, the truth for example which Albertine explains to Julian: "I guess most of us make up things we want, don't get them, and get too old, or too lazy, to make up new ones"—a truth that might almost be the theme of *The Three Sisters*. It is, I think, taken for granted that T. S. Eliot adapted the plots of Greek tragedies for his plays in order to insure himself of perspicuous plots of universal significance. Similarly, it seems possible to say that Miss Hellman takes a story from Chekhov in order to help herself toward qualities which have clearly not been easy for her to achieve: sympathy, objectivity, universal truth.

It is far too soon, of course, to know whether *Toys in the Attic* has anything of the stature of *The Three Sisters*, even though it has unusual magnitude. But it is revealing that this is the first of Miss Hellman's firmly-plotted plays of which such a question can be raised without absurdity. Miss Hellman's plays have always been dramatically powerful, and she has always displayed the virtues of vivid characterization, credible motivation, and an unusually clear and convincing dialogue style; but her work was always too limited in theme and attitude for general or permanent value. In *The Autumn Garden* she displayed something of the qualities she had lacked, but the play misses her characteristic force. In *Toys in the Attic*, with bows to Chekhov and the great fabulists, she has written her first play to combine all her earlier virtues, with compassion, truth, detachment, and tremendous dramatic power.

Notes

1. *Recent American Dramatists* (Minneapolis, 1961), p. 41.

2. "The Rose and the Fox: Notes on the Southern Drama," in *South: Modern Southern Literature in its Cultural Setting*, ed. Louis D. Rubin, Jr., and Robert D. Jacobs (New York, 1961), pp. 349–75.

3. This is a common device in Chekhov's plays (see David Magarshack, *Chekhov the Dramatist* [New York, 1960], pp. 163–64) but is previously rare in Miss Hellman.

4. Quotations from *The Three Sisters* are from *Best Plays by Chekhov*, trans. Stark Young (New York, 1956). Quotations from *Toys in the Attic* from edition of that play (New York, 1960).

The Autumn Garden: Mechanics and Dialectics

Marvin Felheim*

I

Probably no play of the American theater (and I am including that feeble adaptation *The Wisteria Trees*) is more completely Chekhovian than Lillian Hellman's recent and most charming original drama, *The Autumn Garden*.

*Reprinted from *Modern Drama* 3 (September 1960):191–95, by permission of the journal.

Although the piece was only mildly successful when presented during the 1950–51 season on Broadway, to the discerning (and here I quote Alan Downer) it is "Miss Hellman's most original play."

The Autumn Garden is remarkable for its skill. Miss Hellman herself (in her Introduction to *Four Plays*) lists the two faults most enumerated by her critics: that her plays are "too well-made" and that they are "melodramas." These two limitations are strikingly absent from *The Autumn Garden*. As a matter of fact, the play successfully contradicts Miss Hellman's own statements about the nature of drama. In her Introduction, she states: "The theatre has limitations: it is a tight, unbending, unfluid, meager form in which to write." But *The Autumn Garden* is just the opposite kind of drama; it is loose in structure, bends easily but without breaking, is fluid and, far from being meager, overflows with characters and situations; indeed, so diffuse is the play that a first reading presents the same difficulties as does *The Cherry Orchard:* one must keep a finger poised to search out identities in the cast of characters.

In all of Miss Hellman's first six plays, the initial situation is presented in terms of some kind of problem, and in three of these pieces (*Days to Come, The Little Foxes* and *Watch on the Rhine*) the first actors the audience sees and hears are servants behaving in the traditional opening scene fashion. The Negro servants, Addie and Cal, who are on stage in the first scene of *The Little Foxes*, are there to give us a feeling of elegance and richness and a sense of power, all of which help establish the character of Regina Giddens before her delayed entrance allows her really to dominate the stage. In *The Autumn Garden*, the opening is quite different. "On stage at rise of curtain" are six of the main persons of the play. They do not direct their conversation or their actions toward any one situation, but indeed are behaving in a manner which we have come to call Chekhovian. Each is concerned with himself, his own problems. We, the audience, seem to have interrupted a series of activities which have been going on for some time: the marital problems of Rose and Benjamin Griggs; the complex emotional and financial relationships between old Mrs. Ellis, her daughter-in-law and her grandson; the grandson's involvements with a novelist friend and with his fiancée, the refugee, Sophie Tuckerman; Edward Crossman's peculiar and lonely position. Finally, there is the setting itself, "the Tuckerman house in a summer resort on the Gulf of Mexico, about one hundred miles from New Orleans." The house serves a symbolic function, just as do the houses of Madame Ranevsky in *The Cherry Orchard*, of Sorin in *The Seagull* and of the Prosorovs in *The Three Sisters*. It is the old home to which cling many memories but which has grown somewhat shabby with the passage of time; it is the autumn garden where flashes of brightness only emphasize the proximity of wintery sterility.

In both *The Children's Hour* and *The Little Foxes*, widely regarded as Miss Hellman's best plays, once the initial situation has been established, the whole movement of the plays is direct and without embellishment toward the climax. Both are "well-made" plays in the narrow sense that in neither are there any characters or any actions which do not contribute directly to the unfolding of the central incident. Here we might consult Miss Helman's definition; "by the well-made play," she writes, "I think is meant the play whose effects are contrived, whose threads are knit tighter than the threads in life and so do not convince." But all art is contrived and better organized than life. The trouble in *The Children's Hour* and *The Little Foxes* is that the contrivances are too obvious; they are *theatrically* convincing, but they do not have the high artistry which makes them consistent with themselves, true not to life but to dramatic art; the contrivances in these pieces render them merely realistic, good enough for exciting (even meaningful) theater, but not great art. Again, Miss Hellman's words suffice. The dramatist, she asserts, "must represent." These plays do, merely.

The *Autumn Garden* does all this and more. Without seeming to, in this play Miss Hellman organizes her materials in terms of artistic principles, dramatic principles (what Coleridge called "organic" principles). The realism is to the essence of human existence, not to the representation of life. There are many threads of action and of thought playing through *The Autumn Garden*. By the end of act 1, we have established the moral and artistic principle upon which the play is based: people must do the best they can, to do less is immoral. And Miss Hellman, as she hastens to admit, is "a moral writer." But the difference in *The Autumn Garden* is that the moral is within the situation and within the characters, not superimposed upon them by a skillful playwright. (This is the kind of thing David Magarshack refers to in his exciting study, *Chekhov the Dramatist*. Pointing out that "the chorus element" is "an indispensable feature of the play of indirect-action," he maintains that it is the characters themselves who perform the choral function, of moral judgment on the action. "Characters," he asserts, "assume the mantle of the chorus whenever their inner life bursts through the outer shell of their everyday appearance and overflows into a torrent of words." And when this occurs, the characters move from the world of realism into the world of art. For they are then not merely human beings but become also human symbols.) Nick Denery and Rose Griggs are both immoral and selfish people, but their immorality is a matter of degree inasmuch as all of the characters are to some extent tainted (or human). Perhaps one could say it in this way: in this play, Lillian Hellman lets her characters alone to act out their destinies, regarding them only with love and understanding; in her earlier play, she took sides; one can list the characters she admires and those whose behavior and beliefs she dislikes; in *Days to Come*, for example, she admits she even tried to balance characteristics: good against bad, well against sick, complex against simple. In *The Autumn Garden*, she does not make this kind of break-down. The result is true complexity, both in dialectics and mechanics.

II

Mechanically, *The Autumn Garden* has Chekhovian grace. The characters all belong on the set: each has a legitimate reason for being at the Tuckerman house at this particular moment in history; each is searching for the meaning of life, and for love. Some are weak, some a little stronger, but one cannot make lists or easy judgments; this, in other words, is not melodrama, these are people, not puppets. In act 1, Rose and Benjamin Griggs, a retired general, are involved in analyzing their marriage; they have never understood one another, nor do they now; they are doomed perennials. Mrs. Ellis is an aged matriarch using her money for her own selfish pleasures and her tongue to criticize; her dependent daughter-in-law and her grandson are unhappily caught in their emotional mother-son relationship; the grandson is further involved with an unsuccessful (and evidently homosexual) novelist and finally with his fiancée, the refugee Sophie, half European and wise beyond her years; in both relationships young Frederick Ellis is an innocent; he is a good example of the consequences of "momism." Then there is Constance Tuckerman, who runs this genteel boarding house; she is a sentimentalist, living on dreams and good works, understanding neither. Into this charged atmosphere, where indeed the blooms are withering on the vines, come the Denerys, Nick and Nina, cosmopolites and sophisticates, up to their old tricks; they live on her money but they amuse each other by their little cruelties at the expense of other people. Finally, there is Ned Crossman, observer of life, lonely and drunken.

These people arrive and depart constantly. The superficial stage action consists of noise and bustle; the director is provided with inexhaustible opportunities for stage effects of the most varied sort. This movement supplies the external tension, a tension partly produced by confusion and stir, but a tension which accurately mirrors the inner states of mind and emotions of the characters.

This is a Chekhovian cast, appropriately set in the American South; they are upper middle-class people, with their roots in money and traditions, but caught in the essential tragedy, the tragedy of life. This is not Shakespearean; it is Chekhovian. It is social drama, not classical tragedy. As such, it has two necessary dialectical principles. First of all, as Miss Hellman reminds us, it is "sharp comedy. . . . The world these people [she is discussing *The Cherry Orchard*] made for themselves would have to end in a whimper." But, and here is the second significant point, even though the dramatist does foresee the end of this world, he has what Miss Hellman calls "the artist-scientist hope" for a better one. The pity and terror are present, but they are not for the single, noble (however representative) individual, the Hamlet or the Lear; the pity and the terror are spread out, they are for all. Pity and terror have been democratized and made the proper subject for prose.

The Autumn Garden is written in prose. By the very nature of the medium, the tragic intensity and, to a lesser degree, the tragic nobility of the characters and their situations are rendered less magnificent than if the play were phrased in poetry. In one sense, this is a purely mechanical problem. But prose can take on certain of the qualities of poetry, or, I should say, certain poetic devices are available to the prose writer, particularly to the dramatist. Perhaps the most significant of these is symbolism. In *Days to Come* (a play whose shortcomings Miss Hellman admits, but, as she says, "with all that is wrong, all the confusion, the jumble, the attempt to do too much, I stand on the side of *Days to Come*"), one of the characters says: "I don't like autumn anymore. The river is full of leaves and it was too cold to walk very far." This speech, as any clever sophomore could tell us, has symbolic overtones. In *The Autumn Garden,* aside from a few incidental references to roots and trees, there is no mention of a garden, but the title adds a necessary symbolic note to the whole play. Miss Hellman has used a number of such titles, particularly those which emphasize the organic, natural aspects of human existence: in both *The Searching Wind* and *Another Part of the Forest,* she has used the significant relationship between man and nature to extend the meaning of her dramas. So in *The Autumn Garden,* the symbolism inherent in the title adds a poetic dimension to the scope of the play.

In fact, this is my central point: that the kind of drama we have in *The Autumn Garden* is the only kind which makes for modern tragedy. It is not merely psychological (as in Tennessee Williams) nor sociological (as in Arthur Miller) but it is artistic (poetic) and moral—and all in the Chekhovian sense. And so Miss Hellman's movement in this direction is a movement toward seriousness. As one New York critic ironically put it, Miss Hellman is "our most promising playwright."

That Miss Hellman should have moved from the "well-made" play in the direction of Chekhov is not surprising; for a sensitive individual, this was a logical development. Further, it was natural in light of the life-long study which Miss Hellman has made of Chekhov, a devotion which culminated in her edition of *The Selected Letters of Chekhov,* published in 1955. In her various editorial notes, Miss Hellman pays tribute to Chekhov's "common sense," to his workmanship, and to his "deep social ideals"; of all his plays she thinks *The Three Sisters* is the greatest. These opinions throw some light on *The Autumn Garden,* for they support our idea of its careful design and, in particular, they give a point of reference. For the central themes of the two plays are similar: nostalgia for a no-longer existent past and the individual's frustrating search for love and the meaning of life. The central "message" of both *The Autumn Garden* and *The Three Sisters* is also the same: the inevitability of disaster in the kind of world presented. Miss Hellman has quoted this pertinent remark from one of the letters: "A reasoned life without a definite outlook is not a life, but a burden and a horror."

The Adaptations

The Dramatic Adaptations of
Lillian Hellman

Doris Fleischer and Leonard Fleischer*

Lillian Hellman's four stage adaptations from other fictional and dramatic sources simultaneously reinforce and refute certain traditional assumptions regarding her original plays. Two adaptations—*Montserrat* (1949) and *The Lark* (1955)—are based on dramas dealing with historical personalities and events, both focusing on martyr heroes who choose death rather than capitulate to the oppressive institutions (state and church) that they threaten. The other two—*Candide* (1956) and *My Mother, My Father and Me* (1963)—are adapted from satiric works of fiction written two centuries apart, yet both plays contain a typically Hellmanesque, corrosive assault on man's greed and cruelty. Where the first pair reflects the taut dramatic structure normally (if sometimes mistakenly) expected from her, *Candide* and *My Mother, My Father and Me* are chaotic, intentionally episodic works in which the sprawling illogic of dramatized events is consistent with a point of view that sees madness and irrationality as shaping man's destiny. All four adaptations clearly reveal Hellman's tough-minded astringency, here intent on conveying a moral vision that is harsh but uncharacteristically hopeful.[1]

Montserrat, adapted from the French play by Emmanuel Roblès, dramatizes the dynamics of power in nineteenth-century Venezuela. Its straightforward narrative unfolds the dilemma of its title character, a captain in the occupying Spanish army who has become a supporter of the revolutionary leader, Simón Bolívar. Bolivar, who never appears in the play, is being zealously pursued by the Spanish forces, led by a decadent and mysterious general, called "His Excellency," who also never appears on stage. Montserrat's onstage foe is Colonel Izquierdo, who, knowing that Montserrat is aware of Bolivar's hiding place, uses six hostages as pawns and threatens to execute them unless Montserrat reveals Bolivar's whereabouts. Montserrat refuses to betray Bolivar, and the innocent hostages are executed one by

---

*This essay was written specifically for this volume and is published here for the first time by permission of the authors.

one. Like Joan in *The Lark,* Montserrat ultimately chooses death himself rather than betray his cause, his commitment to Bolivar's revolution in the struggle against Spanish imperialism.

In this power struggle the role of organized religion, here represented by Father Coronil, is particularly crucial. For the priest attempts to corrupt Montserrat by offering him physical comfort and escape from martyrdom. As in *The Lark* and *Candide,* the forces of institutional religion represent another manifestation of a repressive society that crushes the heretics and rebels who threaten to undermine their power. When Father Coronil asks Montserrat, "Who are you to set yourself up against your church and your country?" Montserrat replies: "I don't know. That's the truth: I don't know. There is only one thing of which I am certain—we have come a long way from Christianity. I must find my way back."[2]

Montserrat asks that he alone be sacrificed for Bolivar's cause, but Izquierdo, unwilling to permit such a course of action, displays his own dark vision of human behavior by proposing two likely scenarios: in one, Montserrat becomes a villain in the eyes of those innocent hostages he is forced to sacrifice, as they die revealing their own cowardice and degradation; in the other, Bolivar's hiding place is disclosed by the recanting Montserrat, thus illustrating the hollowness of his supposedly lofty ideals. Each alternative is consistent with Izquierdo's contemptuous vision of humanity: "They believe in nothing and are made of mess" (447).

As the hostages are executed, they emerge, in fact, with increasing degrees of stature. It becomes clear that Hellman employs them to evoke a political intensity equal in fervor to religious passion. Montserrat's nobility, shared by some of the other hostages, has been inspired by what Bolivar represents for them. Father Coronil describes how Bolivar changed: "He was a pious man and then he was a dangerous man." Montserrat responds, "He is a pious man today, the most pious man I have ever known" (417).[3]

Montserrat contrasts in striking dramatic terms a life devoted to principle and a vision that will lead to the betterment of man with lives consumed by self-interest and the need to preserve a political hierarchy. Its hero resembles Kurt Müller, the selfless protagonist in *Watch on the Rhine* who chooses to leave the safety of the United States to return to Europe to fight again fascism. The world of *Montserrat* is suffused with evil and injustice; innocence is destroyed and idealism mocked in a society controlled by those eaters of the earth who populate the Hellman dramatic canon, who (as in *Little Foxes, Another Part of the Forest,* and *The Children's Hour*) translate economic power into political subjugation. But in *Montserrat* the temporal victory of the oppressors is to be short-lived. Although Montserrat and the other martyrs are put to death, the cause of Bolivar, whose escape is noted within the context of the play, ultimately triumphs. As in the case of Joan in *The Lark,* the audience's knowledge of events that occur after the play ends supplies a subtly triumphant coda to *Montserrat's* ostensibly grim ending.

Its characters generally portray those extremes of evil and innocence so recognizable in Hellman's original plays before *The Autumn Garden*. The corrupting forces of power—both clerical and secular—triumph within the confines of the action, and the play appears to conclude (as Joseph Wood Krutch once said of her original dramas) "with wrong in the saddle, riding hard."[4] Although *Montserrat* also exposes man's baser instincts, his greed, his lust for power, his hypocritical piety, Hellman here preserves the possibility of heroism, not an empty self-sacrificing martyrdom, but one that achieves the goal of the hero: the betterment of the ordinary, flawed human beings who share his destiny.

Similarly, *The Lark*, adapted from the French play by Jean Anouilh, also focuses on a model of saintly idealism destroyed bodily by clerical and secular institutions of power.[5] Joan's simple devotion and reverence for God's messengers, St. Michael, St. Marguerite, and St. Catherine, lead her to defy a church that has become worldly and accommodating. Combining the persuasiveness of a skilled politician with the gentleness of a saint, Hellman's Joan is pitted against those who defend the church for reasons of expedient necessity (Cauchon), obsession with "private devils" (the Promoter), or pure fanaticism (the Inquisitor). Reminiscent of the courageous priests who ride with Bolivar, Ladvenu represents a humanistic Christianity that celebrates rather than debases mankind.

The world of fifteenth-century France that Hellman dramatizes in *The Lark* is not unlike *Montserrat*'s nineteenth-century Venezuela or the more familiar American terrain of the Hubbards, Tilfords, and Rodmans, where idealism and innocence must struggle to survive. Cauchon, perhaps the most "human" of the churchmen Joan must face, guiltily collaborates with the British invaders and surrenders Joan to them. He aspires to virtuousness but, like most fallible humans, remains unwilling to suffer and die for a cause. Ruled by political expedience, his pragmatic earthly self condemns Joan to death and martyrdom, but he is endowed with the ability to see beyond his own day: "And the time will come when our names will be known only for what we did to her; when men, forgiving their own sins, but angry with ours will speak our names in a curse" (568). The Englishman Warwick, utterly practical and not burdened by spiritual angst, shares Cauchon's awareness of what Joan will symbolize in the future: "Different politics may well require different symbols. We might even have to make her a monument in London. Don't be too shocked at that, sire. The politics of my government may well require it one day, and what's required, Englishmen supply" (551). Later in the drama, stepping even more out of the restrictions of time and place, he predicts Joan's transformation from "a lark into a giant bird who will travel the skies of the world long after our names are forgotten" (601).

Although Hellman (like Anouilh) rejects the kind of epilogue Shaw included in his version of the Joan story, it is clear that her heroine (also like Anouilh's) ultimately triumphs, and her play ends with Joan's greatest success—the coronation of Charles at Rheims.[6] Joan, less the overt champion of the masses than Montserrat, does share his faith in the nobility of the common man and his capacity to discover inspirational sources without the intervention of those who claim to be emissaries of God.[7] And like Montserrat, she argues against the invincibility of institutions that encourage the rich and powerful to enjoy privileges denied to the dispossessed:

JOAN (*to the Promoter*): But if the Devil is beautiful, how can you know he is the Devil?

THE PROMOTER: Go to your priest. He will tell you.

JOAN: Can't I recognize him by myself?

THE PROMOTER: No. Certainly not. No.

JOAN: But only the rich have their priests always with them. The poor can't be running back and forth. (554–55)

Candide and *My Mother, My Father and Me* lack the kind of martyr-hero found at the center of *Montserrat* and *The Lark*. Where the first two works are based on historical events and rely on tight dramatic structures, the later adaptations are far more rambling, though ultimately unified through their satiric tones. The on-stage impact of *Candide*, of course, depended on a variety of collaborative elements, especially the music of Leonard Bernstein and the lyrics of Richard Wilbur and John Latouche. But Hellman's libretto, based on Voltaire's stinging satire, expresses an integral aspect of the work, despite the fact that it was replaced in later revivals by Hugh Wheeler's new book (1974).

In a curious way, the fictional Candide—like Montserrat and Joan—is tested by the vicissitudes of history. An innocent devotee of the ludicrous idealism of Dr. Pangloss, Candide is jolted from the protective world of Westphalia and, in the course of his adventures, repeatedly must confront a real universe where misery and injustice reign. In her version of the story, Hellman stresses the relationship between Candide's misfortune and the capriciousness of historical events. Unlike the Voltaire source where Candide is expelled from Westphalia when caught in a compromising situation with Cunegonde, the Hellman book envisions the country conquered by an invading army. Moreover, Hellman's now lecherous Pangloss is more consciously a cynical manipulator than Voltaire's, finally admitting to Candide near play's end that he probably never believed the everything-for-the-best philosophy that he unswervingly espoused to his pupils. As early as his opening speech, however, Hellman signifies in Pangloss's bizarre choplogic that her dialogue has entered a new and essentially absurdist phase, consistent with the exaggerated theatrical style of the entire production: "It was a long and bloody war, but if men didn't fight they would never know the benefits of peace, and if they didn't know the benefits of peace they would never know the benefits of war. You see, it all works out for the best" (609). Even a kick in the head, according to Pangloss, is worthy of praise:

PANGLOSS: And if you had not stumbled against my head, I would no longer know that I had a head, so weak am I from hunger.

CANDIDE: And I hurt you because I am weak from hunger. The weak kick the weak. That's sad, isn't it?

PANGLOSS: Not at all. If the weak didn't kick the weak, then the strong would kick the weak and certainly that would hurt far more. Things are for the best in the best of all possible worlds. (626)

Such comic dialogue and most of the nonmusical dramatic action are designed to contradict the view of the world according to Pangloss. In the course of the work, Candide must cope with random slaughter, slavery, inquisitions, endless examples of man's boundless craving for wealth and power. Although Hellman omits some of the novel's more bizarre exploits (for example, the cannibals who reproduce with monkeys), her abbreviated versions of Candide's adventures are faithful to the satiric thrust of the novel as they ridicule smug optimism and create a wildly unpredictable and disordered world in which evil runs rampant.[8]

The presence of such behavior notwithstanding, the operetta's tone remains consistently comic and, from Hellman's earlier work, evokes only *Another Part of the Forest,* which also transforms grotesque malevolence into comedy. But where *Another Part of the Forest* rests essentially within the bounds of dramatic realism, *Candide* predicts the absurdist universe she would later depict in *My Mother, My Father and Me.* In this regard, death turns out to be not a dramatic climax of the action (as in *Montserrat* and *The Lark*) but a mere temporary inconvenience. Pangloss, as well as Maximillian, the Sultan and the Marquis, all die—sometimes more than once—but magically reappear. Since the play cannot possess the more leisurely pace of even a short novel, such deaths and resurrections, compressed as they are in the action of the drama, appropriately emphasize the madness of Voltaire's universe, with the added hindsight of two more centuries of world horror.

Pangloss's optimism is balanced by the equally unequivocal pessimism of Martin, who bemoans the venality of man in a world where half the people starve "and the other half diet" (663). But where Voltaire created two contrasting characters, Hellman depicts them as two sides of the same person, played by the same performer. Martin is certainly closer to Hellman's truth than Pangloss, his skepticism more accurately reflecting the world as she portrays it, but her character is a far more fragile individual than Voltaire's. Although his dark vision is caricatured in the novel, the figure of Martin is tempered somewhat in the adaptation. Less resilient than in the original, pained by life's brutality, Martin, in Hellman's version, appears to have the sympathy of his creator despite his lack of the very callousness he espouses as a requirement for survival.[9]

The voice of heartless pragmatism in *Candide* is given to the Old Lady, a survivor and the antithesis of innocent romanticism, whose cynical practicality fits her comfortably within the Hellman canon:

OLD LADY: It is your duty to marry the Governor and save Candide.

CUNEGONDE: But I don't love the man and I don't want to be unfaithful.

OLD LADY: Look. Think of it this way. Marrying another man is no more unfaithful than sleeping with another man.

CUNEGONDE: Oooh! Is that true? You are so worldly. (650)

The play ends with Candide's return to Westphalia. Now recognizing the truth about his companions, he tells Pangloss: "You were my master, and I loved you, and you taught me lies. I was a stupid boy, and you must have known it. (*With great force*) A man should be jailed for telling lies to the young" (675). Not even Cunegonde is spared as he orders her to "go away and let me live" (676). Unlike the original source where Candide is less judgmental and even accepts the now-ugly Cunegonde, Hellman's sobered hero renounces his old values and assumptions: "My head was full of nonsense. But now I am tired of nonsense" (676).[10] Eventually, however, Candide accepts his companions as each attempts to replace empty speculation with concrete, if pathetically comic action: Pangloss cleans a fish, with little success; the old woman carries so much firewood that she resembles a moving forest; Maximillian sweeps the air with a broom; Cunegonde throws a poisoned mushroom into the stew. But, perhaps to accommodate a Broadway audience, perhaps to reassert the possibility of hope expressed in her first two adaptations, Hellman's Candide and his Cunegonde make an effort more romantic than Voltaire's to strip away the sham, to see the world (and themselves) as it (and they) really are. Says Candide: "We will not think noble because we are not noble. We will not live in beautiful harmony because there is no such thing in the world, nor should there be. We promise only to do our best and live out our lives" (678). No longer young nor foolishly idealistic, they take the first tentative step toward productive living.

In her final dramatic adaptation, *My Mother, My Father and Me*, drawn from Burt Blechman's novel *How Much?*, Hellman once again softens the original work, retaining much of its absurdist structure, but muting the acerbic and bitter tone of the source. The play focuses on the Halpern family, a more explicitly grotesque, updated, and urban version of the rapacious Hubbard clan. The father, Herman, and his wife, Rona, live only for their immediate gratification, blind to the motives and consequences of their actions. Rona buys merchandise she doesn't need, and Herman, a crooked but inept businessman, is equally self-absorbed as he maneuvers to keep one step ahead of the law. The "hero" of the drama, their son Berney, tries pitifully to transcend the warped values of his parental home, but his idealism, in its own way, is as comically flawed as Candide's.[11] His liberalism takes the form of worshiping blacks and Indians in an effort to identify with their plight and thus escape the empty materialism of his own surroundings. Berney is clearly a buffoon as he tries to empathize with his black "brothers" by writing folk songs intertwined with his autobiographical musings, which though muddled and empty-headed, possess a certain charm absent in the Blechman original. All the Blechman characters are grotesque and monstrous, while some of Hellman's people (Berney, Jenny), though bordering on caricature, retain a measure of humanity.

Like the action in *The Little Foxes* and *Another Part of the Forest*, the narrative of *My Mother, My Father and Me* dramatizes the unscrupulous behavior of a thoroughly decadent society. The vulgar and opportunistic Dr. Zachary Katz (known as Zatz) runs a nursing home, not to offer comfort to the elderly but to build a personal fortune. Exploiting the aged and seducing Rona to secure business from Herman (shoes for the dead), he manipulates his patients who, though victims of Zatz's greed, are never romanticized and become themselves targets of Hellman's satire.

As in *Candide*, war is accepted as a boon to mankind, bringing with it a sense of adventure and heroism. For Herman and Rona, however, war signifies an opportunity to breathe new life into their dying shoe business, but the prospect never materializes:

HERMAN: The war is over. It never began. (*There is a long pause.*)

RONA: (*softly*) How dare they? How dare they? The dirty little cowards. (812)

Berney's only hope for salvation and escape is his grandmother, Jenny, who represents an indescribable link with a worthy legacy, a tradition that can genuinely nourish the imagination. In the Blechman novel she is another pitiful victim rather than a creative and catalytic force, but in Hellman's hands she becomes a source of inspiration. Knowing that Berney must reject the vulgar travesty that surrounds him and forge some connection with the past, she sells her $500 funeral stipend for $375 so Berney can secure the money immediately and make his own way. Although the novel ends with Rona's being so involved with her shopping that she fails to understand that her mother has died, Hellman's play concludes with a very different image: Berney, dressed in Indian garb, pounding on a tom-tom, selling trinkets. An absurd figure in a lunatic world, Berney, not unlike Pangloss, Maximillian, and Cunegonde at the end of *Candide*, is nevertheless on the right track, seeking something better than the life he has been given. Though the sentiments sound more like Lillian Hellman's than Berney Halpern's, the lines of his poem-in-progress are particularly revealing:

> You find Jerusalem where you find her
> Many a lonely night
> Considered I the crossing of the water
> To join my people
> In the building of Israel.
> But then, decided I, in Jerusalem, Israel,
> There is muscle and strength.
> Here the muscle and strength have gone.

> Here I am needed
> Here they are weak
> And I must teach them to rise again,
> Rise again. (814–15)

Implicit in both *Candide* and *My Mother, My Father and Me* is the belief that mankind can be resourceful in discovering how to cope with adversity. However dark the humor—and Hellman has lightened both originals considerably—these two works are essentially funny, and the mocking laughter renders the human comedy uncharacteristically bearable. Both Berney and Candide make the mistake of striving for roles for which they are unsuited. Their initial environments insulate them from the "real" world, and their journeys to self-discovery form the basic action of the dramas.[12] Both characters are well-intentioned, neither particularly heroic nor even very bright. They lack the passion and the idealism of a Joan or a Montserrat, but they do survive, forced to adjust to worlds that Joan and Montserrat have left. For Candide, this means tending his own garden and assuming the daily tasks appropriate for an ordinary man; for Berney, it means sloughing off his former skin (his parental home) and finding, in however bumbling a fashion, his own creative outlets.

Despite Hellman's deserved reputation as a harsh moral critic, both Berney and Candide illustrate her attempt in dramatic adaptations to find something more hopeful in her characters' lives than their original creators could imagine. While neither hero possesses the stature of Joan of Arc or Montserrat—or Kurt Müller of *Watch on the Rhine*—each is a far more sympathetic figure in his respective dramatic adaptation than in Blechman's or Voltaire's novel. Hellman's Candide is now intelligent enough to learn from misfortune and tend his garden, and Cunegonde, no longer glorified by Candide, may still serve as a suitable mate. Similarly, unlike Blechman's Berney Halpern, who records his experience but fails to understand it, Hellman's hero, absurd as he may be in his Indian garb, at least embarks in a new direction.

In her four adaptations Hellman responds to works that carry with them a vision of a world very much akin to the one she delineates in her original plays. Innocence is destroyed or mocked; power corrupts and is corrupting. It is a harsh vision, but in these adaptations by no means a nihilistic one. For despite corruption and cruelty, there remains an opportunity for heroism and change. Self-knowledge is possible although, as in *Candide*, for example, the price paid is a dear one. Candide's naive idealism may be fruitless but Hellman's character is capable of at least becoming disillusioned, even discerning. As repelled as audiences may be by the Hubbards or the Halperns, they radiate a comic energy that makes them entertainingly vulnerable, even vulgarly lovable. The world is not ready for its saints, as Joan and Montserrat discover. But those figures do, after all, triumph in retrospect.

For all of Hellman's genuine pleasure in dramatic malevolence, her four stage adaptations assert in a variety of ways uncommon in her original plays the notion that meaningful action is both desirable and possible. Political and social goodness (in marked contrast to occurrences that befall the destroyed "good" people of her original drama[13]) is not necessarily equatable with impotence.

Notes

1. Hellman has been criticized for writing plays in which evil figures dominate a morally upright minority who lack the stature to assert themselves. See, for example, Oscar Brockett and Robert Findlay, *Century of Innovation: A History of European and American Theatre and Drama Since 1870* (Englewood Cliffs, N.J.: Prentice-Hall, 1973), 459, 524–26, 567. On the other hand, she has also been attacked as "an arrested child of the 30's, and of its *idée fixe* that the reformation of society produces a better crop of humans" ("Gathering Toadstools," *Time*, 5 April 1963, 56).

2. *The Collected Plays* (Boston: Little, Brown & Co., 1972), 418. Quotes are hereafter cited in the text.

3. A number of critics improperly faulted Hellman for muting the religious element of Roblès's original drama. In fact, it can be argued that Montserrat's real antagonist, the unequivocally villainous figure of the play, is the churchman Father Coronil, not the more complex Izquierdo.

4. "Unpleasant Play," *Nation*, 25 February 1939, 244–45.

5. In an interview during the Boston tryout of *The Lark*, Hellman noted that she tried to stress Joan's principles in preference to Anouilh's attention to feminine vanity. See Murray Schumach, "Shaping a New Joan," *New York Times*, 13 November 1955, sec. 2, pp. 1, 3.

6. Critics are fond of comparing Hellman's adaptation of Anouilh's *L'Alouette* with Christopher Fry's more intellectual translation of the same play. Fry is closer to Anouilh, Hellman considerably freer in her trimming of the original. There is general concurrence that Hellman's adaptation is more personal and emotional than Fry's, her Joan more accessible to American audiences. See, for example, Vance Bourjaily, "Theatre Uptown," *Village Voice*, 7 December 1955, 10; Alan Hewitt, "*The Lark:* Theatrical Bird of Passage," *Theatre Arts* 40 (March 1956):63–64, 96; Alice Griffin, "Books—of a Different Feather," *Theatre Arts* 40 (May 1956):8–10; and, especially, Henry Knepler, "*The Lark*, Translation vs. Adaptation: A Case History," *Modern Drama* 1 (May 1958):15–28, excerpted in this collection.

7. Seymour Peck quotes Hellman's comparison of Shaw's Joan in *Saint Joan* to Anouilh's and her own Joan in *The Lark*. Their Joan, she says, is "gayer, more fragile, less saintly" than Shaw's, more a believer in man's innate strength and courage ("The Maid in Many Disguises," *New York Times Magazine*, 4 December 1955, 28).

8. Despite assumptions that Hellman's book for *Candide* was universally attacked, Brooks Atkinson's vital *New York Times* review considered it a faithful preservation of Voltaire's assault on optimism (9 December 1956, sec. 2, p. 5). Gerald Weales praised Hellman for her contributions to the operetta's satirical effect, maintaining that "she manages to do what most musical adaptations never even attempt to do, retain the artistic intention of the original work in the new form" (*American Drama Since World War II* [New York: Harcourt, Brace, 1952], 152).

9. Certain critics condemned Hellman for identifying too much with Martin's pessimism, in contradiction of the spirit of both Voltaire and the genre of musical comedy. See, for example, Henry Hewes, review of *Candide, Saturday Review*, 22 December 1956, 34–35.

10. In this regard, Hellman's Candide is often considered more the disillusioned modern

hero than Voltaire's jabbering fool. See, among others, Brooks Atkinson, "The Theatre: *Candide*," *New York Times*, 3 December 1956, 40.

11. Interestingly, the full title of Burt Blechman's novel, upon which the play is based, is *How Much? A Novel by B. Halpern As Told to Burt Blechman* (New York: Obolensky, 1961).

12. Frances Rowena Morrison maintains that the unifying principle in Hellman's drama is in fact the theme of self-discovery and the moral necessity for purposeful action ("Seeing and Seeing Again: Self-Discovery in the Plays of Lillian Hellman," Ph.D. diss., University of North Carolina at Chapel Hill, 1978).

13. Consider, for example, among the numerous "good" but ineffectual victims in Hellman's original plays the plights of Birdie Bagtry Hubbard, Horace Giddens, Karen Wright, Martha Dobie, Sam Hazen, and even Julian Berniers.

The Lark, Translation vs. Adaptation: A Case History
Henry W. Knepler*

The main difference between the work of a translator of a play and that of an adapter can be stated simply: a translator will try to reproduce the original intact; he will therefore generally try to find a level of language and idiom which achieves that aim. An adapter tries to find an approximate equivalent for the original, not only in terms of the language but in terms of the whole theatrical tradition to which the adaptation is being made. He therefore has to deal with two elements in addition to the linguistic problem: dramatic technique first of all, and secondly those commonly understood national characteristics or attitudes which are relevant to the particular play. Both of these depend on the traditions and therefore on the expectations of the playgoer; they are bound up with each other and often seem no more than two aspects of the same problem.

Often a play and its playwright are served best by a faithful translation which merely transfers all the meaning and content of the work from one language to another. At times, though, a close translation may not lead to such a faithful transfer; in other words, an adapter may at times keep faith with the intent of the playwright by judiciously departing from the original in order to make it comprehensible to an audience used to a different culture or theatrical tradition.

A play which exemplifies this problem of translation and adaptation has recently been performed in Paris, London, and New York. It provides a more interesting case history than usual because its production occurred in three theatrical traditions, not only two, and because it was translated in one case and adapted in the other, both by major dramatists. It is *L'Alouette* (*The Lark*) by Jean Anouilh; translated by Christopher Fry; adapted by Lillian Hellman.

*Excerpted from *Modern Drama* 1 (May 1958):15–28; reprinted by permission of the journal.

The Lark retells the story of Joan of Arc; this in itself indicates a possible problem in a transfer from one country to another: the national hero of one is not likely to be savored as fully in another. Secondly, there is of course the possibility that the reason for success or failure may lie primarily in the different productions. But both these causes turn out to be quite insignificant in comparison to those which are implicit in the problem of translation versus adaptation. My interest in *The Lark* was aroused by the fact that the play was a great critical and audience success when it was first given in Paris; that it had a mixed reception in London, where it did not last through the season; and that it was as much of a triumph in New York as a historical play is ever likely to be there. The London production was of the translation by Christopher Fry; the production in New York was of the adaptation by Lillian Hellman. . . .

[In the New York production,] Julie Harris is Joan, Boris Karloff is Cauchon, Christopher Plummer the Earl of Warwick, as strong a cast as any, and a great success. The play lasted the whole season, went on tour, and was done on television. Brooks Atkinson spotted the main difference and Walter Kerr the main reason for it in their respective reviews. Atkinson wrote in the *New York Times:* "This is the drama that seemed no more than an intellectual attitude in Christopher Fry's adaptation in London last Spring. It is still basically intellectual, the work of a French dramatist who likes to reason his way through a sacred mystery. But Lillian Hellman's adaptation has solid strength in the theater." And Kerr said in the *New York Herald Tribune:*

> It has remained for a woman dramatist to give us the first really tough minded Joan of Arc. Lillian Hellman is, of course, only the adapter of Jean Anouilh's *The Lark*. But that "only" may be misleading. I have a strong suspicion that a great deal of the biting briskness, the cleaver-sharp determination, the haughty hard-headed candor of this Joan comes from the pen of the Lady who carved out, and carved up, *The Little Foxes*.

It is safe to conclude that the differences in critical receptions were not due primarily to the productions which *The Lark* was given. This paper will try to show that the superiority of the Hellman adaptation over the Fry translation is due precisely to the fact that it was an adaptation. Miss Hellman took cognizance of the differences in traditions and expectations that separate the audiences of Paris from those of New York. Mr. Fry did not do the same for his London public.

Unlike Shaw, Anouilh does not retell the story of Joan in chronological order. His one and only scene is the trial of Joan, which takes place on a fairly bare stage with a neutral setting consisting mainly of several shallow levels. With the trial as his home base, Anouilh takes the characters back in time to re-enact the high points of Joan's life: her departure from home, her agreement with Squire Beaudricourt to send her to the Dauphin at Chinon, her appearance there, and her success in persuading the prince to let her lead the army at Orleans. The play then moves through the trial itself, her defense, her recantation and her denial of it, and finally her execution. But there remained one scene not acted out before—so the play ends, not with her burning, but with the high point of her career, the coronation of the Dauphin at Rheims as King Charles VII.

All these scenes occur in the same place, using only a few props—a throne, a stool, a few faggots—to indicate the particular setting. Most characters are present on stage at all times, and move in and out of the various situations with little éclat. All these details are basically the same in all three versions. Yet whereas Fry adheres closely to Anouilh's directions, Hellman departs from them in ways that are often as subtle as they are significant.

The main change in dramatic technique from Anouilh and Fry to Hellman seems slight at first, but it pervades and modifies the whole play. As the brief synopsis shows, the play relies on a system which we generally call the flashback and know from the film and a few plays like Miller's *Death of a Salesman*. The flashback as we know it takes us from the present back to a previous event, a previous reality; it serves the elucidation of character or some other purpose of exposition. The French flashback, which Anouilh, Sartre and Giraudoux have used to varying degrees before, is not the same at all in technique or purpose. Rather it is a mélange of idea and reality, an often confusing mingling of materials symbolic of past and present, an elusive allusiveness to historical, political, cultural events. It serves character and plot less than the erection of those edifices of historical parallels, cultural undertones and social *double-entendres* which the modern French drama uses extensively (as, for example, in the various modern versions of classic drama). It is therefore not so much a change of scene, like the American type, but a change of character; not exposition, but sophistication. In the American flashback, a character may jump in and out of a scene at the drop of a spotlight. In the French equivalent, he may not only jump out of a scene, but, as a character, out of the whole play—and without benefit of lighting.

This is the most important change in dramatic technique. The others are simpler: compared to the French, the English and American stage has always been more used to physical action and the direct clash of personalities. At the same time, it nowadays prefers fewer words, particularly of the introspective kind. Both of these traditions assist Miss Hellman in heightening dramatic contrasts and other effects at various times—at least in American eyes; but they also lead to a decrease in the subtlety and individuality of characters; Miss Hellman makes type do for individual in some places.

The main transmutation in the less easily definable area of national characteristics is an expected one: various problems connected with sex undergo a great change. But the results are perhaps unexpected. Miss Hellman does not tone things down—Mr. Fry does—but generally substitutes profanity for the more graphically descriptive statements of the original. The other important change concerns religion; here Miss Hellman does tone down some of the anticlericalism of the original. Besides these there are some minor aspects, such as the problems connected with protocol and etiquette, which she has to deal with.

Before I give detailed examples I ought to explain that I shall use the Fry translation whenever it is close enough to the original to point up the contrast to the Hellman version. The original will be referred to only when Fry differs from it.

Two aspects which are important in an analysis of the differences in dramatic technique become apparent in the opening stage directions. In keeping with the film tradition of the flashback Miss Hellman utilizes music to a much greater extent than the original and Fry's translation, which contain short bits of music on only a few occasions. The music for the Hellman version is extensive. It was composed by Leonard Berstein, and is mostly sung by an a cappella choir of seven voices with counter tenor; it is of a liturgical nature, except for a few dances and a marching song, and anyone who heard it in the performance can testify that it was effective in heightening the impact of the play. It does, however, also impart the quality of a pageant to it, which the original does not have. Secondly, Anouilh's stage directions demand a neutral décor in which such later props as the throne of the Dauphin are present from the beginning. Miss Hellman has a cyclorama on which projections are thrown to indicate the change from trial to flashback. The throne appropriately marches on and off stage in darkness. She thereby reinforces the distinction in time and place which the American flashback demands. . . .

With the Inquisitor Miss Hellman had to solve another problem. His part is the most severely cut of all, partly to speed up the action, partly for reasons discussed below in another context. But his defeat by Joan—not her reluctant condemnation by Cauchon and the judges—his defeat by Joan is central to the meaning of the play. His importance has therefore to be established. Near the beginning of the play Joan has said some things which the Promoter (prosecutor) finds terrible. Then

THE INQUISITOR *has risen. He is an intelligent man, spare and hard, speaking with great quietness.*

INQUISITOR: Listen carefully to what I am going to ask you, Joan. Do you think you are in a state of grace at this moment?

Joan tries to evade the question while the court sits in silent expectation of her answer. Brother Ladvenu, her chief defender, interrupts the Inquisitor, who, however, cannot be deflected from his purpose. After he has asked the fatal question of her for a third time, Joan answers:

JOAN: If I am not, may God in His goodness set me there. If I am, may God in His goodness keep me so.

The PRIESTS *murmur. The* INQUISITOR *sits again, inscrutable.*

LADVENU (*quietly*): Well answered, Joan.

Hellman injects additional drama into the scene.

THE INQUISITOR *rises*. THE PROMOTER *stops speaking. The stage is silent.* LADVENU, *a young priest, rises and goes to* THE INQUISITOR.

THE INQUISITOR *whispers to him.* LADVENU *moves to* CAUCHON, *whispers to him.*

CAUCHON (*looks toward* THE INQUISITOR; *very hesitant*): Messire—(THE INQUISITOR *stares at* CAUCHON. CAUCHON *hesitates, then turns toward* JOAN) Joan, listen well to what I must ask you. At this moment, are you in a State of Grace?

Ladvenu immediately intervenes to protect Joan. Cauchon merely repeats his question:

CAUCHON: Are you in a State of Grace?

Joan evades the question in the same way as in the original, but Cauchon continues:

CAUCHON (*softly, worried*): Messire demands an answer. His reasons must be grave. Joan are you in a State of Grace?

Again the question has been asked three times, Joan answers it as in the original, and the scene is over. The Inquisitor has not said one word. In this way Miss Hellman increases his stature and our anticipation of the time when he will finally speak. When he does so in the end she will change and modify his words, too, more than those of any other character in the play. But that involves us with the most complicated aspect of the second area of changes, the one concerned with national attitudes. And before going into it, it may be better to take up its simpler aspects.

Anouilh directs that all characters remain on stage throughout the play, though in the background when they are not needed. He states specifically that Joan's mother is to knit throughout the evening. Both Fry and Hellman leave the placement of the cast more up to the director and omit the knitting instruction (though Fry has it in the mother's scene with Joan). An Anglo-Saxon audience, not aware of the almost ritual connection of the knitting women with the French Revolution and the guillotine, would find the constant action a needless impediment. . . .

In no respect do the shifts between the different versions reflect national tastes more clearly than in matters related to sex. For example, in one scene the Promoter is carried away by his subconscious, as he often is; he describes the Devil, trying to convince Joan that he need not appear as a monster, because he is clever enough to know how to tempt his victims in many ways:

En réalité le diable choisit la nuit la plus douce, la plus lumineuse, la plus embaumée, la plus trompeuse de l'année. . . . Il prend les traits d'une belle fille toute nue, les seins dressés, insupportablement belle. . . .

Fry, not at his luckiest, renders this as:

> I tell you he chooses a moonlit summer night, and comes with coaxing
> hands, with eyes that receive you into them like water that drowns you,
> with naked women's flesh, transparent, white, . . . beautiful—

And Hellman:

> In real life the Devil waits for a soft, sweet night of summer. Then he
> comes on a gentle wind in the form of a beautiful girl with bare breasts—

At which point the Promoter is unfortunately interrupted by the Bishop in
each version—but not before we have had a glimpse at least of the transformation which each of the English versions makes: Fry veers toward the beau
ideal of the English, Hellman towards the pin-up girl.

Virginity and virility are important topics to Anouilh, basic to the struggle which each thinking human being has to wage with himself and with
others in order to achieve some meaningful kind of existence. His presentation of them is remarkably consistent in his plays: The actual situation always
has serious and thought-provoking implications, but the treatment, and the
circumstances in which the problem is brought up, are generally farcical.
The Hellman version tones down that levity and often omits the references
altogether. So she omits a long discourse on the subject made by Warwick in
comparing Joan to his future countess. All references to Charles' possible
homosexuality are also omitted. Fry correctly translates Charles' answer to
the request that he see Joan:

> I don't like virgins. I know, you're going to tell me that I'm not virile
> enough. But they frighten me.

In New York he simply says:

> You know La Tremouille would never allow me to see the girl.

But the neatest example of national attitude may well be this: Charles is
talking to Joan:

> Tu sais que c'est à cause de mes jambes qu'Angès ne m'aimera jamais?

Fry tones down the rational finality of the future tense:

> It's because of my legs that Agnes can't bring herself to love me.

And Miss Hellman makes it:

> It's because of my legs that Agnes can never really love me.

That "really" is, I suppose, a concession to the great American dream that
such a relationship is not possible without at least a little love.

When Joan tells her father about talking to St. Michael, he suspects a
contact of quite another sort, and not with a saint; he beats and abuses her.
Among other things he says to her:

> Et quand tu nous reviendras le ventre gonflé, ayant deshonoré le nom de ton père, tué ta mère de douleur, et forcé tes frères à s'engager dans l'armée pour fuir la honte au village—ce sera le Saint-Esprit, peut-être, qui aura fait le coup!

Fry retains the idea but, as so often, tones down the language:

> And when you can't hide your sinning any longer, and every day it grows bigger for all to see, and you've killed your mother with grief, and your brothers have to join the army to get away from the scandal in the village, it will be the Holy Ghost who brought it on us, I suppose?

Miss Hellman cuts the scene greatly, like many others, and substitutes stronger language, including some picturesque oaths, for the more explicit statements of the original:

> You want to start whoring like the others. Well, you can tell your Blessed Saint Michael that if I catch you together I'll plunge my pitchfork into his belly and strangle you with my bare hands for the filthy rutting cat you are.

Pregnancy is not referred to.

Anouilh is outspoken and matter-of-fact. Sex is among the most important aspects of the conduct of life; and what could be more serious—and more comical—than life? Fry often transforms the necessary spade into an agricultural implement. Miss Hellman also merely implies some of the things Anouilh states directly. But her implication has the virtue, if I may call it that, of providing an emotional equivalent of the original.

It is outside my province to discuss the main differences in religious attitude between France and America. But a few examples from *The Lark* give insight into certain aspects as Miss Hellman took them into consideration. She handles the subject with great care and forbearance, especially when it concerns Catholicism (or at least can be construed to concern it). She avoids the embarrassment, for example, that Anouilh might cause early in the play when Joan tells of her "voices." His Joan actually repeats what the Archangel Michael and others told her and imitates a man's voice in carrying on both sides of the conversation. Miss Hellman keeps it a one-way conversation in which Joan looks towards the sky, listens to an unheard voice, and replies to it.

The main impact of the changes in the sphere of religion, however, is not of this kind. It chiefly concerns the Inquisitor, as mentioned before. His theology is less complex in the Hellman adaptation, and his religious views are softened. His dialectic paradoxes are muted so as not to be misunderstood or misconstrued and give offense thereby. Most of the not untypical anticlericalism of Anouilh and Fry disappear. . . . In the American version child psychology and statistical evidence replace dialectic and paradox; a much more modern Inquisitor, he. It is not surprising that Miss Hellman omits his bitterness and unconscious irony after Joan's recantation, which make him pray:

Will you never grant, O Lord, that this world should be unburdened of every trace of humanity, so that at last we may in peace consecrate it to Thy glory alone?

The end of the play differs in all three versions, as if each writer felt that the proper effect needed to be achieved by different scenes. With regard to the burning at the stake, the original and Fry are close. Joan is dragged to the stake by the executioner followed by a howling mob. "The movement is rapid and brutal." The whole action is "rapid, hurly-burly, improvised, like a police operation." The Inquisitor storms about almost hysterically trying to hurry the execution and experiencing all the time his impending defeat by Joan. In the flames Joan "murmuring, already twisted with pain" speaks her last words, and then the prayer for the dead drowns the voices. . . . Hellman produces a pageant, not a police action, an ascent to heaven, not the execution of a mortal girl. Her concept here is "filmic," one might say De Millean. . . .

The three endings differ greatly and significantly. Anouilh, true to form, spun out to the last his acrobatic mixture of sophistication and studied anticlimax. Fry, with his slight cuts and changes, has diminished the irony of the original and thereby brought out the sentimentality implicit in the final scene. He substituted no effect of his own for the material he omitted.

Hellman has altered the original greatly. As with most of the play, she has simplified structure, characters and language, and has in the process removed much of the sophistication and originality of Anouilh's play. But the ending also shows again that she is somehow able to find, within her self-imposed limits, a rough equivalent of the author's intentions, one that will have an effect on her audience somewhat comparable to the effect of the original. She has worked it along the more orthodox lines of tears than of smiles. She has separated the coronation more fully from the preceding execution, and she has given it an atmosphere reminiscent of much contemporary American fiction, drama, and film: the sentimental element is implicit in the whole situation and its visual presentation, but not in the "tough," unsentimental words spoken by Warwick, Charles, and Joan. This effect is not far removed from that of Anouilh where the silly banalities of Charles, Beaudricourt, and the Father contrast with the (of course) rather ironical school prize picture of an ending. The only difference between Hellman and Anouilh is that the irony of that picture is omitted—it would not be very meaningful in New York. The final words are in both cases of the same hard-boiled school. If Miss Hellman lets the King, the Warrior, and the Maid have the final say, and ends with the Gloria, she does so merely because her whole adaptation has the quality of a pageant, which she knows must be rounded off with a climax of an emotional nature. And she knows also that in the American drama it is better in the end to settle on the side of furtive tears than to stray toward self-conscious smiles.

Reinterpreting the Canon

"Good and Evil" in Lillian
Hellman's *The Children's Hour*

Philip M. Armato*

Critics have often called *The Children's Hour* a melodrama. Those who have done so see Karen Wright and Martha Dobie as "good" characters who are victimized by "evil" Mary Tilford. To Barrett H. Clark and Brooks Atkinson, Mary Tilford is a "monster."[1] Even Hellman's most perceptive critic calls her "the embodiment of pure evil."[2] If *The Children's Hour* is the story of a "sweet little teacher done to death by . . . [a] tyrannical child,"[3] then we must concur with Barrett Clark's reading of the play's ultimate meaning: ". . . here is evil . . . make the best of it.[4]

With great patience, Lillian Hellman has defended her play against the attacks of those who have labelled it a melodrama. In a 1965 interview, for example, she said that it is wrong to view her characters as being entirely good or evil: "You [the author] have no right to see your characters as good or bad. Such words have nothing to do with people you write about. Other people see them that way."[5] The interviewer reminded Hellman that in the preface to the 1942 edition of her plays she had said that *The Children's Hour* was about goodness and badness. To this she replied, "Goodness and badness is different from good and bad people isn't it?" Her assertions suggest that Hellman did not intend to portray a melodramatic conflict between two "good" teachers and an "evil" child when she wrote her play. To clarify the play's substance, we should ask what, within the world of the play, is good and what evil.

Playwrights seldom underestimate the dramatic value of the visual-aural impact at curtain rise. The opening of *The Children's Hour*, in a study-room of the Wright-Dobie school, seems undramatic. Mrs. Lily Mortar, Martha Dobie's aunt, is sleeping, the students are sewing. The action which would catch the eyes of the audience is that of Evelyn Munn, "using her scissors to trim the hair of Rosalie, who sits, nervously, in front of her. She has Rosalie's head bent back at an awkward angle and is enjoying herself."[6] However, the audience sees this stark visual image of the infantile pleasure of exercising

*Reprinted from *Educational Theatre Journal* 25 (December 1973):443–47, by permission of the Johns Hopkins University Press.

cruelty while hearing about mercy, for the first words are those of a student reciting Portia's famous speech in *The Merchant of Venice*. Portia's plea for mercy should make an exceedingly strong impression on the audience, for portions of it are interpolated six times between the dialogue of Mrs. Mortar and her pupils. The visual image of cruelty is juxtaposed with the words "pity" and "mercy," which are repeated seven times during the opening moments of the play.

In *The Children's Hour* Hellman posits mercy as an ultimate good and merciless cruelty as an ultimate evil. But to understand the merciless world of Lancet and its cruelty, one must move beyond the notion that Mary Tilford is the embodiment of it.

The rancorous structure of interpersonal relationships in *The Children's Hour* is patterned after the structure of human association in the Venice of Shakespeare's *Merchant*. This can best be described as a victim-victimizer syndrome, the most concrete representation of which is the relationship between Antonio and Shylock. Antonio is convinced that his harsh treatment of Shylock is "just," because the Jew's interest rates are harsh. As victim, Shylock suffers from spiritual agony, feelings of persecution, and desires revenge. If he is able to consummate his wish, Shylock will become the victimizer of the man who originally victimized him. That the victim-victimizer syndrome is finally self-destructive is seen in the courtroom scene, when each victimizer in turn is reduced to the position of victim. Shylock's demand for Antonio's life is turned against him when Portia reminds the court that an alien Jew must suffer the death penalty if he plots against the life of a Venetian citizen. The Duke and Antonio destroy the vicious circle by showing mercy to Shylock.

In the first two acts of her play, Hellman develops three relationships which are characterized by the circular form and destructive content of the victim-victimizer syndrome; these pairs are: Karen Wright—Mary Tilford, Martha Dobie—Lily Mortar, and Amelia Tilford—Wright/Dobie. In *The Merchant*, a Jew who is socially inferior to a Christian is mistreated by the Christian and attempts to use the Duke—the land's highest authority—as a vehicle for his revenge. In *The Children's Hour*, an adolescent pupil who is socially inferior to an adult teacher is mistreated by the teacher and proceeds to use Lancet's most influential citizen—the powerful matron Amelia Tilford—as a vehicle for her revenge. Finally, in the much criticized third act, Hellman, like Shakespeare, posits mercy as the only solution to the moral dilemma which is created when we deal justly with each other.

Karen Wright's treatment of Mary Tilford has never been sensitively evaluated. No one has noticed that immediately preceding their initial confrontation, Hellman suggests that Karen is perhaps not as compassionate as a teacher of young children should be. For when Mrs. Mortar complains that one of her students does not "appreciate" Portia's plea for mercy, Karen replies: "Well I didn't either. I don't think I do yet" (p. 11). The harshness of her discipline will demonstrate the truth—on a far more literal level than she suspects—of her remark.

Mary Tilford's offense is a minor one. She attempts to excuse her tardiness by saying that she was picking flowers for Mrs. Mortar. The flowers, Karen knows, were "picked" from the top of a garbage can, and Mary's stubborn refusal to admit the truth convinces Karen that she must be punished. First, Mary is told to take her recreation periods alone for two weeks; then, that her friend Evelyn will no longer be her roommate, and that she must now live with her enemy Rosalie. Mary is also ordered not to leave the grounds for any reason. Hellman emphasizes Karen's harshness by adding details—Mary is specifically forbidden participation in hockey and horseback riding—and by one further prohibition. Mary hopes that Karen's rules apply only to weekdays; if so, she may still be able to attend an event she has been looking forward to, the boat-races on Saturday. Unfortunately, she is told that she cannot attend them. While these restrictions might not be extreme deprivation for an adult, they are so for a child.

Mary feels—and rightly—that she is being persecuted. From wanting to tell her grandmother "how everybody treats me here and the way I get punished for every little thing I do" (p. 13), she moves to a sense of her inner agony, objectified in her hysterical "heart problems," and finally to a rebellious attitude: "They can't get away with treating me like this, and they don't have to think they can" (p. 31). She sets out to take her revenge, as is the victim's wont. She accuses Karen and Martha of lesbianism, and persists in her lie. Her behavior is ugly, but has been provoked by Karen's earlier ugliness: she seeks an eye for an eye, a tooth for a tooth.

Karen's inability to deal compassionately with Mary Tilford is paralleled in act 1 by Martha Dobie's attitude toward her aunt Lily. Karen and Martha decide that she must be relieved of her teaching duties, and literally thrown out of school. Their decision is just, for Mortar is a nuisance and an incompetent, yet they do not consider for a moment the effect such a dismissal may have on an old woman whose life has been the school. Again, justice is untempered by mercy, and again Hellman emphasizes the rigidity of the decision's administration. Martha not only tells Lily that she must leave, but makes fun of her—"We don't want you around when we dig up the buried treasure" (p. 20)—and threatens that "You ought to be glad I don't do worse" (p. 20). Mortar pathetically attempts to save face: "I absolutely refuse to be shipped off three thousand miles away. I'm not going to England. I shall go back to the stage. I'll write my agents tomorrow, and as soon as they have something good for me—" (p. 20). This is essentially a plea for mercy cast in a manner that will allow her to retain some semblance of dignity. The old crone is finished on the stage, her "agents" are imaginary, and if she does not leave until they find her a part, she will never leave at all, which is her wish. Her suggestion is brusquely rejected. As Karen isolates Mary, Martha exiles Mortar. Lily's reaction is the same as Mary's: "You always take your spite out on me" (p. 21). As she exits, she casts toward Martha a "malicious half-smile" (p. 23) and the malice of revenge is realized when she refuses to testify on Martha's behalf at the libel trial.

In act 2, Karen and Martha suffer an ironic reversal of fortune; the victimizers become victims themselves. Amelia Tilford, an influential figure in the community of Lancet, misuses her authority over Karen and Martha just as surely as they had taken advantage of the weaker positions of Mary and Lily. When Mary tells Amelia that her two teachers are lesbian, the dowager immediately phones the parents of the children who are enrolled at Wright-Dobie and repeats the charges, thus destroying the school. When Karen and Martha come for an explanation, Amelia makes it clear that she does not want these two lepers in her house: "I don't think you should have come here. . . . I shall not call you names, and I will not allow you to call me names. It comes to this: I can't trust myself to talk about it with you now or ever" (p. 52). Her condescension and her revulsion in the face of her visitors' suspected abnormality pervades the scene: "This—this thing is your own. Go away with it. I don't understand it and I don't want any part of it" (p. 54). Ironically, Karen and Martha now suffer from the same humiliation and ostracism that they so rigorously inflicted on others.

To make the ironic parallel—and thus the lesson—even more explicit, Hellman shows Karen and Martha reacting just as Lily and Mary had. Both think that they are being unjustly persecuted: "What is she [Amelia] trying to do to us? What is everyone doing to us?" (p. 53). Both feel spiritual agony: "You're not playing with paper dolls. We're human beings, see? It's our lives you're fooling with. *Our* lives" (p. 53). Finally, they feel the need for revenge: "What can we do to you [Amelia]? There must be something— something that makes you feel the way we do tonight. You don't want any part of this, you said. But you'll get a part. More than you bargained for" (p. 55).

In act 2, then, Hellman presents a change in relationships, but not a change in the structure of relationships. The rancorous victim-victimizer syndrome is as pervasive in this act as it was in the previous one, the difference being that relationships have now come full circle; those who mistreated others are now mistreated themselves. Clearly, Hellman implies that when one mistreats another, he plants the seeds of his own destruction. This insight is made even more explicit in the third act.

Martha admits to herself that she has always been physically attracted to Karen. Her attitude toward her self is just as harsh as it had been towards others—or as Amelia Tilford's attitude had been towards lesbianism. Indeed, Martha's rancorous attitude toward the imperfections of others is but a reflection of her own self-condemnation. Hellman is making the same crucial point that Sartre makes in *Dirty Hands*, when he has Hoederer say to Hugo, "You, I know you now, you are a destroyer. You detest man because you detest yourself."

As in the other two acts, there is a parallel action, but this time it is the difference that is instructive, not the similarity. Martha's self-condemnation is matched by a new-found self-disgust in Amelia Tilford. She discovers that Mary has lied about her two teachers, and realizes that her hasty phone calls have destroyed two people who are innocent of the charges. Her discovery propels her into the same kind of guilt and self-laceration that we have just seen driving Martha to suicide. Amelia begs Karen to allow her to "do something" for her so that she can in part expiate her sin. Karen extends mercy.

Hellman counterpoints Karen's new-found benevolence with the by now familiar infantile hostility of Lily Mortar, who protests against Amelia Tilford even setting foot in the school: "With Martha lying there? How can you be so feelingless? . . . I won't stay and see it. I won't have anything to do with it. I'll never let that woman—" (p. 83). Martha's suicide, however, has for Karen been both harrowing and educative. Because of it she is, she tells Lily, "Not [young] any more" (p. 81). The brief statement implies that she feels sadness at the loss of her own innocence, but also suggests that Martha's death has introduced her to a new maturity. Her horror at the guilt that caused Martha's suicide leads her to sympathize with the plight of "guilt-ridden" Amelia. In the last moments of the play, she accepts Amelia's atonement and thereby extends compassion—the ultimate good in the world of the play.

MRS. TILFORD: You'll be all right?

KAREN: I'll be all right, I suppose. Goodbye, now. (*They both rise. Mrs. Tilford speaks, pleadingly.*)

MRS. TILFORD: You'll let me help you? You'll let me try?

KAREN: Yes, if it will make you feel better.

MRS. TILFORD: (*With great feeling.*) Oh, yes, oh, yes Karen. (*Unconsciously Karen begins to walk towards the window.*)

KAREN: (*Suddenly.*) Is it nice out?

MRS. TILFORD: It's been cold. (*Karen opens the window slightly, sits on the ledge. Mrs. Tilford with surprise.*) It seems a little warmer now.

KAREN: It feels very good. (*They smile at each other.*) [p. 86]

Karen has destroyed the vicious circle that has characterized human relations; her compassion is the ultimate good in the world of the play.

The two traditional criticisms of *The Children's Hour*'s last act are that Mary Tilford is the central interest of the play and so should not be missing at its conclusion; and that the final "summing up" (Hellman's words) is tedious.[7] However, Mary Tilford is not the central interest of the play; a certain perverse structure of human relationships is. Moreover, if critics paid more attention to what Hellman is "summing up," they would find that the conclusion of the play is a structurally necessary resolution, not a tedious reiteration of previous materials. Jacob H. Adler has noted that *The Children's*

Hour, like *The Wild Duck,* "ends not with . . . [a] suicide but with a brief discussion pinning down the issues as a result of the suicide."[8]

Works as diverse as Aeschylus's *Oresteia,* Shakespeare's *Measure for Measure,* and Melville's *Billy Budd* have dealt with the dichotomy between primitive justice and mercy. Although *The Children's Hour* is certainly a less monumental work of art than any of these, it is within its limits a wholly successful moral play. Hellman suggests that adults are too often "children." While infantile revenge is matter of course in men's dealings with each other, Hellman shows a last-act discovery—Karen Wright's discovery of a more mature concept of compassion.

Notes

1. Clark, "Lillian Hellman," *College English,* 6 (Dec. 1944), 128; Atkinson, "At the Theatre," *New York Times,* Dec. 19, 1952, p. 35.

2. Jacob H. Adler, *Lillian Hellman* (Austin, 1969), 2. Eric Bentley, a little more moderate, merely calls her a "villain" ("Hellman's Indignation," *The New Republic,* Jan. 5, 1953, p. 31), but Edith Isaacs sees her as "the summation of falsity, depravity, and cruelty" ("Lillian Hellman, Playwright on the March," *Theatre Arts,* 23 [Jan. 1944], p. 9).

3. Bentley, p. 31.

4. Clark, p. 128.

5. John Phillips and Anne Hollander, "Lillian Hellman, An Interview," *Paris Review,* 9 (Winter 1965), p. 70.

6. *Six Plays* (New York, 1960), p. 5. All subsequent citations are from this text.

7. For example, Joseph Wood Krutch, "The Heart of a Child," *The Nation,* December 5, 1934, pp. 656–57.

8. Adler, p. 8.

Bohemia Bumps into Calvin: The Deception of Passivity in Lillian Hellman's Drama
Mary Lynn Broe*

Her face like a thousand year old siennese mask sheds time in runnels, etched with the vivacity of a life lived passionately and well. Undaunted, she has visited battle fronts during bombings, foraged bayou country for wild duck, scarfed jambalaya and raccoon stew, whisked contraband in a hatbox across the German border. She is as much at home decapitating snapping turtles as she is captivating the world of high fashion clad in a Balmain dress or a Blackgama coat. Her "spit-in-the-eye" rebelliousness can change mercurially from rampaging anger to demure deference.[1]

*Reprinted with minor revision from *Southern Quarterly* 19 (Winter 1981):26–41, by permission of the author and the journal.

Although at every turn "Bohemia bumps into Calvin" in her character, Lillian Hellman is seldom linked with the concept of passivity. In both the political and literary establishments, she has become one of the foremost authorities on decisive action and pure forcefulness. According to one critic, "Miss Hellman dreams of living successfully by masculine standards: honor, courage, aggression."[2] Yet in *An Unfinished Woman* she admits: "I feel at my best when somebody else drives the car, gives the orders, knows me well enough to see through the manner that . . . was thought up early to hide the indecision, the vagueness." In *An Unfinished Woman* and *Pentimento*, both autobiographical works, the apparent powerlessness that begins as a consistent social pose is a paradoxical one: in incident after incident, the social posture quickly becomes the means to her most penetrating insights. Passivity—both a triumph and a compensation wrested from years of female victimhood—functions as an artistic means to spiritual-moral development in Hellman's writing. "If you are willing to take the punishment, you are halfway through the battle," she announces, recalling herself as a child who, having run away from home, understands the advantageous manipulative power of absence. And later, "I was ashamed that I caused myself to lose so often," she remarks to Hammett, who, when rebuked by her, grinds a burning cigarette into *his* cheek. From characters such as her childhood maid Sophronia, Dash Hammett, Horace Liveright, Dorothy Parker and friend Julia, she learns the vital function of being morally free to be socially passive. Whether she leaves the judgment of others inconclusive, or "refuses to preside over violations against herself," Lillian Hellman employs passivity in the autobiographies as a vehicle for powerful action, compassion, and finally, moral authority.[3]

So, too, in her major plays.[4] Any reevaluation of her drama requires our acknowledgment of her use of passivity in its variegated forms as a catalyst for truth-telling, deception, and most importantly, self-deception: all recurrent themes in her plays.

Lillian Hellman's plays redeem the impediment of a social role of passivity as a calculated artistic choice in a curious, perhaps unlikely, way. It is less Hellman's theme of passivity than her structural *reworking* of the quality within each drama that reclaims these plays from labels of infectious villainy or triumphant duplicity. For it is no longer illuminating to see her characters in the simple categories of initiators of evil, the "despoilers" who execute their destructive aims on the one hand, or the "by-standers" who, because of naiveté or lack of self-knowledge, suggest evil as the "negative failure of good."[5] Rather, passivity redefined to include aspects of deception and moral disguise is both thematically and structurally crucial to any reevaluation of Hellman as a significant contemporary playwright. As Addie in *The Little Foxes* (1939) says: "Well, there are people who eat the earth and eat all the people on it like in the Bible with the locusts. And other people who stand around and watch them eat it. Sometimes I think it ain't right to stand and watch them eat it" (p. 182). The socially negligible female characters, the ones who "stand around and watch them [the locusts] eat," actually control the more brutishly powerful, but often in indirect, unobtrusive ways. As General Griggs (*The Autumn Garden* [1951]) might say of their passive behavior, it is simply a way "to remain in training while you wait" for the big moments, the turning points in life. The minor female characters—Lavinia, Birdie Hubbard, Sophie, Lily Prine and Lily Mortar—candidly, if unwittingly, reveal dramatic "truth" in certain situations. By their revelations they catalyze the outcome of dramatic action. Thus the socially negligible become the dramatically invaluable.

Of course, passivity is not a foreign concept to female authors and characters of the nineteenth or twentieth centuries. Victorian literature is replete with its Mrs. Gamps (professional servants of deaths and entrances), Maggie Tullivers and Edna Pontelliers, whose place is more to suffer than to do. From Thea Elvstead's blond snivellings in *Hedda Gabler* to Blanche Dubois' begging the gallantry of a gentleman caller, to Sylvia Plath's bedding down in a "cupboard of rubbish," at home in "turnipy chambers" among roots, husks and owl pellets, the passive role has become a pejorative image of a lot of handwringers, retiring mealy-mouths, or women playing Galatea to some man's Pygmalion. These female lives seem to guarantee that the meek are not so blessed after all, but simply cursed with social insignificance. No wonder then that one critic has described the circumstance of so many passive women characters as a sentimentally disinvolved torpidity, never deliberate, but always lending a strong impression of sluggish flies hatching indoors in early winter.[6]

But fortunately a number of contemporary thinkers have redefined passivity, retrieving it from the convention of social role to the authority of moral virtue, from a limited stereotype to a limitless capacity for real feeling, intelligence and choice. Mary Ellmann has likened the workings of the stereotype to the dynamics of Negro apathy: once the social restriction is placed on the group, the characteristic inactivity is found and then called innate, not social.[7] And in studying Victorian women, Patricia Meyer Spacks suggests that the lack of social opportunity is less an impediment than a chance for moral and emotional fulfillment. Assuming an unfashionable pose, Spacks defies the old saw that a limited social status necessarily creates a limited personality.[8] Mahatma Gandhi, moreover, elevated passivity beyond either politics or stereotype to a creed of personal ethics that emphasized integrity as a form of struggle. According to Gandhi, one could gain a moral authority worthy of *The Sermon on the Mount* or the *Bhagavad-Gita* by "Satyagraha," an act of the mind and will. If we bear in mind this brief history as we look at five Hellman plays, we see that an apparent social disadvantage actually allows a distinct capacity for being as a *moral* individual, or catalyzes action that permits such moral truth to be recognized.

In *The Children's Hour* (1934), Hellman dismantles the social stereotype of passivity in Aunt Lily Mortar and her parodic distortion, Mary Tilford. Early in the play, the decaying ex-actress Lily Mortar is overheard calling the relationship of the headmistresses of a New England girl's school "just as unnatural as it can be." Her words, repeated to and distorted by Mary Tilford, bring about the suicide of one of the women, who actually does acknowledge so-called unnatural feeling for the other. By shrewdly calculating the cliché of social passivity (the demure silence of an abused child), Mary blackmails and manipulates both her grandmother and a fellow student into the character assassination of Karen and Martha, the headmistresses. She engineers her "great, awful lie" into acceptable truth by exaggerating a social stereotype.

In the course of the play, Aunt Lily Mortar makes a career out of absence, omission, and inadvertence. Living in the days of steamer trunks and roadshows, Lily has made theatrics her domain, chatter her trademark. For Lily the natural thing is the socially customary, courtesy a mere matter of breeding, passivity an unconscious and uncritical way of life. In the play's opening scene, Lily and the schoolgirls are involved in a "great show of doing nothing," their theatrical passivity itself a lie for gainful learning. Here the beaux arts of womanhood become useless, truncated labors, images of incompletion. Hair is being cut as irregularly as Latin verbs are conjugated. Haphazard sewing and basting complement the fake social graces. Theatrics replaces the candor of labor. Unwittingly, Lily herself points out the deception, calling their labors simply women's "tricks."

Perhaps the most critical meta-theatrical moment in this opening scene is Lily's hammy reading of Portia's "mercy" speech from Shakespeare's *The Merchant of Venice*.[9] On Lily Mortar's lips, these celebrated lines dwindle to a mere elocutionary exercise just as the truth she utters central to the outcome of action is but an overheard perception. Portia's moral and verbal disguise contrasts with Lily's inadvertent catastasis of the play's end. (Hellman at once sneers and laughs at the element of "pretend" that infects the stage: as she says the playwright's "tricking up the scene" is the only fitting response.) But ironically, it is the three lines Lily *omits* that seem to anticipate the outcome of the dramatic action in *The Children's Hour:* "Therefore, Jew / Though justice be thy plea, consider this / That in the course of justice none of us / Should see salvation."

No one *does* see salvation in the girl's school where universal deception is rampant. Although Mary Tilford is exposed for her malignant manipulations, and Mrs. Tilford, her rich granny, recants her character slander, both events occur too late to save either Martha's life or the headmistresses' careers. Moreover, Lily's verbal omissions in the first scene foreshadow her crucial absence when Karen and Martha need her witness for their trial. Muttered asides and throwaway lines, Lily's words emerge only indirectly as canny truths about the other characters: "I love you that way—maybe the way they said" (p. 62), Martha admits to Karen following Lily's charge of "unnaturalness"; or Lily's comment that "one master passion in the breast . . . swallows all the rest" (p. 9) accurately describes Mary's maliciousness, Mrs. Tilford's righteousness, as well as Martha's love for Karen before the play ends. In one of Hellman's best deceptions of the intractable theater audience, Lily Mortar has the force of a daft Cassandra.

Mary Tilford is the theatrical caricature and complement to Lily Mortar's genuine social weakness. Mary feigns homesickness, fainting, even a heart attack in a Grand Guignol representation of weakness. Even though this whiner has her facts wrong in the play's Inquisition scene (there is no keyhole in the headmistress's bedroom door, as Mary claims, nor is the other headmistress's room near enough for the girl to overhear anything), Mary turns her calculated passive behavior into a triumph over authority and maturity, as once again moral disguise and meta-theatrics are closely linked. She is coyly frail, consciously retiring in scenes with Mrs. Mortar, her grandmother, and Dr. Cardin. She blackmails Rosalie, her chum, and then defers to Rosalie's facts. As an innocent bystander who sees and hears only inadvertently, she never once utters an incriminating word of her own. But in the end of the play, her mummery of passivity does her in, does not triumph.

Just as meta-theatrics permits moral disguise in Lily's incomplete Portia and Mary's failed Inquisition, so too does it become a metaphor for other forms of playing in *The Children's Hour*. Even structurally, the play proves deceptive. All the truth-revealing scenes are interrupted so that the continuous action of dramatic unravelling and revelation are missing from the play. By such sleight of structure, Hellman shifts the focus from blackmail, extortion, and lesbianism (more melodramatic topics) to the quiet business of redefining a moral capacity. The headmistresses' tense, oblique exchange of feelings about Karen's impending marriage is interrupted by Joe, Karen's fiance, with his talk of the black bulls "breeding in the hills." Eavesdropping girls behind the door halt Lily Mortar's discussion of Martha's "unnatural" sentiments for Karen. And as Mrs. Tilford begins to elaborate that "something horrible" is wrong with Karen, the young woman herself arrives to ask, "Is it a joke, Joe?" mistaking villainy for comedy. Hellman suggests complex new moral possibilities for passivity by giving a dramatically central role to the indirect revelations of Lily Mortar. At the same time, she mocks the theatrics of social passivity by linking it with moral disguise in both Lily and Mary Tilford. She will elaborate these possibilities throughout her playwriting career.

Hellman's general theme of duplicity is more specifically focused on two women characters and their portraits of passivity in *The Little Foxes*. Regina Hubbard Giddens feigns the role of the inept and demure Southern belle in a character study that is, in words Hellman once used to describe Dorothy Parker, a combination of Little Nell and Lady Macbeth. "I don't know about these things," Regina postures. "I shouldn't like to be too definite," she demurs about the family's business bargaining terms (p. 149). But Regina knows both terms and money. She has been systematically juggling her family's lives and fortunes for a long time. She puts her own daughter up for forty percent collateral in a deal, using her also as bait to get an invalid husband home. When told that her husband is dying, Regina can't understand "why people have to talk about this kind of thing" (p. 168). She uses her husband's reticence about committing money and finally even his death as bargaining tools that she wields sharply against her brothers. Outwitting the thieving Hubbards, she gets seventy-five percent of the money for herself, in an actively malignant parody of passivity. Once again, moral dissembling, social passivity, and meta-theatrics are linked in the character of Regina.

The dramatic complement to Regina's feigned passivity is the battered Aunt Birdie. Though Birdie is repeatedly belittled by her family, who claims she'll get a headache if she babbles too much truth—"that's a lie they tell for me," she knows (p. 183)—Birdie reveals the play's central and ironic truth. Flighty and high on elderberry wine, felled by a case of the hiccups, she nevertheless sets the shadowy standard for moral judgment in *The Little Foxes*. Early on, she begins telling more truth than the Hubbards care to hear: she recognizes ethical values. Although her father gave his life as a soldier in the war, she sees through the senseless "killing just for killing." She supports Horace's wishes when he is being pawned by the family's expediency and laments, "If only we could go back to Lionnet." But Birdie's values and her words are not so much nostalgia for an aristocratic past than desire for sources of information and power whereby Horace and Alexandra are able to check Regina's financial and personal manipulations. Birdie, the magpie chatterer who seems financially dominated and personally insignificant, utters the central, empowering moral judgment in the play. What she tells is that Oscar has "made their money charging awful interest to ignorant niggers and cheating them on what they bought" (p. 182). Her emotions are candid and unconventional, even if she does deliver them as pathetic memories and throwaway lines. She hates her own son Leo, warns her niece Alexandra against family dependency ("Don't love me. Because in twenty years you'll just be like me"), and debunks the myth of romantic love between herself and her husband: "Ask why *he* married *me* . . . My family was good and the cotton on Lionnet's field was better. Ben Hubbard wanted the cotton and Oscar Hubbard married it for him" (p. 182).

In the opening scene, Birdie criticizes the unethical behavior practiced by the new Southern industrialists and hints at what will become of the Hubbards in their ruthless use of one another. The information and influence she provides Alexandra and her allegiance to Horace prompt the younger woman's final refusal. Birdie's words give her "the courage to fight" instead of being "one of the people who stand around and watch." While good may not be rewarded or evil sufficiently punished in *The Little Foxes*, Hellman does expand and explore the character of those "little foxes whose vines have tender grapes" through the figure of Aunt Birdie. In Birdie's intoxicated asides, truth is given ultimate, though unlikely, power over apparently active evil. If not redeemed, the passive are victims redefined.

In *The Children's Hour* and *The Little Foxes* both Mary's pose as a battered child and Regina's feigned Southern belle routine set the stage for a very different sort of passivity. These two self-conscious dramas contrast with

Birdie's intoxicated asides that narrate the Hubbard history, and Lily's erratic Portia and words whispered on the staircase—both of which create the circumstances on which the dramatic outcome of each play depends. The real moral quality of passivity (which Birdie in particular represents) triumphs over feigned artifice as it exists in Mary and Regina's meta-theatrics.

In *Another Part of the Forest* (1947), Lavinia claims to have a good memory. And indeed she has. Keeping her all night vigils, wandering about "colored" churches clutching her Bible, Lavinia is easily dismissed as a babbling, mad hanky-wringer. She even lives in silence for a decade on Marcus's promises that "next year they will talk." Like Ghandi, Lavinia literally and morally clings to the truth with an act of mind and will that proves her personal integrity. Unlike the old aristocratic Bagtrys, whose backward nostalgia "got in the way of history," Lavinia's throwaway comments make a curious kind of sense. "It's not easy to send your own husband into a hanging rope," she admits. For despite her dismissal as a crazy pipedreamer, Lavinia knows the truth about the viper's tangle of Hubbard family history. "Imagine taking money for other people's misery," she mutters about Marcus's rise to fortune. Years before, privy to her husband's cheating and lying—now a family trademark—she has recorded events in her Bible. Her facts prove that Marcus has run a blockade to scalp salt to the poor and dying during the war. She also knows that by his action he had been responsible for the Union massacre of twenty-seven Confederate boys in training camp.

Stifled now by a corrupt family, Lavinia tries repeatedly to air her secret, but fails. Instead, she develops an escape fantasy of teaching poor black children "the word" she has never uttered, only clutched. Unlike Mary Tilford's or Regina's postures, Lavinia's pretending functions as an imaginative moral restitution for the deceptive silence she has kept for over sixteen years. "There's got to be one little thing you do that you want to do, all by yourself you want to do it" (p. 332), she insists.

Once again in the Hellman canon, meta-theatrics—now in the form of Lavinia's pipedream of escape—becomes the vehicle for moral disguise. The handwringing, babbling Lavinia is really lucidly oversane. She is immune to bribery and nostalgic myths, just as she knows the difference between sacred vows and a bad marriage. Throughout the play, her asides reveal information about the suspicion cast on the family by Marcus's actions, about the "hot tar and clubs and ropes that night" (p. 377). But the truth she finally utters in act 3 allows her son Ben to check Marcus's power as well as his words, which, as Lavinia reminds them, do *not* match his actions. Supremely guileless, Lavinia toys with that gap between language and reality that has supported Marcus's fictive life: "Why Marcus," she reminds her husband about the incriminating information the prostitute Laurette has just volunteered, "The girl only told the truth. Salt is just a word, it's in the Bible quite a lot. And that other matter, why, death is also just a word" (p. 372).

Lavinia borrows words from her Bible, if not to prompt justice in the play, at least to offer a more lucid understanding of the nature of "truth" on which the dramatic action turns. "I only have what I have," she announces. Truth is neither brute power nor written facts, but "whatever people want to believe," Lavinia knows, "I'm not going to have any Bibles in my school. That surprise you all? It's the only book in the world but it's just for grown people, after you know it don't mean what it says" (p. 391). The chicanery of nearly every member of the family backfires, as Lavinia finally "tells the truth to everybody," clutching her Bible. She deals various members of the family symbolic gifts at the end of the play, proving not only the restoration of her memory, but her degree of moral sense that is not shared by even the shrewd Regina or the greedy Ben. Lavinia, perhaps even more than Mrs. Mortar or Birdie, deceives by redefining a social role of passivity as a capacity for moral understanding, fulfillment, even nuance.

With *The Autumn Garden* (1951), Hellman moves from crass entrepreneurs and claptrap confrontations to the muted haze of middle-life. In a world subtly Chekhovian—and in a play Hellman reluctantly admits is her best—she makes nostalgia a form of consciousness. Pity and compassion are the only bonding possible among weak, aging characters. Under the cabbage roses of the once grand Tuckerman boarding house, each character seems stalled in a particular version of the past—unfinished paintings, mothy romances, worn family legacies. Each is sunken into an after-dinner doze of self-deception: "I think as one grows older it is more and more necessary to reach out your hand for the sturdy old vines you knew when you were young and let them lead you back to the roots of things that matter" (p. 483). But it is precisely this waste that Hellman warns against in *Autumn Garden* through the action of two negligible women characters.

The dramatic situation develops when Nick Denerey, artist manqué with cosmopolitan pretensions, returns to the "summer mansion" of his childhood in order to grab onto those "sturdy old vines" just as they were twenty years before. His memories have never matured, however, only inflated his enormous capacity for myth, philandering, flirting, and do-gooder meddling. One night, on a drunken "rampage of good-will," he compromises the maid Sophie, who is Frederick's affianced. Servants and friends in the provincial town quickly learn the scandal of the boarding house. Ironically, the publication of the news combined with Sophie's ingenuity serves to rescue this indentured Cinderella from a miserable future life with Frederick Ellis and his mother. The outcome of the dilemma depends upon a few pungent perceptions of an old dismissible grandmother, Mrs. Ellis, who warns Sophie about the consequences of the gossip and saves her from a disastrous marriage of convenience with the son.

By virtue of their outcast status or age, both Sophie and old Mrs. Ellis are late examples of Hellman's artistically tooled "passives" who reclaim a social label as a dramatic strength. Both Sophie and Mrs. Ellis join the gallery of Lavinias, Lily Mortars and Birdies, catalysts for action who capitalize on a formerly narrow social quality, dramatically retrieving it. Amidst all the ruin of wasted lives, both of these characters manage to act realistically, not to doze or deceive. They stand in contrast to Rose, the "Army manual wife," who with fluttering eyelids and heart staves off the divorce that her husband the General so desperately wants. Like the faded buttercup Rose, or Ned Crossman, the boarder who makes his valedictories to a bottle of brandy, most of the other characters beg reality never to correct the "indefinite pronouns" of their Southern gentility.

Bored with this passel of self-deceivers, Mrs. Ellis has a strong grasp of the real issues of life—power, sensuality, money: "I say to myself, one should have power, or give it over. But if one keeps it, it might as well be used, with as little mealymouthness as possible" (p. 503). Like Granny in Albee's *American Dream*, who debunks myths by turning them back on the family, Mrs. Ellis is a straight shooter with a razor-sharp tongue who has built a solid financial empire for herself. She uses her power and her overheard words to create the situation that saves Sophie. Walter Kerr has compared her to "the goddess Athena in a snapbrim fedora," delivering her haymakers with aplomb.[10] She knows that it's easy to afford the luxury of morality when somebody else "clips the coupons." She readily admits that the happiest years of her life are those she has spent in solitude since her husband's death. She chides Nick for inflicting his bear hugs, friendly pats, and tiny bursts of passion: "One should have sensuality whole or not at all." Mocking him as one of the "touchers and leaners," she asks if he doesn't find "pecking at it ungratifying." When Frederick discovers that his writer-friend Payson's real attraction to him is money, Mrs. Ellis orders him to "Take next week to be sad. A week's long enough to be sad in" (p. 509). She knows well the system of patronage in which people like Fred, a professional proofreader and simp, must pay for the interest of people like Payson with their literary coteries. Like Lily Mortar's words, Mrs. Ellis's non sequiturs (such as her speech that "nobody in the South has tapeworm anymore") describe candidly the parasitic relationships that surround her—Frederick and Carrie, Nick and Nina, Constance and Nick, Payson and Fred, Rose and the General.

Sophie, another minor female character, has a central dramatic role. She is the impoverished European niece, "indentured" to the family for her cultural and social status. Like Mrs. Ellis, she is far too pragmatic to be arrested in self-deceptions. In the words of General Griggs at the end of the play, Sophie spends her life "in training" for the big moment of her escape. Perceptually, verbally, and morally, she piles up a lot of little moments to stand on. Seemingly tongue-tied and retiring when she first appears, in the course of the play Sophie manages wry words for, and rare understanding of, the others' pretenses. She knows that decisions are made "only in order to speak about changing them." Quite matter of factly she says: "You know it is most difficult in another language. Everything in English sounds important. I get a headache from the strain of listening" (pp. 473–74). And to Constance: "I think perhaps you worry sometimes in order that you should not think" (p. 520). Sophie sees the social facade of Constance's romantic malingering: "Such a long, long time to stay nervous. Great love in tender natures. . . . It always happens that way with ladies. For them it is once and not again: it is their good breeding that makes it so" (p. 480). Sophie admits the bargain she is striking with Frederick (the exchange of social position for sexual cover); knows the prevalent social code for women ("little is made into very much here"); and knows also that "somehow sex and money are simpler in French" (pp. 536–37) than in the indirect metaphors and oblique rhetoric employed by the Ellises and Denerys.

Sophie is shrewd about the female ploys she uses to threaten Nina Denery with exposure of her husband's seduction: her word is ominous, but, held in reserve, carries the power of Lavinia's clutched Bible. "We will call it a loan, come by through blackmail" (p. 537), she says of the five thousand dollars she extorts as escape money with which she will return to Europe. She realistically turns Nick's playful charm-seduction-disposal game back on him by demanding the exact commission he was to receive for doing a portrait of Rose Griggs's homely niece. Most significantly, the trade value of her bargain, that is, her role as marriage counselor, is not lost on Sophie: "How would you and Mr. Denery go on living without such incidents as me? I have been able to give you a second, or a twentieth, honeymoon" (p. 538).

Linked in a socially negligible partnership, but oracular in their throw-away lines, Sophie and old Mrs. Ellis support one another both in dramatic action and verbal power. Now we see the collaboration of the passive, dismissible characters, extremes (impoverished youth to wry old age) on the continuum of life. With realistic savvy about money as power, they use the meta-theatrics of their social roles not for moral disguise, as do Regina and Mary Tilford, but as means to physical escape or greater self awareness. Through their final camaraderie, we realize that *Autumn Garden* issues a stern warning reminiscent of F. Scott Fitzgerald's early stories: life is a valuable and precious trust whose capital must be invested early and wisely, set in a committed direction and tended energetically *before* mid-life, or its returns will never be reaped. If it is squandered, the Sophies of the world will deceive themselves into becoming Rose Griggses.

In *Toys in the Attic* (1960) the demented child-bride Lily Prine wanders about in her slip or with a nightgown over her dress, desperately trying to babble the truth of her suspicions about her roué husband, Julian Berniers. But the world of the Berniers sisters does not promote either candor or truthfulness: they dote on their pasts, on their renegade gambler brother, and on the colognes and candied oranges they trade with each other every week. As Carrie Berniers remarks to her sister, "Funny how you can live so close and long and not know things, isn't it?" (p. 687).

Like flighty Birdie Hubbard or muted Lavinia, Lily has knowledge but not audience, awareness but not articulation. She knows her husband talks every evening at six with "the not such a young lady with the sad face" (p. 701), the same woman seen with him on an Audubon Park bench. Lily cannot quite connect Julian's loss of the Chicago shoe factory with his current wealth that takes him away for so much of the day and permits him to buy ball gowns, pianos, and flaming red mantillas. When she guilelessly asks her questions, whispers her vagaries about the "*not* happenings of the night before," and mutters hallucinatory non-sequiturs, Lily is stifled by her husband Julian. He sends her to her room, locks her in a hotel, or reprimands her that "That's not the way to be married" (p. 702). As Lavinia clutches "the word" in the Bible, Lily Prine totes with her the "sacred knife of truth" (for which she traded her wedding ring in a morphine den), waiting for the moment when she might wield it.

The moment comes when Lily can tolerate no more of her husband's suspected infidelity. She phones Cyrus Warkins, the husband of the elusive other woman. In a babble of typical non-sequiturs, baby talk, and illogical words, she begs him for "just one more year with Julian," thereby revealing the liaison with Warkins's wife. But Lily's action—that slice of the "sacred knife of truth"—cuts grossly, mangles the truth.

The real stakes are far more dangerous than Julian's fictitious adultery. Julian's actual venture is a shady but lucrative business deal based on a tip about a couple of acres of swampland precious to Warkins. Warkins's wife, a sentimental old flame of Julian, has put him onto the scheme to rob her brutal husband of his fortune. Because of Lily's call, Charlotte Warkins is slashed up, Julian robbed and mugged by hired thugs.

Although Lily slices deeply with her knife of truth, she mismanages truth, which seems to have its own aesthetic momentum. She is not the catalyst for the dramatic outcome so crucial to the lives of the Berniers sisters. Curiously, her action returns Julian to a state of passivity, impotence, and dependency on his maiden sisters, who with their cloying affections, paltry fictions, and meagre savings, require his need for their very survival. As Anna says to Carrie after a painful confession scene: "I loved you and so whatever I knew didn't matter. You wanted to see yourself a way you never were. Maybe that's a game you let people play when you love them. Well, we had made something together, and the words would have stayed where they belonged as we waited for our brother to need us again. But our brother doesn't need us anymore, and so the poor house came down" (pp. 745–46).

Like so many Hellman characters, the negligible Lily has the oblique lucidity of the mad, as well as the practical savvy that is, literally, too direct for the Berniers' attic world of mismanaged truth: "I spoke to Mr. Warkins and told him to ask her to wait for Julian for one more year. After that, if Julian doesn't want me—Where would I ever go, who would ever want me? I'm trouble, we all know that. I wouldn't have anywhere to go" (p. 748). Just as the crusty, bohemian Albertine Prine steps in and returns Lily's knife of truth to the gypsy den, fetching back her wedding ring, so, too, does she return her daughter to her husband, counseling her in life-saving deceptions. Like Carrie, whose incestuous feelings for Julian have surfaced through Lily's action, Albertine Prine realizes that "you take your chances on being hated by speaking out the truth." She says to Lily, "Go in and sit by him. Just sit by him and shut up. . . . Can you have enough pity for him not to kill him with truth?" (p. 750).

Lillian Hellman plays passivity in her minor female characters the way a jazz musician ranges over musical notes. She improvises variations on a chordal progression that vibrates from Lily Mortar to Lily Prine; from inadvertent truth-telling to conscious moral restitution and shrewd self-awareness; from moral disguise (Lily in *The Children's Hour*) to physical escape (Sophie in *The Autumn Garden*). Close examination of the negligible women in each of the five plays suggests that Hellman is a consummate trickster both in characterization and in theme—a role for this contemporary dramatist only broached by current criticism. She never appears to be the drum banging melodramatist that critics of her work have insisted. As if to defy what she calls the "pretence of representation" in the theatre, its claptrap as well as its "tight, unbending, unfluid, meagre" form, Hellman cleverly tailors a socially assigned role—passivity—into variegated moral and dramatic authority. And the artistic as well as the moral clout of passive characters has grown increasingly complex as Hellman's playwriting has matured over a quarter of a century. Sophie is surely a more wry, sophisticated blackmailer than Mary Tilford; Mrs. Ellis, more consciously skilled than Lavinia in reversing family events; Lily Prine, a more thorough "undoer" than Lily Mortar. And in the case of Regina's wiles or Mary Tilford's theatrics, Hellman tricks up a counterpoint to the authentic truth-tellers, those who clutch their own word with stubborn personal integrity.

By a painful arithmetic of craft, Lillian Hellman reexamines language, theatrical convention, and the calculated effects of acting and staging, as well as passivity. Shunning "labels and isms," she formally realizes the hazards of moral, verbal, and theatrical absolutes in the effect of these minor characters on the dramatic outcome. Her "spit-in-the-eye" rebelliousness proclaims that the just and the worthy are never adequately credited by social labels, no more than her dismissible women are justly summed up by the inelastic social appearance of passivity. The writer's skill prevails, Hellman insists, not society's foibles: "The manuscript, the words on the page, was what you started with and what you have left . . . the pages are the only wall against which to throw the future or measure the past."[11] Hellman's words—but especially the words and actions of the passive women in five major plays—suggest not only new possibilities for moral being, a new range of expression for female behavior, but also a new approach to reevaluating Lillian Hellman's playwriting skills.

Notes

1. Surely one of the best recent portraits of Hellman as a spunky, rebellious life force is John Hersey's essay, "Lillian Hellman," *New Republic*, 18 Sept. 1976, pp. 25–27. Hersey speaks of her *outside* the formal politics with which she is often associated: "She cuts through all

ideologies to their taproot: To the decency their adherents universally profess but almost never deliver" (p. 27). The phrase "Bohemia bumps into Calvin" is Hersey's.

2. Patricia Meyer Spacks, *The Female Imagination* (1975; reprint, New York: Avon, 1976), p. 381.

3 *An Unfinished Woman* (1969; rpt. New York: Bantam, 1970), pp. 164, 23, 167; *Pentimento* (1973; rpt. New York: New American Library-Signet, 1973).

4. Citations are to *The Collected Plays* (Boston: Little Brown and Co., 1972). Page numbers appear in the text.

5. Doris Falk, *Lillian Hellman* (New York: Frederick Ungar Publishing Co., 1978), pp. 29–34.

6. See Mary Ellmann, *Thinking About Women* (1968; reprint, New York: Harvest Books, 1968), pp. 78–82. Ellmann bases her discussion on Samuel Beckett's *Malloy*.

7. Ellmann, pp. 81–82.

8. Spacks, chapter 2, "Power and Passivity," in *The Female Imagination*.

9. Meta-theatre departs from tragedy or psychological realism to produce, instead, the calculated effects of acting and stage design. In something "meta-theatrical," we are convinced not of reality, but of the reality of the dramatic imagination *before* the playwright has begun to exercise his/her own. In brief, meta-theatre or meta-theatrics suggests the inherent theatricality of life or an event. See Lionel Abel, *Meta-theatre* (New York: Hill and Wang, 1963).

10. Walter Kerr, "A Nearly Perfect 'Autumn Garden,' " *New York Times*, 28 November 1976, sec. D, p. 42, col. 4.

11. *Pentimento*, p. 151.

Lillian Hellman's American Political Theater: The Thirties and Beyond   Timothy J. Wiles*

Along with many American writers from the generation of the 1930s, our "red decade,"[1] Lillian Hellman addressed the Great Depression in her plays of the period, and reflected on its aftermath and her own political awakening throughout her career. Her analysis of American society is essentially Marxist, since it is based on the primacy of material and economic conditions to explain social relations, and emphasizes environmental conditioning, conflict among classes, and the hope that a new person, socialist man, would be born of the conflict through the dialectical collision of opposites.

Her view of her involvement with actual politics of the time changed considerably over the years, particularly her affiliation with Stalin, and in her volumes of memoirs she presents a more ambiguous and complex portrait of the artist engaged with her age than she had presented earlier through the spokesmen for socialism in her plays. But she never recanted her belief in the visionary goal to which socialism aspires, and she came to admire Bertolt Brecht as the master dramatist of the century. Although she never specu-

*This essay was written specifically for this volume and is published here for the first time by permission of the author.

lated about direct influences, a number of resemblances in technique and attitude can be noted between some of her later works and certain Brecht plays. A more significant comparison can be made with Brechtian theory of drama for her best and most explicitly political plays of the late 1930s, works she wrote before Brecht's influence had been felt among American playwrights. The comparison makes Hellman's own dramatic method appear more sophisticated than critics widely assume and may indicate a generic feature of political drama independent of influences.

The themes and forms in Hellman's thirties drama resemble those of noted or notorious playwrights from the decade (and for this discussion I include her plays from the 1940s whose formative influence can be traced to political events that evolved over the two previous decades, particularly the worldwide depression and international fascism). She shared with other thirties writers a belief in collective action and the socialist ideal, the critique of the capitalist personality and condemnation of fascism; as Marxists say, her works' "manifest content" was the same as theirs—strikes, industrial expansion, class warfare, opposition to fascism—and she employed some of their same subgenres, like the strike play, the antifascist play, and the play that indicted the dominant economic class. A simple list of her plays when compared with their thirties counterparts, however, would indicate to readers familiar with this literature how much more complex were her variants of these popular forms.[2] For the strike play, her *Days to Come* (1936) rings far truer as social history than *Stevedore, Black Pit, Marching Song,* or even *Waiting for Lefty.* All her plays indict the dominant social structure, but here the Hubbard plays *The Little Foxes* (1939) and *Another Part of the Forest* (1946), along with *The Autumn Garden* (1951), are matched only by *Awake and Sing!* and *Paradise Lost* for artistic maturity. In the antiwar genre, *The Searching Wind* (1944) and particularly *Watch on the Rhine* (1941) present a better history of the face of fascism than do *Peace on Earth, Bury the Dead,* or *Idiot's Delight;* she wrote them late enough to correct some leftist myths about the war's genesis, but as shall become apparent, all these plays share one central thirties assumption. Perhaps the greatest difference between Hellman's plays and most of these other works is that Hellman addressed her plays more deliberately to the mainstream audience than did her peers during the red decade. She wrote for Broadway, and often achieved success there, or at least a ready production. Most of the other engaged writers remembered from the period wrote for radical fringe stages or the Group Theater, a company of like-minded artists whose political affiliations extended into that fringe. And alone among all of them, her work and career developed and continued to gather respect throughout her lifetime.

With Hellman's memoirs and her uncomfortable emergence as a feminist late in her life, critical attention returned to her, but no study has described the political assumptions in her best plays in any detail or noted how she embeds them in some unique forms, perhaps because her dramaturgy seems relatively old-fashioned.[3] Although her bold female characterizations have been widely admired, the particular nature of these women as political animals still needs to be analyzed. This essay surveys American political themes and forms in a number of Hellman's plays, but it concentrates on her best work. These plays demonstrate that political art is both a product of its age and a force of innovation, one which can lead to wider speculations about the genre (including her kinship with Brecht) and toward a more substantial evaluation of her current reputation as a feminist precursor.

First, however, Hellman's wartime plays must be examined against the backdrop of earlier antiwar drama to isolate a tenet of thirties leftism which indicates how much her social thought was indebted to the period: the role of class conflicts. Since this feature has made much of her drama seem dated, and since it is also a central component of her best play, it is instructive to see how she overcame an ideological blinder to create a memorable heroine who is at war within herself and against some "manifest" dictates from her environment as she simultaneously learns to master the power held by her class and wield it to her own ends. This alludes to Regina, of course, but it really extends to describe Hellman's best heroes, even Alexandra and Birdie, and may most fully describe the role played by Hellman as artist herself.

To maintain the artificial categories "strike play," "antiwar play," and "play indicting social conditions" for just a moment longer, one can note that Hellman's reputation as an engaged political artist rested most explicitly on her campaign against fascism during the actual 1930s and war aftermath. In terms of public actions, she provided financial backing for Hemingway's film *The Spanish Earth* (1937), a documentary made in support of communist-led Loyalists who fought Franco; she refused to support the anti-Soviet Finnish resistance movement by declining to donate proceeds from a *Little Foxes* performance against her own cast's wishes; in *The Searching Wind* she attacked the whole cycle of diplomatic-level appeasements of fascists by U.S. and European statesmen. Most of these gestures were not unusual for leftists of the period, and her antimilitarist drama follows a tradition initiated by earlier pacifist plays written by expressionists (Toller's *Masse-Mensch*, the Green and Weill *Johnny Johnson*, Shaw's *Bury the Dead*), as well as far-left or left-central antiwar plays emphasizing the American context such as *Peace on Earth* or *Idiot's Delight*. She viewed fascism with too much realism ever to indulge in a stance of universal pacifism embraced by the earlier drama. She scorned diplomatic appeasement both at the state level and in specific engagements, even the domestic scene, to the point of condoning in *Watch on the Rhine* the act of an underground resistance fighter when he kills a fascist secret agent.

Hellman, however, did support a major tenet of thirties antimilitarism, a core idea that permeated leftist culture and extended even to U.S. government accounts of the causes of war (such as in the Nye Commission Reports in Congress, which reexamined World War I). This widespread belief was based on Marxist critiques of World War I as well as on popular American perceptions; it held that modern wars among industrial powers were caused by the growth of armaments industries, nationalism as it develops in capitalist countries, imperialist expansion, and subsequent retaliation by owner classes to protect their investments. In short, world wars were caused by the upper classes disputing among themselves, with guiltless proletarian soldiers their victims on both sides. This analysis, a partial explanation of World War I, supported the sentiments held by such diverse groups as doctrinaire Marxists (since it depended on class analysis) and average citizens (since it reflected American weariness with international engagements brought on by high wartime casualties and the gathering economic depression which soon followed). Many took the interpretation not simply as a description of the past war, but as a prediction of the next.

Much of the isolationist antiwar literature written by thirties leftists predicted a second world war that would spring from causes identical to those purported for the first. *Bury the Dead,* an effective expressionist nightmare about "the war that will begin tomorrow" (this in 1936), exhumes not just live corpses but living myths about generals conspiring with businessmen, the advertising sector of the press, and politicians whose eyes are on Wall Street. *Idiot's Delight* brings onstage the promiscuous arms dealer who sells to all the feuding European powers as war breaks out even over Switzerland. It was a sign of Hellman's mature realism that she never proposed a naive pacifism as a means to oppose the National Socialists. Her war drama stems from the late 1930s and early 1940s period of the United Front when communists and various liberals united against fascism. It avoids a doctrinaire explanation for the Nazis' evil ascendency based simply on economics, and dramatizes social forces like the authoritarian personality and ideas like the banality of evil with skill and flair, against a backdrop of diplomats, spies, agents, and resistance fighters. Fascism represented more to her than just an enemy of the Soviet Union; it was a psychological force that could be unleashed in the mass mind by its proponents' conscious manipulation of racial hatred.

Hellman stayed within the limits of dogmatic communist rationalizing, however, when she came to depict the *individuals* who were most to be blamed for fascism's unchecked development. They are people who have outlived an epoch and cannot shake loose from passivity to act effectively, either for their own happiness or the national good—and apart from their politics, they most resemble the figures of Hellman's "Chekhovian" plays *The Autumn Garden* and *Toys in the Attic* (1960). Instead of portraying Germans succumbing to blood-and-soil nationalism, she displays American diplomats conducting unrequited triangular love affairs during the twenty-year rise of fascism; conveniently stationed in key European capitals, 1920–40, they rationalize their failure to request diplomatic censure over Mussolini's putsch, anti-Semitic riots, and the annexation of much of central Europe. Such is the tendentious chronicle found in *The Searching Wind,* which, however, does not fault the Allies for their gullible cooperation with Stalin. The same diplomatic corps, coming from old money and inhabiting the east coast corridor from Boston to Washington, provides the family background for *Watch on the Rhine*. Here also the inertia and complacency indulged by the neurotic rich are exposed as the chief reasons to explain why fascism was looming and America was unprepared to confront it. Somehow, a democratic society's elite is made to bear most of the brunt for World War II's inception, not a fascist society's moral collapse.

This slant dates Hellman's war drama more than the improbable melodramatics involving the union of a Washington society matron's daughter with a resistance fighter, or the maudlin romance central to *The Searching Wind*, or even its subplot in which the son of the love-torn diplomat loses a leg in the war his father's weak foreign policy failed to prevent. But the doctrine that underlies this tendentious slant was a vital component of the thirties socialism Hellman espoused and provides the energy to animate her best play, *The Little Foxes*. Although her communist ethic was inadequate to depict the coming war with any profound fullness, it could inspire her to impart a vision of the creative potential unleashed in people when they define themselves as citizens, one of the chief themes, but the hardest thing to depict, in socialist art. Of course, one reason she succeeded was because she placed the vision in the eyes of characters looking to it in the future (the union organizer Whalen in *Days to Come* and especially Alexandra in *The Little Foxes*); meanwhile she filled the present with fallen individuals who resist curbs to their own greed and self-satisfaction.

The machinations of Hellman's villainous characters certainly entertain us with their sardonic humor and extravagant ruthlessness in treating others in a purely instrumental way, and their crimes do expose the need for a socialist counterreaction. At their best Hellman's villains are fascinating, however, because they represent the highest degree of proficiency in and actualization of certain social models that have succeeded one another under differing economic systems. These models might bear stereotypical names, such as the "robber baron" hero and lone-wolf entrepreneur (Marcus in *Another Part of the Forest*), or the manipulator of corporate capital (Regina). Fortunately, they appear in Hellman's best dramaturgy as sharply defined people, who hunger, behave idiosyncratically, and who resist and eventually triumph over hypocrisy and restrictions imposed by an unself-conscious society. The big foxes in Hellman's plays are self-conscious; their avarice is all the more seductive because it comes tangled with legitimate grudges (like Regina's female subjugation). Her power figures go beyond being thorough models of the social stance that socialism must oppose; they stand forth as the best men of the age and level of social development they inhabit. This means more than to say that the villains in literature are always more interesting than the virtuous, or that Hellman gives us fascinating villains who are worthy opponents for her socialists to battle. One should credit Hellman's thoroughness as a socialist artist as well as acknowledge the real grounds for the positive appeal held by her dynamic villains. As an honest writer influenced by Marxism (an essentially evolutionist doctrine), Hellman was obliged to admire through heroic portraiture the leaders of a given age who had brought their world to the level of development at which it stood, even as she exposed the cost to others and the need to consciously restructure the world beyond this stage.

Marx and Engels had observed in *The Communist Manifesto* that social history consisted of successive class-and-economic configurations, like feudalism, the age of the bourgeoisie, and an age to be dominated by egalitarian workers. At their inception, these economic orders provided the progressive and productive force for their times, but eventually they resorted to holding power by physical force after they had lost creativity and the ability to expand the general wealth. Hellman illustrates this pattern vigorously if uncritically in her best political drama, and she is true to it impartially, neither seeking hidden proletarians in the Middle Ages nor dismissing the entrepreneurial expansionist without admiring his productive energy. She avoids such reductivism and makes her art fuller and closer to uncomfortable reality. It is too limiting to observe that her best villains compare favorably with the plutocrats and employers depicted by O'Neill and Miller, in plays like *The Great God Brown, A Moon for the Misbegotten* (Harder), and *Death of a Salesman* (Howard). These characters seem flat when compared with Hellman's counterparts because she allowed herself the realist's fascination with such citizens, the epitomes of a dominant class configuration. From this perspective, the socialist playwright with whom to compare Hellman is Bertolt Brecht. For all her use of suspense, representational narrative, and the well-knit plot, she bears several significant resemblances to this anti-naturalist; in terms of influence, the parallel development is accidental, but the two writers shared the same politics, even to the matter of their unhappy protracted loyalty to Stalin, and Hellman came to admire Brecht later in her career.[4]

Although politics can be found in most of Hellman's plays, only a few have a stage history beyond their moment or deserve one. Hellman drew her dominant characters and milieux from her own biography, and it is as an autobiographer that she achieved her most sustained quality of writing. She, however, sustained the notion far too long that the spiritual anemia of a gentry class really explained this country's economic woes and foreign policy missteps during the thirties and forties. Her strictly personal plays, *The Autumn Garden* and *Toys in the Attic*, seem like genteel clichés now, which repeat the superficial forms of Chekhov without his hard-edged irony or his universal reduction of our interaction to absurdity. Hellman captures only a localized dying culture, which can be presumed dead and therefore (unlike Chekhov's), no longer a danger to ourselves. The same must be said about the private lives and family plot of her unsuccessful strike play *Days to Come*, which deserves notice as an anthology of thirties gestures and as precursor to *The Little Foxes*, but which otherwise contains only isolated vitality. That the labor organizer Whalen is a rounded and fascinating figure is especially surprising, since this is usually the most insufferable and dogmatically portrayed character in labor drama.

Similarly, Hellman's grudge against her New Orleans and East Coast–urban backgrounds, one that socialist myths from the previous decades abetted, managed to load her wartime plays with the wrong ammunition: The spoiled American rich became the chief villains behind World War II. Her fading southern aristocrats of an earlier century hold little interest as political targets now; they are appropriately submerged in *The Little Foxes* but they almost scuttle *Another Part of the Forest* (which is scuttled by other factors), and indeed, the only time we feel the full danger and power of the foxes is when they prey on each other or threaten us. *The Children's Hour* (1934) suffers somewhat from its being set in a society school milieu, but it addresses problems that expose the tragedy of social existence: a reputation's susceptibility to lies; the power of taboos and the way American culture associates sexual expression with sin and corruption (*vide* the AIDS crisis); and most intractable because technically tragic (that is, irremediable), the desire to merge social approval and success with free expression of one's identity, including the sexual. In other words, *The Children's Hour* only works if one grants that Karen and Martha have lesbian longings at least at the unconscious level; these women want to express their affection if they could acknowledge it, but they also desire the world's approval through its social sanctions such as marriage, career success, and permission to nurture and educate children. This play has come into its own lately because of the feminist and gay rights movements' efforts to have these possibilities extended to all citizens. Yet its politics remain mostly the politics of personal expression. A more interesting analysis can be made of Regina in the feminist mode because she is neither a suffering nor guiltless victim, and because in the Hubbard plays Hellman advances beyond a tacit plea that women be extended certain enfranchisements, and through her portrayal of a female villain suggests that a heightened standard of human enfranchisement be set for all. Actually, *The Children's Hour* emerged to indict public politics (as opposed to the politics of the personal) during the fifties, when it did so to remind Americans of some thirties truths; in its 1952 revival the theme of a lie that blacklists and destroys the socially progressive could be read as a gloss on the McCarthy era, during which Hellman suffered for her principles, and an era that itself was reacting to the excesses and threatening energies of thirties leftism.

Hellman's stage adaptations should be judged separately, of course; they all contain elements of history and politics. Indeed, they are the main works to comprise her politics beyond the thirties (since the war plays really conclude that era and its thematology). Each has elements in common with the social themes found in her original plays, and for reasons of form and the mode of their satire, particularly *Candide* (1956) and *My Mother, My Father and Me* (1963) should be included when considering Hellman's American political theater. Although she allowed several friends (Leonard Bernstein, John Latouche, Dorothy Parker, Richard Wilbur) to write the best jokes in *Candide,* both musical and verbal (through lyrics), she provided a solid sequence of Brechtian episodes (as she did with *My Mother, My Father and Me*) on which to hang the songs and as a platform to argue for a better world—given the contrast manifested by the existing one. And, in what may be the only poem in her dramatic canon, she wrote lyrics for one song, "Eldorado," which summarized the socialist ethic as well as poignantly noting its distance from our present reality.

For her interpreters, Lillian Hellman's prominence as a political dramatist presents a conundrum: that reputation is so well established that new generations may wonder whether it is simply a shibboleth. Furthermore, this reputation became attached to her early and in connection with her best play, which immediately became her most popular play, and later, at least in the eyes of some anthologizers and authors of pocket histories of American drama, her only play. It is not the place of this essay to exhume that whole journalistic debate,[5] but it is necessary to cut through these received ideas while simultaneously acknowledging that the main thrust of Hellman's reception, especially that by audiences, has been essentially accurate. What is left to be said about a work (and a writer for whose reputation it is central) when the play is already well known, accessible to appropriate understanding, and correctly regarded? The reader of Hellman's whole dramatic canon can place her other dramas in relation to this masterpiece and can read more out of their social arguments by showing how the continuity of argument prevails, but coalesces only when *The Little Foxes* remains central. She kept returning to coherent themes and drew characters who bear much family resemblance, even tracing the Hubbard roots to the previous generation in *Another Part of the Forest* and rehearsing in her most overtly political play *Days to Come* the same family relationship that was to have such dramatic force in *The Little Foxes*.[6]

Seen against the canvas of the thirties, virtually all her plays take on more resonance, as direct depiction (*Days to Come*), as an unearthing of the historical roots beneath the crisis of capitalism manifested by the depression (the Hubbard plays), as an extension of this crisis to the world arena (the war plays), or later in her career, as further refinements of some dramatic techniques associated with thirties political satire (her last adaptations). Indeed, the only comparable noted American playwright, in terms of the length of his career, the coherence of his politics, and his willingness to experiment with form and fable, is Arthur Miller, whose vision was also formed in the thirties.

Unlike Miller, however, Hellman's finest political drama is not set directly within the historical period that it intends to illuminate, and ironically, besides *The Little Foxes,* the best of her other original plays—*The Children's Hour, Toys in the Attic*—do not address a period, or politics, very directly.[7] She is also unlike her major theatrical contemporary Clifford Odets, whose fame came during the thirties for his direct and essentially optimistic portrayal of families and workers struggling during the depression, but who lost credit with critics and audiences when that decade's issues lost immediacy and the writer himself lost his talent, such that his critics came to denigrate his early achievements unfairly.[8]

Because of the strength of character that Hellman brought to her public role, and because she maintained her skills and varied her forms throughout her career even while never recapturing the brilliance of her best early play, she gained stature as a writer and as a public artist throughout her career. Although these extrinsic factors are not necessary for a spectator to enjoy *The Little Foxes*, they provide useful guides for the critical reader who wishes to comprehend its lasting impact and attempts to specify the central political themes that this play conveys. Because it makes these themes palatable by embodying them in a gripping melodrama and through several complex characters—all of them women—who command a divided sympathy, the play succeeds as entertainment and impresses an audience that its themes, though none of them are novel as politics, represent social truth. And because the play is such good theater, one never suspects its author would prefer to harangue the audience with a stump speech or read it a moral tract instead of creating drama.

Indeed, *The Little Foxes* is such a good play that it seems reduced when its essential politics are isolated, and the politics seem reductivist when they are listed as tenets within Marxist doctrine: the conflict of base and superstructure; the exposure of social Darwinism; the condemnation of capitalist self-interest; the view of an alternative world sought by some of its characters in rebellion against their harsh surroundings. Any bald recital of such social theses needs immediately to be corrected by a thorough account of how Hellman puts those notions into the passing comments and mundane behavior of vivid characters who, the theater audience never forgets, are caught up in their own life drama and who never betray an awareness that they are expounding dogma. This would be expected from a good political play (even though that is a rare species); what is original to Hellman is that she locates these theories in people who were new to their time (1900 or 1939) and still new to our own, particularly in women whose predicament could be labeled a feminist issue but who themselves refuse the special pleading to which some oppressed minority members feel entitled. They particularly refuse our pity, and by their interactions especially within the female sphere, they block our habitual sympathies (and each other's), and demand of each other and of us that we look at their predicament with critical vision.

"Don't love me," Birdie demands of Alexandra, and we should take her literally, for she gives a key to the subtle technique employed by this political drama, as well as to its original depiction of characters caught in a moment of social transition and crisis. By arguing against our empathy, Hellman intuited a major thrust in Brecht's theories of political art, in a play that, in its surface construction, seems mired in naturalism and enslaved to suspense, to cite two dramatic gambits Brecht railed against. Putting it another way, the elemental Marxist doctrine in Hellman's play would seem to be executed with technical prowess, but little else, if all her characters were men, or were thought of merely as creatures wearing pants more successfully than their brothers and husbands. But because Hellman makes them women and sets them at a time when the struggle between the affective, nurturing role and the rationalizing, self-gratifying one was more clearly divided in our culture along gender lines, she makes us feel the tragedy of the social crisis as it destroys the best representative of a given age, a woman who ironically has won out on the surface and who appears to have succeeded in destroying or thwarting almost all the others in her family. I add, if it is necessary, that Hellman does this not because she is a woman or believes her sex to possess superior virtue, but because she can use the woman issue as it exists in her culture to display a truth about mankind or humankind (and this explains why Hellman always balked when she was labeled "America's leading woman playwright," or later, a feminist writer).

Hellman's women take the center of the stage of ideas only at the play's conclusion, although their longings and needs drive the work from its inception. The spectator may be impressed by Ben's mordant wit as he manipulates the inferior males early on, and may feel a stock sympathy for the pieties Horace speaks from his conventional podium, the sickbed, but one never feels greatly threatened by the former (partly because Ben desires so little, except cash and the control of provincial clerk-relatives), nor particularly moved by the latter (partly because Horace fought back so little for his principles, lacked passion as a lover, provided paternal support for Alexandra's idealism only through proxies like Addie, and lost his own vital energy and generativity around the time when he locked his broken violin away in the strongbox along with his railroad bonds). It is only after the spectator learns all the complications of these people's interrelationships, *and* how their business dealings intertwine to set a complex double mousetrap plot into the dramaturgy, that one realizes that certain characters are more rounded, self-aware (because they have more self), and complexly embedded in a tragedy than are the others, and that the groupings follow gender lines. Therefore, although *The Little Foxes* does not break into two halves in terms of levels of social analysis (received dogma and original variation), this essay considers the play's general politics first in terms of that kind of Marxist social analysis commonly held during the thirties, and, later, through its particular embodiment in the women.

It is the men in *The Little Foxes* who do business and extol it as the business of America. They speak the lines that ironically serve to offer a Marxist analysis of early capitalist expansion. In fact, Ben and Oscar would not be uncomfortable with the first passages in *The Communist Manifesto,* which portray the succeeding orders of social and economic organization as civilization evolved from feudal aristocratic dominance to the age of the bourgeois mercantile class. These new Southerners apply that same reading to their usurpation of the plantation gentry's lands and women, and they couch their reading in evolutionary terms as applied to the social sphere. They are filling a new niche with their entrepreneurial innovation of bringing the mills to the cotton, as they had done earlier by loaning money to blacks at lethal rates, two jobs the older gentry had shunned, and they condemn these weaker competitors for failing to change with the age; Ben boasts to Marshall it is because "the Southern aristocrat can adapt himself to nothing."[9]

The play's social Darwinism extends to embrace that favorite adverb "naturally," as if the conscious self-interest of schemers were the same process by which nature selects improved species for survival. "Naturally" is Ben's simple response to Oscar, when his brother wishes to discuss the possible marriage between Leo and Alexandra that would repay Oscar for the investment percentage that Ben coerces him to sacrifice (151); when Oscar later rationalizes Leo's plot to steal Horace's bonds by proposing that "a man can't be shot for wanting to see his son get on in the world," Leo agrees that this is "natural enough" (160). Regina employs the discourse of nature when her mind turns to business. "It seems only natural," she says in act 1, that a wife should look after her husband's interests by demanding that the silent partner get a bigger share (149), and at the play's end, when she confronts her brothers about their scheme to rob her, her mock sorrow takes the same language: "It's not a pleasant story. I feel bad, Ben, naturally" (194).

If money selects for survival in the human species, it must be the basis of existence. The Hubbards are thorough materialists in a way that Marx would find at least realistic. One primitive tenet he shared with nineteenth-century capitalists was the fundamental separation between material sources of biological survival, called by Marxists the base, and the superstructure of ideas, beliefs, and artistic expressions that man erects about his base as a rationalization for it. The Hubbards dismiss the immaterial realm accordingly, or employ it as a flag of convenience. Birdie's music is superfluous, just one of her graces that she shares with Alexandra and Horace and a symbol of her wasted gentry education; her husband stops her from fetching Wagner's autograph to show Marshall, who he thinks would not be interested. Marshall lets it go, but stops to comment ironically on Ben's credo that a man isn't in business just for profits, but for his heart's good: "You have a turn for neat phrases, Hubbard. Well, however grand your reasons are, mine are simple: I want to make money and I believe I'll make it on you. Mind you, I have no objections to more high-minded reasons. They are mighty valuable in business. It's fine to have partners who so closely follow the teachings of Christ" (142). His bluff called, Ben toasts him by inverting a Henry Frick platitude about railroads being the Rembrandts of investment to propose that now cotton mills will be those Rembrandts. Their dismissal of superstructural ideation extends beyond art and religion to scoff at contemplative thought itself. When Horace recalls that he had spent many weeks in his hospital bed just thinking things over, as if on holiday from life's daily business, Regina is astounded that he would take "a holiday of thinking" in Baltimore when her business needed him here (167).

Even the most elemental kinship ties are but ideas to the Hubbards, links that can be bartered, used for blackmail, eliminated by murder if this serves one's self-interest. Every family bond has its price, as the play demonstrates materially by quoting the figure. Regina pretended to be willing to consider marrying Alexandra to Leo to placate her brother for reducing his profits, she boasts to her husband (and calls the matter "all this business," 167). Ben invented that scheme, and also manipulates Leo to steal his uncle's bonds while arranging to extricate himself from any blame in the affair. When Regina causes Horace's death by withholding his medicine, she is retaliating against his single direct action in the Hubbards' scheme, whereby he would rewrite his will to deny her significant inheritance and excuse her brothers for cheating him.

In the war of all against all, man's chief weapon is unwavering self-interest. Economic life is a battle (people like Ben "struggled and fought" to bring northern-style prosperity to the South, which he calls "patriotism" [141]), in which the decisive weapon is innovation: Ben's real toast to Marshall, delivered behind his back, holds that "God forgives those who invent what they need" (144). Hellman renders this as more than a tract; actually, she makes us admire the chief manipulators for their skill and wit, and impresses on us the ironic dictum that for their time and situation, these protocapitalists represented the most highly developed social species whose greed, for them, constituted a life force. We appreciate their recourse to pieties that we have employed ourselves in not-so-dissimilar situations. Even Oscar gains momentary sympathy when he tells his son "it's every man's duty to think of himself," though this means spying into Horace's strongbox (158). They are merely perpetuating their existence while the weaker men around them uphold the values of a dying class, or seek to die economically or developmentally and drag the vital ones down with them.

Horace has humane reasons for resisting the new cotton development, which he argues to Ben and Regina in act 2 in speeches exposing the social misery their project will yield. He denounces exploitative wages, the ensuing class warfare between poor whites and unlanded blacks, the Hubbards' opposition to unions, and their dividend-derived incomes, all themes that make this play's thirties context explicit. But the Hubbards will not hear his higher values, partly because they float above the economic base of self-interest. To them, Horace's no-growth policy equals death; one must expand or die according to the family's biological progressivism. Regina localizes the attitude by perceiving that his refusal to let her join the mill development constitutes Horace's revenge against her schemes. It is his way of killing her since he must die: "You hate to see anybody live now, don't you. You hate to think that I'm going to be alive and have what I want" (176). As a further irony, while the Hubbards rationalize their own life force by likening it to nature and condemning any values that lack a material base, they treat capital as if it were a fact of nature and intend to live off its self-replicating power. They will "grow rich," Horace notes with the biological metaphor intended, and they marvel at the way their little $75,000 shares will yield a million (171).

All the while Alexandra watches and listens, for all that social theory has been embedded dramatically in confrontations about thievery, confessions of lost dreams, and calls to resistance at the immediate level. Even Addie's credo about the active ones who eat the earth while the others stand around watching (her biblical association refers us back to the play's title) springs from her desire to protect Alexandra and help her resist her family (182). Not surprisingly for a political drama, Alexandra undergoes a conversion in response to promptings from her mammy, aunt, and father, and particularly because she observes how the Hubbards' plots have extended to designs against her freedom, to mutual aggression, and to murder. But her ultimate decisions come within a context of female awakening, one which she does not directly undergo herself (at least, in her speeches, aside from resisting the marriage scheme). The play lets her proclaim the awakening at the end, and articulate it as a collective and social goal: her intention to oppose the earth's devouring and not "stand around and watch [Regina] do it," but "be fighting . . . someplace else" (199). But she is not active otherwise in the drama, nor does she attach feminist intentions to her decision. Hellman's most unconventional gesture with Alexandra is to block the audience's desire to learn her outcome and thus experience closure in terms of the plot. The author never tells us what cause Alexandra might join or how it could prevail. This withheld outcome for Alexandra, along with the denial of any probable opposition to Regina's final triumph, constitutes the major gesture Hellman makes in transferring the solution to this play's problem to the audience.

The feature also constitutes the major deviation from well-made dramaturgy in a play castigated for that, and the major reversal of the expectation that suspense will be solved at the level of ideas as well as plotting, for we never know how the called-for alternative idea to the Hubbards' worldview can prevail. Hellman's refusal to depict the resolution for Alexandra's predicament makes her drama closer to Brecht's dramaturgy than we find in other thirties drama, and Hellman herself called attention to the audience's persistent inability to accept the inconclusive ending for Alexandra.[10] As political theater, *The Little Foxes* preserves by means of its dramaturgy the struggle that Hellman knows is still being waged. But she also remains Marxist in her ideals by implying that this general struggle will yield a progressive outcome, that hope exists, that the world evolves toward greater productivity for more people through a process of dialectical materialism.

Before examining the female awakening that this play depicts more surprisingly through its oppressed woman character Birdie and even through Regina, it is appropriate to survey the earlier and more explicitly political drama *Days to Come*, in which Hellman tried out the family relationships that she perfected with *The Little Foxes*. The play is flawed by its excessive emphasis on the capitalist's neurotic family entanglements and by its maudlin treatment of the strikers, but it does contain one vivid character, the strike organizer. In its broad outlines the play sets forth Hellman's full brief against thirties America.

The plot follows the usual strike play structure: strike breakers are brought in to provoke the strikers out of their passive resistance; a well-meaning owner discovers his complicity through his toleration of venal schemers within the company; the pitiable death of the leading worker's child prompts the man to stop sympathizing with the owner; and the strike organizer attempts to rally the workers, raise their consciousness, and turn their anger away from revenge and toward awareness about class conditions. The general issue that Hellman exposes remains valid: small town values and businesses run on paternalist principles and are incompatible with inherent conflicts within corporate capitalism and its resulting structural problems, though of course, she never states it so baldly in her play. Set in the 1930s, *Days to Come* vividly captures the poignant local version of that breakdown. When a small company that had thrived since the town was settled goes under, its owners and workers stop being peers and for the first time confront their basic antagonism. Union and antiunion tactics infect the town from urban centers, as the national depression touches the small town. Its citizens experience for the first time this country's first systemwide collapse of the industrial boom that had started during the transition from an agriculture-based economy.

In addition to its convincing materialist analysis of conditions at the factory, and in the town and nation, the play posits other materialist assumptions, especially at the level of emotional relations. All the characters are forced to acknowledge how they have fed off each other, and in the denouement the owner-family realizes its emotional parasitism, which took the form of a triangle among owner, wife, and lawyer, abetted by the spinster sister's maintenance of their secret. Hellman enlivens the otherwise uninvolving love crisis by couching each subsequent revelation in terms of "business": Rodman's business to conceal his motives regarding Julie; Cora's business to know the secret; Ellicott's business to invest in its maintenance by seducing his employer's wife. A more interesting twist comes earlier, when the strike organizer Whalen blocks Julie's romantic overtures by admitting that he would treat her instrumentally whenever their class antagonism surfaced: "People like me always make symbols of people like you."[11] Whalen even affronts both owner and chief worker-artisan by suggesting that their business became unprofitable when they persisted in making quality brushes that cost more to produce than the deflated market could bear.

His vulgar materialism, imported tactics, and detachment from the company's paternalism suggest that Whalen may harbor a foreign ideology, a notion supported by his warning to the worker Firth that, with the arrival of the deputized strike breakers, the strikers no longer constitute a peacekeeping force even as passive resisters: "They're law and order now and you're un-American" (104). The play emphasizes that the strikers' values *are* a native product, like that American craftsmanship, that their revolt is as justified as earlier rebellions on the same soil, and that their collective ethic represents the true national spirit. Firth keeps protesting that his people "ain't foreigners" although the strike breakers are, and for a long time he persists in cooperating with Rodman, trying to uphold a democratic ideal of common effort untainted by class antagonism (86–87). The play exists to enlighten him on that, but its recurrent theme of Americanism exposes a common impulse in thirties leftist drama. These writers took pains to represent collectivist unionism as a native product (it was in fact a German socialist import) and to conflate Marxist socialism with democratic revolutionary values as learned from the founding fathers.[12]

Whalen displays his authentic social vision when he explains to Julie his own political conversion, which came neither from reading tracts nor from unworldly love of the squalid souls who peopled his tenement, but from antagonism with his family and frustration at his failure to understand the structures and conditions around him. When he couldn't figure out either the rich or the poor, he took his present job to learn better about both and stop hating either; now he knows that he hates the condition of poverty, even to the extent of hating the meanness and cowardice that come with it, but he loves what the poor could be (107). In addition to debunking a certain folk song populism in this conversion account, Hellman sides with Brecht in his realistic depiction of poor people's squalor and debasement. (Joan of the Stockyards learned there not the evil of the poor but the poverty of the poor, and Setzuan's Good Woman suffered their venality.) She also identifies a tactic promulgated by communists, although not their exclusive invention, that we change our social consciousness by doing and working in the social world, thus realizing the interdependence between praxis and theory.

The most provocative aspect of *Days to Come* lies in its proto-Brechtian dramaturgy, really Hellman's hallmark, of withholding the resolution at the ending. This takes a maudlin shape when the entangled lovers' denouement is left entangled and they will all remain wed to each other, if not married, for all the days to come (128); the title also predicts social revolt. The workers' movement within the mill town is also left unconcluded. Where this dramaturgical tactic takes on real theatrical edge is in the scenes with Whalen, who consistently cuts off closure even of the kind with which an audience might sympathize. He rejects Julie's honest advances, not wanting to revolutionize the boss's wife. He taunts Firth even after Firth's child has been killed, both about the workers' failure to maintain passive resistance and their inability to seize their own fight when its time came; but when Firth makes the easy conclusion that his former friend Rodman was truly the man who killed his child, Whalen blocks that rationalization, telling Firth that this wrong answer will lead him astray and that the individual Rodmans have little to do with the workers' problems (121). Whalen is not the agent who breaks the bonds that hitherto linked people, however badly, in the town, but he exposes the structures and dysfunctions that have sundered them. Any resolution, or any new order, also lies in the days to come.

Another Part of the Forest can also be considered as anterior to *The Little Foxes*, because it is set in the Hubbard family a generation prior to that of Hellman's masterwork. Unfortunately, composed as it was seven years later and as a sequel, it reveals relatively little more of significance about this clan. Full of tumultuous vice and social discord surrounding these native carpetbaggers, the play fails to add much to Hellman's political portrait of America, although it vividly repeats popular myths about southern decadence and breakdown after the Civil War. Judged in its own right the play has vitality as a crackling melodrama infused with vicious wit about rubes and vice figures alike of a kind Hellman introduced more moderately in the earlier Hubbard play.

There, for example, Regina and Ben snigger about the results of a near incestuous coupling in their grandparents' generation—"And look at us" (151)—while *Forest* is larded with such sarcasm, much of it sexual. Marcus dismisses his son's infatuation with a doxy who herself had mused that she always wanted to give up whoring and take up embroidery by exclaiming, "Are you denying the girl makes use of a mattress, do you expect to go through life killing every man who knows she does?" (375). In these terms, with *Forest* Hellman tries out a Jonsonian comedy of humours and creates a sociohistorical satire, initiating a style that she later developed to the same end in her overt satires, the adaptations of *Candide* and *My Mother, My Father and Me*. In fact, the best satire in *Forest* attaches itself to political comments, although Hellman does not develop the political critique of American capital beyond the terms more subtly established in *The Little Foxes*. She exposes the origins of the Hubbards' greed and why they are shunned by Southern society, emphasizing Marcus's sharp trading practices during the Civil War, which leeched off the embattled Southerners while Marcus himself disdained their futile cause—a plot parallel to some action in *Mother Courage*. She creates early visions of his children's future schemes and passions: Ben seeking to control his relatives and hold their assets, although again with no desire to spend or consume the wealth; Regina transfixed by clothes, love affairs, and travel to glamorous Chicago; Oscar consumed with illicit sex and cruelty to black men. Though their Snopesian rape of the local surroundings is more detailed here, its wider ramification is undeveloped.

When contrasted with *The Little Foxes*, the general effect of *Another Part of the Forest* is to underline political themes and criticisms Hellman made more subtly before. For example, she makes the social Darwinism more explicit, both in regard to the succession of generations and the Old South's obsolescence. The whole plot within the action hangs on Ben discovering his father's war secret by coincidences, then manipulating his father into handing him the estate (and thus also cheating Regina, which motivates her desire to restore her inheritance in the next play). Ben repeats his self-justification constantly, claiming not only that his father held him back and underpaid him, but that the man has aged and must move aside for the son. (Regina turns this on Ben at the end of *The Little Foxes*, noting that he is getting old and less adept at his schemes.) Repeatedly, Marcus makes the same social point about the Old South, and in one speech he links this saw to a theory of the zeitgeist: "Well, I disapprove of you. Your people deserved to lose their war and their world. It was a backward world, getting in the way of history. Appalling that you still don't realize it. Really, people should read more books" (368).

This wit characterizes Marcus particularly well, and he develops throughout the first two acts as an unstoppable force, controlling his family and social environment through his greater insight, realism, and enlightened selfishness. He mocks the Southerners' fallen glory, advising a confederate officer to fight in South America on the winning side for a change, noting there is no hero so great as the man who fought on the losing side (367, 372). He calls his own sons' bluffs repeatedly, mocking Oscar's timid sexual rebellions and Ben's ire at being relegated to Bob Cratchit status. Marcus is aware of propriety's value in business. He answers Ben's plea for advancement with a mixed command to "call in some cotton loans or mortgages" and then go to church, but the message is clear that the new cash flow will land in Marcus's pockets, not his sons' (340). In *The Little Foxes*, Ben has inherited most of his father's traits, talents, and holdings, and he impresses us there particularly with his ruthless glee in manipulating others. That capacity shows how he has made a fetish of wielding power in its own right, ignoring the objects that it might bring him to take primal satisfaction in its execution (he first reveals this during *Forest*'s revenge-plot, act 3). The sadistic pleasure of holding power has become its own end. One can observe a political critique about capital perpetuating itself and providing its own pleasure in this characterization.

Aside from this socio-sexual reading, which is further underscored in *Forest* by hints of incest and premarital sex attached to young Regina (implications that are not linked to the play's plot, but that contribute to the atmosphere of Southern Gothic, as do the various secondary characters), *Another Part of the Forest* does not deepen the resonance already contained in the play composed before it. Some flaws in its plotting, both internally and in relation to *The Little Foxes*, weaken its ultimate effect. Too much depends on coincidence, such as hidden papers that are not mentioned until act 3. More serious is Hellman's failure to present a significant antagonist to Marcus and his authority. Ben is too much his likeness, but ironically an inferior copy of his father, less vivid, just finally lucky to uncover the old man's secret. Even his power obsession is mainly known in the play because Marcus demonstrates it in a more fascinating way. It is Marcus, with his idea of history as a zeitgeist that should not be impeded, who bears the identity of that man of his time who is the best of his kind in terms of fulfilling the social destiny of his economic niche. Marcus, intimately linked with young Regina, constitutes the knowing villain whose charisma frightens us as we admire it. So his comeuppance due to accident at the end strikes us not so much as unfair as unfortunately wrong, a betrayal of the play's originating impulse.

These faults would not warrant elaboration were there not a *Little Foxes*. They do point to what Hellman succeeds at in that play, where she maintains the charisma and authority for the appropriate character throughout. Thanks to Hellman's skillful construction, Regina's character does not follow a simple line of aggrandizement or downfall (as does Marcus's), but instead describes a complex trajectory. Regina experiences a complex downfall on one front (the loss of Alexandra) while enjoying her inevitable reign (at least, within her circumscribed society). She even registers mixed emotions when she loses her daughter, since the playwright has plotted that scene in terms of a female awakening both women can share.

It is the women who make *The Little Foxes* a complex classic, and the least complex of these is Alexandra, whose socialist conversion at the end is justified and helps bear Hellman's visionary message. Her aunt and mother serve as female foils to her awakening, but paradoxically put it in partial shadow; ultimately they show that the awakening is not one that only women ought to have, but the goal of the race.

Birdie's contribution is somewhat stereotypical, since the abuse heaped on her repeats conventions about the fate of ineffective women, especially those who depend too much on their weak position, cultural graces, and good breeding when they oppose ruthless aggressors of either sex. What is fresh about this battered woman is her self-awareness and the degree of positive spirit that she has kept alive. She kept it intact by willful alcoholism and can admit that to her family intimates; drinking releases sustaining memories and provides a heightened spirit that the conditions surrounding her stifle when she is sober, vividly demonstrated in act 3 as she deliberately becomes tipsy, freeing herself to deliver Alexandra her most important insight. Here Birdie insists that Alexandra not love her, if the result would be that Alexandra will grow to resemble her, and suffer the same abuse (183). She condemns a pity that renders the sympathizer impotent, a lesson Alexandra applies directly in her final confrontation with Regina, when she rejects her mother's appeals to sympathize with her own stifled desires and refuses to seek or offer solace in Regina's bed.

This Brechtian gesture made before Hellman had heard of Brecht's antiempathic theories is certainly her own hallmark, one that clarifies the uneasy tone maintained in most of her drama. Her best-realized characters have a cold, somewhat cynical, but always intellectual air about them, which may fascinate the spectator, prod him to raise questions, but seldom draws him to them, or if so, it is mainly through intellectual admiration. An audience's complex fascination with Regina may be accounted for this way, as it is with Mother Courage. Her particular story yields little novelty for social analysis: the daughter bypassed in her father's will, saddled with a passive husband whose weak idealism retards her greed and ambition for too long, the immediate objects of her desire little different from any gilded age matron's. She devours her male by withholding her sexuality from him and exploiting it with all the males around her, and her kind would devour the earth. It is not adequate to pity her as a misguided female emancipationist, had she but lived in a better time.[13] She does want to shake off the restraints coming from her culture, but she also wants to impose her will on others.

At the same time, she can admire other fighters who possess their own mind, particularly those of her gender and blood, and she must have a certain awareness of the validity behind Alexandra's socialist rebuttal because she offers no refutation. She may even perceive a zeitgeist (as her father had done), and refuse to deny in words the direction the times are taking, even though she will continue to use her actual power and psychological manipulations against the new forces. Her last lines reveal a new fascination with her daughter, as she explicitly refuses to force Alexandra to side or remain with her, perhaps in response to memories of her own manipulation by others in the past. She knows that she is losing something when Alexandra withstands her arguments on two crucial issues—the domestic one of leaving home, and the social one of taking a stand against her kind—and these have become the most important issues for the play.

This scene is political because it shows people at the moment of transition as one age passes to another. They are not just swayed by the times; they fight out and interact through the roles that the warring orders gave them initially, but which they have developed by their own choices. Alexandra chooses a socialist future, and the play leaves her outcome uncertain. Regina chooses to be to the utmost a man of the present stage of socio-economic development, which in part means that she will be a woman who seizes new openings for her gender, reverses males' expectations and prerogatives when they become too self-confident, embraces change while holding on to obsolete facades of feminine behavior when these serve her advantage. Her tragedy lies in the fact that she cannot possess both the future freedom (reserved for women who define themselves and are allowed to be defined as people) and the present reign simultaneously, since the two are in contradiction, and Regina wants it all. The power she seeks as queen contradicts the full freedom she thought she wanted while she was still held down.

Putting it another way, Hellman's oeuvre succeeded in portraying the complex and potentially tragic interaction of "people's lives together," which was Brecht's ideal for what the theater for a new age would portray, a formula that is essentially political. (The person's life apart, in isolation, and usually destroyed there, is commonly portrayed in other American drama.) Not all her plays have the same quality, but most of them aspire to the same public seriousness. The best of them succeed as entertainment that enlightens because she could use the old tricks of the stage she inherited and shape the ones most crucial to her argumentative ends to new effect. For *The Little Foxes*, these involve the melodrama form, whose conventions Hellman undermined (while retaining its energy) by reversing some of the spectator's usual expectations regarding plot closure and audience empathy. The knowing wit shared by her strongest characters often makes them seem as if they are standing outside the role and commenting on it.

In her drama, the manifest content of her politics remained that of the thirties, but the vision in that politics was not time bound. Some issues she fought in the thirties and beyond returned to the political scene and theatrical stage during her last decades, and although she had turned to the memoir form by then, two of her late theatrical efforts had some stage life and demonstrated that her wit had not abated, meaning both comic prowess and political intelligence. They are both adaptations, and because they are both so extensively collaborative as creations it would be inaccurate to dwell on them as her exclusive or final theatrical statements. But her career is happier because of their performance.

I refer to her last stage work and final adaptation, *My Mother, My Father and Me*, based on Burt Blechman's novel *How Much?*, and her *Candide*, a more lasting theater spectacle. *My Mother, My Father and Me* provided little happiness for Hellman personally, because its run was short, she was dissatisfied with the production, and in general the critics emphasized its shortcomings—too many targets for her satire, too little control of the absurdist form that she had embraced at too late an age. Since both those elements stemmed from the original novel, the fault hardly lies with Hellman unless it lies in her choice to take on the venture. The play contains more comedy and surprising effects than are usually credited, and if viewed not as a would-be American dream but as a continuation of the loosely structured social vaudeville stemming from thirties political musicals and living newspaper satires it can be placed and appreciated better— particularly since that form resurfaced with vitality in sixties plays like those of Jean-Claude van Itallie and Megan Terry, and later flowered with Sam Shepard's exuberances. It presaged the subsequent war economy of the Vietnam period (here the joke is that no one knows where the war is being fought or whether it is really happening), and portrayed the odyssey of a naive idealist who is corrupted by his environment along lines that may still cause discomfort for the present generation.

That same theme of the corrupted idealist who does not know how he has been misled and who still struggles to realize his ideal vision underlies *Candide*. Even more than in her straight play adaptation, in her *Candide* musical Hellman exploits the many techniques and gestures codified by Brecht: picaresque episodism; direct address to the audience; political satire infused with a cynicism that does not simply want to denigrate this world; and particularly, "epic music," or the self-conscious song set apart from the action, which breaks the illusionist frame and comments on its contents and audience emotions by suspending empathy and transforming debased or archaic music, in this case, operatic clichés. Of course, Leonard Bernstein created that element, as Weill had done for Brecht, but within the context devised by the play's author. Hellman's link with Brecht the librettist can be traced through Marc Blitzstein, who in the years prior to the 1956 *Candide* had turned *The Little Foxes* into his opera *Regina,* and rescored and adapted *The Threepenny Opera* for its ground-breaking off-Broadway run, but who in 1936 produced America's greatest political musical *The Cradle Will Rock,* which he dedicated to Brecht. Moreover, Martin's answer to Candide's question of who he is—"A foreigner. A scholar. A beggar. A street cleaner. A pessimist" (644)—echoes some of Brecht's autobiographical poems (such as "To Poor B. B."), which share the same definitionary rhythms, the same protean identity, the same intelligent dismay and realism—and a statement of identity that may be Hellman's own.

My ending point in this survey of Hellman's political theater is to recall her most succinct and evocative statement, at least outside the exhortatory scenes within her explicitly political plays, regarding her social vision for the future. She made it in her one lyric written for *Candide,* the song "El-dorado".[14] Its simple lines, fecund images, and verbal and musical poignancy all project the paradise on earth toward which her socialist heroes aspire, but at which they know they have not yet arrived. The restraint and the withheld directive in "Eldorado" about how to actually get there or what form the socialist future will actually take support Hellman's belief that we will reach Eldorado by creating it ourselves, and then we will know what it looks like. The song resembles Voltaire's conclusion, another withheld resolution that only directs men to start planting their own gardens; in similar fashion, Hellman simultaneously displays and withholds her ending, which is the conclusive arrival at a social utopia.

Hellman's project as a public artist through much of her drama had been to bear witness to the need for our social engagement, considering our present world ("Change the world: it needs it"—Brecht). The goal of that engagement was never far from view, and in one play she articulated it in a perfect song, which shows both her ideal vision and her commitment to mankind now, during this present stage of existence. Hellman's Candide can view and even enter utopia, but he will never be happy until he can find a way to bring his fellow creatures there with him. And it is not just a matter of providing their passage: they must make the march themselves.

Notes

1. Rolf Meyn employed the term to survey social themes in 1930s American fiction, but the label has a long history. See Meyn, *Die "Rote Dekade," Studien zur Literaturkritik und Romanliteratur der dreissinger Jahre in den USA* (Hamburg: 1980).

2. The most influential political plays of the 1930s from the leftist and liberal camps included *Stevedore* (George Sklar and Paul Peters, 1934), *Black Pit* (Albert Maltz, 1934), *Marching Song* (John Howard Lawson, 1937), and Clifford Odets's three plays of 1935, *Waiting for Lefty, Awake and Sing!,* and *Paradise Lost.* Antiwar plays included *Peace on Earth* (Albert

Maltz and George Sklar, 1933), *Bury the Dead* (Irwin Shaw, 1936), and *Idiot's Delight* (Robert Sherwood, 1936). Prominent musicals that offered a leftist political critique included *Johnny Johnson* (Paul Green and Kurt Weill, 1936), *The Cradle Will Rock* (Marc Blitzstein, 1937), and *Pins and Needles* (Harold Rome, et al., 1937). Although these works owed their innovative formal features to several traditions, including agitprop, political cabaret, and constructivist graphics and cinema, probably German expressionism played the strongest role as an influence, as exemplified in Ernst Toller's *Masse-Mensch*, 1920, produced by the Theater Guild in 1924.

3.   She plays a rather small role in major surveys of 1930s drama. See Morgan Y. Himelstein, *Drama Was a Weapon, the Left-Wing Theatre in New York 1929–1941* (New Brunswick, N.J.: Rutgers University Press, 1963); Gerald Rabkin, *Drama and Commitment, Politics in the American Theatre of the Thirties* (Bloomington: Indiana University Press, 1964); and Malcolm Goldstein, *The Political Stage: American Drama and Theatre of the Great Depression* (New York: Oxford University Press, 1971).

4.   In an *Esquire* interview in 1962 she called *The Threepenny Opera* and *Mother Courage* "the great plays of our time." See Thomas Meehan, "Q: Miss Hellman, What's Wrong with Broadway? A: It's a Bore," *Esquire* 58 (December 1926):140–42, 235–36.

5.   A handy survey of the dispute already exists in the form of Mark W. Estrin's annotated bibliography of the entire Hellman criticism to 1980, *Lillian Hellman: Plays, Films, Memoirs* (Boston: G. K. Hall, 1980).

6.   When *Days to Come* was revived in 1978, Terry Curtis Fox noted that its family structure resembled the one later developed fully in *The Little Foxes*. See "Early Work," *Village Voice*, 6 November 1978, 127, 129.

7.   Compare the collapse of capitalist optimism that is Miller's central theme in *Death of a Salesman, A Memory of Two Mondays*, a main segment of *After the Fall, The Price*, and *The American Clock*, all related to the depression.

8.   Perhaps we get more distance on thirties issues in *The Little Foxes* than in Odets's plays because Hellman's work is not set during the immediate era, which makes its anatomy of society seem more universal and not an immediate response to a current crisis (the problem with her war plays). In these terms she is more like Miller, who keeps returning in his dramatized memories to that decade which had already passed before his writing flowered. Her main difference from Odets is her greater toughness of mind, her refusal to tack a conversion scene of unmotivated political enlightenment or activism onto the end of otherwise realistic portrayals of conditions. For a comparison of Hellman and Odets, see Malcolm Goldstein, "The Playwrights of the 1930s," in *The American Theater Today*, ed. Alan Downer (New York: Basic Books, 1967), 25–27.

9.   *The Collected Plays* (Boston: Little, Brown & Co., 1970), 140. Unless otherwise noted, all subsequent quotations from Hellman's plays are from this edition and are cited in the text.

10.   In her *Paris Review* interview, she claimed that she expected Alexandra would grow to become "maybe a spinsterish social worker, disappointed, a rather angry woman" (John Phillips and Anne Hollander, "The Art of the Theater: Lillian Hellman, an Interview," *Paris Review* 33 [Winter–Spring 1965]:64–95; reprinted in this volume). One might liken Hellman's frustration to Brecht's over the persistence with which spectators sympathized with Mother Courage. Mark W. Estrin elaborated the dramaturgical parallel here with Brecht in his introduction to *Lillian Hellman: Plays, Films, Memoirs*, p. 8, where he also collected a number of contemporaneous reviews of *The Little Foxes* that intuited the same structure without being aware of Brecht. Finally, one must note with dismay the major deviation from her stageplay, which Hellman permitted in the 1941 screen adaptation. There, a rival suitor for Alexandra appears in the person of a journalist lover from up north who solves the problem of her withheld happiness for us, and undercuts the force by which her problem is made ours by staying problematic.

11.   This line does not appear in the final version of *Days to Come* found in Hellman's

Collected Plays. It appears in earlier versions and in the collection *Six Plays* (New York: Random House, 1960; New York: Vintage Books, 1979), 119.

12. Most explicitly, when Whalen exposes their fundamental class antagonism to the owners and strikers, he cries, "Don't let 'em tell you that because your grandfather voted for Jefferson, you're any different from some Polack in Pittsburgh whose grandfather couldn't write his name" (121).

13. Honor Moore does not really propound this, but the force of her sympathetic analysis in the introduction to an anthology of new women's drama has that end. See *The New Women's Theater: Ten Plays by Contemporary American Women,* ed. Honor Moore (New York: Vintage Books, 1977), xi–xxxvii.

14. See *The Collected Plays,* 658. Following a poetry reading at Rhode Island College, 16 April 1986, Richard Wilbur, *Candide's* lyricist, confirmed that Hellman was the sole author of "Eldorado," and that he had supported her wish to keep the song included in the score with her lyrics intact. Apparently Hellman herself questioned the sentimentality of the words, but Wilbur countered that the text suited its author's vision precisely. Unhappily, the version of *Candide* currently in general production does not employ Hellman's libretto, but a new version authored by Hugh Wheeler.

THE MEMOIRS

Establishing the Woman and Constructing a Narrative in Lillian Hellman's Memoirs

Pamela S. Bromberg*

Beginning with publication in 1969 of *An Unfinished Woman*, Lillian Hellman created, then re-created a self through a series of four memoirs that differ from the chronological installments of more traditional multivolume autobiographies.[1] Rather, as Hellman grew older and changed, she represented herself and her life in evolving perspectives through acts of revision she identified as examples of "pentimento," the title of her second memoir and an artist's term for the revelation of an initial image through subsequent layers of paint that have aged into transparency. The painter has "repented," changed his mind. "Pentimento," she says, describes "a way of seeing and then seeing again."[2]

There is a large-scale shift from her initial presentation of self to the final portrait in *Maybe*, published in 1980. The first memoir, *An Unfinished Woman*, is the most conventional in its linear, chronological structure and the most conventionally male-identified in its version of Hellman and her life. It reveals Hellman's central, continuing conflict (both as subject and biographer) about her identity and achievement as a woman in a man's world without fully recognizing that conflict as a problem requiring analysis. The successive memoirs reach toward visions, structures, and values that more openly and honestly acknowledge and explore Hellman's conflicts concerning her womanhood. *Maybe* is the most formally daring and theoretically self-aware, by far the most candid about Hellman's inner life and struggles to accept and celebrate her womanhood. Even in *Maybe*, however, where she reveals the most intimate struggles with misogyny and her own gynophobia, Hellman fails to unearth the ideological implications of her life story or to connect her personal experience to sexual politics.[3] The two intermediary memoirs, *Pentimento* (1973) and *Scoundrel Time* (1976), represent dialectical stages on the way toward her final act of re-vision in *Maybe*, where the dual focus becomes the subjectivity of vision and relativity of truth.

In her first three memoirs, Hellman presents two not entirely consonant pictures of herself. The public figure moves confidently, swaggeringly through the largely masculine worlds of theater, international espionage, wartime journalism, even organized crime. She presents herself as the exceptional woman whose gender figures only incidentally in her chronicles of celebrity and success. Hellman's public persona lacks the private, questioning voice typically expected of a woman. Patricia Spacks, citing an exemplary

*Sections of this discussion originally appeared in *New Boston Review* 5 (August–September 1980):5–7. Those sections have been revised and combined with new material to form an essentially original essay, written specifically for this volume and published by permission of the author.

instance of Hellman's bravado in *An Unfinished Woman*, argues that she both creates and judges herself by masculine standards, "rejecting in the process many traditional concomitants of femininity."[4] Still, although Hellman neither portrays herself as a representative woman nor views herself from a consciously female perspective, her memoirs do reveal, at least indirectly, a successful woman's continuing conflicts over her proper gender role.

Furthermore, in some important respects, the memoirs are all distinctively the work of a woman. Hellman fits readily into Mary Mason's theory that women writers discover and disclose self-identity through their identification and relationship with chosen others.[5] Hellman acknowledges the primacy of woman in the creation of her emotional identity and the formulation of a morality of connection and loyalty. At the same time, her work also reveals a primary need for professional approval and sexual recognition from men. Throughout the memoirs, most pronouncedly in the earlier ones, Hellman admires and identifies with male power, although her deference is often undercut by ironic distance. The tone of respect sounds most insistently and continually in—to use her own term—the "cool" style. The irony works in a double way, suggesting both the woman's separation from the male world she observes and her admiration for the world-weary detachment of the Dashiell Hammett detective-hero who maintains his cynical "cool" in the most volatile situations.

Another central tension with Hellman's autobiographical persona is defined by desires for solitude and intimacy, by what she describes as "the stubborn, relentless, driving desire to be alone as it came into conflict with the desire not to be alone when I wanted not to be."[6] Her conflict has been shared by countless strong women who seek to define their own desires and values and who then walk out of narrow paths of social approval. It is the conflict between what Carol Gilligan calls attachment—or the realization of self through involvement with others—and individual achievement, the poles of identity that have characterized women and men in Western culture.[7] Thus, what Hellman herself identifies as a basic conflict is deeply rooted in her womanhood. To seek identity through relationships alone—through the conventional routes of marriage and motherhood—has historically and inevitably involved a corresponding loss of independence and freedom. Hellman's brief marriage—to a man she always described as good and kind—produced in her a state of psychological paralysis, culminating as phobic terror of the drive home to what she repeatedly calls "our ugly house" (*AUW*, 15). But Hellman also needed the intimacy and emotional security of a long-term attachment to a man. Her thirty-year relationship with Dashiell Hammett, with its many interruptions but fundamental loyalty, gave her both distance and dependence. Hellman's complex, often ambivalent portrayals of self all emerge from this "conflict which would haunt me, harm me, and benefit me the rest of my life" (*AUW*, 12).

An Unfinished Woman furnishes the feistiest, coolest, and most public version of herself. Not surprisingly, Hellman in this first memoir is establishing for herself a public image that fits comfortably into the literary culture and mythology of her own era. She writes repeatedly of Hemingway, Fitzgerald, and Hammett. Long excerpts from diaries kept in Spain during the Spanish Civil War and on the Polish front during World War II certify her credentials as a woman who could move anywhere in a man's world. In the passage singled out by Spacks, Hellman relates Ernest Hemingway's grudging admiration for her display of grace under pressure, the kind of bravery that proves you are a man. He tells her, "So you have *cojones*, after all," that is, you have balls (*AUW*, 102–3). Spacks senses Hellman's pleasure in this compliment to her honorary masculinity, but judges her "unaware" of the irony of couching "the possibility of feminine freedom" in such exaggeratedly masculine terms.[8]

But Hellman is careful also to suggest that what Hemingway interpreted as courage was in fact terror. She seems, therefore, to be clearly aware of the ironies in this anecdote and to enjoy both the publicly masculine and privately feminine versions of herself. Ironic awareness does not, however, resolve the essential conflict. Hellman both scorns and aspires to the heroic male code. She revels in successful competition against men, underplaying her own struggles to achieve success while also displaying a more typical woman's diffidence toward her achievement. In all the memoirs she glides over the success of her plays, evades in-depth discussion of her experiences as a writer, and repeatedly turns what should be stories of triumph into stories of failure. She observes this pattern in herself but cannot account for it, asking, "Is it age, or was it always my nature, to take a bad time, block out the good times, until any success became an accident and failure seemed the only truth?" (*AUW*, 191). Hellman capitulates to sexist attitudes, not so much in what she does, but in how she writes about her life; minimizing details of her own struggles and triumphs in becoming a writer, she prefers to focus on petty one-upsmanship among male authors with glittering reputations.

In *Pentimento* Hellman returns to her life as a writer, acknowledging that she has not written about it before. Once again, she avoids talking about what she calls "the part of me [that] struggled" (*P*, 126) and dwells on her failure and her need for Hammett's help far more than her triumphs. Once again, she is unable or unwilling to describe her creative life, to analyze and claim her achievement. In other respects, *Pentimento* is the more coherent and satisfying memoir. Hellman writes with warmth, clarity, and assurance about the people she loved and admired, the chosen others who reveal indirectly the chosen self. *Pentimento*, in contrast to *An Unfinished Woman*, has evoked sympathetic responses from feminist critics.[9]

Scoundrel Time, on the other hand, seems at first glance to be the most public, the most historical, the least private of Hellman's memoirs, and therefore the most removed from the continuing exploration of her life as a woman. She seems to have swung back into the heroic, tough-guy mode as she tells the story of her defiance of the House Committee on Un-American

Activities and of the cowardice and treachery of so many of her liberal acquaintances. Yet the emotional core of *Scoundrel Time* is not Hellman's heroic struggle to do right; rather it is the resulting loss of her beloved farm in Pleasantville, New York, the private world where she could withdraw with Hammett, and apart from society's conflicting messages integrate her identity, create, as she puts it, a house that "fit" her,[10] as opposed to the "ugly house" of her marriage. Furthermore, Hellman articulates her refusal to cooperate with HCUA in terms that place her firmly within Carol Gilligan's theory of women's moral development. She writes: "to hurt innocent people whom I knew many years ago in order to save myself is, to me, inhuman and indecent and dishonorable" (*ST*, 93). Hellman insists that she preferred risk to herself over harm to innocent others.

Maybe puts into clear relief the anxiety about Hellman's femininity that lurks behind the cocky surface of her first three memoirs. She finally reveals in this short, complex book the price she has paid for success in a man's world, an obsessive fear that she will be rejected by men, that there is something "wrong," undesirable about her body, her very being. In *Maybe,* Hellman surrenders the earlier public versions of herself to write a private, confessional narrative. It is fragmented, incomplete, preoccupied with its own uncertainties and lack of coherence, the formal analogue to its picture of a conflicted, confused self. Its tone is evident from the first paragraph: "It was always with Sarah this way and that way all over the place, or maybe I never saw enough to understand. At a few points I know what happened, but there's a good deal I don't, because of time or because I didn't much care."[11] Hellman announces here her own self-conscious anxiety about this excursion into the past and, in fact, the entire enterprise of autobiography. In *Maybe,* subtitled "A Story by Lillian Hellman," she struggles as a writer and a self to establish the possibility of order and meaning in her past life, to distinguish between truth and lies, fact or fiction. Under the pressure of failing eyesight and impending death, Hellman confronts the mysteries of identity and self: "as one grows older, one realizes how little one knows about any relationship, or even about oneself" (*M*, 11). The prospect of final closure to her life story may have helped Hellman to present a less guarded, less "acceptable," but potentially truer picture of that self.

Despite its brevity *Maybe* is difficult to summarize or describe. Of Hellman's memoirs it is easily the densest, the most resonant with metaphor, and the most theoretically profound. The narrative moves with apparent randomness through time, directed by Hellman's stream of consciousness, by inner, psychological patterns rather than linear chronology. Its real subjects do not become apparent until the middle. The opening pages suggest that *Maybe* will attempt to tell the story of Hellman's old acquaintance Sarah Cameron. She assembles the fragments of a narrative from incomplete and obscure memories, trying to make them "fit" into a coherent order. By story's end the reader comprehends that this search for meaning in the past is the book's central concern; the difficulty of finding order and control, of making things "fit" is its real subject.

Sarah and Carter Cameron, the central figures in the book, were tangential, even marginal figures in their chronicler's life. Hellman's encounters with Sarah over the years seem invariably to have been unplanned. They met unexpectedly at restaurants, parties, Italian hotels, and French terraces but rarely sought each other out. And so Hellman's memories of Sarah lack the focus and insight that would have sprung from the choice of friendship. Instead they are scattered, vague, frustratingly evasive, and Hellman's written records are accordingly disjunctive and unresolved. That Hellman remembers her at all seems to be partly accidental, as does her later, tepid affair with Sarah's ex-husband, Carter. At the end of the book, even after assembling and presenting all her material on the Camerons, Hellman still has not achieved and cannot therefore communicate any coherent understanding of who they were or what they finally meant to her.

Eventually the reader comprehends that Hellman remembers Sarah solely for her tangential role in the memoir's central drama: Hellman's crippling obsession with her body odor. The earlier memoirs acknowledge only indirectly Hellman's anxieties about her sexuality and femininity. The prominence of "Bethe" as the opening segment of *Pentimento* signals Hellman's adolescent need for a sexual role model and, along with other anecdotes, suggests that a repressive upbringing had nurtured guilt and anxiety about sex. *An Unfinished Woman* glosses over the pain of her first, loveless affair at age nineteen, but in *Maybe* she returns to look more honestly at the nasty young man who triggered her obsession with her smell. On their fourth night together Alex asks her if she has bathed: " 'Because . . . you always have an interesting but strange odor. So much depends on climate, doesn't it?' " As a consequence of his loathing Hellman writes, "At a good and vigorous age, I couldn't go to bed with anybody with pleasure, without nerves and fear" (*M*, 20).

Then, about six or seven years later her husband Arthur Kober points out to her that she regularly takes three baths a day, thereby confronting her with a compulsion that she has totally denied. After becoming conscious of her three-bath-a-day habit, Hellman suffers a near breakdown as she struggles against knowledge of her self-hatred and gynophobia. She loses sleep, frantically tries to get her parents to tell her if she always took three daily baths without betraying her craziness, realizes she is unhinged, and manages to cut down to one bath and "two over-zealous sponge baths for every curve and orifice." She adds, "I thought of very little else except the bath stuff, certainly not work, or food, which I now barely ate" (*M*, 23). She starves herself in a further, self-destructive attempt to deny her body and her womanhood. Thus, Alex's sadistic misogyny and sexual loathing find a perfect "fit" with Hellman's anxiety over her body and sexuality. The tragicomic obsession plagues her for years until Sarah Cameron confides that Alex had once told her that she too had a "very high odor" in her private parts (*M*, 28).

Thus, Hellman's self-esteem is restored by Sarah Cameron's generously casual confession. Still more years later, however, a vindictive mutual acquaintance destroys Hellman's temporary peace of mind by insisting that Sarah Cameron had lied, that she had never even known Alex. The reader then comprehends that Hellman's quest for knowledge of Sarah Cameron is in truth a quest for knowledge of herself. Sarah had conferred self-acceptance on Hellman by her story; now Hellman needs to know whether or not it was true and thus tries to connect fragmented memories of Sarah and her husband. Hellman requires the pieces of the Sarah Cameron puzzle to "fit" into a coherent whole in order to reassure herself that she is not fundamentally "out of order" (*M*, 39), and that the order, in turn, of the biographer's art is a genuine, not a spurious construct.

Hellman's exploration of this previously suppressed past in *Maybe* goes hand in hand with a more theoretical awareness of the biographical enterprise itself. In two italicized passages she comments openly on the broken narrative of her frustrated quest for insight. In the second of these commentaries, which she places at the book's midpoint, Hellman discusses her choice of Sarah Cameron as subject and the larger problem of telling the truth in a memoir: *"In addition to the ordinary deceptions that you and others make in your life, time itself makes time fuzzy and meshes truth with half truth."* And because the Camerons were such puzzling, secondary figures in her life she was never sure about *"what really happened"* to begin with. She cannot, as a result, locate *"the truth"* (*M*, 51). If *Maybe* is read as a speculative inquiry into the nature of truth and memory, as a way of asking what *can* one know about another person or one's own life, then Hellman's choice of relatively marginal central figures serves to reinforce her interest in how memory works as well as in what it recalls.

But *Maybe* is more than an exercise in epistemology. In the book's first italicized passage—one of her more figurative and difficult pieces of writing—Hellman maintains that without a clear, well-lit, solid sense of the history of self one loses identity, though such a history is elusive, hard-won, and difficult to preserve:

> *So much of what you had counted on as a solid wall of convictions now seems on bad nights, or in sickness, or just weakness, no longer made of much that can be leaned against. It is then that one can barely place oneself in time. All that you would swear had been, can only be found again if you have the energy to dig hard enough, and that is hard on the feet and the back, and sometimes you are frightened that near an edge is nothing. I guess that is what the Camerons are to me. (M, 42)*

Despite or perhaps because of their marginality Hellman needs to know who the Camerons were in order to know herself. She suggests in these two italicized passages that the difficulty of her investigation into the past originates both in them and in her, in the self-deception, inattention, self-mythologizing, and plain forgetfulness that together blur her vision.

Hellman subtitles *Maybe* "a story," but at least some of the characters are identifiably "real" and she classifies it with her earlier "*three memoir books*" when she discusses the impossibility of finding the truth (*M*, 51). This presumably deliberate confusion highlights her central concern with the relation of fiction to fact in autobiography as a genre. By its very disjunctiveness *Maybe* recognizes that the order of the biographer is an artifact. Hellman denies coherence to her stories of the Camerons because she has seen only small parts of their lives and is unsure therefore how they intersect with her own life, which, as the opening narrative of her personal cleanliness compulsion demonstrates, is only partially understood. Thus the structural disorder of the narrative develops into an additional gloss on the text's expressed conflict between the need for order and intelligibility and the desire to find the truth.

Hellman raised but did not confront these issues in her earlier memoirs. *Maybe*, on the other hand, is nearly as much a self-reflexive study of autobiography as it is the story of Hellman's encounters with the Camerons and related acquaintances. As such, it may frustrate the Hellman reader's well-based expectations of stylish and affectionate portraits of her family, lovers, and close friends. What *Maybe* loses in grace and assurance is compensated by its formal and thematic self-consciousness, which invites a more strenuous level of critical inquiry into Hellman's autobiographical corpus.

Hellman continued to retell her own tale because autobiography is by definition an art form that resists closure. A given memoir ends with the writer's present, but its termination is only one of form and convenience, not subject. As long as the chronicled life goes on there may be new endings and new views of the past, until death finally completes the life but silences its telling. Hellman's autobiographies display increasing awareness of this uneasy paradox. As she aged she faced her own vanishing potential, the increasing domination of past over present or future, the ever more pressing need to draw up final accounts, however painful, and the accompanying anxiety that she would finally be unable to possess the truth of her past and life because she was sometimes unwilling or afraid to see it. Her vision steadily darkens over the course of the four memoirs as the prospect of death makes coming to terms with the past more immediately urgent. This thematic movement has a structural correlative as well. The works change from the order of chronological sequence to more associative patterns as Hellman's focus shifts from the events recalled to the cumulative process of recollection itself. *An Unfinished Woman* is the most linear and straightforward, *Maybe* the most convoluted and elliptical.

The titles of Hellman's memoirs offer an instructive paradigm for her process of growth as autobiographer. *Maybe* expresses conditionality and possibility, past or future. Written by an ailing writer in the eighth decade of her life, it evokes the idea of alternate versions of self and experience, the attempt to avoid autobiographical closure by engaging in revisionist, perhaps even fictive, readings of a rediscovered past. One way to resist the claustrophobic shrinking in of failing eyesight and the loss of friends that Hellman describes in *Maybe* is to speculate on what might have been.

In each of her previous memoirs Hellman ended with the hopeful possibility of change in a yet to be chronicled future. *An Unfinished Woman* boldly defies the idea of closure, both in its title and its conclusion. Hellman assures the reader in its final paragraph that ending her memoir on the "elegiac note" of Dashiell Hammett's death does not in any way imply that she foresees her own. Instead she offers her book as self-purgation, as an exploration of the past that, she hopes, will allow her to live the future more wisely:

> But I am not yet old enough to like the past better than the present, although there are nights when I have a passing sadness for the unnecessary pains, the self-made foolishness that was, is, and will be. I do regret that I have spent too much of my life trying to find what I called "truth," trying to find what I called "sense." I never knew what I meant by truth, never made the sense I hoped for. All I mean is that I left too much of me unfinished because I wasted too much time. However. (*AUW*, 280)

The confessional mood of this valediction does not seem fully earned by the relatively unself-critical and guarded autobiography that it concludes. But self-dramatization aside, it does express both Hellman's disquiet over her lifelong desire for truth and understanding and her refusal in 1969 to be bound by the past. That last truncated sentence, "However," indicates forgiveness for the mistakes of the past and more importantly, by its ellipsis, Hellman's forward-looking insistence on the possibilities of the future.

An Unfinished Woman, told in essentially chronological fashion with emphasis on particular eras or individuals, reveals little concern for the idea of shape, of life seen as an intelligible whole. Here Hellman presents her life in and as process, including a number of diary entries; there is no need to see what it adds up to if it isn't finished yet. Despite the misgivings about the possibility of finding truth, which she alleges in the closing paragraph, in the actual telling of her story Hellman betrays no qualms about its or her own reliability.

Pentimento, subtitled and structured as "A Book of Portraits," explores more fully the theoretical and psychological questions about autobiography that Hellman had raised in the closing chapter of *An Unfinished Woman.* Published four years later, it is a more disciplined and self-conscious effort to explore the past in the hope of discovering how Hellman has become the person she is. In a preface explaining the meaning of the title Hellman articulates a new awareness of the doubleness of memory:

> Old paint on canvas, as it ages, sometimes becomes transparent. When that happens it is possible, in some pictures, to see the original lines: a tree will show through a woman's dress, a child makes way for a dog, a large

boat is no longer on an open sea. That is called pentimento because the
painter "repented," changed his mind. Perhaps it would be as well to say
that the old conception, replaced by a later choice, is a way of seeing and
then seeing again.

That is all I mean about the people in this book. The paint has aged
now and I wanted to see what was there for me once, what is there for me
now. (P, 3)

Hellman claims here that the perspective of age has provided her with
clearer vision of her past relationships, which she can now see both as they
were in the past and again through the lens of her own subsequent growth
and change. She shapes the book accordingly, focusing in each chapter on a
person or group of people in her life, then working through the layers of
association and memory to achieve not only an image of the past but also a
sense of the evolution of past into present. Thus, in accordance with her
developing insight into the process of recollection, Hellman exchanges chronology as the principle of order in An Unfinished Woman for a more fluid
structure of associations.

Hellman has, in effect, reformulated Heisenberg's principle of indeterminacy in an autobiographical mode.[12] Even as we recall the past our memories reshape it until it is hard to tell if we remember original experiences or
only earlier memories of them. At the same time, the process of remembering is interpretative and creates new self-understanding, so that we change
ourselves through our recollections. Any quest after objective truth that
employs memory as the tool of vision must of necessity then be frustrated by
the initial selectivity of perceptions, which later furnish memories, then by
the gradual alteration of memory through repetition and interpretation, and
finally by the particular configuration of the self at the moment of actual
recall.

The truth in Pentimento is at least, therefore, double, the truth of then
and now, both seen simultaneously. Yet, while Hellman here acknowledges
the need to see completed shapes in her life, she insists that autobiographical
configurations lack finality; even though the subjects of her memoir are all
now dead, as long as Hellman lives she may "repent" and discover yet new
truths about them and herself. For instance, she only gains access to the
material of the chapter entitled "Turtle," a meditation on Hellman's and
Hammett's attitudes toward life and death, through her own near drowning
twenty-six years later. Both thematically and structurally, then, Pentimento,
unlike An Unfinished Woman, entertains the idea of closure, though it leaves
all acts of interpretation open to future revision and repentance.

Scoundrel Time does not advance Hellman's exploration of the form and
theory of autobiography. Rather, as she explains in the opening sections, it
restores a chapter long missing from An Unfinished Woman, written when
she still found it impossible to confront memories of the McCarthy era. Once
again the title is helpful in defining Hellman's enterprise. It names a discrete
portion of her life, clearly blocked out, now well remembered. There is no

question of truth or fiction here; she participated in a reality larger than her individual experience and is well aware that in this work more than the others autobiography may transcend itself to become political history. "I tell myself that this third time out, if I stick to what I know, what happened to me, and a few others, I have a chance to write my own history of the time" (*ST*, 41). Unlike the two earlier titles, open ended and defiant of resolution or closure, *Scoundrel Time* insists on the act of framing. This book is not so much a quest into the past for identity, an act of discovery, as it is an exorcism of a portion of the past too painful to be forgotten. Hellman writes *Scoundrel Time* not to recall the past, but to put it to rest. This era stands out from her life because it was a time when the truth was not elusive but dangerous: "Truth made you a traitor, as it often does in a time of scoundrels" (*ST*, 85). Focused by political decision and action, her life at that time now seems coherent and clearly memorable. So the barrier to written recollection was not forgetfulness; it was the pain of disillusionment.

The inner plot of *Scoundrel Time* portrays Hellman's confrontation with evil and loss of innocence. *Pentimento* is inhabited by heroes and heroines, people who act with dignity and morality; even its scoundrels are lovable. But in *Scoundrel Time* Hellman must finally articulate the betrayal of her faith in intellectual honor and heroism. She is far more bewildered and pained at the cowardice and self-interest of literary and theatrical colleagues who capitulated to the hysterical anticommunism of the early 1950s by sacrificing their principles and their friends to HCUA than at what she sees as the simple opportunism and lust for power of McCarthy, McCarran, and Nixon. *Scoundrel Time* ends crankily. Hellman still has not recovered from the shock of betrayal, still cannot forgive the intellectuals who failed their country, their honor, and her, still wants them to step "forward to admit a mistake" (*ST*, 155). Her memory thus serves to preserve not only her own past, but also her country's, and perhaps still to goad a collective conscience. Hellman is willing to close her story because it is part of a larger, ongoing national one that she sees as far from resolved.

Maybe returns neither to a suppressed piece of Hellman's public past nor to the long-term relationships she celebrated in *Pentimento*. It looks back instead at the darkness of Hellman's personal history, at shadowy corners peopled by cruel, dishonest, dissipated drifters and, most significantly, at Hellman's own failures of attention, nerve, and moral choice. In *Scoundrel Time* friends and acquaintances fail her, but she herself remains unimplicated; in *Maybe* she finds herself guilty, not of political, but of emotional and moral cowardice. Having confronted evil in her colleagues in *Scoundrel Time*, now she finds it closer to home. *Maybe* is confessional, but not cheaply or self-indulgently so. Hellman displays courage and honesty in acknowledging her close associations with dishonor and evil, no small concession from one who has made so much of honor in her previous writing.

The revelation of a less flattering part of her past goes hand in hand with increased openness about death and the fear of dying. While in her previous memoirs Hellman resisted narrative closure as a strategy to avoid the question of her own end, here she confronts directly her lack of control over time. Her failure to unravel the mystery of the Camerons is emblematic of the ultimate loss of time passed, and now with death approaching the past becomes proportionately more significant. She presents herself, not as unfinished woman, revisionist artist, or noble veteran of ideological battle, but—much less heroically—as an old woman with failing eyesight, frail body and psyche, and most frighteningly, what she fears is an undependable memory. In perhaps the most coherent and moving section of *Maybe*, she describes visiting her beloved Aunt Hannah in a hospital in New Orleans and discovering that she is senile and dying. Clearly, Hannah's loss of comprehension and imprisonment in her past are what Hellman, the writer of *Maybe*, fears for herself: "Ah, how much I had always wanted to be like my aunts and how much I feared being like them" (*M*, 82).

As *Maybe* closes the fear of disintegration has become less abstract. A month after "a losing eye operation," momentarily consoled by the season's first corn and a "fine bottle of wine," Hellman decides to take an evening swim alone. "I guess the wine made me feel capable, a long lost and long regretted feeling" (*M*, 99). She feels rejuvenated, at first enjoys the swim, but loses sight of the shore and panics, not with an immediate fear of drowning, but with the progressive specter of blindness, mental deterioration, and ultimate annihilation: "The word frightened is not the word. I am not frightened in water. Something else was happening to me: I was collapsing in a way that had never happened before" (*M*, 100). Though she manages to climb onto the breakwater Hellman is unable to emerge from the "monumental despair" that engulfs her. Terrified by the idea of blindness, she creates the very situation she dreads by forgetting to turn on her flashlight. She stumbles into a thorny rosa rugosa bush off the path, bumps into her kitchen door, then burns herself in a hot bath. In her panic she telephones a telegram to Carter Cameron:

THERE ARE MISSING PIECES EVERYPLACE AND EVERYWHERE AND THEY ARE NOT MY BUSINESS UNLESS THEY TOUCH ME. BUT WHEN THEY TOUCH ME, I DO NOT WISH THEM TO BE BLACK. MY INSTINCT REPEAT INSTINCT REPEAT INSTINCT REPEAT INSTINCT IS THAT YOURS ARE BLACK. LILLIAN. (*M*, 101)

Hellman interprets neither her motive nor her message, only relating that her own phone call confirms what Western Union tells her two days later: There is no Carter Cameron at that telephone number. Thus *Maybe* ends.

This experience occurred some five years before Hellman wrote *Maybe* and appears to be the incident that triggered her recollections of the Camerons. The telegram links Hellman's despair about old age and death with her sudden instinct that the missing pieces of her relationship with Carter Cameron are "black," that she has never understood him and Sarah because of some unrecognized evil that she had refused to see in the past. The writing of *Maybe* thus becomes a quest for more precise knowledge of that blackness and a response to Hellman's terror that she will lose herself if she loses her past. Her search fails to decipher the dark mystery of the Camerons; Hellman will never find the missing pieces of the jigsaw puzzle. Yet she does uncover an answer to her own "monumental despair." She realizes that the incoherence of her story comes not from the failure of memory but from her earlier failure to see herself clearly and to evaluate the incoherence and "blackness" of the Camerons. Sarah herself articulates the moral of the story most accurately: " 'I've always thought that's the real wages of sin: you never get to know much' " (*M*, 62). Or, in Hellman's own terms: "It's no news that each of us has our own reasons for pretending, denying, affirming what was there and never there" (*M*, 64). Hellman, however, has reached the period in her life when she must attempt to sift out the truth of her past, a stage that Erik Erikson says is characterized by the two poles of integrity and despair. In *Identity: Youth and Crisis* he defines integrity as "the ego's accrued assurance of its proclivity for order and meaning. . . . It is the acceptance of one's one and only life cycle and of the people who have become significant to it as something that had to be and that, by necessity, permitted of no substitutions."[13] For Hellman to overcome her despair and attain the integrity in her private life, which *Scoundrel Time* celebrates in her public one, she must accept and affirm her past with all its blemishes and failures. In *Maybe* she struggles toward that accommodation by portraying herself in a far less complimentary light than she had in the earlier memoirs. She reveals her neurotic fear of her own body and sexuality, a humiliating instance of Hammett's many sexual infidelities and the pain those betrayals caused her, the real indignities of her heavy drinking, and a series of loveless relationships with people of whom she now disapproves. And throughout *Maybe* there is the fear of ending that becomes so clear at the book's close.

But, despite her efforts at truth and honesty, Hellman still engages in a misleading bit of pretense and denial. As if to shield herself against the pain of self-examination, she writes with an almost parodic toughness and disregard for the niceties of diction.[14] Her style functions self-protectively, as a way of distancing the explosive material in *Maybe*, and also dramatically. Taking up where Dashiell Hammett left off, Hellman speaks with the slangy, hard-bitten voice of a detective who presents this part of her life as a mystery in need of solution: "*What I have written is the truth as I saw it, but the truth as I saw it, of course, doesn't have much to do with the truth. It's as if I have fitted parts of a picture puzzle and then a child overturned it and threw out some pieces*" (*M*, 51–52). The subtitle "a story" is as much a clue to *Maybe*'s genre as it is a reflection of Hellman's concern about the relation of truth to fiction in autobiography.

The solution of the mystery in a detective story restores at least a degree of order and intelligibility to the often shabby, decadent world it portrays. The detective, therefore, despite his knowledge of evil and his ability to camouflage himself within the dark world of his prey, is in truth a figure of moral integrity and honor, a knight who slays the dragons of social corruption and individual depravity. For Hellman to write *Maybe* as a detective story without even the possibility of a solution is then to suggest that in reality good does not triumph over evil, that, as she suggested in *Scoundrel Time* in a more narrowly political context, intellect and knowledge, all the brightness of learning and liberalism, may be no match at all for the mystery and tenacity of evil. *Maybe* is disturbing not so much for its revelations about Hellman's neuroses or for its apparent disjunctiveness and coldness, but for its pessimism, its loss of faith in the power of memory and the recovery of the past. Even more sweepingly, it denies the possibility of any discovery at all, of the restoration of meaning and rightness to the world through the detective writer's quest to solve the mystery. Thus *Maybe* lacks narrative closure in a more profound sense than *An Unfinished Woman* and *Pentimento*, which promise either sequels or at least infinite rereadings of the past. *Maybe* records Hellman's discovery that the "missing pieces" are "black," at least concerning Carter Cameron. She cannot know the Camerons because they are elusively connected with evil and hence unreceptive to the order and salvation of understanding. But to resolve her crisis of despair the writer must accept and affirm the darkness of her past as well as the triumphs of love and honor that she celebrated in her earlier memoirs.

In *Maybe* Lillian Hellman explores a self that did not fit into the earlier memoirs or the selves she created in them. In a radical act of penitence, or pentimento, she reveals a hidden self that she had heretofore scrupulously guarded, and in so doing gives voice to the private struggles that characterize women's autobiographies as a genre. *Maybe* reveals at least some of the conflict and anxiety that Hellman suffered as a woman who defied socially prescribed roles. While Hellman may still be too quick to blame herself, *Maybe* can be read as an inchoate critique of the society and values that made her so frightened and guilty about her body, so vulnerable to misogyny, and so dependent on men's approval and acceptance.

Notes

1. Maya Angelou, for example, has written four autobiographical volumes, *I Know Why the Caged Bird Sings* (1970), *Gather Together in My Name* (1974), *Singin' and Swingin' and Gettin' Merry Like Christmas* (1976), and *The Heart of a Woman* (1981). Though each is self-contained, the narratives, in contrast to Hellman's, progress in chronological sequence. Anais Nin's six-volume *Diary* is another serial autobiography written over a period of years in sequential order.

2. *Pentimento* (Boston: Little, Brown & Co., 1973), 3. Subsequent references are cited in the text.

3. See Albert E. Stone, *Autobiographical Occasions and Original Acts* (Philadelphia: University of Pennsylvania Press, 1982), 16.

4. Patricia Meyer Spacks, *The Female Imagination* (1972; reprint, New York: Avon, 1976), 383.

5. Mary G. Mason, "The Other Voice: Autobiographies of Women Writers," in *Autobiography: Essays Theoretical and Critical*, ed. James Olney (Princeton, N.J.: Princeton University Press, 1980), 210.

6. *An Unfinished Woman* (Boston: Little, Brown & Co., 1969), 12. Subsequent references are cited in the text.

7. Carol Gilligan, *In a Different Voice* (Cambridge, Mass.: Harvard University Press, 1982), 163.

8. Spacks, *Female Imagination*, 381.

9. See Stone, *Autobiographical Occasions*, 312; Marcus K. Billson and Sidonie A. Smith, "Lillian Hellman and the Strategy of the Other," in *Women's Autobiography: Essays in Criticism*, ed. Estelle C. Jelinek (Bloomington: Indiana University Press, 1980), 163–79; and Stephanie A. Demetrakopoulos, "The Metaphysics of Matrilinearism in Women's Autobiography: Studies of Mead's *Blackberry Winter*, Hellman's *Pentimento*, Angelou's *I Know Why the Caged Bird Sings*, and Kingston's *The Woman Warrior*," also in *Women's Autobiography*, 180–205.

10. *Scoundrel Time* (Boston: Little, Brown & Co., 1976), 114. Subsequent references are cited in the text.

11. *Maybe* (Boston: Little, Brown & Co., 1980), 11. Subsequent references are cited in the text.

12. Stephen Toulmin and June Goodfield explain Werner Heisenberg's principle of indeterminacy as an unavoidable "theoretical limit on the accuracy with which certain pairs of variables could *simultaneously* be observed. The very act of measuring (say) the position of an electron with extreme precision entailed, according to Heisenberg, a corresponding indeterminacy in its momentum." *The Architecture of Matter* (New York: Harper & Row, 1962), 290.

13. Erik Erikson, *Identity: Youth and Crisis* (New York: Norton, 1968), 139.

14. Hellman's "cool" voice is such a characteristic feature of her memoirs, especially *Maybe*, that I have not singled it out for discussion after my introductory remarks. In *Maybe* she employs numerous sentence fragments and syntactical compressions. A flat descriptive style alternates with more extended, complex passages of analysis and reflection. Diction, as well as syntax, is often informal and slangy.

Lillian Hellman: Autobiography and Truth
Linda Wagner-Martin*

If autobiography is at once a personal and a fictional mode, as William Spengemann has recently suggested, then Lillian Hellman's last four books provide apt illustration of the conflict inherent in that description. *An Unfinished Woman* (1969), *Pentimento* (1973), *Scoundrel Time* (1976), and *Maybe, A Story* (1980) tell and retell the story of parts of Hellman's life, but one telling may differ from the account told elsewhere. Clearly, Hellman is using the process of autobiography both to explore her memories and to challenge the notion that recollection is a means to truth (or, in the words of James Olney, autobiography is a "monument of the self as it is becoming").[1] Hellman writes with recognition of this exploration in *Maybe, A Story:* "What I

*Reprinted from the *Southern Review* 19 (April 1983):275–88, by permission of the author.

have written is the truth as I saw it, but the truth as I saw it, of course, doesn't have much to do with the truth . . . . It's no news that each of us has our own reasons for pretending, denying, affirming what was there and never there. And sometimes, of course, we have really forgotten. In my case, I have often forgotten what was important, what mattered to me most, what made me take an action that changed my life. And then, in time, people and reasons were lost in deep summer grass."

The progression from her first memoir, *An Unfinished Woman*, through *Pentimento* and *Scoundrel Time* to the "story" of *Maybe*, helps the reader chart Hellman's search for personal truth, and for a means of recording it. *An Unfinished Woman* seems to be conventional autobiography, at least the first two-thirds of it. Hellman appears at its center; she is on stage throughout, and she also interprets happenings so that "truth" and "meaning" are in some episodes translated for the reader. *An Unfinished Woman* begins appropriately enough with a lengthy description of Hellman's birth to a prominent New Orleans family, that of the Newhouses, and of her fascination for her father's comparatively poor German family. She makes her fig-tree hideaway come alive, and shows the insecurity of herself as hesitant only child in several scenes. That she takes only twenty-seven pages to bring her persona to her first job—at age nineteen with Liveright Publishers—shows the economy and selectivity of her account.

What must have been the unfortunate circumstances of her marriage— to Arthur Kober, press agent and writer—are understated in the larger context of her sense of the "cool" attitudes toward emotional involvement and display. As Hellman describes the later 1920s, "The shock of Fitzgerald's flappers was not for us: by the time we were nineteen or twenty we had either slept with a man or pretended that we had. And we were suspicious of the words of love. It was rather taken for granted that you liked one man better than the other and hoped he would marry you, but if that didn't happen you did the best you could and didn't talk about it much." Hellman writes about her abortion before her marriage at twenty, her gradual edging into "hard drinking," and the fear and unhappiness of her marriage in much the same tone of flippancy, of distance. For example, "I didn't even understand about my marriage, or my life, and had no knowledge of the new twists I was braiding into the kinks I was already bound round with." By the time of *Maybe*, Hellman would have relinquished the well-turned phrase for the sense of reality—groping, confusion, dismay—which might have made this particular set of memories more effective. Until a third of the way through *An Unfinished Woman*, the reader is bothered by the feeling that there is too much finish.

Once the chronology of the memoir becomes fragmented (Hellman's memories of the 1930s and 1940s coalesce around her relationship with Dashiell Hammett, about whom she seldom speaks directly, and her stays in both Spain and Russia), the style begins to fit the experience in a way different from that of the opening section. The accounts of Spain and Russia are given as journal entries, scene leading to scene, and the presumption seems to be that the reader knows the contexts of the trips. The texture and tone of the experience is the valuable focus, not mere facts and dates. In this scene, for example, Hellman does not tell us where she is or what the political circumstances are:

> "You need to eat."
> I said I didn't need to eat. It has been hard to eat. I can't get used to the smell of the rancid olive oil. Most of the time I feel light and pleasant, but I guess the bad part of hunger is setting in because the last four or five days I have felt weak and irritable. Luis said I could do what I wanted, but he was going to find a place to eat. I said there wasn't much to get from these people along the road, they needed the little they had, so why didn't we wait until we got to Madrid?
> He looked at me. "If they have nothing, they will say it. If they have something, they will give it. That is Spanish."

Hellman by the very mode of telling her story emphasizes the insignificance of factual information. Poem-like, the whole of *An Unfinished Woman* asks the reader to believe that the juxtapositions, the breaks in narrative, the sense of timelessness (scene fused with scene, Hellman's personality recognizable as fragile, dependent yet rebellious, regardless of time) are all calculated to bring the life of Lillian Hellman into comprehension, even if partial. Throughout these books, Hellman ducks the role of author as oracle. In her narrative method of setting scene beside scene, she more nearly assumes the role of observer: here it is; remember the image; appreciate it. And perhaps later, on your own, experience these fragments as a whole. The "knowledge" of Lillian Hellman, both subject and observer, is—and must be—limited. As she writes poignantly in *Maybe,*

> The piles and bundles and ribbons and rags turn into years, and then the years are gone. There is a light behind you certainly, but it is not bright enough to illuminate all of what you had hoped for. The light seems shadowed or masked with an unknown fabric. So much of what you had counted on as a solid wall of convictions now seems on bad nights, or in sickness, or just weakness, no longer made of much that can be leaned against. It is then that one can barely place oneself in time.

The ending of *An Unfinished Woman* conveys this sense of failure at achieving the full memory. Chapters fourteen through sixteen are devoted to separate people, Dorothy Parker, Hellman's maid Helen, and Hammett. There is no attempt to tie these chapters to the body of the memoir. Each a try piece in a different sense, they foreshadow the method of *Pentimento*, as if Hellman had by the ending of her first book of autobiography realized the futility of plot and chronology.

These chapters are less separate than their organization might suggest, however, because Hellman's focus throughout the book has been on other people rather than on herself. Even the title implies that the protagonist will be somewhat vague (why not *This* Unfinished Woman or *The*? The article *An* gives the persona even less importance). And as the events move past, there are many times when Lily's reasons for doing what she does are inexplicable. Hellman's method fits well with the personality motivated by passion rather than logic.

Pentimento is a book made of named "chapters," most of them about individual characters. Continuing on from the closing pages of *An Unfinished Woman*, Hellman perfects her method in "Bethe," "Julia," "Arthur," and others. Again, she tells *her* story by refraction: we are forced to look at Hellman differently in every episode. With Bethe, good German cousin become Mafia girlfriend, Hellman is a fascinated child, strangely drawn by her conviction that passion is a necessity. With Julia, Hellman is unpredictably brave, risking her own life to carry funds for political causes not her own. With Arthur, Hellman is nearly pathetic, looking for affection as she gives it within an unconventional set of circumstances.

Her narrative method is not only effective in that it holds our interest; it more importantly enables her to present multiple facets of her personality. This is near-biography set in an autobiographical frame. It achieves coherence because of the patterns Hellman creates within the separate chapters.

The simplest structural pattern is chronological; the chapters are arranged partly to trace Hellman's life experiences. In "Bethe" she is a young girl who grows older as Bethe does; in "Willy" Hellman is about nine or ten when the account begins of her eccentric Aunt Lily and Willy, her husband who also has an attraction for Hellman. "Julia," the third, deals with the mid-1930s. The retrospective "Theatre" chapter serves as a fulcrum, and then "Arthur W. A. Cowan" takes us to the 1950s and "Turtle" and "Pentimento" move to the 1960s.

The more important structural pattern is that of influences on Hellman as she develops. Each episode allows her a climactic learning experience; central to the entire memoir is Hellman's understanding of Bethe as a woman who loves passionately, beyond reason or safety or moral code. The restaurant scene in which Arneggio touches Bethe's arm is one of the most intense descriptions in any of Hellman's writing, and the memory of that touch spoils Hellman's own wedding day (thinking of the scene, she substitutes "an old ugly gray chiffon" for the dress she had planned to wear) and makes her try to tell Hammett about Bethe as they are first making love:

> As I moved toward the bed I said, "I'd like to tell you about my cousin, a woman called Bethe."
>
> Hammett said, "You can tell me if you have to, but I can't say I would have chosen this time."

Bethe's life itself is important but what is more telling, eventually, to Hellman who suffers all her life from her southern girlhood is the way her aunts Jenny and Hannah have responded to it. For all their outrage about Bethe's living in sin and her involvement with the Mafia—through Arneggio, who is brutally murdered—they never desert Bethe. Secretly, they visit her, give her gifts and money, and spirit her away after her lover's murder. When Hellman takes Hammett back to New Orleans with her to visit Hannah after Jenny's death, Hannah also accepts and befriends him.

"Bethe" shows Hellman's reliance on the determined people of her life—Hannah and Jenny, Hammett, Bethe, her father—and traces enough years that the reader believes her when she comments,

> "In those days" I have written, and will leave here, but I am not at all sure that those days have been changed by time. All my life I believed in the changes I could, and sometimes did, make in a nature I so often didn't like, but now it seems to me that time made alterations and mutations rather than true reforms; and so I am left with so much of the past that I have no right to think it very different from the present.

That permanence of character is implicit too when Hellman says to Hammett, after her cousin's death, that "Bethe had had a lot to do with him and me."

Much less directly than Virginia Woolf, Edith Wharton, or Ellen Glasgow, Hellman faces the problems of being aggressive enough to be a successful woman writer while simultaneously being passive in a male-dominated culture, through her focus on other kinds of experience. Indeed, except for the "Theatre" chapter, *Pentimento* might very well be about any woman, not necessarily a woman writer. Metaphoric as Hellman often is, that tactic here may be germane for the treatment of this theme. It may be too that she saw the conflicts she as writer experienced to be no greater than those Bethe, Hannah, Jenny, and Julia had known.

The primary relationship in Hellman's life—that with Hammett—gave her many opportunities to explore strengths and weaknesses, aggression and passivity. She often presents scenes with Hammett through metaphor. An early scene between them shows Hammett angry about her interest in other men, using a metaphor to give his command to her:

> One day, a few months after we met, he said, "Can you stop juggling oranges?"
> I said I didn't know what he meant.
> He said, "Yes, you do. So stop it or I won't be around to watch."
> A week later, I said, "You mean I haven't made up my mind about you and have been juggling you and other people. I'm sorry. Maybe it will take time for me to cure myself, but I'll try."

Similarly, Hellman chooses an episode in which she and Hammett kill a snapping turtle to try to image their relationship. Hammett's study of turtles has been mentioned throughout both *An Unfinished Woman* and *Pentimento*, so when the "three-foot round shell" appears (in "Turtle") we expect Hammett to be in charge of ridding the farm of it. The conflict between Hellman and Hammett in the process of killing the turtle reveals character as well as interaction: Hellman sees herself as judgmental, happiest when putting people in moral categories she has designed. Hammett is singly-moral, living his life without making judgments. In this instance, however, Hammett is intent on killing the turtle. Even a gun wound behind the eyes and decapitation by ax ("severing the head to the skin") will not do the trick, and in the night the headless turtle moves from the kitchen out to the garden. Once found, the turtle becomes the point of controversy, Hellman insisting that "it has earned its life" and Hammett convinced it is long dead. Hellman finally buries it, against Hammett's wishes; and in the argument that continues, their own individual wills show clearly. Hammett comes to respect her feelings that the turtle's struggle to live, as she interpreted what was a biological post-death heartbeat, was worth commemoration, and when some animal digs up the buried turtle and eats it, he re-buries it for her.

Hellman opens the chapter "Turtle" with a scene about her near-drowning some twenty-six years after the turtle's death, five years after Hammett's. The metaphoric method, then, gives the reader intimations of mortality even in this introductory vignette. She next remembers saying to Hammett, four days after the turtle died, "You understood each other. He was a survivor and so are you. But what about me?" The key to their relationship—Hellman's looking for authority, Hammett's refusing to be that, in most instances—is given in his answer: "I don't know . . . maybe you are, maybe not. What good is my opinion?" And the key to the endurance of their relationship is given suggestively in the metaphor of the turtle's endurance. Past reason, past predictability, Hellman's love lasted. Midway through the turtle-catching scene, Hammett brings up his fear of dependency: "Remind me . . . . Never to save me. I've been meaning to tell you for a long time."

The ending chapter of *Pentimento*, that so titled, shows the full meaning of Hellman's devotion to Hammett, again obliquely. Here, she is teaching at Harvard just a few weeks after Hammet's death in 1961. Because he was to have come with her, but to be housed—because of his extreme ill health—in a nursing home, Hellman often walked at night past the nursing home. Worried about her, Helen—her black friend and companion—followed her, and met a student (Jimsie) who became important to her, and now visits Hellman after Helen's death. Layered images create a mini-pentimento of selfless love: Hellman's for Hammett, Helen's for Hellman, Jimsie's for Helen, centered on Helen's inarticulate statement when Hellman returns from one of her late-night walks, "Death ain't what you think . . . . A rest. Not for us to understand." Hellman replies tersely, "I don't want to talk about death"—but the text of *Pentimento* shows that it is precisely death, more often here defined as the end of loving, that is a primary concern for her.

The tone of this book differs a great deal from that of *An Unfinished Woman*. Just as the method there was ostensibly direct and reasonably factual, the technique in *Pentimento* forces the reader to find the rationale for the choice of images, metaphors, juxtapositions. Hellman herself writes in the 1979 commentaries to the three memoirs, published as *Three* in that year, that

> *Pentimento* was written by what psychoanalysis calls . . . "free association." I did not know from one portrait to another what I would do next, with the exception of "Julia" where, without much hope, I wanted to try once more. I had not, for example, consciously thought of Bethe for perhaps thirty years . . . . I knew I was waiting each time not for what had been most important to me, but what had some root that I had never traced before.

She continues that the importance of the turtle episode was "great" but instead of dwelling on the relationship with Hammett that it represents, moves to a touching paragraph about the deaths of loved ones, again centering on Hammett. The reason this paragraph is so important, I think, is that once again she gives the reader a comparatively oblique and metaphoric image to try to capture the "meaning" of this person (when one thinks of Hammett, for example, a succession of oranges, turtles, and lonely night walks comes to mind—an unusual but not unflattering series):

> I have always regretted that my mother, my father, and Dashiell Hammett died in hospitals, and I was thus closed out from them . . . . I had not wanted Hammett to go away from home and had argued with the doctor against the hospital, losing my nerve when I was told that the proper equipment could not be brought into the house. But I should not have lost my nerve: I should have said what difference does equipment make any longer, what is the difference between Tuesday or Sunday for dying? I am sad that Hammett died away from me . . . . it would have been better for me, if I had taken care of him. If you are involved in a death that means so much to you then you are involved in your own . . . . now all of us give the sick to strangers, in part impressed with what they can do that we cannot do, but also wanting to spare ourselves the pain and the fear, and the reminder of our future. Yes, I helped to kill this turtle, and many others after it, but at least I stuck around.

Whether one speaks out of respect for the past or the dead or out of fear for one's own death, an attempt to come to terms with the full range of life and death is surely one of the main objectives of the autobiographical process. For Régis Michaud, (*The American Novel Today*), such exploration is primary: "This Self of which we take possession . . . is a character we spend our life in designing. . . . Our actions write our autobiography, which is, of course, a fiction." That Hellman chose such a variety of methods makes her series of memoirs one of the most interesting in modern letters.

If *Pentimento* is the process of "repenting," seeing the earlier lines and shapes under the present paint on a canvas, a way of "seeing and then seeing again," *Scoundrel Time*, the third of her memoirs, is almost a scenario for a single episode. Focus is direct: Hellman is to appear before the House Un-

American Activities Committee. (Hammett has already been jailed for his testimony, or refusal to testify.) Context is given, both in Garry Wills' long introduction to the book and in Hellman's account as well, for the McCarthy period. *Scoundrel Time* is almost entirely plot-oriented; it is a record of what happened from March of 1952 through May of that year, especially May 21, the day of the hearing. To be truly moving, the book needs to be read in sequence, following the other two memoirs, because in this one, Hellman says so little about herself or Hammett, or her professional life.

As in *Pentimento*, Hellman gives the reader a characteristically terse explanation for this, her third memoir: "I don't want to write about my historical conclusions—it isn't my game. I tell myself that this third time out, if I stick to what I know, what happened to me, and a few others, I have a chance to write my own history of the time." Mistrust for more general history, dislike of the intellectual poses that accompanied what Hellman and others saw as betrayal, and a return to the method used so effectively in *Pentimento* (the story of a single person both serving its own ends and also illustrating some larger concept important to Hellman) with herself as protagonist: many of Hellman's attitudes are implicit in her comment.

Told in all its innate poignance, the story of Hellman's courageous stand (not to take the Fifth Amendment, except when asked about others; she was willing to answer questions about herself) and the circumstances leading to it makes informative and involving reading. Advised by lawyers Abe Fortas and Joseph Rauh that her stand was legal, she was also told (by Hammett as well as other lawyers) that it was not, and that she would be quickly imprisoned. Her important May 19 letter to the committee—printed here as it was in her *Paris Review* interview—stresses her rights as a human being, at least an American human being. The key issue, which is related to her title, that as time passed and issues changed so that stances previously harmless had become heinous, is stated midway through the letter: "I am not willing, now or in the future, to bring bad trouble to people who, in my past association with them, were completely innocent of any talk or any action that was disloyal or subversive . . . to hurt innocent people whom I knew many years ago in order to save myself is, to me, inhuman and indecent and dishonorable. I cannot and will not cut my conscience to fit this year's fashions."

Allowed to leave the hearing without charges, Hellman yet suffered tremendous financial loss as a result of her stance. In preparation, she had already made plans to sell the beloved Pleasantville farm. (Hammett's income was held until his death; he was penniless for the next ten years.) But as she records: "life was to change sharply in ordinary ways. We were to have enough money for a few years and then we didn't have any, and that was to last for a while, with occasional windfalls. . . . I knew I would now be banned from writing movies, that the theatre was as uncertain as it always had been, and I was slow and usually took two years to write a play. Hammett's radio, television, and book money was gone forever."

The toll Hellman's anxiety about the hearing took on her is clear in her several-day bout of vomiting after the session was over, and in her comment in *Scoundrel Time* that "for almost a year after my hearing before the Committee and after the sale of the farm, I have very little memory and only occasional diary notes." And, later, "I have only in part recovered from the shock that came . . . from an unexamined belief that sprang from my own nature, time, and place"—that people would not betray others, that the intellectuals and artists involved in many of the hearings would not succumb to pressures about their own futures and finances. *Scoundrel Time* is a record of those betrayals, and as such was much maligned in reviews soon after its 1976 publication. Hellman, characteristically, named names; and many of those named resented her forthright charges.

In her 1979 collection, *Three,* the last commentary added to the text of the three memoirs relates to *Scoundrel Time.* A brief note, in comparison with some of the other commentaries, this one is unusually direct, and answers those uncomfortable witnesses once and for all: she begins by saying she had made a mistake in waiting to write the story of the HUAC hearing until she could be "calm" about it. "I misrepresented myself in the book . . . . I am not cool about those days, I am not tolerant about them and I never wish to be." *Scoundrel Time* is, if anything, "too restrained" and Hellman feels that she should have been more open about "the disgraceful conduct of intellectuals." She closes the commentary, and the text of *Three,* by saying: "I am angrier now than I hope I will ever be again; more disturbed now than when it all took place. I tried to avoid, when I wrote this book, what is called a moral stand. I'd like to take that stand now. I never want to live again to watch people turn into liars and cowards and others into frightened, silent collaborators. And to hell with the fancy reasons they give for what they did."

Three was published in 1979; *Maybe, A Story* followed in 1980. If one views *Scoundrel Time* as Hellman's character metaphor much in the same vein as the chapters in *Pentimento,* then the entire book of *Maybe* can be viewed as the Sarah Cameron character in suspended image and metaphor. But Hellman is attempting to do more with *Maybe* than present just Sarah, and her opening chapter suggests the tentativeness of this approach:

> It was always with Sarah this way and that way all over the place, or maybe I never saw enough to understand. At a few points I knew what happened, but there's a good deal I don't, because of time or because I didn't much care.
>
> It's not easy. But not much is easy because as one grows older, one realizes how little one knows about any relationship, or even about oneself.
>
> I don't even know if Sarah is dead, but I am fairly sure she was alive two years ago because I think I saw her come into the lobby of the St. Francis Hotel in San Francisco . . . .
>
> But was it Sarah? My eyesight was getting bad even then and I cannot be sure . . . .

Sure as Hellman was about her ability to tell her own story in *An Unfinished Woman*, sure as she was about her ability to draw the characters in *Pentimento*, sure as she was about the meaning of her HUAC hearing at least for herself, she at this point acknowledges a basic inability to "know" very much about another person (or "any relationship, or even about oneself"). With a revelation that must be important for Hellman, or else she would probably not focus so often on it, *Maybe* is only a mock-chronicle. Parts of Sarah Cameron's life are recounted, always tentatively, always through the eye of some observer other than Hellman, but the explicit meaning of Sarah's story is left for the reader to deduce. As Hellman takes the risk of writing a "story" that is neither biography nor autobiography, that crosses the line between fact and fiction without recognition of that line, one recalls her *Paris Review* (*Writers at Work, III*) comment in the mid-1960s: "You write as you write, in your time, as you see your world. One form is as good as another. There are a thousand ways to write, and each is as good as the other if it fits you, if you are any good. If you can break into a new pattern along the way, and it opens things up, and allows you more freedom, that's something . . . ."

The necessity to break with conventional form, evident throughout these later writings, seems to reflect Hellman's increasing cognizance of the fragility of what had been her earlier convictions. As she muses in *Maybe*, "I am paying the penalty, I think, of a childish belief in absolutes, perhaps an equally childish rejection of them all. I guess I want to say how inattentive I was—most of us, I guess—to the whole damned stew." If she has reached a position closer to that of Hammett, she has not done so easily; and the fragmented sentence patterns and the casual building of paragraphs suggest the groping of the author-persona. As she asked rhetorically earlier in the passage quoted from above, "Why am I writing about Sarah? I really only began to think about her a few years ago, and then not often."

Perhaps Hellman will later write a "commentary" about *Maybe, A Story*, but until she does, let me make this conjecture: Sarah Cameron's life crossed Hellman's in several important ways, important for Hellman's sense of herself as woman. The first was the sharing of Hellman's first lover, the malicious Alex, who suggested in leaving her that she had an unusual body odor. This comment caused a near-obsession with cleanliness (three baths daily) that lasted long into her life; the first third of *Maybe* deals with this obsession in one way or another; it is a connection to several memories of Hammett, to the Pleasantville farm, and to other women friends. Sarah became Alex's lover soon after Hellman and, indeed, was said to have taken Alex from her.

Toward the close of *Maybe*, Carter Cameron, Sarah's former husband, became a lover of Hellman's for an extended period, in a pleasant and non-demanding relationship that was marred (and ended) only when Hellman questioned him about his feelings for Sarah. Both her early and late life as sensual woman was shaped in part by men close to Sarah.

Sarah Cameron herself was a creature of the imagination, a phoenix who might more closely resemble the writer and artist than does Hellman herself. Sheer fantasy wrapped Sarah's life: was the woman seen on the terrace with her dead a decade before? Was Sarah the mistress of a gangster and involved in a murder? Was she a member of the international jet set? Sarah was unpredictable; she was also unforgettable. And in Hellman's mind, she was also a symbol of death. Just after her last meeting with Cameron, Hellman experiences the episode of near-drowning that prefigures "Turtle" in *Pentimento* and finds herself in a subsequent state of collapse. Irrationally, responding to much of the sense of fright and the inexplicable that Sarah has always created in her, she sends to Cameron this telegram:

THERE ARE MISSING PIECES EVERYPLACE AND EVERYWHERE AND THEY ARE NOT MY BUSINESS UNLESS THEY TOUCH ME. BUT WHEN THEY TOUCH ME, I DO NOT WISH THEM TO BE BLACK. MY INSTINCT REPEAT INSTINCT REPEAT INSTINCT RE-PEAT INSTINCT IS THAT YOURS ARE BLACK.

Enigmatic as her response is, even more mysterious is the fact that Carter Cameron is not locatable. No one at "his" telephone number knows anything about him, so the telegram goes undelivered.

The reader moves past the author-persona at the abrupt close of *Maybe:* is it Carter, then, who has the connections with the underworld? Has it been Carter's erratic behavior that has so conditioned Sarah to madness that she must experience it herself? Is Sarah's identity much more intimately bound up with the men in her life than even Hellman's? Trained as we are in what kinds of information to expect from writers, having Hellman leave us with such fragments can be upsetting, until we remind ourselves that Hellman's choices are intentional. The point of *Maybe* is that happenings exist both in themselves and as images which change according to the viewer. For most of her life, Hellman tried to impose order on those happenings (particularly in her plays, but also in the experiences she recounts in earlier memoirs). By the time of *Maybe,* she has relaxed the need for control and is willing to offer the "story" as the mosaic she remembers. An informative paragraph occurs midway in the text: "Maybe the strange mixture is why I don't remember very much. Or, as time and much of life has passed, my memory—which for the purpose of this tale has kept me awake sorting out what I am certain of, what maybe I added to what, because I didn't see or know the people—won't supply what I need to know."

Hellman's willingness to try to tell the Sarah Cameron story, and another part of hers in that process, is proof again of the belief the writer has in the process of coming to words. The text of the story may be vague; she may even call attention to that elusiveness by titling the work *Maybe;* but the process of writing is more valuable than tentative. If Hellman continues to create more characters who figured prominently—whether imaginatively or directly—in her life, she may achieve what few women writers have in literary history: some credible account of the life, anxiety, conflict, love, and death of an important female writer. As Patricia Spacks has pointed out in *The Female Imagination,* "Relatively few women have asserted themselves unambiguously as shaping artists in the act of writing about themselves; even Anais Nin, whose self-glorification as artist and as woman parallels Isadora Duncan's, publishes diaries rather than formal autobiography." Examples of women avoiding the risks of autobiography are rife in this century: the holding of manuscripts for posthumous publication; the changing of names, places, events; and most dramatic of all, Gertrude Stein's wry exchange of apparent biography for autobiography with *The Autobiography of Alice B. Toklas.*

In this context, Hellman's willingness to confront the labyrinth of autobiography/memoir/story is particularly interesting, and particularly commendable. The account of her journey into the writing world and into her own consciousness, now available to us in these four books, seems to be much more than a literary accomplishment.

Note

1. Many books on autobiography were published during the past decade. Among the best are William C. Spengemann, *The Forms of Autobiography* (New Haven, Conn.: Yale University Press, 1980), p. xiii, and James Olney, *Metaphors of Self* (Princeton, N.J.: Princeton University Press, 1972), pp. 35, 29.

Witnesses   Murray Kempton*

This is the third of the meditations of Miss Hellman's memory. Its single theme is her summons by the House Committee on Un-American Activities in 1952, her decision to refuse to yield up the names of Communists she had known, the worse trouble with the Hollywood blacklist that followed that trouble, and the dignity and the shrewdness that carried her through both.

Miss Hellman has developed a style for these discourses very close to the ideal style for letters, say, from an aunt who is envied for her experience of the world and enjoyed for her candor and her comic sense whenever they are directed at persons other than oneself—always a comfortable majority of the cases—amusing, affecting, persuasive, entirely charming, if you don't too much mind being hectored now and then.

Her nieces seem somehow luckier than her nephews. Nieces, I suspect, read her letters for that feminine wisdom condemned to be misunderstood as womanly folly: the sensibility that armors itself with a Balmain dress for the

*Reprinted with permission from the *New York Review of Books,* 10 June 1976, 22–25. © 1976 Nyrev, Inc.

ordeal by the Committee on Un-American Activities, the taste that notices the habit awkward social occasions have of being accompanied by bad food, the gaiety that conquers dread with shopping sprees. It is hard for nephews to find that much unforced pleasure in Miss Hellman; they have to be wary of possible disapproval.

I have never quite understood upon what altar Miss Hellman's moral authority was consecrated, but that authority is there, was there even before the apotheosis of her risky yet grand appearance before the Committee on Un-American Activities. To measure how far and for how long a time her writ has run we need only to consider the case of Elia Kazan, who had decided that it was necessary for him, as they used to say in those days, to "come clean" with the Committee on Un-American Activities. Kazan is one of those persons who would have especially profited from the injunction, "Never Apologize, Never Explain." As it was, in his ignorance, he spread apologies for his small sins and explanations of his vast redemption all over the advertising pages of the *New York Times,* and lifted them like prayers to heaven to Spyros Skouras, president of Twentieth Century Fox.

That was an acceptance of humiliation for the sake of survival in a confiscatory tax bracket, an impulse for which, if we cannot often find enough excuse, we can at least locate an identifiable source. But then, in the midst of his flagellations, Kazan sought out Miss Hellman, who had not yet appeared before the committee, to explain himself to *her*. It was an overture to humiliation for humiliation's own sake that does not now lend itself to reasonable understanding. The scene can only be guessed at among the clouds that surround Miss Hellman's reincarnation in the memoir, but we can glimpse in it the Confederate lady who uplifted the soldier in the heat of his youth and waited in the twilight to receive but in no measure to entertain the veteran's apology for having joined the board of directors of the carpet-bagger's railroad.

Miss Hellman's strength of character is great, but of a kind that is hard to comprehend apart from its candid snobbishness. When she searches for the core of the self that enabled her to resist and left Clifford Odets naked to surrender to the House Committee on Un-American Activities, she can return with no discovery more useful than: "It is impossible to think that a grown man, intelligent, doesn't have some sense of how he will act under pressure. It's all been decided so long ago, when you are very young, all mixed up with your childhood's definition of pride or dignity." Or elsewhere:

Many [American intellectuals] found in the sins of Stalin Communism—and there were plenty of sins and plenty that for a long time I mistakenly denied—the excuse to join those who should have been their hereditary enemies. Perhaps that, in part, was the penalty of nineteenth-century immigration. The children of timid immigrants are often remarkable people: energetic, intelligent, hard-working; and often they make it so good that they are determined to keep it at any cost.

Observations of that tenor somehow suggest that for strong spirits like Miss Hellman's, the Sunday family dinner is material for rebellion in childhood, comedy in middle age, and attitudes in final maturity. What is here intimated is some doctrine of predestination by growing up with servants in the kitchen, but it is not easy to think such a notion prepossessing and impossible to find it serviceable as a measurement for moral development. We are left to wonder why Senator Harry Flood Byrd, whose mother was in every way a Virginia lady, should have arrived at his fullest spiritual bloom ringing changes on the word "nigger" on public platforms, or why John Foster Dulles, grandson of an American secretary of state, should have managed a career whose most striking achievement was the avoidance of any suspicion that the impulse of a gentleman might ever intrude upon his conduct. Let us settle for saying that *Commentary*'s tone was lamentable in the early Fifties, when its editor was Eliot Cohen; for what worse epithet must we thereupon reach to describe *Time,* the Weekly Newsmagazine, in the days when its managing editor was Thomas S. Matthews, son of the Episcopal Bishop of the Diocese of New Jersey?

We move, I think, closer to the truth about those years when Miss Hellman swam against the current and Odets sank beneath it if we think of the Fifties as a time not much different from this one and a majority of others—when most people acted badly, and public faces passed by as a succession of gray embarrassments infrequently illuminated by displays of dignity like Miss Hellman's. Banality is the only sort of chic that always has its fashion; and we need not be surprised that Miss Hellman, thanks to her superb hour of resistance to banal chic, should now be punished with the comfortable indignity of being enshrined by it.

". . . An intense, moving moral," *Time* says of her story now. "She was brave because her private code would not allow her to be anything else. She dabbled in radical politics and befriended Communists because she thought it was her right as an American to associate with whomever she damn well pleased. . . . *Scoundrel Time* is a memorable portrait of . . . a polished stylist and an invaluable American."

The tone of *Time*'s original report on Miss Hellman's encounter with the House Committee on Un-American Activities had, of course, been faithfully cast into the cadences of what Edmund Wilson once called its "peculiar kind of jeering rancor." "Her sympathies [had] led her to attend countless Red-inspired rallies and lend her name to various Communist-front crusades, . . . as the record shows, a skilled playwright and a great meeting goer." Caption on Miss Hellman's photograph, *Time,* May 10, 1976:

Author Hellman: "I cannot cut my conscience to fit this year's fashions."

Caption on Miss Hellman's photograph, *Time,* June 2, 1952:

> Playwright Hellman: "An expert at smooth dialogue."

But after all, as Burke said, "We are very uncorrupt and tolerably enlightened judges of the transactions of past ages. . . . Few are the partisans of departed tyrannies."

So, when Mr. Nixon was in his terminal throes, we were treated to the spectacle of White House Counsel Dean Burch, who had come first to our notice as manager of Senator Goldwater's presidential campaign, complaining to the journalists about the "McCarthyite tactics" of the House Judiciary Committee. A year or so ago, *New York* magazine published an interview with Ted Ashley, the talent agent. Its most inspiring passages recited Ashley's brave, lonely, and, so far as his own memory seemed to suggest, successful struggle to defend Philip Loeb, the actor, against the blacklist. It seems to have been of no consequence to the glory of this Iliad that, if not by Ashley's will certainly with his ultimate compliance, Loeb had been so effectively blacklisted that throughout the year before his suicide he had been able to find no employment above the $87.50 a week Off-Broadway scale. Those who can forget their own history are rewarded by having it forgotten by pretty much everyone else.

When we consider the general practice of using memory so earnestly as an instrument for mendacity, it is a sufficient miracle for Miss Hellman to be so honest a witness; and our admiration for her integrity cannot grow smaller for a final impression that *Scoundrel Time* is not quite true. Honesty and truth are not just the same thing, since the first has to do with character and the second with self-understanding of a cruder kind than hers.

Miss Hellman cannot be blamed for *Time*'s having spoken of her political history as a business of having "dabbled in radical politics." But, even so, the very light brush she brings to her treatment of what must have been a commitment of high self-discipline could well contribute to such a misapprehension. She was, by every evidence, what she most puzzlingly denies she was—one of "those serious, dedicated people"—and she would not have needed to rely so entirely upon herself in her troubles if she hadn't been. It is therefore rather unsettling to come upon musings like: "the mishmash of those years, beginning before my congressional debut and for years after, took a heavy penalty. My belief in liberalism was mostly gone. . . . There was nothing strange about my problem, it is native to our time; but it is painful for a nature that can no longer accept liberalism not to be able to accept radicalism."

Now except for the lonely period when she could have used their good will most, the run of liberals have shown great respect and no little affection for Miss Hellman, and for more substantial reasons than the reverence liberals render to success and the odd pleasure so many of them draw from being scolded. But all the same it would be surprising if Miss Hellman could have been left with many illusions about liberals by the time, long before Mc-Carthyism, when she had completed her apprenticeship with Horace Liveright. By the late Forties, the most prominent liberals were busy antago-nists of her two most heartfelt causes, Henry Wallace's campaign for presi-dent as a Progressive in 1948, and the Cultural and Scientific Conference for World Peace at the Waldorf-Astoria in 1949.

The Waldorf conference was beset with more obloquy than it deserved; but I cannot think that Garry Wills has come quite up to the lofty mark for historical objectivity that he has maintained almost everywhere else when he speaks, in his introduction, of Miss Hellman's having, in her wartime trips to the Soviet Union, "formed friendships there not subject to any government line, so she helped arrange for artists and scholars to meet and discuss what would later (when a new line came in) be called 'detente.' " What had been arranged might less enthusiastically be described as a discussion between Americans who spoke critically of their government and Russians who could hardly have offered theirs any such treatment and safely gone home. It is doubtful that the Waldorf conference provided any historical lesson more significant than that Lillian Hellman got in trouble because she attended it and Dmitri Shostakovich risked worse trouble if he hadn't. But, all the same, there is, I suppose, a case to be made for encounters of this sort, and it seems a loss that Miss Hellman takes note of the affair in terms so cursory as to afford us no reflections upon it at all.[1]

Miss Hellman does tarry longer with the Wallace campaign, but her pause there is not productive of one of her better effects. Very little about Wallace himself seems to have endured in her memory except for "certain embarrassing scenes" in restaurants arising from his inadequacies as a tipper and "the stingy, discourteous supper" (poached eggs on shredded wheat) that he served her when last they parted. Granted that Miss Hellman's generos-ity of spirit is not one of her more remarkable qualities, she is in no way a trivial woman; and it is some trial to the patience to see her reducing what, for someone like her, must have been convictions intensely and even fiercely felt to stuff so trivial as this.

She remembers that she quarreled with the Communists over the con-duct of the Progressive Party's campaign because she would not abate her "constant pleas that we turn attention and money away from the presidential campaign and put them into building small chapters around the country in hope of a solid, modest future." Again there is that uneasy sense of diversion to the marginal. Are we really to imagine that Miss Hellman found the influence of the Communist caucus on the Progressive Party more objection-able when it was merely blundering about tactics than when it was upholding its stern principles by persuading the 1948 convention to reject a motion that the party platform include the statement that "it is not our intention to give blanket endorsement to the foreign policy of any nation"? For the Old Left had principles, good ones and bad ones, or for that matter bad good and good bad ones, and they must have held a substantial place in Miss Hellman's consciousness a long while before the day she embodied the simple and pure principle that she served so well in her troubles. It is an annoyance to have her leave so many mists around them.

We do not diminish the final admiration we feel owed to Dashiell Hammett when we wonder what he might have said to Miss Hellman on the night he came home from the meeting of the board of the Civil Rights Congress which voted to refuse its support to the cause of James Kutcher, a paraplegic veteran who had been discharged as a government clerical worker because he belonged to the Trotskyite Socialist Workers Party. But then Hammett was a Communist and it was an article of the Party faith that Leon Trotsky, having worked for the Emperor of Japan since 1904, had then improved his social standing by taking employment with the Nazis in 1934. Thus any member of the Socialist Workers Party could be considered by extension to be no more than an agent of Hitler's ghost. Given that interpretation of history, Paul Robeson spoke from principle when a proposal to assist the Trotskyite Kutcher was raised at a public meeting of the Civil Rights Congress. Robeson drove it from the floor with a declaration to the effect that you don't ask Jews to help a Nazi or Negroes to help the KKK.

Such recollections, of course, by no means tell all or even much about either Robeson or Hammett. But they do suggest that the matter is not entirely simple; and to appreciate its complexity is to recognize that what was imperishable in the hour of Miss Hellman's witness was that she managed to extract and make incarnate its one important and authentic element of simplicity. Hammett had served a prison term the year before for refusing to surrender to the police the names of contributors to the Civil Rights Congress bail fund. Political considerations had hardly entered into his choice at all; he endured his punishment not for the advancement of Marxism-Leninism but because he felt that to keep inviolate the privacy of those who had contributed to a bail fund for Communists had "something to do with keeping my word."

It would be unjust to Miss Hellman's independence of will to suggest that she was brought to her position by the force of Hammett's example. But all the same, if you presumptuously imagine her offering her objections to his course, if only from tenderness, her words hanging there as though unheard, and being left to argue the dilemma through by herself—then you have to suspect that this was one of those experiences that, however otherwise painful, serve to bring its victim to the confrontation of an essential point, which like most good points was a domestic and not a political one.

The enduring eloquence of her statement to the Committee on Un-American Activities belongs not to rhetoric but to conversation: "I am not willing, now or in the future, to bring bad trouble to people who, in my past association with them, were completely innocent of any talk or any action that was disloyal or subversive. . . . But to hurt innocent people whom I knew many years ago in order to save myself is, to me, inhuman and indecent and dishonorable."

That is not just a fine way of putting the question but the only way, and it seems sufficient to itself. It was enough for Miss Hellman to have done the single great thing of having once and for all defined the issue.

She was by no means the only one who acted well. Arthur Miller acted as well as she—if he could not be said to have performed as superbly—and he took a larger risk of going to prison. If what we call the serious theater otherwise ran short of representatives anxious to enlist as embodiments of its will to resist, comedians like Lionel Stander and Zero Mostel took their places handsomely.

The open Communists absorbed the beatings inflicted upon them by an indifferent official malignity with barely a whimper, not just Robeson and Hammett but scores of others more ordinary. It is ridiculous to give grades in matters like this; but if I had to select just one man who ennobled that age, I think it might be Steve Nelson, Communist Party chairman of western Pennsylvania, to the press then only a piece of boilerplate ("Atom Spy Clams Up"), to prosecuting attorneys only a basic natural resource for the process of conspiracy trials.

Standing on his crutches, he acted as his own defense counsel, questioning with some good humor the newest of the prosecution's witnesses ("Tell me, Mr. Stoolpigeon . . . "). It is unlikely that Steve Nelson had ever known many conscious moments when he had not been a Communist, and by then he may no longer have been entirely certain of the wisdom and kindness of Stalin, but he was dead sure that the one inexcusable act was to be a fink. Miss Hellman did not act better than people like those; but what she alone did had its special grandeur: without mentioning any of them, she drew them about herself and, as none of them had ever been quite able to do, spoke their real reasons for acting as they had.

"I am not willing to bring bad trouble to people. . . ." Rather that I endure my own. That is all that seems finally important about the way she did what she did, and it is a great deal. It would be too much to credit it with any more tangible historical result. The Committee went on just as it had; the blacklist grew if anything more savage and its depredations wider. Miss Hellman's words are memorable not for what they did but for what they said.

It is hard to believe that she ran her course with much risk of going to jail. These doubts have nothing to do with her courage; she would have done her time and been no doubt an excellent con. She might have run serious danger all the same (dignity is always risky) if she had not, quite by accident, come as close as it was ever possible to get to an iron-clad promise of immunity when she retained Joseph L. Rauh as her counsel. She had no way of knowing how seldom an unfriendly witness represented by Joseph L. Rauh ended up convicted of contempt. Rauh's professional skills and high personal honor were the major factors in this record; but it could also be suspected that a less measurable element in his success may have been the general knowledge that Rauh was not inclined to take a client he thought to be a Communist Party member, not because of any want of fervor for the rights of such people but rather because he felt that their difference of temperament might make mutual confidence difficult.

Justice Felix Frankfurter's was the crucial vote on a Supreme Court whose rulings on Un-American Activities Committee prosecutions were by then gyrating so wildly that there seemed to be no way of explaining them except by Justice Frankfurter's solicitude for the liberties of any American so long as it was reasonably certain that he was not a Communist. If Miss Hellman had been indicted, Rauh's name would have been on the brief for her appeal to the Supreme Court, and Rauh's name by then may well have carried for Justice Frankfurter enough assurance that the appellant was not a Communist to permit him to consider the issues in those abstract realms where freedom debates order. There Justice Frankfurter could often be a libertarian.

But if Miss Hellman had been to any degree calculating in her choice of Rauh, she would hardly have treated his advice as starchily as she did. *Watch on the Rhine*, her anti-Nazi drama, had opened in New York, most tactlessly in the Communist Party's view, a few months before Hitler's tanks announced the demise of his friendship treaty with the Soviets. The *Daily Worker* had criticized Miss Hellman for war-mongering and Rauh suggested that this evidence of her independence of the Communist line be submitted to the Un-American Activities Committee as a defense exhibit. (These were days, as Stefan Kanfer has observed, when "the artist was pitiably grateful for bad reviews.") Miss Hellman refused to avail herself of any such umbrella because, ". . . my use of their attacks on me would amount to my attacking them at a time when they were being persecuted and I would, therefore, be playing the enemy's game. . . . In my thin morality book it is plain not cricket to clear yourself by jumping on people who are themselves in trouble."

We would pay Miss Hellman much less than the due such a sense of honor deserves if we credited it solely to a primal innocence. You feel here the operations of a genuine nobility and no small part of a shrewd instinct about the future, an awareness—and such senses have much to do with honor—of how the thing would look in due course. I hardly know Miss Hellman; our only real conversation happened a few days after her testimony. I had read the *New York Times* summary of her statement, and had been moved to express my admiration for it in print, haltingly but with very little competition. Miss Hellman was grateful; but then I was no less grateful to her as I was becoming more and more grateful when members of the Old Left entered my consciousness, reminding me not just of their general humanity but of their personal dignity, and throwing sand into what had for a long time been the mechanical workings of my anti-Communism.

She told me then about her discussion with Elia Kazan, which had preceded his acceptance, and her rejection, of HUAC's demands. She had observed to Kazan at that time, as I remember her account, that they did not, after all, *have* to make as much money as they had over the years and that, if Hollywood was closed to them, there would still remain the theater and the smaller but by no means uncomfortable living it could afford.

It was her recollection at that time that Kazan had replied that it was all very well for her to say that, because she had spent everything she had ever earned, but that *he* had savings. And then she told me that her first thought was of how her aunt used to say that you don't go into capital. In her book she remembers a quite different interior response to Kazan's observations—something her grandmother said. Although her memory is clearly the authoritative one, the years have given me too much affection for my own version to give it up: because it seems to me that one of her most important lessons is that there come times when you have to go into capital, and be ready to face up to the loss of a lot, because you are wise enough to sense that the alternative is to lose everything. You will get through, and there will be a time to come when all that will be remembered about you is whether or not you gave the names.

I have to confess, although it is never gracious to say such things, that Miss Hellman's voice in these discourses does not fall upon my ear as coming from someone I should want overmuch as a comrade. She is too vain about judgmental qualities that seem to me by no means her best ones: she is a bit of a bully; and she is inclined to be a hanging judge of the motives of persons whose opinions differ from her own.[2]

But such feelings, even if they were just, would not finally matter when set against that one great moment of hers. It is her summit. We can ask from her nothing more; I do not suppose that, in the only critical sense, we really need to. The most important thing is never to forget that here is someone who knew how to act when there was nothing harder on earth than knowing how to act.

Notes

1. Cedric Belfrage's *American Inquisition, 1945–1960* (Bobbs-Merrill, 1973), the best perhaps because it is the most radical account that I know of those days, contains a tidy summary of the Waldorf conference, and makes it sound much more interesting than most of us permitted ourselves to imagine. . . .

2. It is a matter of limited moment except to me perhaps, but I cannot contain a desire to express the liveliest resentment of Miss Hellman's statement that James Wechsler "not only was a friendly witness" before the House Un-American Activities Committee "but had high-class pious reasons for what he did." The least offensive thing about this assertion is that it is factually in error. What is far less forgivable is a rancor that Miss Hellman's very eminence and authority ought to instruct her most carefully to ration. Wechsler was never called by the House Un-

American Activities Committee; he was subpoenaed by Joe McCarthy after he was made editor of the New York *Post,* and, far from being a friendly witness, he was a manifestly hostile one. ("I may say," he told McCarthy's committee, ". . . that we have repeatedly taken the position that the New York *Post* is as bitterly opposed to Joe Stalin as it is to Joe McCarthy and we believe that a free society can combat both.")

He did decide that the fight against McCarthy would be damaged if he as a conspicuous opponent did not demonstrate his good faith as an anti-Communist by submitting to the committee a list of persons he had known when he was a member of the Young Communist League. I considered his reasons idiotic and told him so; I thought this action lacking, among other things, in proper concern for his personal welfare, because it is seldom possible to explain the giving of names, no matter how high your motive. But if there have been many occasions when I have wondered about Wechsler's good sense, I have never known a time when I felt the smallest doubt about his honor. Perhaps I have a right to say this, because, as it happens, I was one of the former Communists that Wechsler named in public while he was wrestling with McCarthy. I also think it a duty of fairness to Miss Hellman to say that my strictures on her disposition are inspired in part by personal feelings in this matter.

The Scoundrel in the Looking Glass   Sidney Hook*

Lillian Hellman enjoys a wide reputation: students pay her homage, reviewers praise her books. A recent play on the McCarthy era presents her as a martyred heroine, radiant in the glow of the spotlight. She is also a brilliant polemicist, skilled in moralizing even at the expense of truth, honor, and common sense. And she has spun a myth about her past that has misled the reading public of at least two countries.

Let us imagine the following case.

A woman of some literary talent and reputation who, although not a cardholding member of the Nazi German-American Bund, which flourished in the 1930s, is the mistress of one of its leading figures, and hobnobs with its political leaders in the circles in which she moves. She signs denunciations of the victims of Hitler's purges and frame-up trials as "spies and wreckers" whose degenerate character has been established, and characterizes the Nazi holocaust as a purely internal affair of a progressive country whose "policies have resulted in a higher standard of living for the people." She attacks a commission of inquiry, headed by a noted American philosopher, to discover the truth about juridical affairs in Nazi Germany. At every political turn as Hitler consolidates his power and screws tighter the pitch of his terror against his own people and those of other lands, she lauds his rule. She plays a leading role in organizing cultural front organizations as transmission belts for the Nazi party line. When Berlin launches a phony peace conference, she

*Reprinted from *Philosophy and Public Policy* (Carbondale: Southern Illinois University Press, 1980), 218–37, by permission of the author. This essay (excluding the postscript) originally appeared in *Encounter* 48 (February 1977):82–91.

serves as a keynote speaker denying its true auspices and savagely assailing its critics. When artists and literary figures rally to provide relief for the victims of Nazi oppression, she sabotages their efforts by insisting that charity begins at home. She visits Nazi Germany four times and returns without uttering a single word of criticism of its *gleichgeschaltet* culture, and its concentration camps.

Disturbed by the growing influence of the German-American Bund and other political groups controlled by foreign governments, Congress authorizes one of its committees to investigate their activities and the sources of their plentiful funds. The legitimacy of the inquiry is upheld by the highest courts. It turns out that many members and sympathizers of the Bund are found in the entertainment industry. By this time because the true nature of the Nazi regime has been discovered by many, and because the United States is virtually at war with Hitler, some witnesses subpoenaed and under oath, and therefore subject to penalties of perjury, testify truly about their past involvements and experiences. Some refuse to testify about their membership, invoke the First Amendment, and risk being jailed for contempt. Others invoke the privilege of the Fifth Amendment on the ground that their truthful testimony would tend to incriminate them. Some like the woman in question invoke the Fifth Amendment not on the ground that their truthful testimony would tend to incriminate *them* but that it would tend to incriminate *others*—which really constitutes an abuse of the Fifth Amendment. Some who publicly claim to have been falsely identified as members of the Bund, when invited to confirm or deny the charge, nonetheless invoke the Fifth Amendment.

Much of the interrogation appears, and indeed is, irrelevant or foolish. Some of the committee members are interested in making headlines and (in the changed climate of hostile opinion to Germany) political capital out of the investigation. Nonetheless, considerable evidence is uncovered of penetration by members and sympathizers of the Bund into various areas of American cultural life, especially the entertainment industry. Partly out of conviction and partly out of a sense of guilt at the shabby way they earned their swollen salaries in Hollywood, members and fellow travelers paid large sums of money into the coffers of the Bund. Some of them were well enough organized to place obstacles in the way of outspoken critics of Nazi causes who sought employment.

The entertainment industry is run for profit. Its moguls are exceedingly sensitive to what affects public favor and box-office receipts. Not surprisingly, owners and producers became fearful of employing those identified under oath as members of the Nazi German-American Bund, or who invoked the Fifth Amendment, lest any film, play, or program with which they are associated become the target of a public boycott. An informal blacklist developed and some racketeers sought to exploit the situation. Some economic hardship resulted. Blacklisted writers peddled their scripts under pseudonyms. However, in a few short years, the wartime hostilities with Germany having been forgotten, those who suffered temporary economic hardship resumed their prosperous careers.

What would one think of the woman in this parable who, in 1976, strikes the pose of a heroine who defied the congressional inquisition and empties the vials of her wrath on anti-Fascists in the intellectual and literary community who allegedly stood idly by when she was questioned about her involvement with leading Nazi members and organizations? What would one think of this woman who now lamely asserts that her only fault was being a little late in recognizing "the sins" of Hitler—despite all the evidence that had accumulated over the forty years from the time she had endorsed the first of Hitler's mass purges?

For the Nazi German-American Bund in the above hypothetical account substitute the Communist party. For the woman in question—Lillian Hellman who in her book *Scoundrel Time*[1] seems to have duped a generation of critics devoid of historical memory and critical common sense.

When Lillian Hellman was subpoenaed to appear before the House committee, the United States was in effect at war with two Communist powers—North Korea and China. The threat of involvement with the U.S.S.R. loomed large in popular consciousness. The leaders of the Communist party had declared that in case of conflict with the Soviet Union they would not support the United States. The record of Communist actions, at home and abroad, had generated fear in the American people—and not only among them—of forcible Communist expansion. It began with the violation of the treaties about free elections in Eastern Europe; followed by the revelations of Igor Gouzenko (the code clerk in the Russian embassy in Ottawa) of massive Soviet espionage in Canada and the United States by domestic Communists; the Communist take-over in Czechoslovakia; the arrest and conviction of Klaus Fuchs, Allen Nunn May, Harry Gold, the Rosenbergs, David Greenglass, and other atomic spies; testimony of Communist penetration into some of the most sensitive areas of government; the trials and conviction of Alger Hiss; the Communist blockade of Berlin; the hazardous and costly Berlin airlift; Communist support of rebels in Greece and Turkey; the invasion of South Korea (June 1950). Whatever one thinks of the wisdom of congressional investigations—and despite Lillian Hellman's contention to the contrary, their methods and areas of investigations were *often* criticized by liberals!—they did not create the climate of concern about Communist aggression abroad and Communist penetration within. That was a consequence of historical events. CIO trade-unionists and NAACP Negro leaders were barring Communist-controlled locals from their organizations; leading figures in Americans for Democratic Action and the Socialist party (notably Arthur Schlesinger, Jr., and Norman Thomas) as well as independent anti-Communist liberals, even when criticizing the excesses of the investigating committees, were exposing the unscrupulous behavior of Communist cells in every organization they joined. The concern on the part of the public with security was quite legitimate. One of the great spokesmen of the liberal tradition, Walter Lippmann, even advocated outlawing the Communist party; fortunately it was never done. Certainly the public had a right to know who was financing the Communist party—why nothing had been done to counteract the infiltration of members of its underground apparatus into sensitive government agencies—and what ostensibly neutral organizations, political and cultural, that party had established in order to penetrate the structure of American life.

That Lillian Hellman should have been called as a witness before a congressional committee investigating Communist organizations and activity in the entertainment industry (even if she had not been identified in sworn testimony as present at a meeting organized by Communist party functionaries to enlist prominent writers as members-at-large) was to be expected. The record of her activity as a participant and defender of Communist causes was notorious.

During the 1930s she defended all the Moscow trials, attacked the John Dewey Commission of Inquiry for trying to establish the truth about them, worked hand-in-glove with the party fraction in organizations like the League of American Writers and the Theatre Arts Committee. She went along with almost every twist and turn of the party line. During the Soviet-Finnish War when a theatrical relief committee for the victims of Soviet aggression was organized, it was attacked by Lillian Hellman (among others in the Theatre Arts Committee) on the grounds that "charity begins at home," and that it was a disguised form of intervention abroad—this from the very persons who had been conspicuously active in organizing or supporting committees for Communist relief causes all over the world!

Throughout her self-serving book Lillian Hellman fails to distinguish between two types of witnesses charged with membership before the congressional committees—those who were truly identified as being members of the Communist party, and those who were falsely so identified. To her all investigation of Communist activity was a witch-hunt. One could argue (and many liberal anti-Communists did) that congressional inquiries into education and culture would have a chilling effect upon teachers and other professionals, and that whatever abuses and misconduct by Communists existed in those fields—and there were plenty!—could be dealt with by the practitioners in these fields themselves, without bringing in the state or government. Some took the same position with respect to Communist infiltration in the fields of labor and religion (see, for example, the editorial in the *New Republic* for 20 April 1953, "Communists in the Churches"). But this is not at all Miss Hellman's view. She is opposed to any investigation of members of the Communist party under any auspices. She fiercely attacks any attempt by congressional committees to identify members of the Communist party, even in the most sensitive posts of government, who had slipped through defective and often nonexistent safeguards of the security system. She dismisses the evidence against Alger Hiss in passages that betray her ignorance, really indifference, to the evidence.

According to Miss Hellman the only evidence against Hiss was contained in the documents secreted by Whittaker Chambers in the famous pumpkin. And of these she says that "the only things that had been found in Chambers' pumpkin were five rolls of microfilm, two developed, three in metal containers, most of the frames were unreadable, none of them had anything to do with the charges against Alger Hiss." She could not be more wrong. A great deal of the evidence against Hiss had nothing to do with the contents of the pumpkin (namely, all of the papers that were typed on the Hiss Woodstock typewriter). The two developed microfilm rolls of the five in the pumpkin consisted of photographs of memoranda from State Department office files to which Hiss had access and of mimeographed copies of cables from abroad that were initialled by Hiss. The other three microfilms—which were not introduced in evidence at the trials—contained unclassified material. (Espionage agents never know what the home office already has or might find useful.)

Miss Hellman's reference to the Hiss case is characteristic. On crucial matters, whenever her testimony can be checked by the record it turns out to be misleading or false. The two rolls of developed microfilm bore directly on the charge against Alger Hiss.

Roger Baldwin (the founder and long-time head of the American Civil Liberties Union, and a consistent critic of some of the techniques of congressional investigations) once observed, "A superior loyalty to a foreign government disqualifies a citizen for service to our own." Miss Hellman would have us believe, despite the oaths and pledges that Communist party members took during those years to defend the Soviet Union, that they were no more of a security risk than any others. To be sure membership in the Communist party did not mean that given the opportunity, all members necessarily would be guilty of betrayal of their trust. One may ask, "Are there not some who would refuse to play this role?" The best answer to this question was made by Clement Attlee after the Pontecorvo affair in Britain, "There is no way of distinguishing such people from those who, if opportunity offered, would be prepared to endanger the security of the state in the interests of another power."

Of course there can be no reasonable comparison between the capacities and opportunities for mischief of Communists in sensitive posts in government and Communists in the field of education and culture. Had Miss Hellman recognized this her position would be a little stronger. But her unqualified contention that the investigation of Communists any time and anywhere was a witch-hunt—a subversion of freedom of thought, a persecution of mere heresy rather than of conspiracy and underground secrecy wherever Communist cells functioned—testifies to the faithfulness with which she has followed the official Communist line. She does not regard it as conceivable that one could sincerely oppose *both* the Communists and Senator Joseph McCarthy—the Communists for what they truly represented, the existence and extension of the Gulag Archipelago—and McCarthy for making their work easier by his irresponsible accusations and exaggerations.

Individuals identified as members of the Communist party, and who did not deny it, fell into three main groups—1) those who told the truth, 2) those who refused to answer questions about their membership on grounds of the First Amendment, and 3) those who invoked the privilege against self-incrimination of the First Amendment. In all such cases the motivations for testifying, or not testifying, were mixed; but to Miss Hellman this needlessly complicates matters.

She refers to those who told the truth about their past as "friendly witnesses": These are the "scoundrels." She refuses to believe that anyone who told the truth could have been genuinely disillusioned with Communist behavior or, as the record of Communist penetration and deception unfolded, that they could be shamed by a sense of guilt at having abetted the Communist cause at home and Communist regimes of terror abroad. To her the only "honorable" persons were those who refused to testify if their truthful testimony required that others be implicated. The "betrayers" were only those who did testify regardless of the consequences to others and themselves. But these terms are narrowly defined to fit only the Communist cause.

When the director of the Ku Klux Klan of the state of Alabama was sentenced to jail for refusing to produce Klan records of membership before a grand jury, he pleaded that he was bound by a sacred oath of secrecy, and that to reveal the names of the members would be an act of betrayal. Miss Hellman never raised a murmur against his conviction, and it is not likely that she would characterize his actions as "honorable." She scoffs at the notion that members of the Communist party—even their hardened functionaries—in defending the political and cultural terror of the Soviet regime and its satellites were actually "betraying" the ideals of human freedom and of their own country. Even those like Eric Russell Bentley, who disapproved of the congressional inquiries, wrote apropos of the *Miller* case: "I object . . . to the assumption that what is involved is the question of honor and betrayal with "honor" always meaning the protection of Communists and "betrayal" always meaning the revelation of Communist activity. For after all, there is also such a thing as betrayal of the United States and honorable refusal to betray the United States. Who has been betraying whom?" (*New Republic,* 10 September 1956).

Since writing this and other pieces in a similar vein, and at the time in personal letters to me, Eric Bentley has reversed himself. In his *Thirty Years of Treason* (New York, 1970) he praises both Arthur Miller and Lillian Hellman for the stand they took, and out-McCarthys McCarthy by identifying the position of liberal critics of McCarthy—who attacked McCarthy when Bentley remained silent—with the position of "McCarthyism."

Not only is Lillian Hellman altogether unreliable in describing the "friendly" witnesses before the congressional committees, she does not tell the truth about the liberal and socialist anti-Communists of the time. She gives the impression that with hardly any exceptions they were either sympathetic to the investigations or silent out of fear of losing the perquisites of the high positions they occupied. She states flatly, "No editor or contributor of *Commentary* ever protested against McCarthy." The truth is that several editors and contributors protested at his vicious exaggerations not only in the relatively uninfluential pages of that publication but frequently in the *New York Times*.

The first call for the organization of a national movement to retire McCarthy from public life was published in the *New York Times* (3 May 1953) by a contributor to *Commentary, Partisan Review*, and the *New Leader*—at the height of Senator McCarthy's power. The best book on the subject during that period, *McCarthy and Communism*, was published by James Rorty and Moshe Decter in 1954 under the auspices of the American Committee for Cultural Freedom, and received the encomiums of liberal figures like Reinhold Niebuhr and Elmer Davis.

The manner in which Lillian Hellman refers to these anti-Communist liberals shows that what she cannot forgive them for is not so much their alleged failure to criticize McCarthy but (despite her belated—in 1976!—acknowledgment of Stalin's "sins") their criticism of the crimes of Stalin and his successors during the forty years in which she apologized for them. Her reference to these anti-Communist liberals also betrays the priggishness of the unconsciously would-be-assimilated 100 percent American whose ancestors had reached American shores a few boatloads ahead of other immigrants. Of these intellectuals she writes that "many of them found in the sins of Stalin Communism—and there were plenty of sins and plenty that for a long time I mistakenly denied—the excuse to join those who should have been their hereditary enemies. Perhaps that in part was the penalty of nineteenth-century immigration. The children of timid immigrants are often remarkable people: energetic, intelligent, hardworking, and often they make it so good that they are determined to keep it at all costs."

What she conceals from the reader is that those she criticizes did not wait for the emergence of McCarthy to combat Stalinism at home and abroad. They began in 1933 when Stalin did his bit to help Hitler come to power. She also conceals the fact that McCarthy was elected with the support of the Communist party to the Senate in 1946, defeating the incumbent liberal anti-Communist Robert La Follette, Jr., who had opposed the treaties of Teheran and Yalta. It took McCarthy four years to become an "anti-Communist crusader" of the nationalist, isolationist variety. She conceals the facts that when McCarthy was riding high, like Congressman Martin Dies before him, he lumped together welfare-state socialists and liberals with Communists; that what contributed to McCarthy's influence (before he did himself in by attacking the army) was the spectacle of scores of Communist witnesses remaining silent, or invoking the Fifth Amendment, as the picture of Communist penetration in American life unfolded; that American reaction-aries (who were criticized by those whom Lillian Hellman attacks) seem to have agreed with her that these children of immigrants were the "penalty" for America's past immigration policy; and that few, if any, of these anti-Communist liberals and socialists ever "made it so good" as Lillian Hellman. Indeed, had they been as much concerned with "making it" as she, they would not have taken an open anti-Communist position when Miss Hellman and her Communist associates were running rampant in Hollywood and elsewhere and trying to bar "Trotskyite-Fascists"—as all anti-Stalinists were then called—from getting work or getting published.

Lillian Hellman pictures herself as a heroine defending intellectual and cultural freedom against her inquisitors. But she actually had nothing to fear from them. She claims that she was never a cardholding member of the Communist party. If true she could not by her testimony identify on the basis of her own knowledge anyone else as a member. Anything else would merely be hearsay. She herself was never clearly identified as a member but only as "present" with leading Communists at a meeting fifteen years earlier—a meeting she cannot recall as having taken place. Since she has denied that she ever was a member of the Communist party, to any question about *any other* person's membership she could have truthfully responded that she did not know. The person who placed her at the meeting had admitted his own membership—she certainly could not have hurt him. Two days before her appearance she wrote the committee that she was prepared to answer all questions about herself; but, if questioned about others, she would invoke the Fifth Amendment because she did not want to bring "bad trouble" to anyone else. She claims that she was the first witness to brave the wrath of the committee with this defiant position.

The official records of her interrogation reveal that her entire present account is a compound of falsity and deliberate obfuscation. First of all, it is not true that she was the first of the witnesses to have taken the position that only if she were not questioned about others would she answer questions truthfully about herself—a condition that no court or committee of inquiry can grant. Communists who were identified as members of the party by the sworn testimony of former members had taken precisely the same approach, and Miss Hellman was merely following the pattern with minor variations. For example, on 19 May 1952 (the very day she wrote her letter and two days before her own appearance) a University of Buffalo teacher of philosophy refused on grounds of the Fifth Amendment to answer the question whether he had been a member of a Communist party cell at Harvard during the late 1930s. He, too, had offered (in a letter to the committee earlier in the month) to testify concerning his own "past associations and activities" but not about others.

The reason why members of the Communist party took this tack should be clear. If they refused to answer any question on the grounds of the First Amendment, they risked an action for contempt. If they denied membership (as some members of the Communist party had done in previous investigations in local areas like New York) they risked an action for perjury, if two witnesses who had been former members identified them. By invoking the Fifth Amendment as the ground for their refusal, they escaped answering any questions with impunity. In their case the admission of membership in the Communist party might be self-incriminating under the Smith Act—although no ordinary member of the party was ever prosecuted under it. The first victims of the Smith Act were *Trotskyists* whose conviction Miss Hellman's political allies gleefully applauded. In Miss Hellman's case, since she explicitly claims that she was *not* a member of the Communist party—and that her refusal to say so was motivated only by reluctance to incriminate others—her invocation of the Fifth Amendment was really illegitimate because her truthful testimony could never have incriminated her.

Even more surprising are the details of her testimony. Some questions about her membership in the Communist party she answers without invoking the Fifth Amendment. To the question, "Are you now a member of the Communist Party?" She answers, "No." "Were you yesterday?" She still answers, "No." "Were you last year at this time?" "No." "Two years ago from this time?" "No." But to the question, "Three years ago at this time?" she refuses to answer on the grounds of self-incrimination. She does not explain why a truthful answer would tend to be self-incriminating to the question about her membership in the Communist party in 1949 but not in 1950, 1951, and 1952.

The committee was satisfied with her response and, happily for her, took no legal action, for its apparent strategy was to convince the country that those who invoked the Fifth Amendment had something to hide. Technically, of course, under the law an innocent person could invoke the Fifth Amendment. A police officer, for example, earning $15,000 a year and questioned as to whether the $500,000 in his vault was "graft," could invoke the Fifth Amendment, whether he was guilty or innocent, and stay out of jail. But, after a departmental hearing, he could very well lose his post, unless he could rebut the presumption of unfitness to hold a position of trust created by his refusal to answer a question germane to his professional responsibilities. As Jeremy Bentham pointed out long ago the refusal to answer on grounds of possible self-incrimination creates an inescapable presumption of guilt even if that presumption is rebuttable.

Whether or not one agrees with his politics—which were abominable since he, too, was a committed apologist for Stalin's terror and upheld its necessity as a teacher in the party school—Dashiell Hammett's course in refusing to testify was certainly more straightforward than Lillian Hellman's. The record of her own interrogation as well as of others gives the lie to the artful reconstruction of her behavior as a morally defiant witness. She relates an incident—unreported by anyone else present (newsmen were there in large numbers)—according to which after her letter had been read by the committee's counsel, a journalist loudly exclaimed, "Thank God somebody finally had the guts to do it!" This is implausible on its face. What she did had indeed been done before, and it required no guts at all to invoke the Fifth Amendment. It was a ticket to safety.

Oddly enough, although her reason for refusing to testify truthfully about herself was that she would cause "bad trouble" to others, on the occasions when she proceeded to invoke the Fifth Amendment she could not possibly have compromised or even embarrassed them. When asked if she was "acquainted" with Martin Berkeley she invoked the Fifth. But since Berkeley was a self-confirmed former member whose testimony had identified her as present at a meeting in his house, she could not have harmed him in the least. When asked if she was "acquainted" with V. J. Jerome (who was a member of the Political Committee of the Communist party and in charge of organizing Communist party cells in Hollywood), she also invoked the Fifth. The same for John Howard Lawson. She could not have possibly caused them trouble if, as she now assures us, she was not a member of the Communist party during that time. By denying that she was a member in 1952, 1951, and 1950, and invoking the privilege against self-incrimination for periods earlier, she creates the presumption that she told the truth neither then nor now.

Lillian Hellman is not only disingenuous, to put it mildly, about her defiance of the House committee but also about her "involvement" with the Communist movement even if she is given the benefit of every doubt about whether she was technically a dues-paying member. Throughout her book she gives the impression that she really knew little about the political doings going on around her; that the discussions she heard or overheard made no sense to her; that it sounded like gobbledygook; and that her relations with the Communist party were remote, the result of association with Dashiell Hammett on the one hand, and her opposition to fascism on the other. Yet the internal evidence of this book, and her explicit statement about her political education in a previous book, make it extremely difficult to swallow her artful picture of herself as a rebel and a Bohemian not seriously interested in politics.

By her own account in this book she was up to her neck in politics. She played an important role in both the official and unofficial front activities of the Communist party. She met with "high officials" of the party to discuss the behavior of the party fraction in former Vice-President Henry Wallace's Progressive party. She was privately opposed (she tells us) to the Communist domination of the Progressive party although its role in organizing it was patent even to outsiders. She presents a jeering caricature of Henry Wallace as a kind of eccentric hick and skinflint at a time when the worst thing about him was his invincible political innocence. Subsequently, when he turned against the Communists and denounced them (*New York Herald Tribune,* 14 February 1952) for their "force, deceit, and intrigues," and their activities in the Progressive party, Miss Hellman taxes him with lying—that is, he knew it all along because she had told him that Communists were in the Progressive party when he had asked her about it.

But Lillian Hellman is no more just to Henry Wallace than to others. Wallace had publicly recognized the damage the Communist party was doing to the cause of genuine Progressives when he declared in a speech at Center Sandwich, N.H., in the Fall of 1948, "If the Communists would only run a ticket of their own, the Progressive Party would gain 3,000,000 votes." What Wallace did not know is what Miss Hellman did not tell him—that the Communist party had infiltrated into the strategic organizational posts of the Progressive party, and that she had the evidence of it. What she did tell him when he questioned her was that indeed there were some Communists in the Progressive party and "that the hard, dirty work in the office is done by them. . . . I don't think they mean any harm: they're stubborn men." This was not an accurate account of their role, and she knew it.

In her previous book,[2] Miss Hellman has said enough to make incredible her claim in *this* book that all the strange talk about "dictatorship and revolution" she heard in Communist circles struck her as outlandish. She says she came late to radicalism. But toward the end of the 1930s she undertook a study of Communist doctrine and embarked on an intensive "kind of reading I had never seriously done before. In the next few years, I put aside most other books for Marx and Engels, Lenin, Saint-Simon, Hegel, Feuerbach. Certainly I did not study with the dedication of a scholar, but I did read with the attention of a good student, and Marx as a man, and Engels and his Mary became for a while, more real to me than my friends."

If she could read Hegel we can be sure that she had no difficulty with the catechismic texts of Stalin although she curiously omits his name. Nor did she stop with reading. She checked her knowledge against the superior knowledge of Dashiell Hammett whose Communist political orthodoxy, despite any private doubts, was sufficiently reliable to qualify him for teaching at the party school. "I would test my reading on Dash, who had years before, in his usual thorough fashion, read all the books I was reading and more."

Therefore, when she tells us in her most recent book that precisely during and after this period of intensive study "the over-heated arguments, spoken and printed about dictatorship and repression puzzled me"—as if she were a Marilyn Monroe who had fallen among Marxists—she is singularly unpersuasive. Miss Hellman may or may not have been a member of the Communist party but until Stalin died she was not only a convinced Communist but a Stalinist; and for all her posturing about not really knowing what "dictatorship" means she may still be a Communist. She is no longer a Stalinist but it is not clear when she ceased being one. Communists ceased defending Stalin only after Nikita Khrushchev's revelations at the Twentieth Congress of the Communist party of the Soviet Union in 1956.

Lillian Hellman's most valuable contribution to the Communist cause was her activity on behalf of their front organizations. A few months after the Progressive party imbroglio she was called upon to serve as a keynote speaker at the Cultural and Scientific Conference for World Peace at the Waldorf-Astoria (New York, 25–26 March 1949). This conference was a follow-up of the World Congress of Intellectuals for Peace at Wroclau-Breslau in Communist Poland (25–28 August 1948) and was preparatory to the World Peace Conference in Paris (20–23 April 1949). The Waldorf meeting was held at the height of the Zhdanov purge of Soviet intellectuals. It barred from its program anyone who was critical of Communist party dogma of the class nature of science (including this writer who had, at first, been accepted by a rather careless program committee). The foreign-policy line the conference took was identical with that of the Kremlin: to wit, the United States was the chief enemy of peace and the instigator of the Cold War against the peaceful and freedom-loving Soviet Union. It even refused to give the platform to the Reverend A. J. Muste who was prepared to blame *both* the U.S. and the U.S.S.R. for the Cold War. Lillian Hellman valiantly defended the conference against its critics—whose chief point of protest was the refusal of the conference to speak up for the dissenting or nonconforming intellectuals who were being martyred in Communist countries (although the conference adopted resolutions condemning the court proceedings against Communist leaders under the Smith Act as "heresy trials of political philosophies and attempts to limit and destroy the right of association"). To serve as spokesman for a conference of this kind was a very strange role indeed for a self-denominated life-long "rebel" against organization—at a time when the location and character of the slave-labor camps in the Gulag Archipelago had become public knowledge.

Throughout her book Miss Hellman claims to be aware of "the sins of Stalin" acknowledging only that she was a little late in seeing them. It is only natural to wonder at what point, or when, she saw them; and what she did after she saw them.

It is reasonable to assume that whenever she became aware of them, even if she remained a critic of the sins of her own country, she would not have endorsed measures and organizations that extended the sway or influence of the sinful Stalin and his regime. For otherwise it would have betrayed a degree of hypocrisy and deviousness hard to reconcile with her celebrated forthright nature—so quick to anger when she is bamboozled or pushed around. Nor is it unreasonable to expect that after endorsing in her ignorance so many of "the sins of Stalin"—a curious phrase for "political crimes" since Miss Hellman does not really believe in sin—when she realized their true nature, she would in some way at some point make some public acknowledgment of her discovery. This has been the history of many idealistic Communists and Communist sympathizers who became alienated by some particularly vile outrage or betrayal of the cause with which they had been publicly identified. Certainly, if some former Nazi fellow-traveler were to write in 1976 that, although late, he had become aware of "the sins of Hitler," we would be curious to know when he learned about them, and what he had said or done on making the discovery. (Even Albert Speer has given us thousands of pages of details.)

The record of what Lillian Hellman has written—and not written—

makes it clear that she did not know about the political crimes of Stalin during the purges and Moscow frame-up trials of the thirties, the deportations of the peasants and the resulting famine in the Ukraine; the Nazi-Soviet Pact; the invasion of Poland and the destruction of the Baltic States; the Soviet attack on Finland; the surrender of German Jewish Communists who had fled in 1933 to the Soviet Union by Stalin to Hitler in 1940; the liquidation of the anti-Fascist Jewish leaders, Alter and Ehrlich, by Stalin as "spies for Hitler"; the Katyn massacre of the Polish officers; the mass executions and deportations of returning Russian prisoners-of-war after World War II; the overthrow of the democratic Czechoslovak government in 1948; the Zhdanov purges and executions; the Berlin blockade; the Communist invasion of South Korea; the suppression of the German workers' revolt in East Berlin and East Germany in 1953.

Until Stalin died there is not a particle of evidence that Lillian Hellman regarded any of his actions as sinful or politically criminal. Even after Khrushchev's revelations in which he more than confirmed the findings of the John Dewey Commission of Inquiry, denounced by Miss Hellman twenty years earlier, did she by so much as a word signal her awareness of the nature of Stalin's crimes. She remained mute.

Nor did she speak out when Khrushchev sent in Red Army tanks to crush the Hungarian Revolution of 1956. Nor has her voice been heard in criticism of "the sins" or political crimes of Stalin's and Khrushchev's successors—the construction of (and the shootings at) the Berlin Wall, or the renewed persecutions of Soviet dissenters and their incarceration in insane asylums. After all, Miss Hellman visited the Soviet Union in 1937, 1944, 1966, and 1967. But not a single word of criticism of what she saw or heard or of disavowal of her past tributes to the Soviet Union appeared. Not even the brutal invasion of 1968 by Soviet tanks in Czechoslovakia moved her to public protest. By this time even the American Communist party, the most supine of the Kremlin's pensioners, had shown enough independence to make a feeble protest against Soviet anti-Semitism.

Writing in 1976 she expects us to accept without question her assurance that she had long seen through the horrors and systematic oppression of the Communist regimes. It is hard to do this if only because, as this book reveals, she *still* regards those opposed to the extension of Communist influence as greater enemies of human freedom and the decencies of political life than the Communists ever were. Of the Communists she writes with sadness and pity: of the liberal anti-Communists she writes with virulent hatred. By her attack on them she seeks to distract attention from the many years she faithfully served as an acolyte in the "personality cult," Khrushchev's euphemism for the total terror under Stalin. In this she is banking on the absence of historical memory on the part of most of her readers.

This absence of historical memory is illustrated in the introductions to both the American and English editions of [*Scoundrel Time*] by Garry Wills and James Cameron.

The introduction by Wills, reprinted as an appendix in the English edition, goes further than the most extreme of the revisionist positions on the Cold War. According to him, Truman (despite his opposition to the House Committee on Un-American Activities and to McCarthy) was the true architect of the Cold War. The Communists abroad were blameless, and the Communists at home were merely victims of a reaction to Roosevelt's enlightened policies. Indeed, the Cold War was inspired by domestic considerations. Wills flatly states that "Truman launched the Cold War in the Spring of 1947 with his plan to 'rescue' Greece and Turkey." All unprovoked, of course. There was nothing, or no one, to rescue them from. "We had a world to save with just those plans," he goes on to say, "from NATO to the Korean War." It appears, then, that Truman's plan, with which all of America's Western allies readily agreed, as early as 1947 envisaged the invasion of Korea in the summer of 1950. Wills must believe that either Dean Acheson's declaration that Korea was beyond the sphere of American national interest was a deliberate provocation by the State Department to lure the North Koreans into invading South Korea or that South Korea at the instigation of the United States invaded North Korea. Presumably the United States intimidated the United Nations to support the defense of South Korea. Wills has unconsciously reconstructed the Kremlin's propaganda line. The only omission is the failure to charge the United States with the guilt of conducting germ warfare in North Korea. Wills's account of the domestic political scene in the United States during this period is no more accurate than his flyer in foreign-policy demonology.

It is not likely that Wills will find many credulous readers who are old enough to remember the past. But among them we must number James Cameron who has written the introduction to the English edition. He confesses that he does not know Lillian Hellman, and it is clear that he does not know the United States, its recent history, and the details of the period he writes about with such sublime indifference to the record. He even believes that "Scoundrel Time is come again" in America although he leaves unclear who the scoundrels are this time: The John Deans whose testimony, bartered for immunity from prosecution, helped convict the Watergate defendants? Or those convicted? He is also unclear about the British scene. He asks: "Why did our society never have the McCarthy trauma? Because we were too mature . . . ? Because our constitution, being unwritten, was too flexible? Because we produced no paranoiac like McCarthy? Perhaps—but also because we had too few Lillian Hellmans."

But why should the presence of more Lillian Hellmans generate McCarthyism? Is Cameron saying that if there had been as many Communist fellow-travelers, guilty of the same hypocrisy and duplicity in British cultural and political life as in the United States, the reaction would have been the same? The British Communists, except for those recruited by the Soviets as espionage agents, were never as conspiratorial as the American Communists and were not instructed to penetrate government agencies.

Nor does the English constitution have anything to do with it. If anything its flexibility could lend itself to even greater abuse since there is no Supreme Court to nullify or overrule Parliamentary legislation. English courts have never made absolutes of any right, or tolerated abuses of the privilege against self-incrimination. Actually, in Britain from 1947 on, not only were members of the Communist party completely barred from secret work but also all persons associated with the party in such a way "as to raise reasonable doubts about their reliability." After the defection of Guy Burgess and Donald Maclean the recommendations of a White Paper by Privy Councillors were accepted by the British government in 1956. It reaffirmed the basic principle on which earlier security measures were based that "the Communist faith overrides a man's normal loyalties to his country," and extended them to embrace the much wider circle of "sympathizers" and "associates." These are vague and ill-defined terms, and they required good sense and a genuine dedication to liberal values and individual liberties to apply them without miscarriages of justice. The procedures of American security boards were in some respects much fairer than their British counterparts. Civil servants in Britain who were under investigation were never told of the evidence against them; they were denied rights of legal counsel and even of representation at hearings. They had no right of appeal from the verdict of the tribunal to a higher administrative body or to a court.

Nonetheless, the American procedures worked more hardships and injustices because they were, as a rule, administered by Democratic and Republican party regulars who were politically ignorant of the wide spectrum of beliefs different from their own and who, as I once put it, "found the distinctions between member, sympathizer, front, dupe, innocent, and an honestly mistaken liberal as mysterious as the order of beings in the science of angelology."

Even before Joe McCarthy appeared on the scene, public identification under sworn testimony had been made of individuals occupying the following posts in the American government: 1) an executive assistant to the president; 2) an assistant secretary of the Treasury; 3) the director of the Office of Special Political Affairs in the State Department; 4) the secretary of the International Monetary Fund; 5) the chief of the Latin American Division of the Office of Strategic Services; 6) a member of the National Labor Relations Board; 7) the chief counsel of the Senate Subcommittee on Civil Liberties; 8) the chief of the Statistical Analysis Branch of the War Production Board; 9) a United States Treasury attaché in China; 10) the Treasury Department representatives and adviser in the Financial Control Division of the North African Economic Board in UNRRA, and at the meeting of the Foreign Ministers Council in Moscow in 1947; 11) the director of the National Research Project of the Works Progress Administration.

What would the public reaction in Britain have been if individuals of similar government rank and influence had been identified as members of the Communist party after the Klaus Fuchs case? Probably not as virulent as the American reaction, but it is not altogether excluded that even James Cameron might have been more perturbed than he seems to be. He would have to recognize the difference between nonexistent witches and Communist subversives.

It was in this atmosphere that demagogues like McCarthy seized their opportunity. Ritualistic liberals played into their hands, not by deservedly criticizing their excesses and irresponsibility, but by denying that Communist party infiltration into government existed. The Communists and their sympathizers contributed to eliciting public support for the investigative committees by invoking the Fifth Amendment, even when it was unnecessary, thus generating the impression that the conspiratorial activity was on a vaster scale than it actually was.

The greatest damage done by Senator Joseph McCarthy—whom Miss Hellman never faced—was to the American Foreign Service. His irresponsible charges against a few who may have been guilty of political naïveté—the Chinese Communists were, after all, not mere "agrarian reformers"—tended to inhibit critical independent judgment of American policy among their colleagues. McCarthy headed the Permanent Subcommittee on Investigations which should not be confused with the Subcommittee on Internal Security of the Committee on the Judiciary whose proceedings, in comparison with McCarthy's committee as well as those of the House Committee on Un-American Activities, were fairly meticulously conducted. There is no need to deny, as Miss Hellman does, that the disclosures before the House Committee about Alger Hiss and other key figures named by Whittaker Chambers were genuine. But they would not have been necessary had responsible security officers quietly acted on information which they had long before the hearings. The aura of the Hiss case kept the House committee going for a long time, but it hardly compensated for the vigilantism, cultural irrationalism, and national distrust generated by its successive chairmen and leading members who exploited their roles for cheap political publicity. Their excesses made intelligent criticism of the communism of that period—the heyday of Stalinism—more difficult.

For someone like Lillian Hellman, who loyally cooperated with members of the Communist party in all sorts of political and cultural enterprises for almost forty years, to impugn the integrity of liberal anti-Communists like Lionel Trilling and others of his circle is an act of political obscenity.

The criticisms made by anti-Communist socialists and liberals during these years have been vindicated by events. They insisted on the central distinction between "heresy" whose defense is integral to a free society and "conspiracy" whose secrecy is inimical to it.

This distinction was often ignored by the investigating committees and sometimes by their critics. A heretic is an honest defender of an unpopular idea. A conspirator is one who works stealthily and dishonestly outside the rules of the game. Our moral obligation is to the toleration of dissent, no matter how heretical, not to the toleration of conspiracy, no matter how disguised or secret. When that secrecy is combined with loyalty to a foreign power dedicated to the overthrow of free and open societies, a power that manipulates the activities of conspirators wherever they operate, the pitiless light of publicity must be brought to bear on the situation. Whatever may be the case in these polycentric days, during the years Miss Hellman writes about the evidence is overwhelming that Communists, even though their party was legal, were organized secretly in parallel underground organizations under assumed names working for political objectives framed by the party fraction. To be sure, they sometimes did other things as well, some of them worthy and all of them under deceptively high-sounding phrases, but only to increase their influence in furthering their underlying political purposes. Those who wittingly helped them, even if they paid no party dues, were morally as guilty in the deceptions they practiced. They were engaged in helping to destroy the open society whose benefits and freedoms they enjoyed.

POSTSCRIPT

Since the above was written, Lillian Hellman dramatically confirmed the double-dealing nature of her political judgment, its use of double standards and convenient invention.

In the course of a colloquy with Dan Rather of the Columbia Broadcasting Company, Lillian Hellman was asked about the charge that she could see what was wrong with McCarthy and that whole era but failed to see anything wrong with Stalinism. After all, if considered from the point of view of loss of human life, deprivation of freedom, torture, and suffering of innocent human beings, Stalinism was infinitely worse than McCarthyism.

To which she replied: "I happen never to have been a Communist for one thing, which is left out of this story. I didn't quite understand the argument, I mean I don't really know what has one thing to do with another. I was not a Russian, I was an American." To which Rather responded: "You can't see that the basic argument here is that you applied a double standard? You applied one standard to McCarthy and the United States and another standard to Stalin and the Soviet Union." "No," replied Lillian Hellman, "I don't think I did. I was injured by McCarthy for one thing. I was not personally injured by Stalin, which is not a very high class reason but it's a very—it's a good practical reason."[3]

Lillian Hellman is an eager but unaccomplished liar. She was not German. Nor was she personally injured by Hitler. But she protested vigorously his terror regime. She was not Italian. Nor was she personally injured by Mussolini but she joined liberals in denouncing him. She was not Spanish. Nor was she personally injured by Franco but she was very active in the defense of the Loyalist Spanish cause. Only when called upon to protest against the infamies of Stalin and Stalinism did she suddenly discover that she was not Russian and that as an American she had no business abroad. But then if the fact that she was not Russian and suffered no injury at Stalin's hands exonerates her from failure to criticize Stalin's crimes, why then did she *defend* them, especially the monstrous Moscow frame-up trials, and defame those who, like John Dewey, sought to establish the truth about them?

Lillian Hellman's shabby justification for her sustained role as minnesinger of Stalin's regime is so transparent that it is perhaps needless to point out that "personally" she was never injured by McCarthy (whom she never even confronted) or by the House committee before which she testified.

Notes

1. (Boston: Little, Brown & Co., 1976).

2. *An Unfinished Woman* (Boston: Little, Brown & Co., 1969).

3. Excerpts from the transcript of the interview with Dan Rather as published in the *New York Post*, March 23, 1977.

Scoundrel Time: Mobilizing the American Intelligentsia for the Cold War

Richard A. Falk*

The anti-Communist wing of the New York intellectual establishment has apparently been offended by the unexpectedly intense critical acclaim and popular success of Lillian Hellman's *Scoundrel Time*. If given to conspiracy thinking, I would suppose a plot to denounce *Scoundrel Time* launched at one of those frequent fashionable parties normally given in one of those spacious apartments on Manhattan's West Side. It is at least worth noticing the coincidence of strikingly similar denunciations of *Scoundrel Time* by Nathan Glazer, Hilton Kramer, William Phillips and Irving Howe all published at approximately the same time, and each an essay of acerbic political commentary rather than a review. In addition, we have on a recent front page of the *New York Times* the spectacle of Diana Trilling withdrawing her book from Little, Brown, also the publisher of *Scoundrel Time*, because an editor (probably misguidedly) insisted that some passages critical of Ms. Hellman be removed from her manuscript.

Why this belated outburst? What does it tell us about the book, the issue? At stake, above all else, I believe, has been the realization that the

*Reprinted from *Performing Arts Journal* 1 (Winter 1977):97–102, by permission of PAJ Publications.

success of *Scoundrel Time* would, if not challenged, endow its views of the McCarthy period in the early 1950s with an authoritative status. Particularly galling, of course, was the impression Ms. Hellman unmistakably creates that the anti-Communist intelligentsia was complicit, allowing its ideological passion to take precedence over its defense of democratic rights here at home. Let me be clear. Lillian Hellman regards the Congressional witch-hunters and their explicit allies as "the scoundrels"; in her view "the Trilling set" (that roughly encompasses those who now take issue with Ms. Hellman), by its ambivalence to red-baiting official style, helped make it "a scoundrel time" and bear some measure of responsibility for the worse things done later in the name of anti-Communism. Had the intelligentsia stood firm in the 1950s, in other words, the cold war mentality might not have gripped the country and we might now be struggling to loosen the bonds speciously wrapped around our citizenry in the name of "national security."

The main argument of the cold war intellectuals against Ms. Hellman centers on the character of "the Communist threat" at the time and what should have been done about it. Ms. Hellman's indictment is largely directed elsewhere, at the careerism and weakness of those who "caved in" and told the government everything they knew, and sometimes more, about themselves and their friends. Such an official "smear" campaign had its personal, as well as its political effects, and the issue of principle can be drawn in various ways. For those who stand, as I do, with Ms. Hellman the balance of indecency was clearly on the side of McCarthyism, with its digusting effort to discredit dedicated, serious citizens and its mindless campaign to whip up fear and hatred. Part of this determination had to do with the extremist motivations of the investigators, but part also had to do with the absence of a genuine "internal security threat." The country was not endangered nearly so much by those with left affiliations and leanings, as it was by those who would help launch this country on an overseas anti-Communist crusade culminating in the Vietnam defeat abroad and the Watergate collapse at home. It was these cold war warriors who legitimized huge peacetime defense budgets, formed the cadres of "the best and the brightest," were ready to fight Communists on any battlefield in behalf of any ally, that by and large reject Ms. Hellman's reconstruction of the McCarthy years as "imbalanced" and "distorted."

It is not that the *Commentary/Partisan Review* world, which is explicitly attacked in *Scoundrel Time* and is fighting back, endorsed McCarthyism as such. On the contrary, as Glazer and Phillips correctly emphasize, the magazines in question, especially *PR*, deplored the red-baiting approach of Congress to internal security. But what was also true was that these anti-Communist outlooks regarded the Soviet Union as "the main enemy" and reserved their principal hostility for those Americans who resisted this judgment. It was this kind of self-righteous and uncritical anti-Communism that converted an unexceptionable anti-Stalinism into a mandate for America's global role as guardian at the gates, especially in the Third World. For this reason, I think, Ms. Hellman is basically correct in connecting the ambivalent response to McCarthyism on the part of anti-Communist liberals with the full excesses of cold war diplomacy. These "decent" anti-Communists, who now attack Ms. Hellman as a popular exponent of revisionist historiography, by and large lent support to or failed to oppose the American involvement in Vietnam, at least up through the Tet Offensive in February 1968, because they accepted the desirability of keeping South Vietnam out of the Communist orbit. They long overlooked, or blinked at, the massive evidence of systematic atrocities of war decreed by United States policy-makers during the Vietnam years. Again such cold war intellectuals were not altogether for the war, some like Howe generally opposed it, but they were at all points far more intensely preoccupied with their opposition to the anti-war movement here at home. And so growing out of those McCarthy years we have, I think, the lines of battle drawn that continue to divide Americans as to the character of "security" and "justice" in a world of revolutionary turmoil.

In some ways it is odd that Ms. Hellman's book was such a popular success, and now is on its way to having a second career as a storm-center. Of course, she is well-known and writes well. There is about her account a pervasive charm and modesty that lends her views an aura of authenticity, and then, of course, she has been vindicated. Almost everyone now repudiates the McCarthyism of the 1950s just as they now condemn Vietnam as a national disgrace. And there is, I think, a widespread intuitive appreciation that the failure to protect citizens against official inquiries into their political beliefs and activities was somehow connected with the excesses of later years. In other words, if the public and its intellectual leadership tolerated the abuse of Constitutional rights at home in the name of anti-Communism, then it seems likely that it will go along with napalm, free-fire zones, antipersonnel weaponry, and the like in remote places if done beneath the banner of anti-Communism. And the American polity surely went along until the prospects of victory dimmed and the domestic and global costs of continuing rose so high. Remember that even Gene McCarthy and war critics in Congress failed to break ranks until the military situation began to look bleak for the American side in February 1968.

Scoundrel Time is built around an episode in this period of red-hunting. Ms. Hellman was called in 1952 to be a witness before the House Un-American Activities Committee, chaired at the time by Congressman John S. Wood. She reacted in a humane way, filled with anxiety about the adverse personal consequences of her stand and yet appalled by the prospect of being a friendly witness. Lillian Hellman does not conceive of herself as a heroine. She frankly portrays her stand as one that aimed to avoid either martyrdom or prison. After much soul-searching she decides to tell the Committee about her own beliefs, activities, and affiliations, but to refuse any responses that will endanger her friends. Her tactic works, although it is not clear why. The Committee could have pressed for a contempt citation as she had no legal grounds for her position. The Fifth Amendment privilege against self-incrimination is available only for oneself and if not so invoked is considered waived. And yet the Committee pressed no charges and kept her in the witness chair for less than an hour. The Committee may have regarded Ms. Hellman as a tough customer. After all she was a nationally popular playwright who was, at worst, naive. Her willingness to talk openly about the extent of her own activities underscored the moral character of her opposition to what the Committee was trying to do—that is, ask citizens to incriminate their friends and colleagues by reporting on their opinions, activities, and affiliations. Surely compelling such disclosures went against the American grain and the Committee may not have wanted to do battle against Lillian Hellman on such an issue. And so Ms. Hellman emerged from her ordeal untarnished, creating an impression at once moderate and decent. At the same time the hysteria of the times imposed some sanctions. Although she was neither ruined, jailed, nor disgraced, she did suffer some loss of professional opportunities and economic status in the next decade, and was forced to sell a country farm that had meant a great deal to her.

One of the most moving sections of the book is an intensely personal description of her performance in New York, only a few weeks after the hearings, as narrator in a Marc Blitzstein concert presentation of *Regina*, his opera based on Hellman's play *The Little Foxes*. Fearing to be hissed off-stage, Ms. Hellman admits that she needed several bourbons to get her before the audience. She then encountered, not hostility, but deafening applause. In truth, red-baiting was never popular with the intelligentsia as such, but only with a vocal, influential anti-Communist minority, and therefore it was not surprising that the cultured public should manifest its solidarity with such a widely admired artistic personality as Lillian Hellman.

Through the experience, as recounted in *Scoundrel Time,* there is an underlying sense of a decent person holding out for the sake of decency against pressures of indecency building up around her. At one point in the book she says, ". . . I was not a political person and could have no comfortable place in any political group." Yet she did generally support political causes, being involved in Henry Wallace's campaign for the Presidency in 1948 and taking a position favoring friendship with the Soviet Union, including a prominent role in the Cultural and Scientific Conference for World Peace, held at the Waldorf Astoria Hotel and widely attacked at the time as a Soviet propaganda event. In the end, accurately I think, Lillian Hellman emerges as a disillusioned left liberal who, despite progressive inclinations, remains incapable of adopting a more radical position. In her words: " . . . the mishmash of those years, beginning before my congressional debut and for years after, took a heavy penalty. My belief in liberalism was mostly gone. I think I have substituted for it something private called, for want of something that should be more accurate, decency." And yet she is not entirely satisfied with her solution—"One sits uncomfortably on a too comfortable cushion."

In assessing Hellman's memoir one is struck, in our world of torture and terror, by the relative tameness of the experience. Optimistically one can say Americans were not really tested in those years, and the absence of heroes then reflected the moderateness of the repression. More pessimistically, in the vein of Ms. Hellman's own reflections, one notices that without any serious forms of intimidation, most intellectuals and cultural figures either ran for cover to protect their careers or were so preoccupied by their anti-Communist animus as to be ambivalent about their resistance to an anti-Communist witch-hunt. With this in view it becomes clear why Ms. Hellman believes that our failure to resist more forcefully the contemptible encroachments of the McCarthy period paved the way for the more consequential experiences of Vietnam and Watergate. *Scoundrel Time* avoids any political analysis of this process and offers no diagnosis more profound than noting a cultural tendency to avoid at all costs past unpleasantness, a trait that has the consequence of leaving in place the social forces that produced the earlier evil. Surely, this refusal to learn from failure is serious, but it hardly cuts deeply into the mythic or socioeconomic imperatives that have throughout our country's history impelled American leaders to seek out "enemies" within and without in an almost obsessive fashion; it is the American compulsion depicted by Herman Melville in *Moby Dick* and generalized as cultural criticism in Richard Slotkin's *Regeneration through Violence*.

In the end *Scoundrel Time* is a book about the failure of civility in American society, especially about the failure of supposedly liberal intellectuals to step forward in defense of those in political trouble. Lillian Hellman acknowledges that people like herself "took too long to see what was going on in the Soviet Union," but contends that such mistakes did no real harm, whereas the intellectuals who joined in anti-Communist cold war activities often, it turned out, under CIA auspices, did contribute to that consensus that led our leaders and people to support a murderous war in Indochina and to build up a national security state in Washington. Of course, here is where the current controversy commences. Was it worse to be slow about the sins of Stalinism or the menace of the CIA? I tend to consider both evils of awesome magnitude, but agree with Ms. Hellman that our opportunities and failures are much greater in relation to that which we could, in theory, influence. The victims of Soviet repression are largely beyond our reach, and although it is important to strip away illusions and to lend support where possible to Soviet dissenters, there is little that can be done from the outside. On the other hand, to convert anti-Stalinism, or even anti-Sovietism, into a free-wheeling American mandate for an imperial foreign policy is to wage war against the generally progressive tendencies of revolutionary nationalism throughout the world. And this is exactly what the United States has done (is doing) in the name of anti-Communism, and never facing up along the way to the extent to which this global role is dictated, not by ideological or security motives, but by an almost mythic mixture of the sacred and the profane, the mythic drive to expand and hunt down evil forces and the secular drive to assure the well-being of the multi-national corporation. And so now we find the United States, ever more isolated and beleaguered in world public opinion, a bastion of reactionary policies, and a tacit or outright ally of a new, alarming drift toward militarism and fascism in Latin America, Asia, and Africa.

In the end, I am not sure what we can expect from American intellectuals, nor should we lump them together, nor exhaust the category by reference to this anti-Communist clique. Perhaps, slowly, the lesson is being learned that resistance to political evil is essential for the life of the imagination. Perhaps, despite his reactionary impulses, this is one message that Solzhenitsyn has effectively transmitted: "If we wait for history to present us with freedom and precious gifts, we risk waiting in vain. History is us—and there is no alternative but to shoulder the burden we so passionately desire and bear it out of the depths." Lillian Hellman's witness is more gentle, as are our circumstances, but read carefully, she too is warning us that we risk everything by risking too little.

The Legend of Lillian Hellman   Alfred Kazin*

On September 28, 1976, The *New York Times* reported on its front page, under photographs of Lillian Hellman and Diana Trilling, that Little, Brown had refused to publish a book of essays contracted with Mrs. Trilling. Lillian Hellman had made critical references to Lionel and Diana Trilling in her best-selling memoir of the McCarthy period, *Scoundrel Time;* Mrs. Trilling had replied to these and now explained to The *Times* that her contract had been canceled because of her refusal "to delete or modify four passages." The passage most objected to came from an essay on "liberal anti-Communism," written for the inevitable symposium. Mrs. Trilling's offense was to say: "Since the publication of this symposium in 1967, the issues which come within its orbit have continued to divide the intellectual community with ever-increasing acuteness, albeit with always-diminishing intellectual force. The most recent document of the division is Lillian Hellman's *Scoundrel Time*, published in 1976." The publisher demanded she delete "albeit with always-diminishing intellectual force."

The writing is careful to the point of being immobile, but what a brouhaha among the literary teacups! The president of Little, Brown stated that "Miss Hellman is one of our leading successful authors; she's not one of the big so-called money-makers, but she's up there where we enjoy the revenue." Mrs. Trilling, who does not often get on the front page of The *Times*, was glad to report that her telephone had been ringing all morning with offers to publish her book. Miss Hellman said that she didn't know what Mrs.

*Reprinted from *Esquire* 88 (August 1977):28, 30, 34, by permission of the author.

Trilling had written and didn't wish to know, but added, to The *Times*, "I was told it contained a hysterical personal attack on me." The *Times* read the objectionable passage to her on the telephone, and "she burst out laughing when she heard the proposed deletion. 'I don't give a damn,' she said. 'My goodness, what difference would that make?' "

Diana Trilling's book of essays has finally appeared—*We Must March My Darlings* (Harcourt Brace Jovanovich, $10). Although the imbroglio is funny enough in its way—both women are in their seventies and have been great friends, and both are known for controversy and for having a whim of iron—neither book has any significance beyond heating up the war on the left between pro- and anti-Communists. But that unending war in the intellectual community goes to the heart of the McCarthy period, the Hiss case, a lot of stormy American history and even Carter's short-lived effort to protect Soviet dissidents.

Lillian Hellman's *Scoundrel Time* has been more than a big seller: it has convinced the generation that has grown up since the Fifties that the author was virtually alone in refusing to name past or present Communist party members to the House Un-American Activities Committee, that the only issue in 1952 was whether you were personally a baddie instead of a hero like her great love Dashiell Hammett. Hammett went to jail for refusing to name the donors of a fund set up to support Communists, the Civil Rights Congress.

It was not only the young who adored *Scoundrel Time;* it was that great body of liberal Americans who are either inattentive to historical facts or have never known them. Studs Terkel said of Hellman, "Let it be recorded that she is merely great." The many adoring reviews of *Scoundrel Time*— most of them quoting Hellman's remark "I cannot and will not cut my conscience to fit this year's fashions"—were ignorant and simpleminded; Hellman's celebration of herself and Hammett was accepted uncritically. The book was sentimental and evasive in its portrait of Hammett. It was totally in error in stating that the documents in Whittaker Chambers' famous pumpkin that nailed Alger Hiss were of no significance. (The pumpkin contained microfilms—two of them reproductions of State Department memoranda to which Hiss had access—plus copies of cables initialed by Hiss.) Hellman obfuscated the fact that H.U.A.C. dismissed her after a little more than an hour because she took the Fifth Amendment when there was no need to: she steadfastly denied ever having been a Communist party member, so there would have been no legal force to her naming anybody. And the book featured a historical introduction by Garry Wills, formerly an extreme rightist and a proponent of war against the Communist forces of evil, who now acclaimed Hellman as the greatest woman dramatist in all American history and, with the same discrimination, proceeded to blame the cold war and McCarthyism entirely on Truman.

The snappy but rather pointless title of Mrs. Trilling's book refers to a long, solemn essay in disapproval of the living habits of Radcliffe students. There is no "hysterical personal attack" on Lillian Hellman. There is a stiffly courteous, reasoned and documented critique of Hellman's long-standing inability to understand the nature of Soviet society.

Alas, Mrs. Trilling is not likely to persuade anyone not already in agreement with her. She is a heavy, totally humorless writer, with a mannered style and an abstract vocabulary, who never moves away from such well-worn subjects as Freud, D.H. Lawrence, the barbarity of the young. In returning to her old college, Radcliffe, for the principal essay in the book, she interviewed the boys and girls, who without fuss now occupy the same dormitories and bathrooms, as if she were Grandma Moses entering a massage parlor. But her real fault is not her rigidity and New York parochialism in constantly invoking the "educated class," the "advanced intellectuals," the "literary intellectuals"; it is her inability to distinguish between culture—the customs and ideas that can be so superficial and irrelevant—and government, which, since the Thirties and the war, has expanded so wildly as to become virtually autonomous. Government—the state—exercises mysterious powers that are far more damaging to our culture than Radcliffe boys and girls brushing their teeth at neighboring washbasins.

The success of *Scoundrel Time* is due in part to Hellman's long-standing grievance against government in America. This cannot but please a generation sickened by Vietnam, Watergate, governmental snooping, taxation on every civic level. The young, unlike old leftists and ex-leftists now in their seventies, have no interest in Russia but are understandably suspicious of their own government, so overgrown, unwieldy, secretive, demanding, hideously costly. And whereas Mrs. Trilling's essays are virtuous, unimaginative and written in a style so highfalutin that they make me think of a letter to the editor written in Henry James's most mandarin style, Lillian Hellman has been dramatizing herself ever since she stopped writing plays. She can dramatize anything about herself, and she has done herself, Dashiell Hammett, her old retainers, the many people she hates, with a Broadway skill that is a mixture of social snottiness and glib liberalism. A large audience—it includes many people who disagree with her if they ever think about it—finds her so-called memoirs irresistible.

If you wonder how a nonfiction book can have so much dialogue and why there should be so many baddies in her innocent life, the answer is that Broadway will rewrite anything. The Diana Trillings just sound aggrieved. Damned unfair. But there is nothing in *We Must March My Darlings* that tells you anything concrete about Diana Trilling, her honest troubles as a human being or the famous husband to whom she was married for forty-five years. Whereas Hellman has made a love movie out of her long relationship with Dashiell Hammett, the ex-Pinkerton, the tough writer of thrillers, the perfect Southerner, the fearless American maverick.

Scoundrel Time even opens as a movie. February 21, 1952. When Miss Lillian was subpoenaed to appear before the House Un-American Activities Committee, she occupied a "lovely neo-Georgian house on East Eighty-second Street." She also owned a superb working farm in Westchester. She sometimes made as much as $140,000 a year from her Broadway plays and Hollywood scripts.

Close-up. The process server was "an over-respectable-looking black man, a Sunday deacon, in a suit that was so correct-incorrect that it could be worn only by somebody who didn't want to be noticed." Notice what a crafty type the poor man represents. Could it be that, black or not, the man was just making a living and picked a suit off the rack at Howard's? But Hellman comes from a German-Jewish business family in New Orleans and, revolting against (especially eastern European) Jewish timorousness in the South, feels an upper-class protectiveness about blacks and has special expectations of blacks. Readers of *An Unfinished Woman* and *Pentimento* will remember her long, loving conversations with black servants. Blacks even in New York should never become process servers. That is siding with the enemy. Hellman's famous temper is always on the side of the liberal virtues. "I opened the envelope and read the subpoena. I said, 'Smart to choose a black man for this job. You like it?' and slammed the door."

Hammett, whom she had lived with since the early Thirties and to whom she remained passionately attached even when they did not share a house, had joined the Communist party in 1937 or 1938. He had been sent to jail for the last six months of 1951. Hellman does not say that the civil-rights fund, whose donors he refused to name, was set up to protect C.P. members. It refused aid to James Kutcher, a paraplegic veteran who had been dismissed as a government clerical worker because he belonged to the Trotskyite Socialist Workers Party. Nor does she say that Hammett was asked for names only after several indicted Communists had jumped bail. But she makes very vivid Hammett's lung trouble and the fact that he owed the Internal Revenue so much money that they attached his income from everything. She and Hammett were alone with the U.S. government as their persecutor.

Joseph Rauh, Hellman's able lawyer, was head of Americans for Democratic Action, an organization of New Deal liberals that did not admit Communists. But like many men who felt the power of her personality, Rauh was so concerned for Hellman that at first he allowed her to send a letter to H.U.A.C. in which she declared her determination to tell anything about herself but nothing that would bring "bad trouble" to others. H.U.A.C. declined to accept these conditions. Since she could not answer questions about herself without being legally compelled to testify about others, she took the Fifth Amendment on every question at her appearance before H.U.A.C. on May 21, 1952. She had bought herself a Balmain dress and a new hat. She was excused after an hour and seven minutes. The committee may have been less impressed by the new dress and hat than by the usual implication that those who took the Fifth had something to hide. But they surely noticed the dress. She made a vivid, gallant, lonely figure. But since she claimed never to have been a member of the C.P., there was no possibility of self-incrimination and no need to take the Fifth.

Communist leaders also took the Fifth. But Hellman somehow seemed different from them and more distinguished than Larry Parks, Zero Mostel, Elia Kazan, Clifford Odets, etc., etc., who had once joined the C.P. as their protest against Hitler, Franco, mass unemployment. Not only was she a woman amid all these shambling and shamefaced witnesses and congressional inquisitors, she was vivid, as always, brave yet somehow wistful, *and* a famous playwright. She had a distinct influence over people prepared to disagree with her. Even such bitter anti-Communists as Diana and Lionel Trilling had been friends for years. You might disapprove of her political sympathies, but you could not overlook her; and after a while even her sympathies seemed generous, lovable, American.

Lillian Hellman recently modeled a mink coat for an ad that read: WHAT BECOMES A LEGEND MOST? The force of her personality is such that an editor friend who disagrees with her turned down a critical review of *Scoundrel Time*. It is hard to go up against Lillian. Diana Trilling was right when she said to a publisher: "Lillian will come out of all this smelling like roses." The reason is that Hellman projects a picture of herself as totally good and brave without being in the least simpleminded. Indeed, her snobbishness helps. The Balmain testifying dress is as vivid in *Scoundrel Time* as her account of Clifford Odets's (who ratted to H.U.A.C) choosing a bad restaurant and spilling the wine. Her plays usually take place in settings that flatter the audience while satisfying its hatred of injustice and cruelty. In *Watch on the Rhine*, an anti-Nazi exile finds refuge in a country house outside Washington that belongs to the patrician family he has married into. He commits murder for his cause but says as he goes back to the European underground: ". . . why must our side fight always with naked hands. All is against us but ourselves."

Hellman grabbed the readers of *Scoundrel Time* with the starkest black-and-white picture of America but forgot to say anything about the despotism that Khrushchev himself was to document in 1956. Hammett made Hellman the sassy, heartbreakingly honest and true Nora Charles in *The Thin Man*. Hellman then made Hammett the lone-cowboy hero of the left. Hammett was an ex-Pinkerton whose labyrinthine thrillers betray just how complex, dark and secretive his own career must have been. Hellman was angry with him when he confessed that he had been offered money to murder a labor leader. But in her untrustworthy memoir she turns him into such a parfit gentil knight, taking on all comers, that when he goes off to jail we get this applause-making line from Kitty, the Irish maid, who also adored him: "We're Irish, Miss Hellman. Jail's nothing." Jews are too lower-class to do so well. Hammett made Hellman walk out of Odets's *Awake and Sing*: "Once outside I said I liked the play, why didn't he, and he said, 'Because I don't think writers who cry about not having had a bicycle when they were kiddies are ever going to amount to much.'" And if that doesn't take care of Odets (or the Trillings, Sidney Hook and other anti-Communist children of eastern European immigrants), you can see from the following why Mrs. Trilling's fact and reason won't prevail against the public that ignorantly swallowed *Scoundrel Time* as the last word on McCarthyism (Hellman never went up against McCarthy):

Many of them found in the sins of Stalin Communism—and there were plenty of sins and plenty that for a long time I mistakenly denied—the excuse to join those who should have been their hereditary enemies. Perhaps that in part was the penalty of nineteenth-century immigration. The children of timid immigrants are often remarkable people: energetic, intelligent, hardworking; and often they make it so good that they are determined to keep it at any costs.

Hellman is easy on herself and Hammett, exquisitely nasty to those with whom she disagrees. Henry Wallace didn't seem to know that Communists were running his 1948 campaign until she told him. What she does then is mark him down for being dumb; pushes him down even more for being a stingy rube in restaurants; scorns his wife for serving a ridiculous supper of one egg on shredded wheat. She then caps the performance by explaining to Wallace that the Communists running him " 'don't . . . mean any harm; they're stubborn men.' 'I see,' he said, and that was that." But it isn't. *Scoundrel Time* is historically a fraud, artistically a put-up job and emotionally packed with meanness. Oh, these ancient positions and position takers! These glib morality plays about goodies and baddies in a world where millions have died, will go on dying, for not taking the correct "line"!

It cannot be said of Lillian Hellman, as was said of Henry James, that she has a mind so fine that "no idea can violate it." She is full of ideas. She is saddled with ideas. So, in another bad time, her book has pleased all those who think that Stalin lived in the time of Ivan the Terrible and that her taking of the Fifth Amendment in 1952 gives political sanction and importance in the 1970's to her self-approval and her every dogged resentment.

Close Encounters of the Apocryphal Kind
Martha Gellhorn*

> Apocryphal. a. Of the apocrypha; of doubtful authenticity; sham, false.
> —*The Concise Oxford Dictionary of Current English*, Oxford at the Clarendon Press, 1925.

Apocryphal stories would not be worth worrying about if their inventors stuck to the spoken word. What's a bit of bragging or slander among friends? But when these tales reach print they become accepted fact. No matter how implausible or self-serving, how spiteful or absurd, they are believed. Distin-

*This essay, reprinted by permission of the author, is an abridged version (limited to material on Hellman) of "On Apocryphism," originally published in *Paris Review* 79 (Spring 1981):280–301. The author wishes it noted that "Close Encounters of the Apocryphal Kind," the intended title of the essay, was published in Hellman's lifetime.

guished professors, scholars, biographers repeat and thus validate the fantasies of apocryphiars (new word). Built-in falsehood, children, is bad.

The form for apocryphiars is to wait until witnesses to the apocryphal episode are dead. The motive for an apocryphal story is the build-up of the inventor or the put-down of the subject or both. There has to be something very odd about apocryphiars. Undigested grudges? Vanity out of control? Historical social climbing?

A second new word is needed: *apocryphism,* a meld of apocryphal story and apocryphiar. I stop reading wherever apocryphism rears its two-faced head. If what I know about is untrue, why trust the parts I cannot check? For that reason, long long ago I stopped reading anything on the Spanish Civil War. . . . Apocryphiars thrive on it to this day. I would not have touched apocryphism with a twenty foot pole but for . . . a current literary *cause célèbre*[1] in which I have not the slightest personal interest. Over forty years ago, I met briefly the plaintiff; I have never met the defendant. The goings-on of the stars of the literary world do not concern me. The literary world is not my home ground. But all of a sudden I knew how that camel felt about the last straw: enough is enough.

I am definitely not dead and may be the sole surviving witness to a few years during the Spanish War. Who knows, these painfully researched pages might filter far from the *Paris Review* and warn off present or future apocryphiars. How could they ever be sure that a forgotten witness is not lurking by a typewriter?

And so to a selection of apocryphisms. It is astonishing that they have not been noticed and mocked before.

[Here follows the author's refutation of statements made by Stephen Spender in an earlier issue of *Paris Review.*]

We move on . . . to that famous personage of American letters, Miss Lillian Hellman, whose memoir *An Unfinished Woman* I read with unfathomed amazement.[2] Goodness to Betsy, I said to myself, what an *important* lady. How marvelous for Miss Hellman to be Miss Hellman. This book reads like a novel, I thought, and then found that *Pentimento* reads like excellent short stories. In my specialized study of apocryphism, Miss Hellman ranks as sublime.

Let us begin on page 56 of *An Unfinished Woman,* hereinafter referred to as AUW for speed. Miss H. starts a long anecdote: "*In 1938, after I had been to Spain* [my italics], and was back in Hollywood for a short stay, Ernest and Joris brought the final cut of *The Spanish Earth* to California." For two and a half pages, Miss H. describes this evening which—with her usual importance—she makes very much her own. "We invited a few well-heeled people," etc. After the film, she writes, Mrs. Parker asked some friends to her house, far from a pleasant occasion because Hemingway in an unexplained rage smashed a glass in the fireplace. Miss H. was lovely and comforting to a shaky Scott Fitzgerald and persuaded him to come to that party despite his fear of Hemingway. The glass smashed at the moment Miss H. and Scott arrived.

This apocryphism is a whopper. Hemingway and Ivens took *The Spanish Earth* to California on July 10, 1937. Since Miss H. writes, truthfully (p. 63, AUW), that she met Hemingway for the first time in "those pre-Moscow Paris weeks," *August or September, 1937,* she could not have been present at Hemingway's only showing of the film in Hollywood. (I cannot figure out where or when Miss H. ever met Joris Ivens but would welcome exact information.) Miss H.'s Hollywood story grows in apocryphal size when we read of that evening in the King James Version of Hemingway's life by Carlos Baker. "Fitzgerald, who was present, was full of admiration. The next day he wired Ernest that 'THE PICTURE WAS BEYOND PRAISE AND SO WAS YOUR ATTITUDE.' The attitude, as Scott soon wrote Max Perkins, 'had something almost religious about it.' Ernest was keyed up to a kind of 'nervous tensity' that sent him into and out of Hollywood 'like a whirlwind' leaving thousands of dollars in his wake." I have found many errors of fact in the King James version, where I was involved, but Baker got the facts I know of wrong from ignorance; he is not an apocryphiar.

As we progress in this increasingly learned treatise, I would like you to note that this is apocryphal put-down number one of Hemingway in AUW; more await you.

On page 59 of AUW, Miss H. begins another long anecdote.

A year or so later, we were in the Stork Club, and the table grew, as it so often did until it included Ernest and Gustav Regler, a German writer I had known in Spain. . . . *The Spanish War had just ended* [my italics] and many Republicans and their supporters had been caught in France or in northern Spain and had to be bailed or bought out. We had all given money to make that possible but Ernest was in a bad humor. . . . People began to leave our table until nobody was left but Ernest, Regler, Dash and me.

This fantastic tale takes up two pages; the burden of it is that Hemingway, bullying and vicious, "crumpled" a tablespoon "between the muscles of his upper and lower arm" and challenged Hammett to do the same. It would be impossible not to feel contempt for Hemingway, reading that story, but everything in it is untrue.

The Spanish War ended officially on March 31, 1939, and it is clear that Miss H. had no idea of the enormous tragic exodus into France which preceded the end, nor of the abominable French treatment of the soldiers of the Republic. I do despise her facile "we had all given money." To whom? To bail or buy out uncounted thousands? "The Spanish war had just ended" can be any date you choose, a week, two weeks, a month. It does not matter because neither Regler nor Hemingway was anywhere near New York. Regler was at the bridge from Catalonia into France with Herbert Matthews in the first heartbreaking days of the exodus; after that he was in France with his great love Marie Louise, free and as happy as anyone could be in those terrible times, until he was arrested as a German and sent to a concentration camp at Vernet in August, 1939. From which, with no help from Miss H.— but unstinted help from Mrs. Roosevelt—he was rescued before it was too late. He and Marie Louise reached New York towards the end of May, 1940. Hemingway was in Cuba writing *For Whom the Bell Tolls*, had been there since February, 1939, and did not visit New York at all until July, 1940. Since neither Regler nor Hemingway was at the Stork Club, the spoon story is the second apocryphal put-down of Hemingway.

I doubt that Miss H.'s spoon trick is physiologically possible. . . . The spoon trick has the added absurdity of being seen only once by Miss H. Mr. Hammett was dead, as were Regler and Hemingway, when AUW was published. If Hemingway had ever been able to do such a thing, he would have crumpled tablespoons, proudly, in bars all over the world. Scott Donaldson, in good faith but perhaps without enough good sense, picked up this Hellman apocryphism and repeated it, in one sentence on page 264 (Penguin edition) of *By Force of Will*, as proof of Hemingway's great physical strength. Thus rubbish lives.

Gustav Regler, who was not at the Stork Club, appears again on page 234 of *Pentimento*.[3] From internal evidence, the time of this anecdote, in "Arthur W. A. Cowan," must be the early fifties; again the exact date does not matter. Miss H. is with Mr. Cowan (not specified where) and silent and when asked why and told "Spit it out," she writes: "I told him about a German who had fought in the International Brigade in the Spanish Civil War, been badly wounded and was now very ill in Paris without any money and I had sent some but not enough." Miss Hellman documents her generosity meticulously in both books. The anecdote continues on page 235, wherein Mr. Cowan gives her a check for $1000 ending with "I sent the money to Gustav and a few months later had a letter from his wife," etc. etc.

But Regler was not ill and penniless in Paris. He had been perfectly healthy if never entirely happy in Mexico since 1940. Marie Louise died there of cancer in 1945. Later, Regler married a very nice American woman who was not penniless. He could not get an entry visa to the U.S. due to his long-past Communism, though I think he finally did. Still healthy, he certainly went to Europe in 1957. His autobiography, *The Owl of Minerva*, was published in Germany in 1958, in England in 1959, in the U.S. in 1960. He names all his helpful friends but Miss Hellman is not among them. Where did that money of Miss Hellman's and Mr. Cowan's go?

Miss Hellman is the very devil to pin down on dates which is peculiar in non-fiction where facts and dates are essentially linked. I find this puzzling in view of her authoritative detail about everything except time. Fascinated, I tried to make a chronology of Miss Hellman's travels in 1937. To start we have one sure fact: Miss H. and Mrs. Parker and her husband, Alan Campbell, and I did cross on the *Normandie* from New York to France (p. 63,

AUW), arriving on August 23, 1937. I had not met them before but was kindly invited for a drink in first class, liked Dottie and Alan and thought Miss H. a somewhat sullen presence. This slight acquaintance netted Miss H. two quick cat jabs at me which I receive with a catlike smile. How long then did Miss H. stay in Paris?

P. 62, AUW: "about the third week in Paris." P. 63, AUW: "in those pre-Moscow Paris weeks." P. 103, *Pentimento:* "that month in Paris." P. 143, *Pentimento:* "I said I had seen Julia in October." As all must know, this was during the stopover between trains, Berlin-Moscow. P. 112, *Pentimento:* "But I trust absolutely what I remember about Julia." What shall we decide? Miss H. left Paris for Moscow in early October, if she is "absolutely" certain about anything that concerns Julia? Until Miss H. proves a date, let us say she left Paris on October 1, though it can just as well have been later.

Two statements are repeated in both books. P. 67, AUW: "When the trunk did arrive from Berlin two weeks later." P. 143, *Pentimento:* "the trunk did arrive in Moscow two weeks later." So Miss H. spent at least two weeks in Moscow, bringing us to October 14, if the train sped from Paris to Moscow in only one day. Parenthetically and irresistibly, consider this tidbit. P. 68, AUW: "I did not enjoy the Moscow Theatre Festival except for a production of *Hamlet,*" etc. Perhaps this can be explained by the fact that The Fifth Soviet Theatre Festival took place in Moscow from September 1 to September 10, 1937. Foreign visitors then had the choice of proceeding to Leningrad for further performances from September 11, for five days, or of travelling to the Ukraine for ten more theatre days. Intourist ran a four week trip, leaving London on August 25, price from £32.15s—makes you think. The Society for Cultural Relations with the USSR in London (ah research, research) knows in boring length of only one *Hamlet* production during 1937, in *Leningrad,* precise date unavailable. Maybe a special performance was laid on for Miss H. in Moscow though the Theatre Festival was long over.

Miss H. then left Moscow on October 14, the earliest possible date from her curiously muddled evidence, presuming that she left Moscow immediately upon getting her trunk. P. 63, AUW: "I went back to Paris after a few weeks in Prague." P. 143, *Pentimento:* "I wrote to her [Julia] from Moscow, again from Prague on my way back to Paris." What is a few weeks? Surely two at a minimum? That brings Miss H. back to Paris on October 28—we are hurrying the lady, allowing always the least amount of time said to be spent here and there. She then rested a few days in Paris and went to Spain. She arrived in Valencia on October 13, "From a diary, 1937," p. 71, AUW, one of the diaries she has not lost. I must say I don't see how she did it.

A riveting mix-up is added on p. 183, *Pentimento:* "I had been in Helsinki in 1937 for two weeks." I cannot fit that in anywhere since there is no other reference to foreign travel in 1937 except for p. 56, AUW: "I decided to join Ivens in Spain but I came down with pneumonia in Paris and came home," etc. Her self-issued invitation "to join Ivens" relates to a corporation I never heard of until now, on becoming a reluctant researcher. It was called

"Contemporary Historians," formed apparently in February, 1937, its members being MacLeish, Dos Passos, Hellman and Hemingway, its purpose "to produce" what became *The Spanish Earth*. I don't know how the other three members of the group aided *The Spanish Earth*.

Hemingway did not speak of them; I can find no record of any group meetings. The single printed connection between Miss H. and Hemingway to emerge from my present delving is as a cofounder or member of "Contemporary Historians." Perhaps Miss H. caught pneumonia in Helsinki in February or March, 1937, before she made her abortive attempt to "join Ivens" from Paris? Perhaps Helsinki was another year? The short Helsinki episode is puzzling in more than its date.

This wearisome effort to attach Miss Hellman to some firm dates has a purpose. My favorite apocryphal story comes next. It begins on the last line of p. 63, AUW: "I liked Ernest." Hemingway had not "just come out of Spain" (p. 64, AUW). He had sailed from New York on the Champlain two days ahead of me; in that pre-historic past, we tried steadily though in vain to be discreet. On p. 65, AUW, Miss H. writes: "Hemingway and Parker, who did not like each other but who in those weeks were trying hard to mask it from the Murphys." We are meant to think that Hemingway spent night after night with Miss H., Dottie and Alan "in those weeks." "I don't remember that Martha Gellhorn joined us, perhaps she was not in Paris." I was, and with Hemingway; we had six merry hiding days and did our chores for the return to Spain.

One day Hemingway felt he had to call on Dottie Parker as some sort of anti-gossip ploy. He went alone (more discretion) for an evening drink; Herbert Matthews and I met him in the lobby of their hotel—the Meurice according to Miss Hellman—to go to dinner. He loped toward us, closely resembling a horse that has escaped from a burning stable, with a smear of lipstick on his collar. I went to Le Lavandou to swim for a few days and returned to Paris. Hemingway and I left for Spain on September 6, arriving in Valencia on September 7. Spain was the focus of his life then, not auld lang syne. He never mentioned seeing them after that one drink-time meeting; but I cannot prove how he passed three nights at the beginning of September. So much for Miss H's buddyhood with Hemingway "in those weeks."

Miss H's story picks up speed on p. 65, AUW: "One night after dinner, when we usually parted, the Campbells and I, led by Ernest moved around Paris," etc., Miss H., feeling "drunk and headachy," returned to her hotel room. After she had been asleep for two or three hours, Hemingway pounded on her door (what was the night concierge at the Meurice thinking of?) with whiskey and a package, the proofs of *To Have and Have Not*. Thereafter Hemingway sat in her room all night, while Miss H. read the proofs. When dawn came she made some highly perceptive but rather critical remarks about the ending of the book, which annoyed Hemingway. In the hotel hall, on his way out, he said, "I wish I could sleep with you but I can't because there's somebody else. I hope you understand." Furious at this presumption, Miss H. woke Mrs. Parker who, bright as a button in the dawn's early light, spoke knowingly but improbably about Max Perkins and Hemingway's bad cutting to shorten the book, and soothed Miss H's wrath over the half-offer of sexual intercourse. As dawn conversations go, it is a winner. This anecdote runs from p. 65 through p. 67. It ends: "The next day I left for Moscow, changing trains in Berlin."

Now turn to *Pentimento*, p. 108: "I left a note for them [Dottie and Alan] saying I was leaving early in the morning and would find them again after Moscow . . . Now I lay down, determined that I would not sleep until I had taken stock of myself . . . In any case, I slept through the night and rose only in time to hurry for the early morning train." Turn next to p. 112, *Pentimento;* "I think I have always known about my memory; I know when it is to be trusted and when some dream or fantasy entered on the life, and the dream, the need of dream, led to distortion of what happened . . . *But I trust absolutely what I remember about Julia."* (My italics.)

Which Miss Hellman shall we believe, if any? For the third time, Hemingway was not there. On the night before Miss H. left for Moscow, as she so clearly states, whether at the end of September or October, we were in Madrid safe from apocryphiars until Miss H. arrived. Hemingway read his proofs in America before sailing. Again Miss H. has devised a malicious apocryphism about Hemingway. There are too many, they have a queer ring.

I can hardly bear to discuss Miss H's ego trip in Spain. First, there is a peculiar omission. Though so full of Dottie and Alan in Paris, Miss H. neglects to mention that they had preceded her to Spain, safely blazing the trail. An AP news item, dated Valencia, October 10 (1937), reports that "Dorothy Parker, well-known American poet" and her husband Alan Campbell "will leave by air for Paris tomorrow. They have been travelling in Spain for several weeks." Did the friends meet in Paris before Miss H. set out bravely to war? Obviously Miss H's journey becomes less impressive when we know that Mrs. Parker, whom Miss H. defines as not "my generation" (nine years difference in age), had already survived several weeks in Spain without fuss or mishap.

A letter from Madrid to my mother, dated October 8, 1937, says "Dottie Parker is here and very nice and we had a marvelous dinner at Matthews." My clear memory is that Dottie and Alan stayed in Madrid briefly, less than a week, and that Miss H. stayed even more briefly. Madrid had a bad reputation for danger though it was quiet that October. The three friends, like most visitors, were based in Valencia, in every way a more comfortable city.

Take a deep breath.

Miss H. arrived in Valencia on October 13, 1937. On October 14, she presented her credentials at the Press office (AUW, p. 73). She was "pleasantly welcomed by Constancia de la Mora, had two telephone calls from her suggesting I come back to the office and meet people who might like to meet me, and have not gone. This is nothing new; *part the need to make people come to me, part not wanting to seem important.*" The italics are mine and those words say more about Miss H. at that war than anyone else could ever think up. It was Constancia's job to take polite care of all visiting foreigners. The great New York playwright (*The Children's Hour* and a second unsuccessful play) imagined that her clippings and fame had preceded her and she did not want to seem important in Spain. Dear God. No hint of conceit marred Mrs. Parker's acts and attitudes in Spain, but then she was not a conceited woman.

On this same page 73, AUW, an air raid starts, the day after the important Miss H. arrived. Being a dramatist, Miss H. describes the air raid dramatically through page 76:

A child screamed; women ran. (I was always impressed by the Spaniards' quiet reaction to danger.) A policeman (an imbecile?) pointed to a bench and gave Miss H. a shove. She "crawled" [rolled? wriggled?] under it for protection from bombs. Until now I have never heard of and of course never seen anyone under a park bench during an air raid but Miss H. is unique, and humor is not her most notable trait. Somehow this sizeable city empties; Miss H. is all alone; it is practically her private air raid. She left the park bench, too frightened to stay by herself. Running, she reached the convent wall next to her hotel where she saw that "the planes were overhead, flying fast"; how else. Two Spanish soldiers were standing in the convent door; one said, in English, "Italian bastards." "As he spoke, one plane dropped down and from it slowly floated what looked like a round gift-wrapped package."

I don't know what to make of this. Like millions of others, I have been on the ground during various air raids but never glimpsed a bomb "slowly" float. I am also bewildered by "one plane dropped down." The big silver Italian bombers, flying from the Balearics, were not dive bombers; habitually, their pilots kept to a very prudent height. Bomb bays did not open to eject one bomb, like an auk's egg, or a gift-wrapped package. The trip would not be worthwhile, would it, when the object was to cause as much indiscriminate death and destruction as possible, in minutes.

Air attacks on civilian populations, and the artillery attacks on Madrid, were then a novelty of war, exhibited for the first time in Spain, later spreading and continuing violently throughout the world, a vile commonplace of our time.

But there is no record anywhere of an air raid on Valencia on October 14. And I have searched above and beyond the call of duty. The (London) *Times* from Valencia reports "the worst air raid so far . . . on the harbour district" on October 3. At least sixty bombs and heavy casualties. An AP dispatch to the *New York Times*, dated October 3 from Madrid corroborates the date. From Madrid, on October 4, the (London) *Times* correspondent wired "reports are reaching Madrid" of bombers along the Mediterranean coast and "between last Friday and Sunday" (*viz:* October 1–3) casualties at Barcelona and Valencia had mounted to "triple figures." The air raid of October 3 on Valencia is definitely established.

At the bottom of a page in the *New York Times* for October 15, there is a ten line paragraph headed "Valencia, Spain, October 14, AP." The man on the spot reports a daylight raid by "five Insurgent warplanes" on "the Government's Mediterranean naval base at Cartagena." Cartagena, as the crow or bomber flies, is approximately one hundred and twenty miles south and west of Valencia. The AP man in Valencia would surely have noticed bombs dropping around him on October 14, the date of Miss H's air raid. The (London) *Times* does not mention that Cartagena air raid or any other for that date.

On October 16 the *New York Times*, but not the (London) *Times*, carried a dispatch dated "Madrid, October 15, AP," stating that "insurgent airmen attacked Cartagena, Barcelona and Valencia, government cities on the eastern coast, causing heavy damage and casualties." That one looks very dicey, a correspondent filing loose news. The Madrid AP man had to get his information second hand; the AP correspondent in Valencia was there. If Valencia itself had been bombed on October 15, the AP man there would have cabled a report about it. Valencia was the capital of Republican Spain, the seat of government, not an inconsequential village. The lack of corroboration by the AP or the (London) *Times*, from Valencia, rules out the fact of an air raid there on October 15.

After that, no attacks on Valencia are reported until December 11, when Fascist ships shelled the port without casualties for a change.

Apart from the wrong date and the absence of solid proof of any air raid on Valencia after October 3, how come that Miss H. did not visit the scene of the crime, the "section around the port" . . . where "the Italian bombers killed sixty three people" (p. 74, AUW). If she ignored the obligation to write about wanton killing of civilians, Constancia de La Mora would most certainly, gently, firmly have arranged for her to see what war looks like. One must conclude that Miss H. was told of the very bad raid on October 3 and her imagination then took over, placing her a bit off key at the center of the apocryphal action.

On October 22 (p. 80, AUW), Miss H. sets out for Madrid at 7 A.M., arriving there after 8 P.M. that night. She is sorely tried by the strain and fatigue of the journey, by the road and its perils. "Hot and aching, I groaned my way out of the car and sat down suddenly on the running board . . . hoping the dizziness would go away" (p. 83, AUW). "Weak and dizzy" is such a frequent phrase in AUW that one can only admire the will power that kept Miss H. going. Of course thousands of less sensitive people travelled that road regularly; it was the main route for civilian and military supplies to Madrid. In the late afternoon, the village where Miss H. sat down suddenly provides a splendid anecdote (pp. 83–86, AUW), featuring a woman with peroxided hair, an English-speaking evacuee from Madrid, in itself a rare lucky break for Miss H. who did not speak Spanish. The "bleached lady" told Miss H. that she disliked this village "where they were bombed almost every day." Can Miss H. have met a nameless Spanish apocryphiar? A few bombings would have left any village a heap of deserted rubble.

Miss H. was again generous (p. 86, AUW). "We kissed each other and the four ladies of the table followed us downstairs. I had left my shoes for the blonde lady under the chair." Presumably none of the four ladies noticed that their foreign guest, who might more usefully have left some canned food, walked on stocking feet. Her gift was not observed until Miss H. saw the blonde lady at a window "as she shouted for me to come back for my shoes, and then, as I waved no from the car, she clapped her hands in applause." As do we all; Miss H's repeated munificence is beyond praise. I wonder how Miss H. knew that the shoes would fit.

I have only one folder of notes on the Spanish War. By chance, I made very full notes for October 15, 1937 which begin: "We started off in a fury." Obviously I don't remember what that quarrel with Hemingway was about but it soured the whole day and night. Sefton Delmer, Herbert Matthews, Hemingway and I spent a long useless day trying to see some section of the front near Aranjuez. The notes make little sense to me now and most of the names in them have become only names.

> We drove rapidly back to Chinchon hoping for permission from the Colonel to visit the lines and see what had been done. But the Colonel was asleep after three exhausting but unsatisfactory days of fighting . . . and finally we realised that they did not want us to go to the lines because the operation had been a failure. So there was nothing to do but return to Madrid . . . The end of the afternoon at the Censura [press office] is a tedious affair, with waiting people and dim lights and nothing much to do and no news these days, but often visiting firemen. Miss Hellman was amongst those present . . .

Having no reason whatever to fudge dates, I think you can accept as fact that Miss H. had arrived in Madrid by October 15, and I think her own later date of arrival on October 22 has the purpose of making her Spain visit seem longer than it actually was. Her record on dates is far from perfect. There is no other mention of Miss H. in my notes nor in any letter to my mother.

AUW, p. 86: "Madrid October 23 . . . Early this morning a young man from the Spanish Press Office came to tell me that Columbia Broadcasting had agreed to give them radio time for me that night and the government people were very pleased because they hadn't had much luck getting air time in America." Broadcasting from Madrid was not really such a big deal. Even I did it, had done so on October 9, though I hated it from stage fright. Miss H's account of how these broadcasts were arranged enhances her importance but is incorrect.[4] Foreign radio networks, of any country, asked someone in Madrid to broadcast. "The government people" agreed to the time if the station was free. The written broadcast had to be passed by the censor.

How remarkable that Miss H., so replete with detail about herself, did not mention writing her broadcast that day and seeing it through the Censura. In my scant notes, I read bad-tempered complaints about the nuisance of the Censura, when you had to get last minute changes accepted as the witching hour at the microphone drew near.

Instead of writing her broadcast, Miss H. says (p. 86, AUW): "I wanted to see University City but I got tired before I got there." Based on her official birth date, Miss H. was a young woman of thirty-two that year, not frail in appearance. From the Telefonica to the trenches and smashed buildings of University City, Madrid's front line, was an easy walk, perhaps half an hour. Miss H. uses "I" meaning "we" the way royalty formerly used "we" meaning "I." She could not have gone alone, but it was not her type of outing. A warren of shallow trenches connected the remnants of buildings; sandbags in holes in these buildings indicated where the enemy had the clearest view of movement. Though it was a stable front then, periodic bursts of anger caused it to come alive with machine guns and mortars. The lines were so close that the men on both sides taunted each other by megaphone at night; by day that amusement was too risky. One detail I remember (who am not big on detail like Miss H.): the Fascists had a good gramophone, they played records at night. "Kitten on the Keys" was much appreciated by the Republican troops. They disliked Fascist songs and took pot shots in the direction of the sound.

P. 86, AUW: " . . . when I came back to the hotel, Ernest was in the lobby with a bottle of whiskey for me and an invitation to have dinner that night," etc. I am surprised Miss H. did not say Ernest had brought his right eye for her, whiskey being of that value in Madrid. AUW, pp. 87–88 are devoted to that dinner party which I remember but not at all as Miss H. remembers it.

My memory is so much simpler that I'll give it first. I have no date for it. (Miss H's date is October 23.) We four, Delmer, Matthews, Hemingway and I, pooled cans from our invaluable and ever-decreasing supply to make a good dinner for Miss H. Delmer had become a first-class can cook. Miss H. brought nothing but herself and unlike Dottie she was not funny. The object was to please Miss H. and encourage her zeal for the Republic. Evidently we three Americans, zealous but not apocryphiars, felt this was necessary, and the Englishman, Delmer, went along because he shared the apartment with Matthews. I remember it as a dull, grumpy dinner, and afterwards we heard that Miss H. said the correspondents in Madrid lived off the fat of the land and we were suitably irritated. That is my memory. I did not see Miss H. after that evening whenever it was. My guess is that Miss H. was no longer in town.

Her sojourn in Spain was not sufficiently vital to the Republic to be documented in any book I can find. Mrs. Parker named Miss Hellman as her literary executor and might as well have left her papers to Fort Knox. Until Miss H. releases Mrs. Parker's papers, there is no way to prove how long

Miss H. actually stayed in Spain. I estimate ten days at most, and mostly in Valencia.

Miss H. however has a memory (p. 86, AUW) of eating beef at our dinner, given by "Madrid bullfight people." Her incomprehension of that war is near idiocy. How could she think there were ever bullfights in wartime Madrid, let alone beef? What a target a bullfight crowd would have made for the German artillery on Garabitas hill. "When I arrived Ernest was already there and Martha Gellhorn, looking handsome in her well-tailored pants and good boots." The best-dressed woman at a war: that is a delightful put-down which I enjoy for its open bitchery. In a spirit of fun, I return it here: if Miss H's beauty had matched her brains, she would have been a more cuddly personality. "I took along two cans of sardines and two cans of paté," generous as ever; it's my word against Miss H. on that one. "I dropped my spoon and Ernest told me that I was hearing my first bombardment." What follows has to be quoted in full though it takes a lot of space but it is Miss H. at her noble best. Everyone else, not to mince words, is a shit.

> The Englishman, Ernest and Martha went out to the balcony to watch—[Miss H. forgot Herbert Matthews but he too is dead now, as is Delmer; no witnesses left except me.]—every night at almost the same hour the Franco people bombarded the telephone building—and I sat on the couch in the living room with my head bent low and my eyes shut, hoping I could control the panic I felt. Several times Ernest called to me to come out on the balcony, it was a beautiful sight, he said, and once Martha called, and once the Englishman came to the door and stood looking at me and went mumbling back to Ernest. Ernest came to the door, stared at me, opened his mouth as if to speak, changed his mind, and went back to the beauty of the shelling. After a while the phone rang, and the Englishman said the man at the radio station said the station itself was being hit, it would be too dangerous for me to come there, so would I tell the chauffeur who was already on his way to take shelter somewhere?
>
> About ten minutes later the doorbell rang, a servant admitted the chauffeur, and I went down the stairs with him.
>
> When I was a few flights down, Ernest shouted to me, "You can't go into that shelling." He ran down the steps toward me. "Come back here."
>
> I said I wasn't going to come back. It was important for me to do the broadcast, they probably couldn't get the time on another night. Ernest was holding me by the arm. Then he dropped my arm and said softly, "So you have *cojones* after all, I didn't think so upstairs. But you have *cojones* after all."
>
> I said, "Go to hell with what you think."
>
> When the broadcast was over and I was back at the hotel, Ernest knocked on my door. We had a few drinks and I kept wanting to tell him that I would have gone into far more dangerous places to get out of that apartment that night but I didn't tell him.

Oh man, one might even say *Wow!*

I am having trouble with dates. The (London) *Times* report, dated

Madrid, October 22, says "the city was again shelled during the night, although less intensively than recently." An unusually long paragraph in the *New York Times* (two Congressmen were in town) dated October 22, reports a bombardment beginning at 10:45 P.M. on October 21, ending at 12:05 A.M. on October 22. In Madrid, pencilled on scrap paper, I wrote October 11—biggest shelling. October 13–14 (night)—2nd shelling. October 25th—3rd shelling. November 24—4th shelling. Checked against the (London) *Times* and the *New York Times* my dates agree, except October 21–22 (them) and October 25 (me). I can't win an argument with both the *Times*, so I have to accept October 21–22. The precise timing of the bombardment in the *New York Times* is doubtless correct, due to the presence of the Congressmen which gave importance to what was by then routine news.

If the date of Miss H's alleged unlovely evening with us monsters was October 23, as she states, no shells hit Madrid that night.

Miss H. writes (p. 67, AUW): "every night at almost the same hour the Franco people bombarded the telephone building." By her own timetable, she must have slept through a bombardment on her first night (October 22) in Madrid. Who can credit that? But as she was in the city on October 15 according to my disinterested notes (it made no difference to me when Miss H. arrived) she had to know that "the Franco people" did not bombard every night. A regular artillery schedule would have spoiled their terror tactics. Instead nobody ever knew when shelling would begin and though the Telefonica was often hit, the whole city was the target. There were too many times when bombardments were fearful continuous hell for all the inhabitants of Madrid. In the typescript of an old article I see that we counted 600 shells with a stopwatch in less than an hour one night; and described the effect on people and homes the next day. October 1937, and through to the last week of November, was relative peace by Madrid standards.

The venom in Miss H's story is directed mainly against Hemingway who urged her to come on the balcony to see "the beauty of the shelling." Miss H. is a crazy mixed-up kid about Hemingway; she wants us to think she was great buddies with him and that he danced attendance on her yet she cannot stop knifing him. At night, there was nothing to see during a bombardment; phosgene (incendiary) shells were unknown in Spain. Windows were opened against the risk of blast because window glass was irreplaceable. Like the entire population of Madrid, we could tell by the sound of incoming shells whether there was immediate danger, and by the noise of explosions we could gauge where shells were landing and the pattern of the bombardment. Like everyone else we listened carefully. All of us foreigners had as our model of behavior the stoicism and the jokes of the people of Madrid. If there was a bombardment on any night when we were in that apartment we would certainly have been listening from the balcony where Miss H. has us gloating over non-existent fireworks.

If the radio station "was being hit" (p. 87, AUW), no one could have made a broadcast that night. The station was an ordinary almost soundproof room in the diplomatic quarter, the safest part of town. Miss H. cannot have rushed out into a rain of shells to do her superb bit for the Republic at a microphone that was not operational. As a newcomer, Miss H. had a perfect right to "panic" if she was experiencing her first artillery bombardment though not on October 23 when there was none.

But could Miss H. have passed over—without a word—the pointed scream of incoming shells, the explosions—a rumbling roar confined in that stone city, her emotions in the car on the dark deserted streets alone with the only chauffeur in Madrid as brave as John Wayne, her climb through the rubble (the station "being hit" must mean several shells) to reach the microphone where the intermittent thunder of high explosive echoed in that almost soundproof room? Does such modest silence, such a waste of truly dramatic detail sound like our Miss H? That is, if she ever heard the big guns aimed at Madrid.

The only purpose I can see in her story is to heap scorn on the rest of us while displaying her own magnificent courage. "I would have gone into far more dangerous places to get out of that apartment . . . " (p. 88, AUW). Perhaps that was revenge for not having charmed us? Specifically for never having charmed Hemingway? Carlos Baker could not have overlooked so important a woman if she had had any relation to Hemingway's life. Is Miss H. suffering heartburn from an old undigested grudge?

Whose account of that dinner party are you disposed to believe? Mine (nothing much) or Miss Hellman's (high though highly dubious drama)? In my opinion, Miss H. has the *cojones* of a brass monkey.

Here is another apocryphism (p. 90, AUW). "November 4." "Walking back to the hotel, I was shocked to see that a whole block was almost completely destroyed since I had been past it a week before. I stopped in front of what had been a fine nineteenth century house converted to apartments and asked a woman who was standing in the broken doorway when it had been destroyed. She said that *the night before* [my italics] twenty-seven people had been killed and nine wounded." Miss H. also spoke to a man and two children (p. 91, AUW). Had she learned Spanish since arriving in Valencia on October 13? Miss H. describes her perilous entry to and exit from the smashed building and what she saw, in graphic detail. She collected some souvenirs, two china bottles and the daguerreotype of a young girl. I forgot to report that Miss H. gave away a can of beef soup to a seamstress, en route to this dwelling.

There was a vast number of wholly or partially destroyed buildings in Madrid, dating all the way back to the murderous German air raids in the summer of 1936. Miss H. might have explored any of them. She might also have been accompanied by a guide/translator from the Censura, as was usual for passing visitors. The woman in the broken doorway cannot have told Miss H. or a hypothetical translator that "a whole block was almost completely destroyed," or even a portion of a block, on the night of November 3. Surely to God Miss H. would have heard the artillery uproar and surely to God she would have behaved heroically during it. But there was no artillery fire in that October and November, as I am weary of saying, except on the four dates I have listed. Hunger and cold were far worse for the people than high explosives, in the autumn and winter of 1937. Hence Miss H. seeing, in her destroyed house, that "a bowl of limp lettuce was sitting on a chair" (p. 90, AUW) is ludicrous incomprehension. Lettuce, of all improbable unseasonal non-nourishment in an abandoned apartment in Madrid, where the daily sandy bread ration was just over five ounces.

"Valencia, November 6" (p. 91, AUW). "It was nice to come back to Valencia maybe because air raids frighten me less than the nightly bombardments in Madrid." By now I must have made abundantly clear the one confirmed date of the one (and pre-Hellman) air raid on Valencia and the three dates (October 11; 13–14; 21–22) of bombardments in Madrid, thus proving that sentence to be sham and false.

Miss H. has written a great part for herself throughout AUW, with special skill in her Spanish War scenes. She is the shining heroine who overcomes hardship, hunger, fear, danger—down stage center—in a tormented country. The long endurance of the Spanish people and the men who fought to defend the Republic was true heroism. Self-serving apocryphisms on the war in Spain are more repellent to me than any others.

I observed at the beginning of this tome and observe again—there is no harm in making your point twice or as often as you can get away with it—that one clear apocryphal story is good reason for not trusting the other stories you are unable to verify. Questions about the rest of AUW, outside Spain, and even about "Julia," swim in my mind like a shoal of sardines. I am only certain that Miss H. is a wonderful storyteller and writes fast vivid prose. . . .

Hemingway became a shameful embarrassing apocryphiar about himself, which I believe damaged him as a man, but he was not like that in Spain nor in China. Or, since I can only testify to what I know, never in my hearing. He had a fair amount of hyena in him, as he admitted, but he made good jokes and was valuable cheerful company in those wars and no more boring than we all are the rest of the time. In Cuba, in World War Two, I watched with anger the birth and growth of his apocryphisms about the spy factory, the Pilar submarine patrol. As far as I could see, apocryphisms grew like Topsy until I stopped being there to see. Perhaps his own boastful apocryphisms have brought on him the apocryphisms of others that surround his name.

Now, for the first time, this article has obliged me to consult the Hemingway scholars. The eye roams beyond the needed page, and I wish it hadn't. The Hemingway saga, probably swelling with each new book on Hemingway, is bad news. His work sinks beneath the personality cult and the work alone counts, the best work from the beginning through A Farewell to Arms. He was a genius, that uneasy word, not so much in what he wrote (speaking like an uncertified critic) as in how he wrote; he liberated our written language. All writers, after him, owe Hemingway a debt for their freedom whether the debt is acknowledged or not. It is sad that the man's handmade falsehoods—worthless junk, demeaning to the writer's reputation—survive him.

Nothing excuses apocryphism by anyone about anything. No good comes of it. It is cheap and cheapening. The world would be a far far better place if people—especially writers and politicians—stuck to fact or fiction. Not fiction passed off as fact. Literary apocryphiars, it seems to me, confuse and distort the record; political apocryphiars can be fatal. Consider, for instance, the Tonkin Bay story. Alas, the chances for a far better world are as usual slim but we might train ourselves, our heirs and descendants to be wary of all apocryphism.

Notes

1. The lawsuit for one million dollars in libel damage Lillian Hellman brought against Mary McCarthy.

2. All page references to *An Unfinished Woman* are taken from the Bantam Books paperback, U.S. 10th printing, January 1979.

3. All page references to *Pentimento* are taken from Quartet Books paperbacks, U.K., 1980.

4. CBS has no program records as far back as 1937. In spite of the importance Miss H. attached to her broadcast there is unfortunately no mention of it in the *New York Times* for October 24 or 25 but possibly Miss H. got her date wrong.

Who Was Julia?   Alexander Cockburn*

> I think I have always known about my memory: I know when it is to
> be trusted and when some dream or fantasy entered on the life, and the
> dream, the need of dream, led to distortion of what happened. And so I
> knew early that the rampage angers of an only child were distorted night-
> mares of reality. But I trust absolutely what I remember about Julia.
> —*Lillian Hellman*, Pentimento

On February 6, only a few months after the woman who denied having borrowed her life, Muriel Gardiner died at the age of 83 in Princeton, New Jersey. On reading her obituary in the *New York Times* I was once again struck by the oddity of the whole Julia saga and the behavior of Lillian Hellman. How to explain it? I think the life of yet another exceptional woman who died last year may help us through the labyrinth.

But first, Muriel Gardiner. She was heiress to an immense fortune. One of her grandfathers founded the Union Stockyards in Chicago, and the other

*Reprinted with permission from the *Nation*, 23 February 1985, 200–1. © 1985 the *Nation* magazine/The Nation Company, Inc.

started the meatpacking firm of Swift and Company. She attended Wellesley College, studied literature at Oxford University and then went to Vienna and tried to enter analysis with Freud. Although she failed in this plan, she did stay in Vienna to study medicine and psychoanalysis. She married Joseph Buttinger, leader of the Austrian Revolutionary Socialists. As the Nazi tide swelled, she joined the antifascist underground and, with money, false documents and a safe house, helped organize the escape of hundreds of fugitives from Nazism. She was a founder of the International Rescue Committee.

She came back to the United States in 1939. After the war she was a practicing psychoanalyst and assembled the marvelous "Wolfman" papers. She helped establish the Freud Museum in London, in the house to which the Freuds moved from Vienna in 1938. The museum will open next year. One of her legacies is *Children's Express,* which she helped found and fund, and another is *Dissent,* for which she and her husband put up half the starting capital, in 1953, and whose deficits she helped pay off for many years.

Lillian Hellman published *Pentimento,* subtitled *A Book of Portraits,* in 1973, and in one of its stories, "Julia," she describes the eponymous heroine, her friend in childhood and adolescence. She was an heiress who had studied at Oxford before going to Vienna, there becoming a "patient-pupil of Freud"; becoming also a socialist, "sharing her great fortune with anyone who needed it" and getting involved in underground rescue work for fugitives from Nazism.

In 1983 Gardiner published her memoir, *Code Name "Mary."* Her publishers drew attention to the similarities between Hellman's Julia and her own life, most particularly her underground work in Vienna. Gardiner wrote that friends had pointed out these similarities but that she had never met Hellman, though they had shared the same lawyer. Hellman, in turn, asserted that Gardiner was "certainly not the model" for her Julia.

A week after Gardiner's death, a friend of Hellman's told me a story was going around to the effect that just before she died, Muriel Gardiner had confided to William Abrahams, Hellman's official biographer, that she did not, after all, feel she had been the basis for Julia and that her publisher, Yale University Press, had stressed the similarities to draw attention to *Code Name "Mary."* In the two days before I was able to contact Abrahams, I talked to a number of people who knew both Hellman and Gardiner, and after I sat down and reread "Julia," I felt there was a way of looking at the affair that people had so far missed.

Those who are sure in their own minds that Gardiner was the model for Julia and that Hellman, as some of them put it, "stole her life" say flatly that Julia simply could not have been anyone else and that as a historical account, "Julia" fails to hang together. Amid the furor at the time of the publication of *Code Name "Mary,"* Herbert Steiner, head of the Documentation Archive of the Austrian Resistance, said he had looked up the records of the University of Vienna and found Gardiner to be "the only American woman who studied medicine and psychology at the time." He added that friends in the Resistance all certified that events in "Julia" could "have been experienced only by Muriel Gardiner."

But if they never met, how did Hellman know of Gardiner's exploits? They were pretty well known in many circles in New York City, and, furthermore, when she came back to the United States in the fall of 1939, Gardiner shared some property in New Jersey with Wolf Schwabacher. Schwabacher, now dead, was a theatrical lawyer who knew Hellman well, and it was Gardiner's supposition that he had been the bearer of her tale.

William Wright, who is well along in his unofficial life of Hellman—there is yet a third being written by Hilary Mills—says he talked to Gardiner a few months ago: far from feeling that she had been the pawn of publicity-hungry publishers, she told Wright she thought she had let Hellman off too easy. She'd written a letter to Hellman after the publication of *Pentimento,* saying that a lot of friends had told her that she was Julia and asking if it was a composite portrait. Hellman had never replied.

I talked to Hellman's lawyer, Ephraim London, who said that she had once told him who Julia was (not Gardiner) but "I took good care to forget the name." Then I took another look at "Julia." It's a very odd piece of work. The material about smuggling the money to Berlin is labored. Much the strongest part is the evocation of Hellman's adolescent relationship with Julia and of Julia's emotional and physical allure: "I cannot say now that I knew or had ever used the word gentle or delicate or strong, but I did think that night that it was the most beautiful face I had ever seen. . . . I have had plenty of time to think of the love that I had for her, too strong and too complicated to be defined as only the sexual yearnings of one girl for another. And yet certainly that was there."

It was the association of Freud and an attraction between women that reminded me of Bryher and H.D.

In 1927 a woman of enormous wealth flew across the Alps to Vienna to visit Freud, who was excited to hear that she had come to him on an airplane and who accepted with pleasure her gift of a book by Norman Douglas. In the early 1930s she successfully recommended her lover to enter analysis with Freud. In the late 1930s she helped rescue fugitives from Nazism and visited Vienna to that end.

The heiress was an Englishwoman, Winifred Ellerman. She was the daughter of the shipping tycoon Sir John Ellerman, and she later took the name "Bryher," from an island in the Scillys, to escape the association of her family name. In 1918, at the age of 24, she met H.D., the imagist poet Hilda Doolittle, who was then 32. At that time H.D., an American who had gone to Bryn Mawr College and, in 1911, followed Ezra Pound to London, was living in Cornwall. She was looking after her daughter, fathered by Richard Aldington, and getting very near the end of her tether. Bryher took up H.D. and they became lovers. H.D. was known around the Ellerman family house in London as "that woman." Between 1927 and 1933 H.D. helped Bryher edit the film magazine *Close Up,* and in 1933, on Bryher's prompting, began to see Freud. H.D.'s extraordinary evocation of her analysis, *Tribute to Freud,* was published in 1956.

Bryher published two volumes of autobiography. The first, *A Heart to Artemis,* published in 1962, had a passage describing her work in helping refugees from Nazism: "I was the receiving station in Switzerland. It was considered too dangerous for me to enter Germany but I went several times to Vienna and Prague to interview applicants and bring out documents they needed for their visas. . . . I used to smuggle them out in copies of the *Times*. This newspaper was considered so pro-Nazi at the time that its readers were usually unmolested at the frontier." (One of the people Bryher helped was Walter Benjamin, who later committed suicide on the Spanish frontier, fearing he was about to be captured.)

I'm not suggesting something so straightforward as that Bryher was Julia and that Gardiner was not, or even that Hellman knew Bryher personally, any more than she knew Gardiner. It seems to me that much of *Pentimento* is fantasy, in the respectable creative sense of an imaginative working of biographical material. "Julia" is an amalgam of both sexual and heroic fantasies in which Hellman assumes the role of H.D. (her beautiful polar opposite) and renders Gardiner/Bryher as Julia but appropriates some of Julia's heroism for herself. The Julia figure crops up in *An Unfinished Woman* under another name, this time killed in the Vienna riots of 1934, which were described in a long poem by Stephen Spender, quondam lover of Muriel Gardiner.

One of the stranger aspects of Hellman's account of Julia is the savage way the author physically destroys her subject. First, Julia's leg is amputated (neither Gardiner nor Bryher suffered this), and then Hellman describes the body, hacked by Nazi knives, and the slashed and battered face which, in the mortuary, Hellman declines to kiss. This works neither as biography nor as art, and seems to me explicable only as the abrupt rejection and destruction of a fantasy. In the story, Hellman furiously slaps the face of a man who suggests that she and Julia had had a sexual relationship. It is, by the way, worth remembering that *The Children's Hour,* Hellman's first, very successful play, was all about lying and lesbianism. In January 1940 Hellman began seven years of Freudian analysis with Gregory Zilboorg and retained, with intermittent consultations, a deep interest in Freud and psychoanalysis to the end of her life.

There's one more aspect to the *Pentimento* fantasy. Julia tells Hellman she's had a child (" 'Freud told me not to' . . . . the baby seemed to like being called Lilly"), and the story ends with a relative of Julia telling Hellman that he had never heard of such a child. In interviews with Hellman on PBS in 1981, Marilyn Berger pressed Hellman about the fate of this child. Hellman said she had followed the trail to a village in Alsace, only to find that the child had been murdered by the Nazis. Amid tears, she told Berger she was glad, in a way, to have learned that the child had died, since this knowledge diminished her sense of guilt about not having tried to find the child earlier. Hellman herself was childless. Incidentally, H.D.'s daughter, Perdita, was adopted by Bryher and now lives in New York City. Like Hellman, Bryher died last year.

I finally got hold of William Abrahams, the official biographer. It turned out that the story about his meeting with Gardiner was nonsense. He'd never known her—though he once met Stephen Spender in her New York apartment. He didn't want to talk about *Pentimento* "because I was Lillian's editor at the time and I want to preserve my own material zealously until I publish in four or five years. I know a great many things are true. I'm firmly convinced she took money to Berlin and was very brave. Why is she put on the witness stand? The zeal on the part of her detractors is interesting." Finally I asked Abrahams if he knew who Julia was, and after a long pause, he said, "I can't tell you."

I think Hellman told us, in her definition of the word "pentimento." It is a "repenting" by the artist, she wrote, a change of mind: "Perhaps it would be as well to say that the old conception, replaced by a later choice, is a way of seeing and then seeing again. That is all I mean about the people in this book. The paint has aged now and I wanted to see what was there for me once, what is there for me now."

"Lies Like Truth": Lillian Hellman's Autobiographies   Timothy Dow Adams*

> Everyone's memory is tricky and mine's a little trickier than most.
> —Lillian Hellman[1]

Lillian Hellman's four autobiographies embrace several hybrid forms of life-writing in a deliberate effort to thwart the process of identity formation associated with traditional autobiography. Instead of arriving at the end of the autobiographical act with the most current version of herself, she reversed the process, beginning with an "unfinished" self and ending with "maybe," progressing not toward the creation of a monument but toward its deconstruction. Hellman's pattern—yes, no, maybe so—is constantly reflected by her persona's movement, not toward a sense of reconciliation, of finally having gotten down in writing what happened, but increasingly toward a conviction that, as she wrote about her memories in the introduction to *Three* (the collected and annotated version of *An Unfinished Woman*,

*This essay is published here for the first time by permission of the author. Portions will appear in another form in a book-length study entitled "Telling Lies: Lying in Modern American Autobiography," to be published by the University of North Carolina Press.

Pentimento, and *Scoundrel Time*), "often parts of them now seem to have been written by a woman I don't know very well."[2]

Her subtitles confuse her autobiographies' precise generic home. *An Unfinished Woman* is called a "A Memoir," *Pentimento,* "A Book of Portraits," and she refers to those works along with *Scoundrel Time* as "memoir books" in *Maybe,* which is itself subtitled "A Story." In interviews she vehemently denied having written autobiography, maintaining that she chose the word *memoir* because no other term seemed right, because "the word autobiography should be about yourself and should have some space control—when this happened and how it happened and what followed next."[3]

The traditional distinction between autobiography and memoir is expressed by Roy Pascal, who admits that "no clear line can be drawn": "There is no autobiography that is not in some respects a memoir, and no memoir that is without autobiographical information; both are based on personal experience, chronological and reflective. But there is a general difference in the direction of the author's attention. In the autobiography proper, attention is focused on the self, in the memoir or reminiscence on others."[4] To the extent that her books focus on others, Hellman has written memoirs, but with an individual twist. The traditional memoir is often written by a less famous person who tells what it was like to have been an observer of the famous. But Hellman's focus frequently reverses the pattern; she is the famous person observing a series of obscure lives in what Richard Poirier's introduction to *Three* calls a group of "essays in recollection," featuring "a gallery of people nearly anonymous" (viii).

Scoundrel Time, on the other hand, resembles a more traditional memoir, focusing on the famous at an important historical juncture. According to Marcus Billson, the distinction between autobiography and memoir is not the outward or inward focus of narration, but "the length of time of the narration and the dynamic nature of the author's represented self."[5] Although *Scoundrel Time* partly satisfies this definition, it strays from the world of memoir because its emphasis is finally not on Joseph McCarthy or Richard Nixon, nor on the historic figures who usually delineate the genre, but on Hellman herself.

An Unfinished Woman begins as classic autobiography, with the traditional recitation of its author's time and place of birth, parents, and childhood memories, all told in straightforward chronological fashion. But the narrative is broken in chapter 8 with the introduction of large sections extracted, apparently unedited, from diaries. If the first two-thirds of *An Unfinished Woman* is autobiography supplemented by modified diary entries, the last third consists of what she refers to in *Pentimento* as portraits. Like a traditional biographer, Hellman employs letters, newspaper clippings, magazine pieces, personal interviews, her own diaries and those of others, and her "writer's book"; yet her choice of subjects (often obscure people about whom facts are impossible to obtain, for whom a logical story is impossible to tell), her repeatedly expressed doubt of the authenticity of her portraits, and the fact that each of her subjects is intimately related to her—all these turn her biographies into partial autobiographies. Richard Poirier remarks that one of her favorite stories was "Bartleby the Scrivener," and that Hellman once contemplated writing a biography of Melville while a student at Columbia (xx). And like the lawyer-narrator of Melville's story, Hellman combines story, biography, autobiography, memoir, and obituary into a personal form of life-writing that best exposes the enigmatic nature of both life and the attempt to record it. Her frustration, like that narrator's, in putting life onto paper tells as much about the biographer as about the subject.

Like Gertrude Stein's, Hellman's autobiographical writing produced a series of "manifestos" labeling the author a liar. The attacks on Hellman's veracity originally focused on her version of events remembered in *Scoundrel Time* (see, for example, Sidney Hook's *Encounter* attack[6]) but broadened considerably with publication in the *Paris Review* of Martha Gellhorn's "On Apocryphism," a detailed, bitterly humorous rebuttal to *An Unfinished Woman* prompted by an interview with Stephen Spender in an earlier issue.[7] Spender himself was among those charging that Hellman's portrait of Julia in *Pentimento* was not only fictional but also based on the life of Muriel Gardiner, author of an autobiography entitled *Code Name "Mary."* (According to William Wright, Hellman's unofficial biographer, Mary McCarthy—Hellman's longtime foe—pointed out to Gellhorn and Spender certain discrepancies in *Pentimento*.[8])

Samuel McCracken's " 'Julia' and Other Fictions by Lillian Hellman" argues that Julia was indeed modeled on Gardiner and maintains that the eventual portrayal of Hellman's reputation "will tell us a good deal about the health, intellectual no less than moral, of our literary establishment."[9] In "The Life and Death of Lillian Hellman," which sounds like the title of a biography, Hilton Kramer accuses Hellman of being a "shameless liar" whose *Scoundrel Time* was "one of the most poisonous and dishonest testaments ever written by an American author."[10] For Kramer, the reviews of Hellman's autobiographies, along with the politically and personally motivated writing against her by such authors as William Phillips, Diana Trilling, and William F. Buckley, plus the Gellhorn-Gardiner-Spender-McCracken arguments, all constitute "a sweeping exposé of the falsehoods that formed the very fabric of Hellman's autobiographical writings."[11] Like the arguments of other Hellman antagonists, Kramer's charges stem partially from his misunderstanding of autobiographical truth, and from his confusion of the interrelated terms *fiction, nonfiction, memoir,* and *autobiography.*

Confusing claims emerge from the key words used in these attacks: Gellhorn sees Hellman as an "apocryphiar," Spender implies she is a fiction writer and a plagiarist, and Kramer and Hook and other anticommunists of the Right escalate the literary charges one turn by naming her a liar and a perjurer. In contrast, left-wing anticommunists with literary roots, like Diana Trilling, correctly see part of the conflict as a problem in defining literary rather than political terms. Trilling considers *Scoundrel Time* "a narrative that should have commanded attention as a work of autobiography, one among several volumes in which Miss Hellman, an imaginative writer of established gift, looks back upon her past, [but which] is being read as a political revelation innocent of bias."[12] Throughout her counterargument, Trilling bases her remarks on the assumption that *Scoundrel Time* should be treated within its literary genre, "if Miss Hellman's narrative is to be properly assessed as historical reporting."[13]

The variety of generic labels attached to Hellman's personal narratives becomes more than a problem in academic classification if A. O. J. Cockshut's distinction between reading autobiography and memoir is valid:

> There are two ways of reading autobiography. The first . . . is to take it as a work of art, to judge it from within by the standards which an actual reading of it suggests. Thus one may note interior inconsistencies or falsities of tone, but relegate external evidence of untruth or exaggeration to mere scholarly footnotes. Or one can read it as a historical record which it is right to criticize in the light of the available evidence from all sources. It would seem, on the whole, that autobiography lends itself naturally to the first kind of reading, and memoir to the second.[14]

Distinctions between historical reporting and personal narrative, as well as between true and false, fiction and nonfiction, are inherently complicated, without reversals of previous political positions, the encroachment of time, deliberate and accidental falsity of memory, and the differing requirements of veracity in various genres. Halfway through *Maybe* Hellman wrote: "It goes without saying that in their memoirs people should try to tell the truth as they see it or else what's the sense? Maybe time blurs or changes things for them. But you try, anyway."[15] But this assertion of trustworthiness—which includes a rhetorical appeal to veracity by admitting the possibility of failure of execution of the intention to tell the truth—occurs within a book that is labeled "A Story." *Maybe*'s generic situation is further confused by its physical appearance as a book: the standard paperback edition continues the color scheme of *Three*—black cover, title in gold accented with red stripes—making it seem to be part of the same package. Hellman posits her attempt at telling the truth in her autobiographical trilogy as being different from what she had done in *Maybe*:

> In the three memoir books I wrote, I tried very hard for the truth. I did try, but here I don't know much of what really happened and never tried to find out. In addition to the ordinary deceptions that you and others make in your life, time itself makes time fuzzy and meshes truth with half truth . . . . What I have written is the truth as I saw it, but the truth as I saw it, of course, doesn't have much to do with the truth. (*M*,50–51)

Hellman's distinction between her subjective version of truth and the absolute truth of "what really happened," her contrast between the first three books and the last in terms of "history" and "personal history," is unnecessary according to Billson, who persuasively argues that all *memoirs* are subjective: "The memorialist's real intention, despite all claims to being an objective observer, is to use this source for subjective ends—to embody his own moral vision of the past. It is not the memorialist's desire to present men and events as they were (although he invariably thinks he is doing so), but rather to represent them as they appeared to him, as he experienced them, and as he remembered them."[16]

The contentions of her most antagonistic critics that Hellman is, at best, a tricky and disingenuous simplifier, at worst, a fraudulent liar should be addressed with the understanding that her four autobiographical works are literary documents, works of art that combine a variety of life-writing's forms (autobiography, biography, memoir, and diary). The major charges against her autobiographies can be summarized: she obscures her life by chronological discontinuity and a tendency toward reticence; she lies by omission because of her elliptical style and her too-meticulous attention to surface finish; she is falsely modest and naive, manipulating her position in history so that her political faults are diminished, her personal heroism augmented; she misrepresents her historical position before the House Committee on Un-American Activities (HCUA) and the split between anticommunists and anti-anticommunists; and most damning, she makes herself look heroic by claiming to aid "Julia" when actually she took the idea for "Julia" from another person's life. Although there are times in her autobiographies when Hellman is less than forthcoming, misleading, annoyingly moralistic and exasperatingly mean spirited, ultimately her autobiographies are exceptionally authentic portraits of America's greatest woman playwright, a woman whose life story has significance far beyond its literal events.

Because her major adverse critics have been political analysts, writing with a historian's approach, rather than literary critics well versed in contemporary autobiographical theory, her autobiographical writing has generally been misinterpreted, primarily because those who have criticized her have misunderstood her tone, failed to consider her four books as one unit, and overlooked the subtitles of her autobiographical performances. Those who have written favorably of Hellman's memoirs are primarily novelists and playwrights like Marsha Norman, who said of Hellman, "I am not interested in the degree to which she told the literal truth. The literal truth is, for writers, only half the story."[17]

AN "UNFINISHED WOMAN"

You are a gallant little liar. And I thank you for it.
                                        —Kurt Müller in *Watch on the Rhine*

For some, the "unfinished" in the title of Hellman's first memoir suggests the missing parts of her life that were to be recorded in later memoirs. Others, praising her candor, gloss "unfinished" to mean "unvarnished," the direct statements of an author who never went to finishing school. For critics like Martha Gellhorn "unfinished" would imply incomplete, inaccurate, untrustworthy.

Gellhorn's reading of *An Unfinished Woman* depends upon point-by-point refutation of virtually everything Hellman wrote about the Spanish Civil War and her relationship with Ernest Hemingway—who at the time had been married to Gellhorn—and upon cruelly witty attacks on the Hellman persona. ("Goodness to Betsy . . . What an important lady. How marvelous for Miss Hellman to be Miss Hellman"; "If Miss Hellman's beauty had matched her brains she would have been a more cuddly personality."[18]) Much of Gellhorn's argument is based on differences between *An Unfinished Woman* and *Pentimento* in terms of dates and places.

"What a word is truth," writes Hellman in her preface to the reprinted version of *An Unfinished Woman*. "I tried in these books to tell the truth. I did not fool with facts. But, of course, that is a shallow definition of truth. I see now, in rereading, that I kept much from myself, not always, but sometimes" (9). The words "fool with facts" are ambiguous; they could mean, "I didn't deliberately alter any facts so far as I'm aware" or, alternately, "I didn't bother to check up on facts, to worry much about exactness of date and location." Throughout all four of her autobiographies, she reiterates that she is not striving for fidelity to fact. Her books are replete with disclaimers: "perhaps," "maybe," " 'in those days,' I have written, and will leave here," "that's the way I remember it," and, of course, the "however" that ends the first book.

In Gellhorn's reading of *An Unfinished Woman*, Hellman is falsely noble, too much "the shining heroine who overcomes hardship, hunger, fear, danger—down stage center—in a tormented country."[19] But those who see the Hellman persona in these terms misapprehend the ironic, tongue-in-cheek tone she so often adopts when trying to hide her embarrassment and ineptness, while simultaneously maintaining the detached, unemotional, tough-guy stance she so admired in Hammett. In a voice that is not always successful, she often pretends to be pretending, as when she opens her "biography" of Hammett by writing, "And so this will be no attempt at a biography of Samuel Dashiell Hammett, born in St. Mary's County, Maryland, on May 27, 1894" (276).

In one sense, Hellman *is* right; the chapter that follows is not biography since it follows too closely the "Bartleby the Scrivener" pattern, focusing as much on Hellman as on Hammett. The piece in question is not really biography because it was first presented as an introduction to Hammett's collected writing, and in its appearance in *An Unfinished Woman* it takes on many of the characteristics of an elegiac eulogy. And yet it *is* biography, both because it begins with biography's customary facts about the birth of its subject, and because in writing it as she has Hellman validates Hammett's claim that her biography of him—in a manner similar to Stein's *The Autobiography of Alice B. Toklas*—"would turn out to be the history of Lillian Hellman with an occasional reference to a friend called Hammett" (276).

Hellman's portrayal of herself in *An Unfinished Woman*, like the Henry

Adams of *The Education of Henry Adams,* is the portrayal of a relative failure. Much of what Gellhorn sees as boasting self-importance is actually intended as ironic self-deprecation. As a young girl, Hellman assimilated certain moral stances: "I was taught, also, that if you gave, you did it without piety and didn't boast about it" (28). This inherited trait is combined in the author with Hammett's characteristically understated code: "Hammett's form of boasting was always to make fun of trouble or pain" (283).

Hammett, who once worked in advertising, summarized his calculated, understated advertising style as follows: "Meiosis . . . has nothing to do with modesty or moderation in speech as such. . . . It is a rhetorical trick, the employment of understatement, not to deceive, but to increase the impression made on the reader or hearer. In using it the object is, not to be believed, but to be disbelieved to one's advantage."[20] Together these related forms of inverted bragging became important ingredients in the Hellman-Hammett persona, resulting in a unique form of nonboasting about boasting, making mainly negative claims for personal bravery. Hellman's meiosis is intended, not to deceive, but to underplay her naturally bold personality. As Pascal tells us, in contrast to overwriting, "the untruth of under-writing is of course much more bearable, since it is allied with qualities of modesty or shyness that in their turn win our sympathy."[21]

Hellman is aware of her understating tendency "to take a bad time, block out the good times, until any success became an accident and failure seemed the only truth" (210) but she is apparently not aware that her self-deprecating sometimes comes across as the reverse. For instance, Gellhorn cites Hellman's explanation for not going to the press office in Valencia, although asked: "I . . . had two telephone calls . . . suggesting I come back to the office and meet people who might like to meet me," writes Hellman, "and have not gone. This is nothing new: part the need to make people come to me, part not wanting to seem important" (95). These words, from a diary entry written thirty-two years earlier, were included to amplify the author's general presentation of herself, not as an heroic figure, but as an inept radical, unsure of how to act.

"Not wanting to seem important" is followed in the passage attacked by Gellhorn with the following words, which Gellhorn omits: "But then why have I come here, what will I see, or do, what good will I be to these people as I eat their food or use their cars or lie on a bed reading Julian Green? I settle it by going for a walk" (95). The tone is intended half-ironically. It is the same tone used throughout Hammett's *The Thin Man,* in which Nora Charles, who was based on Lillian Hellman, is always in the way of the real detective, stumbling onto clues accidentally, solving part of the mystery while pretending to be asleep.

A central reason for the attacks on Hellman's veracity, however, lies in her critics' failure to see that the "unfinished" of the title is meant to suggest the author's sense of herself as unfinished politically, awkward and incomplete in situation after situation. Throughout *An Unfinished Woman,* Hellman undercuts her effectiveness through a repeated pattern of accidents and sicknesses. Ironically, she uses the traditional device of Hollywood to signify heroism for women—the twisted ankle. Like so many movie heroines being carried in the strong arms of a man from burning buildings, Hellman is constantly awkward, stumbling through her autobiography, twisting her ankle just at the wrong time. Her first memory, as a child, of the persistent anger she so often attributes to herself—what other people see as the quality that makes her a "difficult woman"—is undercut by an ankle injury: "I tried to get up from the couch, but one ankle turned and I sat down again, knowing for the first time the rampage that could be caused in me by anger. . . . I knew that soon after I was moving up the staircase, that I slipped and fell a few steps . . . " (31). This episode, like so many to follow, ends in her vomiting.

Back in Spain, she records in her diary the following description of her actions following an aerial bombardment: "(The planes had been around all afternoon and the mess was new and looked hot.) The filthy indignity of destruction, I thought, is the real immorality, as I slipped and turned my ankle" (99). Questioned at a dinner party about the passionate emotion she had derived from her stay in Spain—emotion she said she had "little right to . . . from so short and relatively safe a visit" (130)—she responds with the same pattern, "My life, all I felt in Spain, is going out in drip-drops, in nonsense, and I was suddenly in the kind of rampage anger that I have known all my life" (132). As a result, she "slipped to the floor, had a painful ankle, and didn't care" (132). On this occasion, her ankle is broken, and years later, en route to Moscow, she notes, "I turned my once-broken ankle in the ice ruts" (141).

In addition to the repeated ankle accidents, as well as many other physical injuries, including the story in "On Reading Again" about falling from a taxi and cutting her knee (6), Hellman's picture of herself in action is often accompanied by humiliating physical details—tears, excessive sweat, constant dizziness, and vomiting. She is constantly clumsy, falling off running boards of cars (107), "falling over and over again" while walking in new boots in Moscow (194), stupidly giving away her position on the Russian front line by allowing the sun to reflect off field glasses (170), confessing "two minor accidents and once I killed a rabbit" while driving home to Hollywoodland (70), and always depicting herself acting incoherently: "as others grow more intelligent under stress, I grow heavy, as if I were an animal on a chain" (166).

Because Hellman reminds her readers that much of her heroic stance when faced with fear is a pretense, she signals that her frequent clumsiness is not ironic, is not meant to glorify herself. From the first paragraph of *An Unfinished Woman*, when she says "even as a small child I disliked myself for the fear and showed off against it" (13), through her depiction of her generation as being "pretend cool" (45), to her admission that in terms of money she "cared too much, in fact, that I pretended not to care" (190), Lillian Hellman repeatedly undercuts the Hammettesque hard-boiled detective style so often attributed to her. Caught between the masculine standard of heroic action, especially at time of war—the Hammett/Hemingway grace under pressure—and its traditional feminine counterpart, fainting and feistiness, Hellman adopts a personal style somewhere in between, an impassioned form of action in which, angry beyond control, she is hampered by traditional feminine physical weakness with a masculine twist, a literal turn or trope: an ankle turned, not out of weakness but in anger, almost deliberately, in an attempt to demonstrate her ability to fluctuate between the male and female worlds.

Virtually every published interview with Hellman reports that her physical bearing was surprisingly feminine. Although she pictures her own body movements as stumbling and jerky, she is seen by others of both sexes as being, unconsciously, gracefully seductive. In a *New Yorker* profile Margaret Case Harriman called her "neither cute nor tough. For a woman with militant undercurrents, her surface behavior is more often mild than not, and she is genuinely feminine to a degree that borders on the wacky."[22]

In actual life Hellman seems to have combined the apparently contradictory traits of physical gracefulness and a lack of coordination that rendered her clumsy in numerous physical activities. She is described as unable to open a safe or shoot a gun: aiming at a flying duck, she hit a wild lilac bush; aiming at a large deer right in front of her, she hit a dogwood tree behind her. Her sense of geography is often amiss, as is her sense of direction. Essential to understanding the tone of *An Unfinished Woman*, as well as her other autobiographies, is a realization of this combination of grace and awkwardness, a combination that is paralleled in Hellman's personality and that often manifests itself in an apparently boastful tone when modesty is intended, a form of self-mockery that sometimes appears to be the opposite, a character trait that renders her an unfinished rather than completed woman.

"MY JULIA": *PENTIMENTO*

> Harke newes, O envy, thou shalt heare descry'd
> My Julia; who as yet was ne'r envy'd.
> To vomit gall in slander, swell her vaines
> With calumny, that hell it selfe disdaines,
> Is her continuall practice; does her best . . .
>
> —John Donne, "To Julia"

Pentimento acts as the missing half of the first autobiography, or its subtext; it fills in gaps and provides reasons for their initial existence, but retains the earlier book's mistrust of memory. In using this painterly term, combined with the subtitle "A Book of Portraits," Hellman emphasizes the biographical rather than the autobiographical nature of *Pentimento*. If biography is to portrait as autobiography is to self-portrait, then her title/subtitle combination raises this question: What would the painterly analogy be for memoir? One possibility might be the Claude-glass, a device from the romantic period in England that allowed the user to capture in reflection a picturesque scene resembling a studied, panoramic landscape painting. The Claude-glass "was a black convex mirror held in such a way above one's shoulder that it could capture the reflection of the countryside just passed."[23] Another answer might be a photograph of an artist in the act of painting, something like the picture labeled "Pleasantville" included in *Three*. This photograph, taken by Hammett, shows Hellman looking at herself in a mirror, neither meeting her own gaze, nor focusing on either her real or her mirror image, emblematic perhaps of her repeated statement that a psychiatrist told her "something very revealing. . . . I look at myself as though I'm a total stranger."[24] And in *Pentimento* she has managed to produce portraits that continually reflect on the photographer, self-portraits in a convex mirror.

As in most of Hellman's work, she uses an artistic term in a metaphorically individual way. In the world of art history, *pentimento* suggests an effort by the artist to cover a portion of the original painting, to obliterate a mistake. The artist has "repented" in the act of creation, realized the error, and apparently hidden it from view. The discovery of pentimenti represents an invasion of the artistic process, a failure of the medium to convey the message, an accidental parallel to the use of the Xerox machine to determine a painting's authenticity.

In contrast, Hellman achieves a kind of reverse pentimento by simultaneously layering old and new paint, deliberately exposing the pentimenti behind her portraits. Where a painter repents at failure and covers it up, Hellman repents at having covered up failure. Instead of realizing an error and attempting to hide it, she deliberately creates a context in which both old and new coexist. Examples include her consistent pattern of mixed tenses, such as "the letter *said*, says now" (311), or "I thought, I think now" (511), and her repeated use of extended parenthetical statements that undercut the sentences they follow. In one sense Hellman's diaries and writer's book are the original works of art that over time have come to seem inaccurate (hence her frequent comments about their untrustworthiness), but the errors have been superimposed rather than composed, though sometimes one diary entry is quoted within another. Hellman's pentimento comparison is not meant to refer so much to the autobiographical act; for her, pentimento becomes a metaphor for memory, an analogy to the particular difficulty of artistically remembering a life, telling the truth despite memory's unreliability.

Because her books are nonchronological, crossing and recrossing the same time period, sometimes the same events, Hellman (like the Nabokov of *Speak, Memory*, who writes "I like to fold my magic carpet, after use, in such a way as to superimpose one part of the pattern on another"[25]) relies on documents such as Bethe's partially legible letter, its pages torn in the folds, to compose her multiple redactions. In book after book, including the author's comments and comments on comments, she eventually demonstrates the pentimento of her memory. For *Pentimento, An Unfinished Woman* acts as a pentimento, the original lines having been covered by the second memoir, just as *Scoundrel Time*'s version of the HCUA's effects on Hellman's life partially covers up the earlier versions given in the first two memoirs.

Hellman's pentimento technique reaches its conclusion in *Maybe* where she repents, not that she has revealed too much in her memoirs, but that she has covered up the original lines, pretended that her memory was more precise, more trustworthy than she now realizes: *"There is a light behind you certainly, but it . . . seems shadowed or masked with an unknown fabric"* (*M*, 42). In this description of a veiled light, Hellman echoes Nabokov's description of memory's uncertainty: "The individual mystery remains to tantalize the memoirist. Neither in environment nor in heredity can I find the exact instrument that fashioned me, the anonymous roller that pressed upon my life a certain intrinsic watermark whose unique design becomes visible when the lamp of art is made to shine through life's foolscap."[26]

In transferring the pentimento concept from painting to writing, Nabokov emphasizes another aspect of the autobiographer's use of the painter's metaphor. For an autobiographer the false starts and rough drafts, which sometimes become available to researchers in special collections of libraries, are something like pentimenti. But for a writer like Hellman, pentimento can also be thought of in literary terms from two completely different periods. The first is a palimpsest, "a writing surface . . . which has been used twice or more for manuscript purposes. . . . With material so used a second time, it frequently happened that the earlier script either was not completely erased or that, with age, it showed through the new.[27]

The second literary example of pentimento is found in the writing of Heidegger and Derrida. For both philosopher and literary-linguistic theorist, the concept of putting a word under erasure, signified by printing with x's superimposed, is clearly explained by Gayatri Chakravorty Spivak, in her "Translator's Preface" to Derrida's *Of Grammatology:* "Now we begin to see how Derrida's notion of 'sous rature' differs from that of Heidegger's. Heidegger's ~~Being~~ might point at an inarticulable presence. Derrida's ~~trace~~ is the mark of the absence of a presence, an always already absent present, of the lack at the origin that is the condition of thought and experience."[28] For Hellman then, a pentimento is a personal palimpsest, a Heideggerian metaphor for the self whose integrity she is simultaneously proud and scornful of, an ambivalent self most markedly displayed in the Julia portrait.

Samuel McCracken's " 'Julia' and Other Fictions by Lillian Hellman" contends that extensive research into the memoirs raises grave doubts about Hellman's credibility, especially because she "manipulated millions of readers and moviegoers into admiring her as an ethical exemplar, and as a ruthlessly honest writer."[29] That McCracken uses "fictions" in his title suggests the apparent equation of *fiction* with *lie*. It is one thing to claim that "Julia" is a fiction, another to claim, as he eventually does, that Hellman has plagiarized an actual person's life. Although Hellman admits that she uses "a lot of principles of fiction" in her personal narratives, she is insistent that she did not alter essential facts and that "Julia" is a true story.

Because Hellman initially transformed her personal experiences into drama—a literary form that is not susceptible to the usual fiction/nonfiction dichotomy—her dramatic story of Julia in a nonfictional memoir results in a particularly problematic situation, especially since Hellman admits that the character Kurt Müller in *Watch on the Rhine* "was, of course, a form of Julia" (489). Part of McCracken's attack stems from unfulfilled expectations concerning autobiography, the nature of which Paul John Eakin so aptly describes in a theater metaphor: "When we settle into the theatre of autobiography, what we are ready to believe—and what most autobiographers encourage us to expect—is that the play we witness is a historical one, a largely faithful and unmediated reconstruction of events that took place long ago, whereas in reality the play is that of the autobiographical act itself, in which the materials of the past are shaped by memory and imagination to serve the needs of present consciousness."[30]

Basically, those who attack the Julia section of *Pentimento* make two arguments: first, "Julia" does not ring true; and second, while Hellman may have had "Julia" as a childhood friend, the story of Hellman's carrying money to Berlin for antifascist purposes is a fabrication because "Julia" is actually based on American psychoanalyst Muriel Gardiner, whose own autobiography, *Code Name "Mary,"* recounts *her* life as an underground anti-Nazi fighter in Vienna.

The major point of the Julia episode is not, as her critics seem to believe, to turn Lillian Hellman into a brave, heroic radical who risks her life for the antifascist cause. Part of Hellman's interest is to mock her actions by presenting them with comic overtones. She is not a character in a spy novel; she is a character in an autobiography who remembers the entire incident, like so many of her stories of evil, in an ironic, half-comic way, which is not to suggest that she is less than serious.

Essential to the story is her lack of understanding of what was happening. She wants to contrast her own inept bungling—her failure to recognize how safe she really was, and her lack of a sense of direction (politically as well as geographically)—with Julia's genuine commitments and sacrifices. Julia allowed her friend to experience a safely controlled version of political espionage—a grown-up version of the playacting they had indulged in as girls—in an effort to spur Hellman into giving up playwriting for radical action, and because Julia wanted to say farewell to a friend and provide a protector for her child.

Hellman's detractors focus on inconsistencies of travel accounts and street names in both *Pentimento* and the earlier sections of *An Unfinished Woman*, which present roughly parallel versions. To those who knew Hellman's total lack of geographic awareness—as related in John Hersey's tribute when she received the MacDowell Medal, or Dashiell Hammett's story of her repeatedly getting lost on her own Pleasantville farm—the picture of her clumsy foray into underground activity rings true. Attempts to pin down specific dates and names in a book of portraits ignore Hellman's clear warnings: "I have changed most of the names"; and "whenever in the past I wrote about that journey, I omitted the story of my trip through Berlin because I did not feel able to write about Julia" (441). In the additions included in *Three* she explains further that she changed street names and addresses at the suggestion of her lawyers. That she chose to present "Julia" in *An Unfinished Woman* as "Alice," or that the "Anne-Marie" and "Sammy" of *Pentimento* are called "Marie-Louise" and "Hal" in the first book, further indicates that the authenticity of the story, what it tells us about Lillian Hellman, should not be determined by the literal accuracy of its nouns. Hellman herself admits to having accidentally confused the issue because she could no longer remember which names she changed, which are original. It makes little sense to question an autobiographer's veracity because of nominal inconsistencies when the author labels her work a portrait and warns that names have been changed, not only to protect the innocent, but also because one of Hellman's most consistent moral positions is her repeated refusal to name names.

The second major argument, that Julia is based on Muriel Gardiner's autobiography, is considerably more complex. She had been an American medical student in Vienna; was both a student and a patient with Dr. Ruth Mack Brunswick, a pupil and colleague of Freud's; worked underground for the Social Democrats; and eventually married Joseph Buttinger, a socialist leader and later author of *In The Twilight of Socialism*, a history of Austrian socialism in the 1930s.[31]

When *Pentimento* was published, Gardiner wrote to Hellman, asking about the coincidences, but received no reply, which is not surprising given that her letter, however polite, implied plagiarism and included the words, "I hope you don't find this letter an intrusion. There is no need to answer it."[32] Hellman later remarked, "Miss Gardiner may have been the model for someone else's Julia, but she was certainly not the model for my Julia."[33]

In his published *Journals* Stephen Spender makes a curiously contradictory claim about the Gardiner controversy. He first calls "Julia" "fiction written in autobiographical form with a narrator who purports to be Hellman"; but once he has actually read *Pentimento* he writes, "Some of the events described and the general idea . . . are presumably taken from Muriel's life, but the character bears little resemblance to Muriel."[34] Spender, who was also accused by Martha Gellhorn of being an apocryphiar, is a biased witness. His *Journals* are dedicated to Gardiner who was his lover in Vienna, as recorded both in Gardiner's and his own autobiographies. The whole issue of names is further confused because Muriel Gardiner, known by the underground name "Mary" and later "Elizabeth" and "Gerda," is called "Elizabeth" in Spender's autobiography. There are other discrepancies between Spender's account of his life with Gardiner and her account, including his claim that she had twice been married when they met, which contradicts her mention of only one marriage in *Code Name "Mary."*

Though Spender only claims that Hellman fictionalizes Gardiner's life—not in itself a dishonest action, especially for a playwright whose first production, *The Children's Hour*, was based on an historic case—most damaging of all is Gardiner's research, which includes a statement from Dr. Herbert Steiner, director of the Documentation Archives of the Austrian Resistance, stressing that no records show any other American women "deeply involved in the Austrian anti-fascist or anti-Nazi underground."[35] To this charge Hellman has answered, "underground socialist workers don't keep archives."[36]

Because the Hellman Collection at the University of Texas has been closed to all researchers except William Abrahams, Hellman's literary executor, it is impossible to determine the exact answer to this controversy, but it is possible to speculate. One immediate answer may be that Julia lied to Hellman. Moreover, Gardiner, like all autobiographers, admits to memory lapses. She is not certain in which year she met Freud, nor whether she actually met his mother or if she saw her only in her "mind's eye," although meeting Freud, not to mention his mother, would seem fairly memorable for a psychoanalyst. Gardiner remarks that she "was never really part of the psychoanalytic community until my last years in Vienna."[37] Throughout her book, she mentions that few people were aware of *her* involvement in underground activities and that she was surprised to discover the involvement of acquaintances.

Another explanation lies in the nature of Gardiner's politics. She was deeply involved in *socialist* anti-Nazi activity, but highly suspicious of *communist* anti-Nazi endeavors, a fact which makes more sense out of Hellman's claim that she was reluctant to reveal Julia's name because she was "not sure that even now the Germans like their premature anti-Nazis" (401). The term "Premature anti-Fascist," or PAF, is connected, as McCracken observes, with those "associated with the *Daily Worker* and other communist and procommunist publications."[38] Hellman's wariness seems retrospectively less paranoid in light of Mary McCarthy's 1985 suggestion that Hellman was "an operative for the KGB," an echo of an earlier implication in McCarthy's short story "The Perfect Host," in which a semifictional McCarthy accuses a semifictional Hellman of being a spy for the Soviets.[39]

Another way of explaining the entire Julia controversy, then, might be to argue that in a situation where names and nationalities are constantly being altered for reasons of politics and survival, Gardiner either did not know she knew Julia, or was not aware of her because Julia was working for the communist underground to which Gardiner was antithetic. A less historical and more psychological approach to the problem has also been suggested or assumed by a number of commentators. Spender, among others, sees Hellman as writing fiction, but apparently overlooks the possibility that she adopted the device he admits to using in his own autobiography, where characters "are portrayals of types and not of real personalities."[40] Gardiner first thought Julia a composite portrait, and Hellman's portrayal of Julia as Kurt Müller in *Watch on the Rhine* opens the possibility that the childhood friend—called Alice in *An Unfinished Woman*—and the adult Julia were two different people, one female, the other male, combined by Hellman, not just to protect her memory and to assuage her guilt over having told Julia's story (which she believed would not have pleased her friend), but also as a psychological projection of her lifelong need for an heroic other against whom she could measure her own lack of political commitment.

McCracken observes that Freudians will have much to make of the fact that "having inserted Alice/Julia into the narrative of her own life, Miss Hellman kills her off—in *An Unfinished Woman* in 1934, in *Pentimento* four years later (after first mutilating her by the loss of a leg)."[41] Another who sees Julia in Freudian terms is Alexander Cockburn, who notes that the Julia controversy reminds him of yet another wealthy American woman connected to Freud and involved with rescuing political refugees from the Nazi *Anschluss* in Vienna—the poet H.D.[42] As Janice Robinson notes in her biography of Hilda Doolittle, "H.D.'s whole orientation during the thirties had been antifascist, antitotalitarian, and anti-Hitler."[43] Robinson notes of H.D. and her lover, Bryher (Winifred Ellerman), that they were involved in funding the Jewish emigration from Austria and Germany and were instrumental in helping Freud escape.[44]

Although Bryher was British, H. D. was an American, and together they constitute another indication that Gardiner was not aware of everyone working underground against the Nazis, since neither Bryher nor H.D. appears in *Code Name "Mary,"* even though Bryher's 1962 autobiography, *A Heart to Artemis,* reports her presence in Vienna. Cockburn's argument is not that Julia was Bryher or H. D. or some combination of the two, though he might be interested to know that H. D.'s name in her self-described *roman à clef, Bid Me To Live,* is Julia.[45] Instead Cockburn suggests that much of *Pentimento* creatively reworks biography. 'Julia' becomes "an amalgam of both sexual and heroic fantasies in which Hellman assumes the role of H. D. (her beautiful polar opposite) and renders Gardiner/Bryher as Julia but appropriates some of Julia's heroism for herself."[46]

Cockburn's linking of Julia/Hellman with Bryher/H. D. also brings up the question of homosexuality, which acts as a subtext to the whole controversy. Hellman writes that she was angered when "Anne-Marie's" brother "Sammy" drunkenly remarks that "everybody knew about Julia and me" (420), apparently a reference to lesbianism. There is a hint of such a relationship later when Hellman notes, "I have had plenty of time to think about the love I had for her, too strong and too complicated to be defined as only the sexual yearnings of one girl for another—and certainly that was there" (414).

However deep the homosexual connection might have been, it provides another reason why Hellman deliberately obfuscated the story. Although Hellman asserts that her relationship with Julia did not include a physical aspect, Spender writes that "the heroism of Julia is partly a device for flattering herself since she portrays herself as Julia's dearest friend, in fact lover."[47] Pauline Kael, in reviewing the movie version, implies lesbianism when she writes, "the friendship between Hellman and Julia was obviously the emotional basis—the original material for *The Children's Hour*."[48] This last is an interesting observation for several reasons: *The Children's Hour* at first looks like the story of a "big lie"—a child maliciously labels the main characters lesbians—but at the end we discover that unknown to one of the women, the other *was* apparently a lesbian, and the lie turned out to be true, especially complicated since many later saw the play as an allegory, not for homosexuality, but for the whole McCarthy era. Lillian Hellman's sexual preferences appear considerably more ambiguous, adding another layer of obfuscation to her whole autobiographical performance.

Cockburn and Spender, among others, do not see that the story of Julia is the usual story of Hellman's inability to understand what has happened, even as it is happening, the story of her difficulty in understanding what she means because nurses, hotel clerks, telephone operators, doctors, and others all speak in foreign languages and in cryptic ways. Hellman's story is not so much a record of Julia's bravery as it is a record of her own characteristic inability to resolve the mysteries of the lives to which she is attracted, or to reconcile the shifting political movements that made Stalin and Hitler allies at one moment, Russia and America allies at another, followed by a period of bitter renunciation of each other—all of which is embodied in the shifting grounds of Julia's identity and such irreconcilable facts as John Von Zimmer's alliance with Julia at one moment in Vienna, his marriage to "Anne-Marie"at another.

The inability to "finish" the Julia story is reflective of dozens of stories in her four autobiographies in which Lillian Hellman realizes she has no way to trace someone from her past because she has lost the address, forgotten the name, or the person has unexpectedly died: Horace Liveright, Sergei Eisenstein, the Russian captain who reads American novels, Pascal (the young Frenchman with whom she comes out of Spain), and Julia's daughter, Lillian. That this pattern is important to Hellman is reinforced by the stories of Arthur Cowan and Sarah Cameron, both of whom lead contradictory, illusory lives that end ambiguously. She needed to present the Julia episode as she did; for all its confusion, inaccuracy, incompleteness, possible fictive components, the most telling aspect of the story resides in the fact that at age sixty-seven Lillian Hellman felt compelled to write the story so as to deliberately point up its shadowy "unfinished" nature. True to the unfinished pattern of her books, she died before her McCarthy suit came to trial.

NOT NAMING NAMES: *SCOUNDREL TIME*

I'd rather lie to him than have him think I'm lying.
—Nick Charles,
in Dashiell Hammett's *The Thin Man*

"Are you now or have you ever been a Member of the Communist Party?"—the classic question of the House Committee on Un-American Activities—parallels in grammatical structure the classic question asked by all autobiographers: how much of what I am as I write depends on what I once was? The HCUA question also parallels, stylistically, Lillian Hellman's natural autobiographical rhythm—her simultaneous layering of past and present—the "I didn't understand it then and I don't now" (701) style that begins with the dedication of *Scoundrel Time:* "For Barbara and John / Ruth and Marshall / in gratitude for then and now" (602).

Like the earlier books, *Scoundrel Time* is informed by notebooks, diaries, memos, and the official record of the HCUA, but Hellman insists that she is after a personal rather than a historical version of what happened: "IT IS IMPOSSIBLE to write any part of the McCarthy period in a clear-dated, annotated form; much crossed with much else, nothing obeyed a neat plan" (642). This autobiographical rather than memoiristic focus stresses that for Hellman what is important about her experiences with McCarthyism is not her past's emphasis on political activity, but her present's belief that she is considerably less politically astute than the record might indicate.

Where her physical clumsiness often produced an ankle turn, Hellman reveals in *An Unfinished Woman* that her political stumbling was characterized by similar difficulties with turns. "All through my childhood and youth I had an interest in all sharp turns of history" (204); however, she admits in *Scoundrel Time,* "I cannot make quick turns . . . cannot ever adjust fast to a new pattern; have not the mind or the nature to do one thing, maybe wiser, when I am prepared for another" (668). For such a person, the period after the Spanish Civil War was particularly problematic. Having been attracted in varying degrees to communism, liberals of all persuasions, suddenly made aware of Stalin's purges and the Nazi-Soviet Pact in 1939, were faced with a dramatic political turn, made more confusing when Russia later became an American ally in World War II. As Frank Warren asserts in *Liberals and Communism,* "If Trotsky were not guilty and the trials were a monstrous frame-up, one could not distinguish morally between Communism and Fascism."[49]

Like the majority of those who supported communism in this period, Hellman can offer few answers to her own blindness. That she shares the generic liberal failure to imagine the most monstrous of political machinations is one answer. Another lies in the realm of psychoanalysis, "the impulse to obscure dark facts" that Daniel Goleman defines as those "vital lies" that "come from the need to preserve the integrity of the self."[50] Hellman repeatedly describes herself as exhausted, dizzy, on the verge of vomiting, disoriented, accident prone, following clues that lead nowhere, often unable to communicate at crucial moments because of comical ineptness at understanding. These psychological, sometimes physical traits, grow stronger until in *Maybe* they become physically linked through literal blindness to overwhelming despair. While swimming she is inexplicably unable to locate the shore: "I am not frightened in water. Something else was happening to me: I was collapsing in a way that had never happened before" (*M*, 100).

Actually, something similar had happened before. Throughout *Three* there are examples of Hellman's loss of bodily control, physical parallels to her lifelong rages, as when her discovery of Bethe's connection to the Mafia brings her to a state of "conscious semiconsciousness, as if I were coming through an anesthetic, not back into a world of reality, but into a new body and time" (345); or when, testifying before the HCUA, she moves her "right hand as if I had a tic, unexpected, and couldn't stop it" (674).

The controversy that followed *Scoundrel Time*'s publication takes its shrillest form in William F. Buckley's "*Scoundrel Time:* And Who Is The Ugliest of Them All?" a title that suggests both Buckley's idea that Hellman lacked self-reflection and an *ad hominem* argument about Hellman's facial features, an echo of the claims that her face resembled the figurehead of a ship, a primitive statue on Easter Island, or George Washington, although her detractors hardly claim that she cannot tell a lie.[51] The more moderate attacks against *Scoundrel Time* generally charge that Hellman falsely presented herself as a model of integrity by simplifying the complex nature of the period and underplaying her commitment to Stalinism in a book characterized by a tone of obfuscation, self-righteousness, and a lack of forgiveness.

Hellman answered most of her detractors within *Scoundrel Time*, agreeing with their objections before they had been voiced: "I am, of course, making my political history too simple" (613), she admits, after having confessed that "the traceries from what you were to what you became are always too raw and too simple" (612). To her antagonists, her apologies seem inadequate—too little, too late. But to Hellman and the other victims of the blacklisting period, the demand for a public statement of remorse smacks of what Victor Navasky, in his *Naming Names*, calls "degradation rituals," one of the main purposes of the HCUA purge.[52] It is true that Hellman simplifies her mistakes, but she also simplifies her apologies. Repeatedly she confesses her errors; of "Stalin communism" she acknowledges that "there were plenty of sins and plenty that for a long time I mistakenly denied" (606). In her most straightforward retraction, she admits: "I thought that in the end Russia, having achieved a state socialism, would stop its infringements on personal liberty. I was wrong" (612).

Many of Hellman's critics are also guilty of oversimplification. William Phillips, for instance, notes that "Lillian Hellman's question as to why we did not come to the defense of those who had been attacked by McCarthy is not as simple as it appears. First of all some were communists and what one was asked to defend was their right to lie about it."[53] With the phrase "the right to lie" Phillips is alluding to the taking of the Fifth Amendment, the legitimate refusal to answer a question that might be considered incriminating and a perfectly legal strategy, stemming from an ethical tradition established long before the HCUA. In 1907, for instance, in his "Classification of Duties—Veracity," Henry Sidgwick stated that "It is obviously a most effective protection for legitimate secrets that it should be universally understood and expected that those who ask questions which they have no right to ask will have lies told to them."[54]

This philosophical version of "Ask me no questions, I'll tell you no lies" is amplified by Sissela Bok's contention, in her "Lying to Liars" chapter of *Lying,* that not only is there "an undoubted psychological easing of standards of truthfulness toward those believed to be liars," but also "if, finally, the liar to whom one wishes to lie is also in a position to do one harm, then the balance may shift; not because he is a liar, but because of the threat he poses."[55] During the HCUA inquests of the fifties, the actual words of the Fifth Amendment shifted their surface meanings depending on the audience. To HCUA members and defenders, invoking the Fifth Amendment meant, "I refuse to answer because I'm really a Communist, since no one who was not would hide behind such an obvious legal out."

Even to Hellman, this tactic was suspect. Instead of replying with the standard "I refuse to answer . . . " Hellman often said, "I *must* refuse to answer . . . " thereby expressing her contempt for a legalistic trick forced on her by the inverted rules of the game. Because she made certain errors in her testimony—she says "At times I couldn't follow the reasoning" (674)— her antagonists further view her as a liar rather than as a person who repeatedly states that "there was no question of heroics. There was a question of legalities."[56]

Hellman's letter to the HCUA in which she pledges to waive her Fifth Amendment rights if not required to testify about others, a strategy she attributes to Abe Fortas, was an attempt on Hellman's part to maintain one of the most consistent patterns of her life, the refusal to name names, especially when someone is in trouble. "Don't go through life making trouble for people" (25), said Sophronia Mason on the occasion of young Lillian's having discovered her father was having an affair. Using this black woman as her only inviolable standard, her life's lodestone, Lillian Hellman—who as a child once tried to pass for black by claiming she was related to Sophronia— is consistent in not naming names. She will withhold Julia's name now, as she refused earlier, at the time of her abortion, to reveal the name of her lover, though they eventually married.

Hellman asserts that she is unhappy with her HCUA stand and the excessive admiration it eventually evoked. Of an earlier version of her letter, with its famous line "I cannot and will not cut my conscience to fit this year's fashions," Hellman noted, "I didn't like it much because it didn't sound like me" (658). Like Henry Adams, who saw his autobiographical protagonist as a manikin whose clothing is tailored by his narrator, Hellman frequently uses clothes metaphors throughout *Scoundrel Time* to describe both the events of the blacklisting era and her subsequent attempts at understanding what they meant. "If facts are facts," she writes, "and should not be altered, then which of us, as individuals or in groups, did the alterations and why?" (650). For Hellman, who is most inaccurate when she deals in facts—and who later appeared in a controversial advertisement for a full-length Blackgama mink coat, under the heading "What Becomes a Legend Most?"—clothes are a suitable metaphor, both for concealment and for the difference between the way things were and the way they appear in retrospect.

Hellman agrees with those who question elements of *Scoundrel Time*, adding later in *Three* that she "misrepresented" herself in the book (725). She means both that she made herself too heroic and that her tone appears too restrained. But most of her errors are the result of the complex, conflicting motives behind her writing of *Scoundrel Time*, her searching for a truth she "couldn't name" (344), yet another example of her difficulty in naming names in the process of resurrecting the past.

When Pauline Kael asks about the word "pentimento" in a review of the film *Julia*, "Of what is Hellman repenting?"[57] she echoes those antagonists who have failed to see that throughout her autobiographies Hellman is repenting virtually everything, confessing in the traditional autobiographical sense that she really was never the brave and decisive figure she appeared to be. Her nature was given to rages and rash acts, motivated by a stern sense of social injustice, powered by angry passion rather than logic; yet brusqueness and anger were often simply the covering mask for a constant inner feelng of vagueness and indecision. "Simply, then and now, I feel betrayed by the nonsense I had believed" (608), she writes, placing the blame on herself.

Unlike her critics, who have never publicly admitted their political errors in not standing more firmly against the HCUA, Hellman says repeatedly that she was wrong because she was slow to recognize her errors. Throughout her account she shows herself to be slow in understanding, late at letting go, a sort of person on whom, politically, everything is lost. "It took me months to understand what I was listening to" (607), she says of overt anti-Semitism in pre-World War II Germany. "It is comically late to admit that I did not even consider the fierce, sweeping, violent nonsense-tragedies that break out in America from time to time" (615), she says in distinguishing her romantic notions of radicalism from Hammett's pragmatic approach. Speaking of the anticommunist writers who oppose her, she writes, "such people would have a right to say that I, and many like me, took too long to see what was going on in the Soviet Union" (720). In always linking her admissions to a sense of bad timing, Hellman is consistent in *Scoundrel Time*, both with her statements in *An Unfinished Woman* and *Pentimento* about these pro-Stalin charges, and with her recurring, self-accusatory theme of personal and political awkwardness.

CONCLUSION: "WHAT IS REMEMBERED"

> Autobiography is stranger than fiction which as everybody knows must be stranger than life.
>
> —Jane Lazarre, "The Art of Lying, or a Slight Distortion of the Truth"[58]

Alice B. Toklas's autobiography *What Is Remembered,* a title that deliberately omits a question mark, would make an apt summation for the four volumes of Lillian Hellman's autobiography. In moving from the first sentence, "I was born" to the last, "I hung up"—from "the sweetest smelling baby in New Orleans" to an adult forever unsure about the spuriousness of a misogynist's charge that she had a particularly strong personal odor— Hellman, in one sense, deconstructed herself. But in another, she has reconstructed her self, ratifying A. O. J. Cockshut's claim that "it is the privilege of a great autobiography to give us data for disagreeing with its conclusions."[59] Throughout the four books she repeats the self-directed charge that she must pay a price for having once believed in absolute truth. The price, she explains, is having "gone through my life blaming myself for almost anything that harmed me: what anybody did to me, what work failed, what meanness or malice was given . . . it was I who was the fool for not guessing it in time, for accepting lies I should have known to be lies . . . " (19).

In writing her four autobiographies, however, Lillian Hellman finally triumphed over the lies she told herself; in the end, she gained "the final courage to say that I refuse to preside over violations against myself" (213). She gained the personal courage so long falsely ascribed to her by the legend of Lillian Hellman through the writing of her autobiographies. Her lifelong struggle between being alone and acting on political feelings is illustrated in the shape and direction of these four books, and in her final breakthrough in *Maybe,* an autobiography that is satisfied with its own inconclusive rhetorical stance.

For Lillian Hellman, a woman who once thought of her own life as unfinished, the act of repenting through mastery of the art of palimpsestic autobiography, ultimately produced a completed woman, at home with an ordering of memory, not into an idealistic "yes," or a Hawthornian "no in thunder," but into a resolute, self-satisfying, self-defining *maybe*.

Notes

1. Christine Doudna, "A Still Unfinished Woman: A Conversation with Lillian Hellman," in *Conversations with Lillian Hellman*, ed. Jackson R. Bryer (Jackson: University Press of Mississippi, 1986), 195.

2. "On Reading Again," in *Three: An Unfinished Woman, Pentimento, Scoundrel Time* (Boston: Little, Brown & Co., 1979), 9. Parenthetical references in the text are to this edition.

3. Fred Gardner, "An Interview with Lillian Hellman," in Bryer, *Conversations,* 176.

4. Roy Pascal, *Design and Truth in Autobiography* (Cambridge, Mass.: Harvard University Press, 1960), 4.

5. Marcus K. Billson, "The Memoir: New Perspectives on a Forgotten Genre," *Genre* 10 (1977):265.

6. Sidney Hook, "Lillian Hellman's *Scoundrel Time*," *Encounter* 48 (February 1977):82–91. Reprinted in this volume.

7. Martha Gellhorn, "On Apocryphism," *Paris Review* 79 (Spring 1981):280–301. Reprinted in this volume.

8. William Wright, *Lillian Hellman: The Image, the Woman* (New York: Simon & Schuster, 1986), 395–96.

9. Samuel McCracken, " 'Julia' and Other Fictions by Lillian Hellman," *Commentary* 77 (June 1984):43.

10. Hilton Kramer, "The Life and Death of Lillian Hellman," *New Criterion* 3 (October 1984):2.

11. Kramer, *The Life and Death*, 4.

12. Diana Trilling, *We Must March My Darlings* (New York: Harcourt, Brace Jovanovich, 1977), 42.

13. Trilling, *We Must March*, 46.

14. A. O. J. Cockshut, *The Art of Autobiography in 19th and 20th Century England* (New Haven, Conn.: Yale University Press, 1984), 6.

15. *Maybe: A Story by Lillian Hellman* (Boston: Little, Brown & Co., 1980), 50. Parenthetical references are to this edition.

16. Billson, "The Memoir," 264.

17. Marsha Norman, "Lillian Hellman's Gift to a Young Playwright," *New York Times*, 27 August 1984, sec. 2, p. 7.

18. Gellhorn, "On Apocryphism," 286.

19. Gellhorn, "On Apocryphism," 297.

20. Cited in Diane Johnson, *The Life of Dashiell Hammett* (New York: Random House, 1983), 317.

21. Pascal, *Design and Truth*, 79.

22. Margaret Case Harriman, "Miss Lily of New Orleans," *New Yorker* 17 (8 November 1941):22. Reprinted in this volume.

23. Janet Varner Gunn, *Autobiography: Towards a Poetics of Experience* (Philadelphia: University of Pennsylvania Press, 1982), 77.

24. Cited in Rex Reed, "Lillian Hellman," in Bryer, *Conversations*, 181.

25. Vladimir Nabokov, *Speak, Memory: An Autobiography Revisited* (New York: Putnam's, 1966), 139.

26. Nabokov, *Speak, Memory*, 25.

27. C. Hugh Holman, *A Handbook to Literature*, 4th ed. (Indianapolis: Bobbs-Merrill, 1980), 315.

28. Gayatri Chakravorty Spivak, "Translator's Preface," in Jacques Derrida, *On Grammatology* (Baltimore: Johns Hopkins University Press, 1976), xvii.

29. McCracken, " 'Julia' and Other Fictions," 43.

30. Paul John Eakin, *Fictions in Autobiography: Studies in the Art of Self-Invention* (Princeton, N.J.: Princeton University Press, 1985), 56.

31. Cited in Muriel Gardiner, *Code Name "Mary": Memoirs of an American Woman in the Austrian Underground* (New Haven, Conn.: Yale University Press, 1983), 69.

32. Cited in Linda Witt, "Nazi Era Saga: A Real 'Julia' Disputes History," *Chicago Tribune*, 25 November 1984, sec. 2, 11.

33. Cited in Wright, *Lillian Hellman*, 404.

34. Stephen Spender, *Journals 1939–1983*, ed. John Goldsmith (New York: Random House, 1986), 483.

35. Gardiner, *Code Name "Mary,"* xv.

36. Cited in Spender, *Journals*, 483.

37. Gardiner, *Code Name "Mary,"* 43.

38. McCracken, " 'Julia' and Other Fictions," 40.

39. Cited in Wright, *Lillian Hellman*, 388.

40. Stephen Spender, *World within World: The Autobiography of Stephen Spender* (London: Reader's Union, 1953), 165.

41. McCracken, " 'Julia' and Other Fictions," 41.

42. Alexander Cockburn, "Who Was Julia?" *Nation* 240 (23 February 1985): 200–1. Reprinted in this volume.

43. Janice S. Robinson, *H.D.: The Life and Work of an American Poet* (Boston: Houghton Mifflin, 1982), 304.

44. Ibid., 303–4.

45. Cited in Robinson, *H.D.*, 133.

46. Cockburn, "Who Was Julia?," 201.

47. Spender, *Journals*, 483.

48. Pauline Kael, "The Current Cinema: A Woman for All Seasons?" *New Yorker* 53 (10 October 1977):94. Reprinted in this volume.

49. Frank A. Warren, *Liberals and Communists: The "Red" Decade Revisited* (Bloomington: Indiana University Press, 1966), 163.

50. Daniel Goleman, *Vital Lies, Simple Truths: The Psychology of Self-Deception* (New York: Simon & Schuster, 1985), 239–40.

51. William F. Buckley, "*Scoundrel Time:* And Who Is the Ugliest of Them All?," *National Review* 29 (21 January 1977):101–6. Tallulah Bankhead is responsible for the George Washington remark, Geoffrey Wolff for the Easter Island comparison, and John Hersey for the ship's figurehead.

52. Cited in Thom Andersen, "Red Hollywood," in *Literature and the Visual Arts in Contemporary Society*, ed. Suzanne Ferguson and Barbara Groseclose (Columbus: Ohio State University Press, 1985), 159.

53. William Phillips, "What Happened in the Fifties," *Partisan Review* 43 (1976):338.

54. Quoted in Sissela Bok, *Lying: Moral Choice in Public and Private Life* (New York: Vintage, 1979), 154.

55. Bok, *Lying*, 140.

56. Cited in Marilyn Berger, "Profile: Lillian Hellman," in Bryer, *Conversations*, 254.

57. Kael, "The Current Cinema," 94.

58. Jane Lazarre, "The Art of Lying or a Slight Distortion of the Truth (A Story)," *Feminist Studies* 12 (1986):110.

59. Cockshut, *The Art of Autobiography*, 101.

THE HELLMAN PERSONA

Miss Lily of New Orleans:
Lillian Hellman
Margaret Case Harriman*

A good way to annoy Lillian Hellman, if you happen to be someone who wants to annoy Lillian Hellman, is to call her a woman playwright. This simple descriptive term, applied to Miss Hellman, author of *The Children's Hour, The Little Foxes, Watch on the Rhine,* and *The Searching Wind,* sends her into a strange rage, often interesting because, although it may be accompanied by a stamping of the feet, it is not without a cool, unanswerable logic. Being called a woman playwright bores and exasperates her for the same reason, she explains, that a man who writes plays would be bored and exasperated by being continually called a man playwright. Her admirers argue that few people could tell, anyway, whether her plays are written by a man or a woman, since they are all distinguished by the kind of intellectual indignation that must be sexless. This is honest tribute, but Miss Hellman has suffered from such praise. People who meet her for the first time are apt to come away murmuring in astonishment, "She's sort of cute, isn't she?" and interviewers who find her in a hostess gown write dazed pieces about her feminine draperies and fail to disclose much else about her. There has been one notable exception among the interviewers. After Miss Hellman's first success, *The Children's Hour,* in 1934, a feature-writer for a New York paper called on her and apparently surprised her in a tailored suit and a crisp mood. "She's the kind of girl who can take the tops off bottles with her teeth!" this analyst wrote enthusiastically afterward.

Actually, Lillian Hellman is neither cute nor tough. For a woman with militant undercurrents, her surface behavior is more often mild than not, and she is genuinely feminine to a degree that borders engagingly on the wacky. Although her writing is sure and pointed, she has no geographical sense of direction whatever, and last summer, after she had got lost twice in one week on the 130-acre farm in Pleasantville, New York, where she has lived for the past six years, Dashiell Hammett, an old and solicitous friend, undertook to teach her how to take her bearings. "Look," he said, pointing, "that's north. When you face north"—he grasped her by the shoulders and pointed her north—"east is on your right hand, west on your left, and south behind you." He then drew a little map indicating that the house was east of the chicken farm, west of the woods, and so on. Next day, Miss Hellman got lost for three hours. "You told me," she said accusingly to Hammett when he found her in the woods, "that north was in front of me, so naturally I followed

*Reprinted from *Take Them Up Tenderly,* by Margaret Case Harriman (New York: Alfred A. Knopf, 1944), 94–109. Originally published as a *New Yorker* "Profile," 8 November 1941, 22–26, 32, 34–35. Copyright 1944 by Margaret Case Harriman. Reprinted by permission of Alfred A. Knopf, Inc.

my left hand from where I was facing." Her approach to scientific phenomena is equally baffled and baffling. One evening, Herman Shumlin, who has produced all of Miss Hellman's plays, happened to remark that heat rises. Miss Hellman thought that over, and suddenly glowed with the light of reasonable argument. "If that's true," she said, "why doesn't your hand get burned worse if you hold it a foot above a radiator than it does if you put it right on top?" There is nothing coy about Miss Hellman's helplessness in the face of geography and physics. Defeated by them, she dismisses them with a word, generally of four letters.

Lillian Hellman's face and appearance are not well known to the public in spite of her three hit plays, the Drama Critics Circle Award for 1941 to her *Watch on the Rhine,* and the various pictures she has written or adapted for Hollywood—*Dead End, The Dark Angel, These Three* (a movie version of *The Children's Hour*), *The Little Foxes,* from her stage play of that name, and *The North Star*. She is five feet three inches tall, and slim, with reddish hair, a fine, aquiline nose, and a level, humorous mouth. When she is in repose or talking business, her nose and mouth give her a fleeting and curious resemblance to the familiar Gilbert Stuart portrait of George Washington. Her voice is flexible and interesting, and her hands, feet, and legs amply reward the candid pleasure she takes in them. She likes clothes and is so sensitive to them that the right or wrong dress has been known to produce a momentary success or disaster in her social career.

A week or so after the opening of *The Little Foxes,* she was invited to dine with Mr. and Mrs. Henry Luce at their Waldorf Towers apartment. Mrs. Luce is famous as Clare Boothe, a woman who would just as soon be called a woman playwright. Another guest was Dorothy Thompson, the columnist and firebrand. After dinner the ladies, leaving the men to their cigars and brandies, fluttered to Mrs. Luce's powder room, and a conversation sprang up between the hostess and Miss Thompson about a remark Dorothy Parker had made to Somerset Maugham when she had met him a week or so before. "I am a great admirer of your style," Mr. Maugham had said to Mrs. Parker, and Mrs. Parker had replied, "Thank you, Mr. Maugham. I have always admired you because you have no style." This, a true compliment from one discriminating writer to another, was construed by Mmes Luce and Thompson as a deadly insult to a dean of English letters. Miss Hellman, whose best woman friend is Dorothy Parker, listened in silence as long as she could and then mistakenly tried to explain to the two what Mrs. Parker had meant. They stared at her and, it is said by other witnesses, giggled. A few minutes later, in the drawing room, they approached her in tandem, so to speak, drawing up chairs to the couch where she rather miserably sat.

"We're going to *heckle* you, Miss Hellman," said Mrs. Luce archly. At this, Miss Hellman simply got up and fled blindly back to the bathroom. "Ordinarily, I might have coped with those—ah—beauties," she says now. The reason she was routed, it seems, was that they were sleek in satin and she, that night, was wearing an expensive error in yellow organdie, threaded with black velvet ribbon tied in girlish bows at the throat and wrists.

Revenge is sweet, especially when it's on Dorothy Thompson, and such an opportunity is not given to many women. A few weeks after the dinner party, however, Miss Thompson telephoned Miss Hellman. Metro-Goldwyn-Mayer had made motions toward buying Miss Thompson's play about refugees, *Another Sun*, which had run eight days in New York in 1940, on condition that Miss Hellman adapt it for pictures, and they had sent it to her to read. Miss Hellman, studying the manuscript, found that Miss Thompson, in a welter of nostalgia for the old Germany, had flung into the dialogue a good many *gemütlich* phrases in the mother tongue. When Miss Thompson called up about the play, she was ready for her. "I suggest first that you translate it from the German," she said coldly. Nothing ever came of this incipient collaboration.

Lillian Hellman, at thirty-nine, is the youngest successful woman playwright, or woman successfully writing plays, in the United States, and therefore probably in the world. She was born in New Orleans and was cared for as a child by a Negro mammy—two facts that have embarrassed certain playgoers and critics, who denounced her Negro characters in *The Little Foxes* as being artificial and overdrawn. Her father, Max Hellman, was a prosperous shoe merchant with a store on Canal Street in New Orleans; her mother had been Julia Newhouse of Alabama. Mrs. Hellman died nine years ago. Mr. Hellman, living with a gusto his daughter has inherited, has retired from business and spends most of his time playing pinochle with cronies in Atlantic City. He confesses a mild amazement but practically no awe when he thinks how his little girl has grown up to be a famous playwright.

When Lillian was five, a partner of her father's absconded with the company's funds, and Max Hellman came to New York with his wife and only child to start over again as a travelling salesman for a clothing firm. For many years afterward, Lillian spent her summers in New Orleans, visiting her aunts or her grandmother. In New York, the Hellman family lived on West Ninety-fifth Street near the River, and from this base Lillian soon established a widening circle of activities. America entered the first World War when she was twelve, and in an excess of patriotism she and a friend named Helen Schiff took to trailing people who they thought looked like German spies. Long-haired fellows carrying brief cases or violin cases (handy for holding machine guns and bombs) were especially suspect, and once the girls chased two men ten blocks and reported them to a police sergeant, who, after considerable trouble, discovered them to be a professor of Greek from Hunter College and a second violinist from the Palace Theatre. Lillian and Helen had a stooge, a timid blonde who was detailed to eavesdrop on conversations of suspects and report them to the two head spy-catchers. Her reports were dull and her superiors grew bored. "It's got to be more *interesting!*" Lillian exclaimed one day, and she and Helen then twisted the stooge's arm until she managed to think up something worth hearing. A version of this incident appeared in *The Children's Hour*, but Miss Hellman says that she did not remember it consciously while she was writing the play.

When Lillian was fourteen her budding taste for sitting in a chatty group around a table led to her first open rebellion. A boy in his second year at Columbia asked her to go to a fencing match with him and another boy and girl, and after the match the four repaired to Constantine's ice-cream parlor on upper Broadway. The Columbia student was nineteen, the other girl and her beau were at least seventeen, and Lillian, irked by her own youth and her father's order to be home by eleven, brooded herself into a state of defiance and stayed out until after midnight. The stern reception she got when she did turn up further inflamed her, and next day she left home for good, with seventy-five cents in her pocket. She spent an agreeable afternoon a couple of miles to the south, talking to strangers and eating candy, but by nine o'clock that night most of her money and her spirits were gone, and she called up the Columbia sophomore with her last nickel. "I have left home," she told him romantically. "Come and look after me." Columbia came all right, but Lillian was depressed to note that instead of looking gallant and protective, he looked protective and very bored. He took her home and shoved her in the door, and Lillian reluctantly entered, to find her mother in tears from grief and worry. "Are you all right, my baby?" she kept saying, and this gave the wanderer an idea. She assumed a frail look, waited for a pause, and announced, "Mother, I have heart trouble."

When Lillian entered Wadleigh High School in 1922, her dramatic instinct easily surpassed that of the dramatic coach, who carelessly gave her the role of the villainess in a school play, *Mrs. Gorringe's Necklace*. This character actually had few lines to speak, but at Lillian's final exit the night of the play the door stuck and she couldn't get off the stage. Pleased by the happy circumstance, she returned calmly to the panic-stricken members of the cast, who were grouped about a drawing-room set and, arranging herself on a sofa, proceeded to invent a dazzling scene, which fattened up her own part by a number of showy remarks and lasted a good five minutes after the stricken coach had got the door unstuck and started to wave wildly at her from the wings. Lillian appeared in no more plays, but she soon got around to writing a column for the school paper. The column was called *It Seems to Me, Jr.*, and, since it appeared before either Heywood Broun or Lillian Hellman had become the people's friend, it was light, chatty, and without social significance.

Miss Hellman has been called a Communist almost as often as she has been called a woman playwright, and her political viewpoint is about the only thing toward which she has a regrettable tendency to be coy. Pinned down to a statement of her allegiances, she says vaguely that she would like to be a liberal if she could tell, these days, exactly what the hell a liberal is. Reminded of Dorothy Thompson's crack in her 1940 valentine column, which suggested "To the Communist Party of America—*The Little Foxes*," Miss Hellman says candidly, "I stuck my neck out there." Miss Thompson's reproof was inspired by the row, familiar along Broadway, between Miss Hellman and Tallulah Bankhead over the benefit performance of *The Little Foxes*, which Miss Bankhead, the star of the play, proposed to give for Finnish relief. Miss Hellman, backed up by Herman Shumlin, producer of the play, objected on the ground that Miss Bankhead and the cast had refused, some months earlier, to play a benefit Miss Hellman had asked them to give for the Spanish Loyalists. "And besides," Miss Hellman added, cannily, as it turned out, "I don't believe in that fine, lovable little Republic of Finland that everybody gets so weepy about. I've been there, and it looks like a pro-Nazi little republic to me." The battle, gentled along by Richard Maney, Shumlin's press agent, got into the headlines, and public sympathy was with Miss Bankhead, since Finland was then being attacked by Russia. People reasoned that Miss Hellman, being opposed to aiding Finnish relief, must be a Red. The knowing ones pointed out that she had been in Russia and in Spain in 1937 and had published pieces about her trip in the *New Masses* and the *New Republic*. Miss Hellman now says mildly that she submitted the pieces first to several slick magazines, which turned them down. The detached biographer, looking through the record, will find that the longest and most heartfelt of these articles was called *A Bleached Lady* and was a semi-fictional piece about a Spanish woman refugee who, noticing that an American lady traveller's hair had begun to turn dark at the roots, recommended a friend who ran a hairdressing shop in Madrid and had a skillful hand with *teinturerie*, if she was still alive.

People who know Lillian Hellman well say that what some theorists consider her Communist tendency is actually more a violent anti-Fascism and an equally strong instinct to fight for the little people who can't fight for themselves. She is a woman who hates to see anybody pushed around, they say. Miss Hellman agrees with this explanation, but she is an arguer at heart. Once, in her presence, a friend of hers set out to prove to a heckler that Lillian was not even sympathetic to the Communists, and gave a number of convincing reasons. "Isn't that true, Lillian?" the friend said, turning to her rather breathlessly. "Well . . ." said Miss Hellman.

The easy riches of the 1920's, of which she had no share, may partly explain her curiously split social attitude, which combines a sensible fondness for money with a violent dislike for people who wallow in it. Graduating from Wadleigh High, she entered N.Y.U., where her reaction to culture seems to have been entirely normal. She admired Lewis Carroll and Dante and thought of writing a biography of the latter, but got no farther than a line in her notebook stating, "Dante is okay." Graduated from N.Y.U., she took a course in journalism at Columbia, as an indirect result of which she was engaged to write several one- and two-column book reviews for the Sunday *Tribune*, at about $4.70 a column. In the middle twenties, still living with her family, she worked at a series of jobs—as a reader for Horace Liveright, the publisher, as a play-reader for Anne Nichols, who was then trying to find a worthy successor to *Abe's Irish Rose*, and as a press agent for something called *The Bunk of 1926*. Through her theatrical contacts she came to know Herman Shumlin and Arthur Kober, who shared an office in the Selwyn Theatre Building and worked, as general manager and press agent respectively, for Jed Harris, the most fabulous producer of that period. In 1925, Miss Hellman married Kober. Kober later became a successful Hollywood writer and author of the play *Having Wonderful Time*.

Divorce ended the marriage in 1932, but it did not affect Kober's attachment to Miss Hellman. A man whose cherubic appearance conceals hell's own inner turmoil, he was probably the first to appreciate her great common sense and capacity for shouldering burdens, and certainly the last to want to give them up entirely. His friends (and Lillian's) grew accustomed to the familiar sight of Arthur seated in a dim corner of some *boîte* mentally wrestling with himself in an effort to get along without Lillian's advice about a new play, a new apartment, or whatever was torturing him. It was always a losing battle. Whenever Kober returned to New York from Hollywood and began looking at furnished apartments to sublease, he would say to the occupant, "May I bring my friend to see it?" The householder, expecting another man, would naturally consent, and soon Kober would reappear with his ex-wife, whom he nervously introduced as "my friend." Miss Hellman would then inspect closets, stove, plumbing, and other important details, and finally state her opinion to the startled tenant. "It stinks," she would say agreeably more often than not. When Kober eventually decided to remarry, four years ago, he brought his fiancée for Lillian to see, in the most natural way in the world, and Miss Hellman was so pleased with the prospective Mrs. Kober that she stood up with the bride and groom at the wedding as matron of honor.

By 1933, Herman Shumlin had become a successful producer with *Grand Hotel* and *The Last Mile*, and Miss Hellman went to work for him as a reader. She had written one play, *Dear Queen*, in collaboration with Louis Kronenberger, now dramatic critic of *PM*, but it was never produced, chiefly, Miss Hellman thinks, because she and Kronenberger had a hilarious time writing it. As writers keep on sorrowfully finding out, the kind of writing that entertains its authors is generally not the kind that entertains the public. One night, at a party at Ira Gershwin's, she said to Shumlin, "What would you think of a play about a couple of schoolteachers accused of being Lesbians by a brat pupil?" "I wouldn't waste any time on it," he answered kindly. Miss Hellman had already spent several months on such a play, and after she had spent six or eight more, she laid the manuscript on Shumlin's desk. "Here's that play I mentioned," she said. "Oh," said Shumlin, "all right, I'll read it." Miss Hellman said, "When?" Shumlin said, "Now." Miss Hellman said, "I'll wait." She sat down in a corner of the office and appeared to read a magazine while Shumlin read *The Children's Hour*. He made three comments: "Swell!" at the end of the first act, "I hope it keeps up" at the end of the second, and "I'll produce it" when he had finished the third. Miss

Hellman looked at him in astonishment. "You really mean that?" she demanded. This has been her invariable remark each time Shumlin has eagerly agreed to produce a play of hers, and it is often followed by the dour prophecy "Well, this is *one* play you'll lose your shirt on." Her confidence in her own work is unaffectedly shaky, in strange contrast to her almost reckless poise in private life.

Miss Hellman had fifty dollars in the bank the day Shumlin first read *The Children's Hour*, and made about $125,000 out of the play, which ran twenty-one months in New York, another year on the road, and was produced in London and in Paris. Its tours, although not its publicity, were frequently interrupted by censors, who objected to the theme. Once, in Chicago, a test performance was given for the local censor, a lady, who brought a woman friend. In the middle of the scene in which one teacher confesses her illicit love for the other and goes offstage to commit suicide, the censor, who had been silent throughout the performance, turned to her friend, and Shumlin and Miss Hellman, sitting tensely in the row behind, leaned forward anxiously to listen to what she might have to say. "I like that suit she's wearing," the lady censor said. *The Children's Hour* was officially banned in Chicago, but it was put on there anyway by the Actors' Company, a high-spirited group of amateurs.

In 1936, Miss Hellman turned out a drama about labor called *Days to Come*, a harrowing flop. On the opening night, as the play's doom became increasingly clear, Miss Hellman plodded from her seat in the last row to the door of the theater and dispatched the doorman with a ten-dollar bill for a quart of brandy. When he came back with it, she retired to the lonely box office and took several deep, consoling drinks. A few minutes later a form of death attacked her. No amount of failure or brandy could account for the way she felt, she thought dimly, trying to unclench a clammy fist. As her fingers slowly loosened, the change the doorman had returned to her from the ten-dollar bill fell from her hand; it was $9.06. The effect of the ninety-four-cent brandy was not lessened by the party Ralph Ingersoll, now editor-on-leave of *PM*, gave for Miss Hellman after the show that night. It was grisly, like all festivals after a failure. Dashiell Hammett, apparently choosing frankness as the best policy, sat down beside Miss Hellman and told her that in his opinion the play was terrible. "But when you read it," she reminded him desperately, "you said you thought it was the best play you'd ever read." Hammett rose and called for his hat and coat. "I have changed my mind," he said coldly and left.

Although Miss Hellman's next play, *The Little Foxes*, established her as a sure-fire playwright (if there is such a thing), she continued to give each manuscript to friends to read and trembled each time for their decisions. She takes criticism uncomplainingly and writes so many drafts of every play— from four to as many as ten—that the script that finally goes into rehearsal seldom requires any change. She finished the first version of *The Little Foxes* in the summer of 1937, in a cottage she had taken on an island off South

Norwalk, and gave it to Hammett, who happened to be a weekend guest. Writing about the South she knew, she had evidently been carried away in the first draft into composing lengthy dialogues of a local color between the two Negro servants in the play. Hammett read it in bed Sunday night and left for town in a cowardly fashion before his hostess was up next morning, leaving the manuscript and a note. "Missy write blackamoor chitchat. Missy better stop writing blackamoor chitchat," the note said. Miss Hellman went for a grim swim after she read this and, she says now, thought of drowning herself. That afternoon, however, she started work on a new version. It took her ten months of writing and rewriting to complete *The Little Foxes*, and as long, or longer, to write each of her other plays.

Her notebooks for a play are monumental, running to two or three volumes of four or five hundred typed, single-spaced pages each, containing data on contemporary history, local customs, factual anecdotes, political aspects, celebrities of the time, and long lists of likely names for characters. In one of her notebooks for *Watch on the Rhine*, three pages are filled with German first and last names—Kathe, Werner, Maxl, Pilar, Willy; Lange, Brech, Reger, Unruh, Rochow, and so on—all of which she studied and discarded before she decided to name the German, played by Paul Lukas, Kurt Müller, and his wife, played by Mady Christians, Sara. Other pages carry details of the age, life, and background of the characters before their entrance into the play. Frequently there are notes like "What was he doing in Germany? Scientist? Trade Union Movement? Maybe China? What was going on 1920–1932? Maybe they have only been here about 6 months? What was he doing here?" All of this research, in which Miss Hellman is assisted by one secretary, is the usual task of a careful writer, but even in the case of a careful writer it is uncommon to find notes that could be expanded, as the notes for *Watch on the Rhine* could be, into a detailed and accurate history of a period covering twenty-five years. Miss Hellman leaves the direction of her plays to Shumlin, but her thirst for perfection sometimes leads her to wander into a theater during a play's run and take a look at the performance. When *The Little Foxes* was playing to capacity in New York, she appeared silently one night and made the following notes in pencil on a program: "Sound over air system. No thank you from Collinge too quick. Dingle—no looks to audience. Bankhead cuts in on important lines. Don't clutch Horace. Leo—you too cute." These flaws were corrected before the next performance.

Miss Hellman works at a typewriter perched on a rickety table that, in search of solitude, she drags around from one room to another of her Pleasantville house, which is generally full of guests. Not long ago, with a job to do, she posted the following notice outside the room where she was working:

This room is used for work
Do not enter without knocking
After you knock, wait for an answer

If you get no answer, go away and don't come back
This means everybody
This means you
This means night or day
By order of the Hellman-Military-Commission-for-Playwrights.

Court-martialling will take place in the barn, and your trial will not be a fair one.

The Christmas Court-martialling has now taken place.

Among those:

Herman Shumlin, Former *régisseur*.
A Mr. X, former insurance man.
Miss Sylvia Hermann, aged three, former daughter of a farmer.
Miss Nora, former dog.
Mr. Samuel Dashiell Hammett, former eccentric.
Mr. Arthur Kober, former itinerant sweet-singer.
Mr. Louis Kronenberger, born in Cincinnati, lynched by me.
Emmy Kronenberger, wife to Kronenberger, died with him.
Mr. Felix Anderson, former butler.
Irene Robinson, former cook and very pretty.

Note: Mr. Max Bernard Hellman, father, is a most constant offender.
His age has saved him. This sentimentality may not continue.

When posted warnings fail to keep visitors out, Miss Hellman comes into town, rents an apartment in a quiet street, and writes there, doing her own housework and cooking. She is a fine, resourceful cook, specializing in crab gumbo and other New Orleans dishes, and skillful at turning even a domestic annoyance into a *plat de résistance*. Last summer the lake on her Pleasantville place was invaded by snapping turtles, and Miss Hellman, burned up because this threatened to spoil her swimming, sharply ordered her farmer to set traps and deliver all the turtles he caught to the kitchen door. Then she made a superior soup out of them. She has a gourmet's interest in food and will bedevil any hostess who serves her a new and succulent dish until she has got the recipe for it. The food in her own house is beautifully cooked and served, under her fairly gloating direction, by Irene and Felix. Irene is a woman of such exceptional tact that it is a source of wonder to her employer. Not long ago she asked Miss Hellman, politely and rather deviously, to tell Felix to wash the living-room windows for the party. "What party?" inquired Miss Hellman, who had not planned any. No special party, Irene said, going on to explain that Felix was simply the type of man who works better with a definite object in view. Miss Hellman especially admires Irene's way with people because she knows that her own tactfulness is often less than consummate. In 1940, for example, she went to Philadelphia to cover the Republican Presidential Convention for *PM*. In a hotel lobby one day she ran into Thomas E. Dewey, an acquaintance of hers. "Hello!" she said to him cordially. "You going to be here all week?" After Dewey had wanly passed on, a friend who was with Miss Hellman gazed at her and said, "Look, dear. The poor guy just hopes to get nominated. Remember?"

Like most independent women, Lillian Hellman has more men friends than girl friends. A few of these men, with Miss Hellman, form a solid, affectionate group whose friendship for one another is never disturbed by the fact that most of the men have, at some time, been in love with Lillian. Miss Hellman presides over the brotherhood like an exceptionally maternal Maintenon. Her house is permanently open to the boys, and they like to go there and stay for weeks, perhaps, taking their work with them and often turning out a book, a play, a set of editorial memorandums, or a production schedule for the new season. She is a good hostess, casual and entertaining, and her advice about business and artistic problems is sure to be either wise enough or just screwy enough to be exactly right. Among the headaches she has shared is *PM*, which she helped Ralph Ingersoll formulate. She was one of its original stockholders—"mainly," she explains, "because I lent them some money to pay the electric-light and telephone bills once or twice when they were broke, and got paid back in stock." She also thought up the name *PM* after a series of conferences during which Ingersoll kept doggedly insisting that the paper be called simply *Newspaper*, on the peculiar theory that people habitually walk up to a newsstand and say, "Give me a newspaper." She was concerned because Dashiell Hammett didn't write a new book after *The Thin Man*, eleven years ago, and she was warmly proud of him when he enlisted as a private in the Army in 1942, and went overseas. When Herman Shumlin needs relaxation, she goes on fishing trips with him and his admiration for her increases because, he says, she always knows what every goddam fish is planning at the other end of the line. She likes to gamble with men for manly stakes and once won twelve thousand dollars in an evening at *chemin de fer*. She ordered two ambulances for the Spanish Loyalists next morning, lost the twelve thousand dollars in another game that night, but bought the ambulances anyway.

In spite of Miss Hellman's liking for masculine company, she has none of the phony impatience with her own sex so often affected by female literary celebrities. She is fond of a number of women and likes to send them unexpected and interesting presents, half a *prosciutto* ham or a silver bowl for mixing New Orleans *café diable*. She is not above loud and bitter complaint if she doesn't get enough presents in return. A week before her birthday last year, she sent a telegram to some twelve or fifteen friends. "A birthday present for Lillian Hellman is a blow against Fascism," it suggested. When the friends came through nobly with gifts, Miss Hellman wept frank and grateful tears. Although she is subject to attacks of sentiment, her aspect is not always tender. "When Lillian gets mad," Dorothy Parker will tell you in her soft, deprecating voice, "I regret to say she screams." This talent for making a noise is partly responsible for Miss Hellman's success in Hollywood, notably with Sam Goldwyn, who is no whisperer.

In 1935, Mrs. Parker and Miss Hellman were among the leaders of a group of Hollywood writers who wanted to revive the moribund Screen Writers' Guild and were therefore enthusiastic about the proposed Wagner Act, which guaranteed collective bargaining and the right to strike. One day the two ladies called on Goldwyn. "Sam," said Miss Hellman, "why don't you come out in favor of the Screen Writers' Guild and help us revive it? You would be the first producer to do it, and it would give you tremendous distinction." "That's right, Sam," added Mrs. Parker, who does not always speak in epigrams. Goldwyn thought it over, and finally replied, "I can't do it, girls. I can't come out in favor of the Screen Writers' Guild, but I tell you what I *will* do for you. I will definitely," he said with a ringing sincerity, "come out against the Wagner Act." Miss Hellman's screams echoed through Hollywood then, but by the time she got back to New York, a few weeks later, they had dwindled to a murmur far more deadly. One night, Charles MacArthur said to her, "A fine thing, you twenty-five-hundred-a-week Hollywood writers wanting to strike for more pay." The truth was that Miss Hellman and the other supporters of the Guild felt they had been fighting for the little people again, the anonymous forty-dollar-a-week writers, and she suspected that MacArthur knew that. Although she has a gentlemanly quality of never being rude to anyone unintentionally, she can sometimes hit below the belt. "Let me see," she said to him idly. "You used to write for pictures, too, once, didn't you? Whatever became of you?" The Wagner Act was passed in 1935, and the Screen Writers' Guild was reestablished shortly afterward. Miss Hellman's standing with Goldwyn, which is exalted, antedates those events, however, by at least a year. Some people say it goes back to the time she made *The Children's Hour* into a good, uncensorable movie, *These Three,* by replacing the Lesbian theme with the simple triangle; others, including Dashiell Hammett, maintain that her success with Goldwyn springs from a mutual gift they have for causing people to vanish by not looking at them. "When Sam doesn't look at you, you cease to exist," Hammett explains. "Lillian solves that by just not looking at *him.*" Miss Hellman's contract with Goldwyn pays her thirty-five hundred dollars a week for as many weeks as she wants to work, whenever she wants to.

From this cushioned ease, she worries harder than ever about the hope and doom of the world these days. Once or twice lately she has quoted T. S. Eliot's lines from *The Hollow Men:*

> This is the way the world ends
> Not with a bang but a whimper.

She will repeat them in conversation, looking thoughtful and faraway. But she never stays dreamy long. Her zest for living soon recalls her to the realities of food, clothes, friends, work, war, enemies, love, hate, and indignation, and when she returns to them it is not with a whimper but a bang.

Lillian Hellman: An Interview

John Phillips and
Anne Hollander*

Miss Hellman spends her summers in a comfortable white house at the bottom of a sandbank in the town of Vineyard Haven, Massachusetts, on the island of Martha's Vineyard. There is none of old Cape Cod about it; a modern house, newly built with lots of big windows and a wooden deck facing on the harbor. Miss Hellman observes the ferries of Woods Hole–Martha's Vineyard–Nantucket Steamship Authority, weighted down with passengers and automobiles, push through the harbor on their midsummer schedule and disgorge ever more visitors upon this teeming, heterogeneous resort. It is a measure of Miss Hellman's dedication to her work that she achieves so much in her exposed situation, not half a mile from the ferry dock. Here she stays with her maid, and a big barking poodle that discourages few of the peak-of-the-season visitors who troop through her parlor.

Behind this new house and out of view on top of the sandbank is the old one, which Miss Hellman sold after Dashiell Hammett died. A frame house with yellow painted shingles and climbing roses, plainer and more regional in its architecture, like a Yankee farmhouse of the last century, it had a complex of boxlike rooms where Miss Hellman's guests thronged. Removed from these, on the far east wing of the house, stood a tower formed by the shell of an old Cape Cod windmill. Up in this windmill tower was the room where Dashiell Hammett lived; he always escaped there when company came. He had been an invalid since the war; he became a recluse and at the end of his life talked to almost nobody. Hammett was a thin, finely built man and very tall—when he was seen walking in delicate silence, in the cruel wasting of his illness, down a crowded sidewalk on his way to the library, unrecognized, unknown, forgotten, the proudness of his bearing set him off from the summer people.

Occasionally a stranger would come in the house uninvited and catch Dashiell Hammett off guard. He might be reading in an easy chair. Miss Hellman would introduce him, and he would elegantly rise and shake hands. Like many a famous writer who detests being disturbed in his private self, a million miles from any social confrontation, he had learned to scare off the intruder with his smile. Here he was luckier than most, for rather than looking pained and fraudulent, rather than a predictable Sam Spade/ Humphrey Bogart hard-guy leer, the smile Dashiell Hammett produced on his clear-eyed, lean, aristocratic face was so nearly beatific that it disarmed the intruder long enough for Dashiell Hammett, with no more than a how-do-you-do, to vanish from the room. The armchair or the book gave his only

*Reprinted from *Writers at Work: The Paris Review Interviews*, 3d series, ed. George Plimpton (New York: Viking Press, 1967), 115–40. Originally published in *Paris Review* 33 (Winter–Spring 1965):64–95. ©1967 by The Paris Review, Inc. Reprinted by permission of Viking Penguin Inc.

evidence. Even the invited dinner guest coming punctually into the room would know the same ectoplasmic presence, when Miss Hellman, the laughter mingled in her greeting, would immediately explain what Dash had said—what his joking exit line had been on, it seemed, the instant of your entrance. He was elusive but never aloof. Through the medium of Miss Hellman it was possible to carry on a running extrasensory conversation. A question to him, put through to her, on one evening (as how to clean a meerschaum pipe) or a request for an opinion (on somebody's writing, on something President Eisenhower did) was sure to be answered on another. And five years before the meeting with Miss Hellman, a request had been put in writing for a Paris Review *interview. He was by then at the end of his tether, often too weak to take his meals at the table. An answer came: "Sorry. Don't think it would work. Lilly will explain." Which she does, though neither by design nor by coincidence, in this interview. On a table in the parlor where she talked was a framed snapshot of Dashiell Hammett as he looked in World War II as a corporal in the Army Service Forces. He is lighting his cigarette on a PX-Zippo lighter and looking every inch a soldier in his impeccably creased suntans and overseas cap tilted toward the right of his head of white hair.*

Miss Hellman's voice has a quality, not to be captured on the page, of being at once angry, funny, slyly feminine, sad, affectionate, and harsh. While talking here she often allowed her laughter, like an antidote to bitterness, to break into her thoughts and give a more generous dimension to her comments, which, in print, may seem at first glance merely captious. These pages are compiled from three afternoon conversations in the more than usually harrying conditions of the Labor Day weekend on Martha's Vineyard, while Miss Hellman was driving herself to finish a movie script for Sam Spiegel. There were many interruptions—telephone calls and people coming and going in the room. Such circumstances cannot excuse but may in part explain some of the interviewers' unrehearsed and too eagerly "literary" questions.

INTERVIEWER: Before you wrote plays, did you write anything else?

HELLMAN: Yes, short stories, a few poems. A couple of the stories were printed in a long-dead magazine called *The Paris Comet* for which Arthur Kober worked. Arthur and I were married and living in Paris. Let's see, about 1928, 1929, somewhere in there. They were very lady-writer stories. I reread them a few years ago. The kind of stories where the man puts his fork down and the woman knows it's all over. You know.

INTERVIEWER: Was it Dashiell Hammett who encouraged you to write plays?

HELLMAN: No. He disliked the theater. He always wanted me to write a novel. I wrote a play before *The Children's Hour* with Louis Kronenberger called *The Dear Queen*. It was about a royal family. A royal family who wanted to be bourgeois. They kept running away to be middle class, and Dash used to say the play was no good because Louis would laugh only at his lines and I would laugh only at mine.

INTERVIEWER: Which of your plays do you like best?

HELLMAN: I don't like that question. You always like best the last thing you did. You like to think that you got better with time. But you know it isn't always true. I very seldom reread the plays. The few times I have, I have been pleasantly surprised by things that were better than I had remembered and horrified by other things I had thought were good. But I suppose *Autumn Garden*. I suppose I think it is the best play, if that is what you mean by "like."

INTERVIEWER: Somebody who saw you watch the opening night in Paris of Simone Signoret's adaptation of *The Little Foxes* said that through the performance you kept leaving your seat and pacing the vestibule.

HELLMAN: I jump up and down through most performances. But that particular night I was shaken by what I was seeing. I like *Little Foxes*, but I'm tired of it. I don't think many writers like best their best-known piece of work, particularly when it was written a long time ago.

INTERVIEWER: What prompted you to go back to the theme and the characters of *The Little Foxes*? Only seven years later you wrote *Another Part of the Forest*.

HELLMAN: I always intended to do *The Little Foxes* as a trilogy. Regina in *The Little Foxes* is about thirty-eight years old, and the year is 1900. I had meant to take up with her again in about 1920 or 1925, in Europe. And her daughter, Alexandra, was to have become maybe a spinsterish social worker, disappointed, a rather angry woman.

INTERVIEWER: In the third act of *The Little Foxes* is a speech which carries the burden of the play. It says there are people who eat the earth and all the people on it, like the locusts in the Bible. And there are the people who let them do it. "Sometimes I think it ain't right to stand by and watch them do it." At the end of this play Alexandra decides that she is not going to be one of those passive people. She is going to leave her mother.

HELLMAN: Yes, I meant her to leave. But to my great surprise, the ending of the play was taken to be a statement of faith in Alexandra, in her denial of her family. I never meant it that way. She did have courage enough to leave, but she would never have the force or vigor of her mother's family. That's what I meant. Or maybe I made it up afterward.

INTERVIEWER: These wheelers and dealers in your plays—the gouging, avaricious Hubbards. Had you known many people like that?

HELLMAN: Lots of people thought it was my mother's family.

INTERVIEWER: Might you ever write that third play?

HELLMAN: I'm tired of the people in *The Little Foxes*.

INTERVIEWER: In *Regina*, the opera Marc Blitzstein based on *The Little Foxes*, the badness of Regina is most emphatic.

HELLMAN: Marc and I were close friends but we never collaborated. I had nothing to do with the opera. I never saw Regina that way. You have no right to see your characters as good or bad. Such words have nothing to do with people you write about. Other people see them that way.

INTERVIEWER: You say in your introduction that *The Children's Hour* is about goodness and badness.

HELLMAN: Goodness and badness is different from good and bad people, isn't it? *The Children's Hour*—I was pleased with the results—was a kind of exercise. I didn't know how to write a play and I was teaching myself. I chose, or Dashiell Hammett chose for me, an actual law case, on the theory that I would do better with something that was there, had a foundation in fact. I didn't want to write about myself at the age of twenty-six. The play was based on a law case in a book by William Roughead. I changed it, of course, completely, by the time I finished. The case took place in Edinburgh in the nineteenth century, and was about two old-maid schoolteachers who ran a sort of second-rate private school. A little Indian girl—an India Indian—had been enrolled by her grandmother in the school. She brought charges of Lesbianism against the two teachers. The two poor middle-aged ladies spent the rest of their lives suing, sometimes losing, sometimes winning, until they no longer had any money and no school.

INTERVIEWER: As a rule does the germ of a play come to you abstractly? Do you work from a general conception?

HELLMAN: No, I've never done that. I used to say that I saw a play only in terms of the people in it. I used to say that because I believed that is the way you do the best work. I have come now to think that it is people *and* ideas.

INTERVIEWER: Have characters invented themselves before you write them?

HELLMAN: I don't think characters turn out the way you think they are going to turn out. They don't always go your way. At least they don't go my way. If I wanted to start writing about you, by page ten I probably wouldn't be. I don't think you start with a person. I think you start with the parts of many people. Drama has to do with conflict in people, with denials. But I don't really know much about the process of creation and I don't like talking about it.

INTERVIEWER: Is there someting mysterious in what a play evokes as art and the craft of writing it?

HELLMAN: Sure. That is really the only mystery because theories may work for one person and not for another. It's very hard, at least for me, to have theories about writing.

INTERVIEWER: But you had to begin with a clear idea of what the action of the play would be?

HELLMAN: Not always. Not as I got older. It was bright of Hammett to see that somebody starting to write should have a solid foundation to build on. It made the wheels go easier. When I first started to write I used to do two or three page outlines. Afterward, I didn't.

INTERVIEWER: Do you think the kind of play you do—the well-made play, one which runs the honest risk of melodrama for a purpose—is going to survive?

HELLMAN: I don't know what survives and what doesn't. Like everybody else, I hope I will survive. But survival won't have anything to do with well-made or not well-made, or words like "melodrama." I don't like labels and isms. They are for people who raise or lower skirts because that's the thing you do for this year. You write as you write, in your time, as you see your world. One form is as good as another. There are a thousand ways to write, and each is as good as the other if it fits you, if you are any good. If you can break into a new pattern along the way, and it opens things up, and allows you more freedom, that's something. But not everything, maybe even not much. Take any form, and if you're good—

INTERVIEWER: Do you have to do with the casting of your plays?

HELLMAN: Yes.

INTERVIEWER: Do you feel you were well served always?

HELLMAN: Sometimes, sometimes not. *Candide* and *My Mother, My Father and Me* were botched, and I helped to do the botching. You never know with failures who has done the harm. *Days to Come* was botched. The whole production was botched, including my botching. It was an absolute horror of a failure. I mean the curtain wasn't up ten minutes and catastrophe set in. It was just an awful failure. Mr. William Randolph Hearst caused a little excitement by getting up in the middle of the first act and leaving with his party of ten. I vomited in the back aisle. I did. I had to go home and change my clothes. I was drunk.

INTERVIEWER: Have you enjoyed the adaptations you have done of European plays?

HELLMAN: Sometimes, not always. I didn't like Anouilh's *The Lark* very much. But I didn't discover I didn't like it until I was halfway through. I like *Montserrat*. I don't seem to have good luck with adaptations. I got nothing but pain out of *Candide*. That's a long story. No, I had a good time on *Candide* when I was working alone. I am not a collaborator. It was a stormy collaboration. But I had a good time alone.

INTERVIEWER: *Candide* was a box-office failure, but obviously it was a success. The record is very popular.

HELLMAN: It has become a cult show. It happens. I'm glad.

INTERVIEWER: Do you think *My Mother, My Father and Me* was a cult show?

HELLMAN: It opened during the newspaper strike, and that was fatal. Yes, I guess we were a cult show. Oddly enough, mostly with jazz musicians. The last week the audience was filled with jazz musicians. Stan Getz had come to see it and liked it, and he must have told his friends about it. I hope it will be revived because I like it. Off Broadway. I had wanted it done off Broadway in the beginning.

INTERVIEWER: Can you comment on your contemporaries—Arthur Miller?

HELLMAN: I like *Death of a Salesman*. I have reservations about it, but I thought it was an effective play. I like best *View from the Bridge*.

INTERVIEWER: *After the Fall?*

HELLMAN: So you put on a stage your ex-wife who is dead from suicide and you dress her up so nobody can mistake her. Her name is Marilyn Monroe, good at any box office, so you cash in on her, and cash in on yourself, which is maybe even worse.

INTERVIEWER: In an important subplot of this play a man who was once briefly a communist names a close friend before a congressional committee.

HELLMAN: I couldn't understand all that. Miller felt differently once upon a time, although I never much liked his House Un-American Committee testimony: a little breast-beating and a little apology. And recently I went back to reread it and liked it even less. I suppose, in the play, he was being tolerant: those who betrayed their friends had a point, those who didn't also had a point. Two sides to every question and all that rot.

INTERVIEWER: And Tennessee Williams?

HELLMAN: I think he is a natural playwright. He writes by sanded fingertips. I don't always like his plays—the last three or four seem to me. to have gone off, kind of way out in a conventional way. He is throwing his talent around.

INTERVIEWER: Mary McCarthy wrote in a review that you get the feeling that no matter what happens Mr. Williams will be rich and famous.

HELLMAN: I have the same feeling about Miss McCarthy.

INTERVIEWER: She has accused you of, among other things, a certain "lubricity," of an overfacility in answering complex questions. Being too facile, relying on contrivance.

HELLMAN: I don't like to defend myself against Miss McCarthy's opinions, or anybody else's. I think Miss McCarthy is often brilliant and sometimes even sound. But, in fiction, she is a lady writer, a lady magazine writer. Of course, that doesn't mean that she isn't right about me. But if I thought she was, I'd quit. I would like critics to like my plays because that is what makes plays successful. But a few people I respect are the only ones whose opinions I've worried about in the end.

INTERVIEWER: There is a special element in your plays—of tension rising into violence. In *Days to Come* and *Watch on the Rhine* there are killings directly on stage. Was there possibly, from your association with Dashiell Hammett and his work, some sort of influence, probably indirect, on you?

HELLMAN: I don't think so, I don't think so. Dash and I thought differently and were totally different writers. He frequently objected to my use of violence. He often felt that I was far too held up by how to do things, by the technique. I guess he was right. But he wasn't writing for the theater and I was.

INTERVIEWER: You have written a lot of movies?

HELLMAN: Let's see. I wrote a picture called *The Dark Angel* when I first started. I did the adaptation of *Dead End*. I did the adaptation of *The Little Foxes*. Right now I'm doing a picture called *The Chase*.

INTERVIEWER: Did you ever worry about Hollywood being a dead end for a serious writer?

HELLMAN: Never. I wouldn't have written movies if I'd thought that. When I first went out to Hollywood one heard talk from writers about whoring. But you are not tempted to whore unless you want to be a whore.

INTERVIEWER: The other night when we listened to Pete Seeger sing his folk songs you seemed nostalgic.

HELLMAN: I was moved by seeing a man of conviction again.

INTERVIEWER: We aren't making them like that any more?

HELLMAN: Not too many. Seeger's naïveté and the sweetness, the hard work, the depth of belief I found touching. He reminded me of very different times and people. There were always X number of clowns, X number of simple-minded fools, X number of fashionables who just went along with what was being said and done, but there were also remarkable people, people of belief, people willing to live by their beliefs. Roosevelt gave you a feeling that you had something to do with your government, something to do with better conditions for yourself and for other people. With all its foolishness, the thirties were a good time and I often have regrets for it. Many people of my age make fun of that period, and are bitter about it. A few do so out of a genuine regret for foolish things said or foolish things done—but many do so because belief is unfashionable now and fear comes with middle age.

INTERVIEWER: Do people still mention your statement before the House Un-American Activities Committee: "I can't cut my conscience to fit this year's fashions"?

HELLMAN: Yes.

INTERVIEWER: Did that put you in contempt of Congress?

HELLMAN: No, I never was in contempt. They brought no contempt charges at the end of that day. My lawyer, Joseph Rauh, was so proud and pleased. He was afraid I would be harmed because I might have waived my rights under the Fifth Amendment.

INTERVIEWER: You took the stand that you would tell the committee all they wanted to know about you, but you weren't going to bring bad trouble upon innocent people no matter if they had been fooled?

HELLMAN: We sent a letter* saying that I would come and testify about myself as long as I wasn't asked questions about other people. But the committee wasn't interested in that. I think they knew I was innocent, but they were interested in other people. It was very common in those days, not only to talk about other people, but to make the talk as interesting as possible. Friendly witnesses, so-called, would often make their past more colorful than ever was the case. Otherwise you might turn out to be dull. I thought mine was a good position to take—I still think so.

INTERVIEWER: Was it something of a custom among theater people in those days, when they were going to name some old acquaintance to a committee, to call him beforehand and let him know? Just to be fair and square, as it were?

HELLMAN: Yes. They would telephone around among their friends. In several cases the to-be-injured people actually gave their permission. They understood the motive of their friends' betrayal—money, injury to a career. Oh, yes, there was a great deal of telephoning around. Kind of worse than testifying, isn't it?—the fraternity of the betrayers and the betrayed. There was a man in California who had been barred from pictures because he had been a communist. After a while he was broke, this Mr. Smith, and his mother-in-law, who was getting bored with him— anybody would have been bored with him—said that he could have a little piece of land. So he started to build a two-room house, and he borrowed the tools from his closest friend, his old college roommate, Mr. Jones. He had been working on his house for about seven or eight months and almost had it finished when Mr. Jones arrived to say that he had to

---

*Following the interview is the text of this letter. The Committee rejected the proposal contained in the letter.

have the tools back because, he, Mr. Jones, was being called before the committee the next day and was going to name Mr. Smith and thought it was rather unethical for Mr. Smith to have his tools while he was naming him. I don't know whether the house ever got finished. Clowns, they were.

INTERVIEWER: A little-known aspect of Lillian Hellman is that she was the inspiration for Dashiell Hammett's Nora Charles, the loyal wife of Nick Charles, the detective-hero of *The Thin Man*. That marriage is beautifully evoked in the book and was played by William Powell and Myrna Loy in the movies.

HELLMAN: Yes.

INTERVIEWER: Didn't it give you some gratification?

HELLMAN: It did, indeed.

INTERVIEWER: When Myrna Loy turned into her, then she became the perfect wife.

HELLMAN: Yes. I liked that. But Nora is often a foolish lady. She goes around trying to get Nick into trouble.

INTERVIEWER: And that was about you both?

HELLMAN: Well, Hammett and I had a good time together. Most of it, not all of it. We were amused by each other.

INTERVIEWER: Was it because of that book that Gertrude Stein invited you to dinner?

HELLMAN: Miss Stein arrived in America and said that there were two people that she wanted to meet. They were both in California at that minute—Chaplin and Dash. And we were invited to dinner at the house of a friend of Miss Stein; Charlie Chaplin, Dash and myself, Paulette Goddard, Miss Toklas, our host and hostess, and another man. There was this magnificent china and lace tablecloth. Chaplin turned over his coffee cup, nowhere near Stein, just all over this beautiful cloth, and the first thing Miss Stein said was, "Don't worry, it didn't get on me." She was miles away from him. She said it perfectly seriously. Then she told Dash he was the only American writer who wrote well about women. He was very pleased.

INTERVIEWER: Did he give you any credit for that?

HELLMAN: He pointed to me, but she didn't pay any attention. She wasn't having any part of me. I was just a girl around the table. I talked to Miss Toklas. We talked about food. It was very pleasant.

INTERVIEWER: Did you know Nathanael West?

HELLMAN: He managed a hotel, the Sutton Hotel. We all lived there half free, sometimes all free. Dash wrote *The Thin Man* at the Sutton Hotel. Pep West's uncle or cousin owned it, I think. He gave Pep a job out of kindness. There couldn't have been any other reason. Pep liked opening letters addressed to the guests. He was writing, you know, and he was curious about everything and everybody. He would steam open envelopes, and I would help him. He wanted to know about everybody.

Dash had the Royal Suite—three very small rooms. And we had to eat there most of the time because we didn't have enough money to eat any place else. It was awful food, almost spoiled. I think Pep bought it extra cheap. But it was the depression and I couldn't get a job. I remember reading the manuscript of *Balso Snell* in the hotel. And I think he was also writing *Lonelyhearts* at that time. Dash was writing *The Thin Man*. The hotel had started out very fancy—it had a swimming pool. I spent a good deal of time in the swimming pool . . . I had nothing else to do with myself.

Then the Perelmans* bought a house in Bucks County. We all went down to see it. There was a dead fish in a closet. I don't know why I remember that fish. Later we would all go down for weekends, to hunt. I have a snapshot of the Perelmans and Dash and me and Pep and Bob Coates.

Even in a fuzzy snapshot you can see that we are all drunk. We used to go hunting. My memory of those hunting trips is of trying to be the last to climb the fence, with the other guns in front of me, just in case, Pep was a good shot. He used to hunt with Faulkner. So was Dash.

INTERVIEWER: Did Faulkner come around a lot in those days?

HELLMAN: Faulkner and Dash liked each other. Dash's short stories were selling, the movies were selling. So we had a lot of money, and he gave it away and we lived fine. Always, he gave it away—to the end of his life when there wasn't much, any more. We met every night at some point for months on end, during one of Faulkner's New York visits. We had literary discussions. A constant argument about Thomas Mann. This must have taken up weeks of time.

INTERVIEWER: Was Faulkner quiet?

HELLMAN: He was a gallant man, very Southern. He used to call me Miss Lillian. I never was to see him much after that period, until a few years ago when I saw him a couple of times. We remembered the days with Dash, and he said what a good time in his life that was and what a good time we had had together.

INTERVIEWER: Was any play easy to write?

HELLMAN: *Autumn Garden* was easier than any other.

INTERVIEWER: At the very end of the play, the retired general, Griggs, makes one of the rare speeches in your plays that is of a remotely "philosophic" nature.

HELLMAN: Dash wrote that speech. I worked on it over and over again

*S.J. Perelman was West's brother-in-law.

but it never came right. One night he said, "Go to bed and let me try." Dash comes into this interview very often, doesn't he?

INTERVIEWER: "That big hour of decision, the turning point in your life, the someday you've counted on when you'd suddenly wipe out your past mistakes, do the work you'd never done, think the way you'd never thought, have what you'd never had, it just doesn't come suddenly. You trained yourself for it while you waited—or you've let it all run past you and frittered yourself away."

HELLMAN: Yes, the basic idea was his. Dash was hipped on the subject. I think I believe that speech . . . I know I do. . . . Dash worked at it far harder than I ever have, as his death proved. He wasn't prepared for death, but he was prepared for the trouble and the sickness he had, and was able to bear it—I think, because of this belief—with enormous courage, and quietness.

INTERVIEWER: What is the sensation the writer has when he hears his own words from the mouth of somebody else? Of even the most gifted actor?

HELLMAN: Sometimes you're pleased and the words take on meanings they didn't have before, larger meanings. But sometimes it is the opposite. There is no rule. I don't have to tell you that speech on the stage is not the speech of life, not even the written speech.

INTERVIEWER: But do you hear dialogue spoken when you are writing it?

HELLMAN: I guess I do. Anyway, I read it to myself. I usually know in the first few days of rehearsals what I have made actors stumble over, and what can or cannot be cured.

INTERVIEWER: Do you have disputes with actors who want their lines changed?

HELLMAN: Not too many. I took a stubborn stand on the first play and now I have a reputation for stubbornness.

INTERVIEWER: Is that because you have written always to be read, even more than to be acted?

HELLMAN: Partly. But I had learned early that in the theater, good or bad, you'd better stand on what you did. In *Candide* I was persuaded to do what I didn't believe in, and I am no good at all at that game. It wasn't that the other people were necessarily wrong. I just couldn't do what they wanted. With age, I guess, I began to want to be agreeable.

INTERVIEWER: Would you mind if your plays were never produced again but only read?

HELLMAN: I wouldn't like it. Plays are there to be acted. I want both.

INTERVIEWER: The famous Hemingway dialogue, the best of it, turns to parody when actors speak it verbatim in adaptations of his work.

HELLMAN: That's right. It shows up, it shows up. That's just what I meant by listening to the actor. Writing for the theater is a totally different form. But then, if you want to be good and hope people will also read the plays, then it becomes a question of making sure the two forms come together. Very often in the printed form, you must recast a sentence. I do it—when I'm not too lazy—for the published version. But in minor ways, like changing the place of a verb, or punctuation. I overpunctuate for theater scripts.

INTERVIEWER: Do you think the political message in some of your plays is more important than the characters and the development?

HELLMAN: I've never been interested in political messages, so it is hard for me to believe I wrote them. Like every other writer, I use myself and the time I live in. The nearest thing to a political play was *The Searching Wind*, which is probably why I don't like it much any more. But even there I meant only to write about nice, well-born people who, with good intentions, helped to sell out a world.

INTERVIEWER: Maybe this was one play in which you were more concerned with a situation of crisis than with your characters?

HELLMAN: Yes. But I didn't know that when I was writing it. I felt very strongly that people had gotten us into a bad situation—gotten us into a war that could have been avoided if fascism had been recognized early enough.

INTERVIEWER: What were you doing in those war years?

HELLMAN: In 1944 I was invited by the Russians to come on a kind of cultural mission. Maybe because they were producing *Watch on the Rhine* and *The Little Foxes* in Moscow.

INTERVIEWER: What were those productions like?

HELLMAN: *The Little Foxes* was an excellent production. *Watch on the Rhine* was very bad. I had thought it would be the other way around. I would go to rehearsals of *Watch on the Rhine* with Serge Eisenstein, and when I made faces or noises, he would say, "Never mind, never mind. It's a good play. Don't pay any attention to what they are doing. They can't ruin it." I saw a great deal of Eisenstein. I was very fond of him.

INTERVIEWER: When did you discover that you could no longer earn money by writing for the movies?

HELLMAN: I learned about the black-listing by accident in 1948. Wyler and I were going to do *Sister Carrie*. Somebody, I think Mr. Balaban, told Wyler that I couldn't be hired. That unwritten, unofficial, powerful black list stayed in effect until two or three years ago.

INTERVIEWER: Weren't you offered clearance if you would sign something? If you made an appropriate act of contrition?

HELLMAN: Later. Shortly after the first black-listing I was offered a contract by Columbia Pictures—a contract that I had always wanted—to direct, produce, and write, all three or any. And a great, great deal of money. But it came at the time of the famous movie conference of top Hollywood producers. They met to face the attacks of the Red-baiters and to appease them down. A new clause went into movie contracts. I no longer remember the legal phrases, but it was a lulu. I didn't sign the contract.

INTERVIEWER: What did you think about what was happening?

HELLMAN: I was so unprepared for it all, so surprised McCarthy was happening in America. So few people fought, so few people spoke out. I think I was more surprised by that than I was by McCarthy.

INTERVIEWER: People in the theater or pictures?

HELLMAN: Yes, and literary people and liberals. Still painful to me, still puzzling. Recently I was asked to sign a protest about Polish writers. I signed it—it was a good protest, I thought—and went out to mail it. But I tore it up when I realized not one of the people protesting had ever protested about any of us.

INTERVIEWER: What did you think was going to happen?

HELLMAN: I thought McCarthy would last longer than he did. I thought the whole period would be worse and longer than it was. You know, I was very worried about Dash. He was a sick man and I was scared that he might go back to prison and get sicker—I lived for a long time in fear that he would go back and not get good medical treatment and be alone and— But jail hadn't worried him much or he pretended it hadn't. It amused him to act as if jail was like college. He talked about going to jail the way people talk about going to college. He used to make me angry. . . .

INTERVIEWER: *The Maltese Falcon* was taken off the shelves of the U.S.I.S. libraries when Roy Cohn and David Schine were riding high. Dashiell Hammett was called before Senator McCarthy's committee.

HELLMAN: Yes. It was on television and I watched it. They called Dash, and Dash was a handsome man, a remarkably handsome man, and he looked nice. One of the senators, I think McCarthy, said to him, "Mr. Hammett, if you were in our position, would you allow your books in U.S.I.S. libraries?" And he said, "If I were you, Senator, I would not allow any libraries." A good remark. McCarthy laughed. Nobody else did, but McCarthy did. Dash had an extremely irritating habit of shrugging his shoulders. For years I would say, "Please don't shrug your shoulders." I don't know why it worried me, but it did. He was shrugging his shoulders like mad at the committee. He'd give an answer, and he'd shrug his shoulders with it. And when he was finished and got to the airport he rang me up and said, "Hey, how did you like it? I was shrugging my shoulders just for you."

INTERVIEWER: Did that period—and its effect on people—appeal to you as a subject?

HELLMAN: I've never known how to do it. It was really a clownish period. It was full of clowns talking their heads off, apologizing, inventing sins to apologize for. And other clowns, liberals, who just took to the hills. Ugly clowning is a hard thing to write about. Few people acted large enough for drama and not pleasant enough for comedy.

INTERVIEWER: Then you went to England to do a movie?

HELLMAN: I used to try to explain that it wasn't as bad as they thought it was. And it wasn't. They were exaggerating it because they don't always like us very much. So much talk about fascism here and how many people were in jail. The only time I ever met Richard Crossman, he didn't know I knew Hammett. Hammett was in jail, and Crossman said what a disgrace that was. "What's the matter with all of you, you don't lift a finger for this man? It couldn't happen here, we'd have raised a row." I told him I had lifted a finger.

INTERVIEWER: Did you ever think of living abroad as other Americans were doing?

HELLMAN: I was tempted to stay in England, but I couldn't. I like this country. This is where I belong. Anyway, I don't much like exiles. But I used to try to persuade Dash to go away, just to save his life. He had emphysema. He caught tuberculosis in the First World War and emphysema in the Second. He had never been to Europe. He used to laugh when I suggested his leaving here. He had a provincial dislike of foreigners, and an amused contempt for Russian bureaucracy. He didn't understand all of our trotting around Europe. Thought it was a waste of time.

INTERVIEWER: Did he laugh at the idea that they admired him over there?

HELLMAN: No. He liked it but it didn't interest him much. When I told him that André Gide admired him, he made joke which you can't print.

INTERVIEWER: Let's be bold.

HELLMAN: All right. He said, "I wish that fag would take me out of his mouth."

INTERVIEWER: Whom did he want to admire his work?

HELLMAN: Like most writers he wanted to be admired by good writers. He had started off as a pulp writer, you know, and had a wide audience— he wrote a lot for a pulp mystery magazine, *The Black Mask*. But I believe Dash took himself very seriously as a writer from the beginning.

INTERVIEWER: He helped you with your work. Did you help him with his?

HELLMAN: No, no.

INTERVIEWER: Did he show you his novels while he was writing them?

HELLMAN: *The Thin Man* and some stories, and a novel unfinished at his death. The other novels were written before I met him.

INTERVIEWER: But he worked very painstakingly with you, on your work.

HELLMAN: Oh, yes, and was very critical of me. The rules didn't apply the other way. I had many problems writing *The Little Foxes*. When I thought I had got it right, I wanted Dash to read it. It was five o'clock in the morning. I was pleased with this sixth version, and I put the manuscript near his door with a note, "I hope *this* satisfies you." When I got up, the manuscript was outside my door with a note saying, "Things are going pretty well if you will just cut out the liberal blackamoor chitchat."

INTERVIEWER: He meant the Negro servants talking?

HELLMAN: Yes. No other praise, just that.

INTERVIEWER: So you knew you were all right?

HELLMAN: No, I wrote it all over again. He was generous with anybody who asked for help. He felt that you didn't lie about writing and anybody who couldn't take hard words was about to be shrugged off, anyway. He was a dedicated man about writing. Tough and generous.

INTERVIEWER: Was he always reasonably successful?

HELLMAN: Oh, no. He earned a kind of living at first, but pulp magazines didn't pay much. He was not really discovered until shortly before I met him, in 1930. He had been writing for a long time.

INTERVIEWER: He read constantly?

HELLMAN: Enormously. He had little formal education. He quit school at thirteen to work. He was the most widely read person I ever knew. He read anything, just anything. All kinds of science books, farm books, books on making turtle traps, tying knots, novels—he spent almost a year on the retina of the eye. I got very tired of retinas. And there was a period of poisonous plants and Icelandic sagas and how to take the muddy taste from lake bass. I finally made a rule that I would not listen to any more retina-of-the-eye talk or knot talk or baseball talk or football talk.

INTERVIEWER: Do you consider yourself to be closely tied to the theater and to "theater people"?

HELLMAN: In the early days I didn't think it out, but I stayed away from them. I was frightened of competing. I felt that the further I stayed away, the better chance I had. No, I don't know too many theater people.

INTERVIEWER: A man who has known both breeds said that on the whole writers are even more narcissistic and nastier and more competitive than people in show biz.

HELLMAN: Hard to know the more or less. But people in the theater are usually generous with money and often with good will. Maybe the old-troupers world—having to live together and sharing. Writers are interesting people, but often mean and petty. Competing with each other and ungenerous about each other. Hemingway was ungenerous about other writers. Most writers are. Writers can be the stinkers of all time, can't they?

INTERVIEWER: The playwright knows dangers that are different from those the novelists know?

HELLMAN: Yes, because failure is faster in the theater. It is necessary that you not become frightened of failure. Failure in the theater is more dramatic and uglier than in any other form of writing. It costs so much, you feel so guilty. In the production of *Candide,* for the first time in my life, I guess, I was worried by all this. It was bad for me.

INTERVIEWER: Writing about the Lincoln Center Repertory in the *New York Review of Books,* Elizabeth Hardwick said that the trouble with the present theater is that it is all professionalism and is divorced from literature.

HELLMAN: Yes, of course she was right. There shouldn't be any difference between writing for the theater and writing for anything else. Only that one has to know the theater. Know it. To publish a novel or a poem one doesn't have to know print types or the publishing world. But to do a play, no matter how much one wishes to stay away from it, one has to *know* the theater. Playwrights have tried to stay away, including Shaw and Chekhov, but in the end, they were involved. Chekhov used to send letters of instructions and angry notes. A play is not only on paper. It is there to share with actors, directors, scene designers, electricians.

INTERVIEWER: Do you believe there are many talented writers working at present?

HELLMAN: Yes, but nothing like the period when I was very young, in the twenties. That was a wonderfully talented generation, the one before mine. But, you know, I think there's talent around now. Maybe not great talent, but how often does that occur anyway? It is good that we have this much. And there are signs now of cutting up. They are not always to my taste, but that doesn't matter. Cutting up is a form of belief, a negative expression of it, but belief.

INTERVIEWER: The hard professionalism in writers of that generation, like Ring Lardner, Dashiell Hammett, or Dorothy Parker, seems very unfashionable now. Young writers take themselves very seriously as highbrows and artists.

HELLMAN: The writer's intention hasn't anything to do with what he achieves. The intent to earn money or the intent to be famous or the intent to be great doesn't matter in the end. Just what comes out. It is a present fashion to believe that the best writing comes out of a hophead's dream. You pitch it around and paste it up. So sentimental.

INTERVIEWER: Sentimental or romantic?

HELLMAN: Romantic and sentimental. I am surprised, for example, at the sentimentality in much of Genet, and surprised that people are romantic enough not to see its sentimentality. I mean a sentimental way of looking at life, at sex, at love, at the way you live or the way you think. It is interesting that the "way-out" is not the sharpness of a point of view or the toughness, but just tough words and tough actions, masking the romantic. Violence, in space, is a romantic notion. Antibourgeois in an old-fashioned sense.

INTERVIEWER: Philip Rahv said the old idea of *épatisme* is dead. You can no longer scandalize the bourgeois. He may be vicious about defending his property; but as to morality, he is wide open to any and all nihilistic ideas.

HELLMAN: Yes, indeed. He has caught up. That is what words like "the sexual revolution" mean, I guess—the bourgeois sexual revolution. I agree with Philip. "Epataying" is just a sticking out of the tongue now, isn't it? The tongue or other organs.

INTERVIEWER: You have seen a lot of the contemporary theater in Europe. How does it compare with ours?

HELLMAN: The British have more talented young men and women than we have here, but I doubt if they are major talents. Genet and Ionesco are interesting men, but they are not to my taste in the theater. Beckett is the only possibly first-rate talent in the world theater. But he must grow larger, the scale's too small. We don't know much about the Russian theater. Obviously, it hasn't produced good playwrights. Certainly not when I was there. But Russian production, directing, and acting are often wonderful. But that's a dead end. When the major talents are directors, actors, and scene designers—that's dead-end theater. Fine to see, but it ain't going nowhere. You have to turn out good new writers.

INTERVIEWER: What about the revival of Brecht?

HELLMAN: Brecht was the truest talent of the last forty or fifty years. But a great deal of nonsense has been written about Brecht. Brecht himself talked a great deal of nonsense. Deliberately, I think. He was a showman and it is showman-like in the theater to have theories. But that doesn't matter. What a wonderful play *Galileo* is. Writers talk too much.

INTERVIEWER: What do you want to do next?

HELLMAN: I am going to edit that anthology. I had a struggle with myself because Dash would not have wanted it. He didn't want the short stories

printed again. But I decided that I was going to have to forget what he
wanted. Someday even the second copyrights will expire and the stories
will be in public domain. I don't really know why he didn't want them
reprinted—maybe because he was too sick to care. It will be a hard job. I
have already started the introduction and I find it very difficult to write
about so complex a man, and even I knew so little of what he was. I am
not sure I can do it in the end, but I am going to have a try. But I don't
know his reasons. Probably when you're sick enough you don't care much.
He went through a bad time.

May 19, 1952

Honorable John S. Wood
Chairman
House Committee on Un-American Activities
Dear Mr. Wood:

As you know, I am under subpoena to appear before your Committee
on May 21, 1952.

I am most willing to answer all questions about myself. I have nothing
to hide from your Committee and there is nothing in my life of which I am
ashamed. I have been advised by counsel that under the Fifth Amendment
I have a constitutional privilege to decline to answer any questions about
my political opinions, activities and associations, on the grounds of self-
incrimination. I do not wish to claim this privilege. I am ready and willing
to testify before representatives of our Government as to my own opinions
and my own actions, regardless of any risks or consequences to myself.

But I am advised by counsel that if I answer the Committee's questions
about myself, I must also answer questions about other people and that if I
refuse to do so, I can be cited for contempt. My counsel tells me that if I
answer questions about myself, I will have waived my rights under the Fifth
Amendment and could be forced legally to answer questions about others.
This is very difficult for a layman to understand. But there is one principle
that I do understand: I am not willing, now or in the future, to bring bad
trouble to people who, in my past association with them, were completely
innocent of any talk or any action that was disloyal or subversive. . . .

But to hurt innocent people whom I knew many years ago in order to
save myself is, to me, inhuman and indecent and dishonorable. I cannot
and will not cut my conscience to fit this year's fashions, even though I long
ago came to the conclusion that I was not a political person and could have
no comfortable place in any political group. . . .

I am prepared to waive the privilege against self-incrimination and to
tell you anything you wish to know about my views or actions if your
Committee will agree to refrain from asking me to name other people. If
the Committee is unwilling to give me this assurance, I will be forced to
plead the privilege of the Fifth Amendment at the hearing.

A reply to this letter would be appreciated.

Sincerely yours,
LILLIAN HELLMAN

Lillian Hellman   John Hersey*

Lillian Hellman has long been known as a moral force, almost an institution of conscience for the rest of us—but my view is that her influence, and her help to us, derive rather from something larger: the picture she gives of a *life* force.

It is the complexity of this organism that stuns and quickens us. Energy, gifts put to work, anger, wit, potent sexuality, wild generosity, a laugh that can split your eardrums, fire in every action, drama in every anecdote, a ferocious sense of justice, personal loyalty raised to the power of passion, fantastic legs and easily turned ankles, smart clothes, a strong stomach, an affinity with the mothering sea, vanity but scorn of all conceit, love of money and gladness in parting with it, a hidden religious streak but an open hatred of piety, a yearning for compliments but a loathing for flattery, fine cookery, a smashing style in speech and manners, unflagging curiosity, fully liberated female aggressiveness when it is needed yet a whiff, now and then, of old-fashioned feminine masochism, fear however of nothing but being afraid, prankishness, flirtatious eyes, a libertine spirit, Puritanism, rebelliousness. . . .

Rebelliousness above all. Rebelliousness is an essence of her vitality— that creative sort of dissatisfaction which shouts out, "Life ought to be better than this!" Every great artist is a rebel. The maker's search for new forms— for ways of testing the givens—is in her a fierce rebellion against what has been accepted and acclaimed and taken for granted. And a deep, deep, rebellious anger against the great cheat of human existence, which is death, feeds her love of life and gives bite to her enjoyment of every minute of it. This rebelliousness, this anger, Lillian Hellman has in unusually great measure, and they are at the heart of the complex vibrancy we feel in her.

But all the attributes I have listed are only the beginnings of her variousness. She has experienced so much! She has had an abortion. She has been analyzed. She has been, and still is, an ambulatory chimney. She drinks her whiskey neat. She has been married and divorced. She has picked up vast amounts of higgledy-piggledy learning, such as how to decapitate a snapping turtle, and I understand that as soon as she completes her dissertation, said to be startlingly rich in research, she will have earned the degree of Doctor of Carnal Knowledge. This is in spite of the fact that during a long black period of American history she imposed celibacy on herself. She will admit, if pressed, that she was the sweetest-smelling baby in New Orleans. As a child she knew gangsters and whores. She has been a liberated woman ever since she played hookey from grade school and perched with her fantasies in the hidden fig tree in the yard of her aunts' boarding house. She is so

*Reprinted from the *New Republic,* 18 September 1976, 25–27, by permission of the journal. John Hersey wrote this homage to Hellman on the occasion of her receiving the Edward MacDowell Medal, previously awarded to Edmund Wilson, Eudora Welty, Norman Mailer, Edward Hopper, and Georgia O'Keeffe.

liberated that she is not at all afraid of the kitchen. She can pluck and cook a goose, and her spaghetti with clam sauce begs belief. She can use an embroidery hoop. She knows how to use a gun. She cares with a passion whether bedsheets are clean. She grows the most amazing roses which are widely thought to be homosexual. She speaks very loud to foreigners, believing the language barrier can be pierced with decibels. She scarfs her food with splendid animal relish, and I can tell you that she has not vomited since May 23, 1952. She must have caught several thousand fish by now, yet she still squeals like a child when she boats a strong blue. I know no living human being whom so many people consider to be their one best friend.

She is not perfect. Her chromosomes took a little nap when they should have been giving her a sense of direction. "We can't be over Providence," she said, flying up here this morning. "Isn't Providence to the south of Martha's Vineyard?"

I told her it was to the northwest of the Vineyard.

"But when you drive to New York, you go through Providence," she said, "and New York is to the south of us."

I said that the only way to drive directly to New York from Martha's Vineyard would be to drive on water, and that I could think of only one person in history who might have been able to do that.

She said, "You mean Jews can't drive to New York?"

God gave her a gift of an ear for every voice but her own, and when she tries to disguise that voice on the telephone, as she sometimes does, the pure Hellman sound comes ringing through the ruse. "No, Miss Hellman is not here," the voice will say. "Miss Hellman is out." The only thing you can be sure of is that Miss Hellman is in.

She is, I believe, the only National Book Award winner who can claim to have had a father who cured his own case of hemorrhoids with generous applications to them of Colgate's tooth paste.

I am fairly certain that she is the only member of the American Academy of Arts and Letters, female or male, who has thwarted an attempted rape by staging a fit of sneezing.

She also has the distinction of being the only author at or near the summit of the best seller lists who has publicly stated that she has always wanted to go to bed with an orangutan.

She is surely the only employee of Sam Goldwyn who ever refused to attend two conferences with the great mogul because of being too busy rolling condoms. (Perhaps I should add, in case you are wondering why this activity was taking place, that it was in the interest of a practical joke.)

Miss Hellman has changed the lives of many people, as teacher or exemplar or scold, and a few people have changed hers. Among these, two stand out:

The first is Sophronia, her wet nurse and the companion of her childhood, and, her father would say, the only control she ever recognized. "Oh, Sophronia, it's you I want back always," Miss Hellman cries out in one of her books. As a kind of pledge of her debt to Sophronia, Miss Hellman sent her the first salary check she ever earned. There is a photograph of this remarkable figure of pride in *An Unfinished Woman,* and looking at it one sees the force of what Miss Hellman writes: "She was an angry woman, and she gave me anger, an uncomfortable, dangerous, and often useful gift." Once, when the child Lillian had seen her father get into a cab with a pretty woman not her mother, Sophronia counselled keeping her mouth shut, saying, "Don't go through life making trouble for people." We all know the stern and dazzling resonance of that advice in Miss Hellman's appearance before the House Un-American Activities Committee in Joe McCarthy's time.

The other person was Dashiell Hammett. With that handsome, sharp-minded, and committed man she had a relationship, off and on, for over 30 years, one which, as she has said, often had "a ragging argumentative tone," but which had "the deep pleasure of continuing interest" and grew and grew into "a passionate affection." Hammett was—and he remains to this day—*her* conscience. He was her artistic conscience, as ruthless with her as he was with himself in his own work, for 10 of her 12 plays. She still makes many a decision by asking herself, sometimes out loud: What would Dash have wanted me to do about this? Death took Hammett and became her enemy.

I have spoken, she herself has spoken, of a religious streak in her. It is hard, perhaps dangerous, to trace or describe it. She is profoundly yet also skeptically Jewish—more in culture and sensibility, obviously, than in faith. She tells of an indiscriminate religiosity that her mother had, dropping in on any handy house of worship. Hers is certainly not like that—yet there is a weird ecumenical something-or-other going here. She writes somewhere of Bohemia bumping into Calvin in her. Calvin! When anything seems unspeakable to her, she will shout "Oy!" and cross herself. When all her beliefs and rituals, serious and playful, are rendered down to their pure state, just this remains: she insists on decency in human transactions.

This places her—a lonely, lonely figure—at the nowhere crossroads of all religions and all politics.

She *is* a moral force, but take a firm grip on your hat!—for the moment will come when the force, operating at high pitch, will suddenly go up in smoke before your eyes, and in its place will stand pure caprice. This is sometimes a mischievous 13-year-old girl.

Nothing gives this girl greater pleasure than to be shocking. She knows I was born in China and love and respect the Chinese, so whenever I'm around, her universe is suddenly thronged with chinks. Niggers, kikes and idiot WASPs crowd tales told to prim folks. Bad food—even if it is bad lox and bagels—is always "goy dreck." She incessantly offers TL's—"trade lasts," compliments spoken by absent parties and offered on a barter basis (there was one in *The Children's Hour*)—but again, be wary; what she gives in exchange often has an ironic barb in it.

If she says, "Forgive me," my advice is to back away. This is a signal for the final blunt blow in an argument. In Vineyard Haven, she and my wife and I have a mutual neighbor, a willful lady whom I shall call, as Miss Hellman calls all women who should be nameless or whose names she has forgotten, Mrs. Gigglewitz. Miss Hellman met Mrs. Gigglewitz downtown one day, and the latter began to complain about the noise certain neighborhood dogs made. One of them, she said, was that awful Hersey dog. The fact of the matter was that our dog could bark—but seldom did. Miss Hellman's powerful senses of loyalty and justice were instantly mobilized.

"I don't think you hear the Hersey dog," she said.

"Oh, yes," the woman blithely said, "it makes a hell of a racket every morning."

"No," Miss Hellman said, "their dog is exceptionally quiet."

"*Quiet?* It barks all day."

"I think you're mistaken." Any ear but Mrs. Gigglewitz's would have heard the sharpness in the voice.

"I'm not mistaken. It makes a terrible racket."

"Forgive me, Mrs. Gigglewitz, "Miss Hellman then said. "I happen to know that the Hersey dog has been operated on to have its vocal cords removed."

Miss Hellman's powers of invention are fed by her remarkable memory and her ravenous curiosity. Her father once said she lived "within a question mark." She defines culture as "applied curiosity." She is always on what she calls "the find-out kick." How long is that boat? How was this cooked? What year was that? All this questioning is part of her extended youthfulness. More than three decades ago she wrote, and it is still as fresh in her as ever, "If I did not hope to grow, I would not hope to live."

We must come back around the circle now to the rebelliousness, the life-force anger, with which Miss Hellman does live, still growing every day. There was a year of sharp turn toward rebelliousness in her, when she was 13 or 14. By the late 1930s or early '40s, she had realized that no political party would be able to contain this quality of hers. Yet the pepper in her psyche— her touchiness, her hatred of being physically pushed even by accident, her out-of-control anger whenever she feels she has been dealt with unjustly—all have contributed in the end to her being radically political while essentially remaining outside formal politics. Radically, I mean, in the sense of "at the root." She cuts through all ideologies to their taproot; to the decency their adherents universally profess but almost never deliver. "Since when," she has written, "do you have to agree with people to defend them from injustice?" Her response to McCarthyism was not ideological, it was, "I will not do this indecent thing. Go jump in the lake." Richard Nixon has testified under oath that her Committee for Public Justice frightened J. Edgar Hoover into discontinuing illegal wiretaps. How? By shaming.

Lillian Hellman is popular now, and needed now, because her stern code touches the national nerve at just the right moment—after Nixonism . . . before what?

Important as this is, our need for her, as I suggested at the outset, is far larger than that. In her plays, in her writings out of memory, above all in her juicy, resonant, headlong, passionate self, she gives us glimpses of *all* the possibilities of life on this mixed-up earth. In return we can only thank her, honor her, and try to live as wholeheartedly as she does.

She and I share a love of the sea. We fish often together. Coming back in around West Chop in the evening light I sometimes see her standing by the starboard coaming looking across the water. All anger is calm in her then. But there is an intensity in her gaze, almost as if she could see things hidden from the rest of us. What is it? Can she see the years in the waves?

A Woman for All Seasons?   Pauline Kael*

To say that *Julia* is well lighted doesn't do Douglas Slocombe's cinematography exact justice. It's *perfectly* lighted, which is to say, the color is lustrous, the images so completely composed they're almost static—picture postcards of its heroine Lillian Hellman (Jane Fonda) as a national monument. This is conservative—classical humanist—moviemaking, where every detail of meaning is worked out, right down to each flicker of light in the bit players' eyes. The director, Fred Zinnemann, does all the work for you, the way George Stevens did in *A Place in the Sun*. He does it beautifully—and there are very few directors left who know how to do it at all; the younger directors who aspire to this style, such as Alan Pakula or Dick Richards, don't achieve anything like the smoothness of Zinnemann's control, the glide of one sequence to the next. The man who made *From Here to Eternity* and *The Nun's Story* and *The Sundowners* hasn't forgotten his trade. Yet there's a cautiousness and reserve in his control now. Though Zinnemann takes a very romantic view of his two heroines—Lillian and Julia (Vanessa Redgrave)—the film is impersonal, its manner objective. Zinnemann's imagery isn't as inflated as David Lean's; he doesn't hold the frames too long; *Julia* is never ponderous. But this is important-motion-picture land, where every shot is the most beautiful still of the month. *Julia* is romantic in such a studied way that it turns romanticism into a moral lesson.

"Julia," one of the stories in *Pentimento, A Book of Portraits* (1973), Lillian Hellman's second volume of memoirs, is an acccount of how her childhood friend Julia involved her in smuggling fifty thousand dollars into Nazi Germany ("to bribe out many in prison and many who soon will be"). Of the stories in the book, it comes closest to Hellman's plays and scenarios; it's the one most like a movie—specifically, the anti-Nazi adventure movies

*Reprinted from *When the Lights Go Down* by Pauline Kael (New York: Holt, Rinehart & Winston, 1980), 304–10. © 1980 by Pauline Kael. Reprinted by permission of Henry Holt & Company, Inc. This essay originally appeared in the *New Yorker*, 10 October 1977, 94, 99–102.

made in Hollywood in the forties. The author uses the smuggling operation as a suspense mechanism, and as a framework for her recollections about Julia. Zinnemann lets this suspense element slip between his fingers, indifferently, as if it would be vulgar to grip the audience's emotions. The Georges Delerue score is lovely, in Delerue's special, under-orchestrated way, and gives the imagery a reminiscent edge, but *it* doesn't provide suspense, either. Trying to be faithful to Lillian Hellman's recollections, Zinnemann and Alvin Sargent, the screenwriter, construct an ornate superstructure of narration, dissolves, flashbacks spanning decades, and telepathic visions. Yet without suspense this superstructure has no engine inside. The film is all mildly anticipatory; it never reaches a point where you feel "This is it." Sargent has demonstrated his craftsmanship in the past (the most gifted writers sometimes regress to the poetic follies of adolescence, and that probably explains his other Lillian, in *Bobby Deerfield*), and he's really trying this time. There's some shrewd, taut writing, but you can see that he's harnessed. The script fails to draw you in, and the invented scenes of the heroines as young girls are flaccid—a literary form of calendar art, and photographed like *September Morn*. The constraint and inertness must go back to the decision to treat the story as literary history, as a drama of conscience, a parallel to Zinnemann's *A Man for All Seasons*, with Lillian Hellman herself as a legendary figure, and the relationships she has written about—with Dashiell Hammett (Jason Robards), Dorothy Parker (Rosemary Murphy), Alan Campbell (Hal Holbrook), and others—assumed to be common knowledge. Pity the screenwriter impaled on the life of a living person. And Sargent is bound by that person's short account, to which a high degree of art has already been applied. He might have been liberated if he could have changed the names and fictionalized the story; that way, he could have plugged the holes in the material and supplied what's missing in the characters, and some skepticism. But then the film would have lost its air of importance, history, lesson. And, of course, its selling point. What other movie has had its trailer built into an Academy Awards presentation, the way *Julia* did last March, when Jane Fonda made a speech introducing Lillian Hellman, who, head erect, acknowledged a standing ovation?

The film opens with Jane Fonda's recitation of the epigraph to *Pentimento*, a passage about old paint on canvas aging and revealing what was underneath, what was obscured "because the painter 'repented,' changed his mind." Speaking as the elderly Lillian Hellman, she ways, "I wanted to see what was there for me once, what is there for me now." The flashback structure, too, suggests that there will be shifting perspectives, and throughout the movie we wait for the revelation of something lost from sight, displaced, hidden. Yet the narrator also tells us, "I think I have always known about my memory: I know when it is to be trusted . . . I trust absolutely what I remember about Julia." And actually there are no shadings that change, nothing brought up that was painted over, no hint of "repentance." Except for some needed exposition and some filler scenes, the movie limits itself to what the author provides, and her terse style locks her view of the past in place; there's no space for us to enter into it—not even any junk rattling around for us to free-associate with. What, then, is the point of the first quotation? This sort of fidelity—presumably for the sake of a polished, literate tone—fuzzes up whatever chances the film has for clarity in its first, complicated half hour. Lillian's memories of the years shared with Hammett and her efforts to write are interspersed with her memories of Julia, the opening night of *The Children's Hour*, the play that made her famous, and scenes on the train when she's carrying the bribe money across Germany to Berlin. You need to stare at the wigs to locate yourself in time. After a while, it becomes apparent that the filmmakers are trafficking in quotations and too many flashbacks because they can't find the core of the material.

They trust the author's memory, but can *we?* Who can believe in the Julia she describes—the ideal friend of her early youth, the beautiful, unimaginably rich Julia who never fails to represent the highest moonstruck ideals? If ever there was a character preserved in the amber of a girlhood crush, she's it. The gallant, adventurous Julia opens the worlds of art and conscience to the worshipful Lillian. She recites poetry and is incensed at the ugliness of the social injustices perpetrated by her own family; she goes off to study at Oxford, then to medical school in Vienna, intending to work with Freud; she plunges into the dangerous opposition to Hitler, writes letters to Lillian explaining the holocaust to come, and in the middle of it all has a baby. This saintly Freudian Marxist queen, on easy terms with Darwin, Engels, Hegel, and Einstein, might have been a joke with almost anyone but Vanessa Redgrave in the role. Redgrave's height and full figure have an ethereal, storybook wonder, and she uses some of the physical spaciousness that she had on the stage in *The Lady from the Sea;* she can be majestic more fluidly than anyone else (and there's more of her to uncoil). She has a scene all bandaged up in a hospital bed; unable to speak, she points with maybe the most expressive huge hand the screen has ever known. She handles the American accent unnoticeably—it's not that awful flat twang she used for Isadora. In closeups, Vanessa Redgrave has the look of glory, like the young Garbo in Arnold Genthe's portraits; her vibrancy justifies Lillian's saying that she had "the most beautiful face I'd ever seen." Redgrave is so well endowed by nature to play queens that she can act simply in the role (which doesn't occupy much screen time) and casually, yet lyrically, embody Lillian Hellman's dream friend. Zinnemann has very astutely cast as the teen-age Julia a young girl (Lisa Pelikan) who's like a distorted Vanessa Redgrave—a fascinating, dislikable, rather creepy look-alike, who suggests that the intellectual goddess didn't appear out of a white cloud.

It's the dark cloud—Jane Fonda's stubborn strength, in glimpses of her sitting at the typewriter, belting down straight whiskey and puffing out smoke while whacking away at the keys, hard-faced, dissatisfied—that saves the film from being completely pictorial. It's a cloud-of-smoke performance; Bette Davis in all her movies put together couldn't have smoked this much—

and Fonda gets away with it. It's in character. She creates a driven, embattled woman—a woman overprepared to fight back. This woman doesn't have much flexibility. You can see that in the stiff-necked carriage, the unyielding waist, even in the tense, muscular wrists, and in her nervous starts when anything unexpected happens. Her clothes are part of her characterization: Anthea Sylbert, who designed them, must have taken her cue from photographs of the author. These are the clothes of a woman who didn't choose them to be flattering—she chose them with a sense of her position in the world. They're expensive, selected with an eye to drama and to fashion—also not to get in her way. Outfitted in a style that combines elegance and impatience, Jane Fonda catches the essence of the Irving Penn portrait of Lillian Hellman reproduced in her first book of memoirs, *An Unfinished Woman* (1969). When she's alone on the screen, Fonda gives the movie an atmosphere of dissension, and she sustains this discordant aloneness in her scenes with everyone except Julia, with whom she's soft, eager, pliant. Her deliberately humorless Lillian is a formidable, uningratiating woman—her hair sculpted out of the same stone as her face. If you like her, you have to like her on her own implacable terms. How does a viewer separate Jane Fonda's Lillian Hellman from the actual Lillian Hellman? It's impossible to make clear distinctions between the live woman that Jane Fonda draws from (the performance could be called an inspired impersonation), the self-portrait in the story, and the semi-fictionalized activities on the screen. Almost anything one thinks or feels about this character seems an intrusion on a life, yet an intrusion that has been contracted for by Lillian Hellman herself—perhaps somewhat unwittingly.

The story itself has a *submerged* core: all of Hellman's attitudes, everything that goes into her woman's variant of Hemingway-Hammett stripped-down, hardboiled writing. Her prose is strong and clear, and also guarded, reluctant, pried out of a clenched hand. In the kind of situation-centered play Hellman writes, she doesn't give much of herself away. Her memoirs are dramatized, too, yet they're more exciting as drama than her plays are, since you can feel the tension between what she's giving you and what she's withholding. One expects a writer to trust his unconscious, to let go sometimes—not always to be so selective. Lillian Hellman carries thrift and plain American speech to a form of self-denial. The clue to some of the tension in the story "Julia" comes elsewhere in *Pentimento*—in "Turtle," the most compact Hemingway-Hammett story in the book, yet the one that reveals the cost of being hardboiled. In "Turtle," there are only two important characters—Hellman and Hammett, with whom she lived off and on for almost thirty years—and it's evident that for him strong and clear and definite meant masculine, while doubts and unresolved feelings were weak nonsense: feminine. Lillian Hellman tried to write (and to live) in a way that Hammett would approve of; he rejected much of what she actually felt, and she accepted his standards. (The question of why a woman of such strength and, in many ways, of such ruthless honesty should have deferred to the judgment of a man of lesser gifts than her own—that's the sexual mystery that would make a drama.)

The movie is about Hellman's career and doesn't really exist independently of one's knowledge of that career. The friendship between Julia and Lillian is obviously the emotional basis—the original material—for *The Children's Hour*. In that play, scandalmongers spread a sexual rumor about the relationship of two young women teachers, destroying their friendship and their hopes. Here, in *Julia*, Lillian is out drinking in a restaurant with Sammy (John Glover, who shows a nasty vitality, like an American Edward Fox), the brother of a former schoolmate. He says that "the whole world knows about you and Julia," and she slugs him, knocking him back in his chair and then slamming the table over on top of him as she leaves. (People in the theatre applauded.) In the melodramatic Victorian code that is integral to hardboiled writing, the suggestion of homosexuality is a slur—it sullies the purity of the two women's relationship. Only contemptible people—curs like Sammy—think like that. They don't know how to behave; they lack standards. (This was the theme that came out all too nakedly in Hellman's third book of memoirs, the 1976 *Scoundrel Time*.) The failure to look beyond "right" and "wrong" has limited Hellman as a dramatist, and in "Julia" (though not in other stories in *Pentimento*) she thinks in the same terms—judgmentally. "Julia" is an expression of outraged idealism—sexual, political, and in all areas of personal conduct. It is in this story that she shows the beginnings of her own political conscience, started and nurtured, according to her account, by Julia. And it is Julia's dedication to fighting Fascism and her subsequent mutilation and murder that serve as the concrete justification—the personal experience—behind Lillian Hellman's embittered attitude toward those she regards as cowardly or dishonorable. The motive force of the story is that those who have not lived up to her conception of honor stand morally condemned for eternity.

In the film, at the last meeting of Lillian and Julia, in a café near the railroad station in Berlin, Lillian turns over the money she has smuggled in, and Julia says to her, "Are you still as angry as you used to be? I like your anger. . . . Don't you let anyone talk you out of it." There's no way for viewers to understand what Julia is referring to: in their scenes together, Lillian has never demonstrated any anger. Julia has been the daring leader, railing at injustice, going off and doing something about it. Lillian has been the docile follower, the naïf. In the movie version of *A Man for All Seasons*, a respectable job of monument-making, Zinnemann enshrined the martyred Sir Thomas More as a man of conscience; audiences weren't forcibly reminded that what More got himself beheaded for was the belief that the Pope represented divine law. What people could take away from the film was that More stood by his principles and died for them. In *Julia*, it isn't nearly as clear why Lillian is a monumental figure. In the episode of carrying the money to Berlin, she's more of a hazard than anything else; the operation is so efficiently organized and she is supported by such resourceful anti-Nazi underground aides that she hardly seems to be needed at all.

And so it has to be from Lillian's mentors that we get her measure. As Hammett, Robards, who is gruff and funny at the beginning, has nothing to do once the film gets under way—he's just the all-wise, all-knowing Dash standing by, with love. But Dash is there for a reason: he's a judge of writing of such supreme authority—a Sainte-Beuve at the very least—that when he tells Lillian that *The Children's Hour,* which she has just finished, is "the best play anyone's written in a long time," there can be no question about it. Julia is the saintly political activist who certifies Lillian's anger as instinctive morality, and Dash is the stamp of approval that certifies her greatness.

The most difficult thing for an actor to suggest is what goes into making a person an artist—the tensions, the richness. And this is particularly difficult in the case of Lillian Hellman, who doesn't have that richness, and who in her own account makes herself so innocent of intellectual drives that anger seems to be her creative fount. If Julia's last advice to Lillian actually was to hang on to her anger, it was bad advice. Anger blinds Lillian Hellman as a writer. But anger is what holds the story "Julia" together, and the movie doesn't have it. At moments, Jane Fonda supplies something better, because she understands how to embody the explosive Hellman resentment. She gets at what anger does to you. It won't let you relax. It boxes you in: you're on your own. When—as Lillian—she walks into Sardi's on the opening night of her hit, twitching slightly from drunken nervousness, revelling in the attention she's getting while stiffly living up to her own image of herself as the distinguished playwright, you want more of her. You feel that Fonda has the power and invention to go on in this character—that she could crack this smooth, contemplative surface and take us places we've never been to. The film's constraint—its not seizing the moments when she's ready to *go*—is frustrating. Perfectionism has become its own, self-defeating end.

Starring . . . the Writer   Martin Knelman*

In "Turtle," my favorite section of *Pentimento,* Lillian Hellman tells about a remarkable snapper that she and Dashiell Hammett once trapped on her farm in Westchester County. They left its corpse on top of the kitchen stove, waiting to be made into turtle soup the next day. But during the night, with its head attached to its body only by a slender piece of skin, that turtle managed to get down a staircase and up a wall to the garden, where it was found in the morning. Hellman was so shaken by this development that Hammett mockingly referred to it as a religious experience, and they had a memorable battle. Years after both the man and the snapper were dead,

*Excerpted from *Atlantic Monthly* 240 (November 1977):96–98; reprinted by permission of the author.

what was left for Hellman was the echo of what she had said to Hammett four days later. "You understood each other. He was a survivor and so are you. But what about me?"

Lillian Hellman turns out to be the greatest survivor of them all, but she has endured in unexpected ways. . . . Who could have predicted that the glory of Lillian Hellman's career would be not the plays to which she devoted most of her life or even the movies she worked on for money, but the memoirs she wrote when she had more or less retired from the rest? An irony is that, wonderful as the memoirs are, nobody would have wanted to publish them if she hadn't already been famous for something else. And yet perhaps, as V. S. Pritchett has observed, it was her training in the theater that taught her to break up the story of her life into short, strong scenes and to present herself with stunning directness. *The Little Foxes* was carried by the perverse energy of its queen vampire, Regina, played on Broadway by Tallulah Bankhead and on the screen by Bette Davis. But even giving Regina her due, the most unforgettable character Lillian Hellman has ever created is Lillian Hellman, the tenacious, vulnerable, half-Jewish girl from New Orleans, who emerges in the brilliant self-portraits of *An Unfinished Woman* and *Pentimento*.

The transformation of Lillian Hellman into a popular phenomenon is made complete with the arrival of *Julia*, an intense, engaging movie based on a section of *Pentimento*. Jane Fonda's portrayal of her will make Hellman a heroine even to audiences who have never read any of her books or seen any of her plays. But this is not just a slick, commercial entertainment. It's a movie that can be enjoyed by those for whom Lillian Hellman already symbolizes something important. Having reread the "Julia" story and wondered how it would be possible to get a workable script out of it, I take this movie as a happy surprise—a reversal of those cases when you watch a literary property being wrecked in the name of popularity.

It's obvious why *Julia* could be made just now. The times are thought to be right for a strong feminist story: the tough woman is making a comeback in mass culture. In a sense, this is the second time around for the Hellman character. Hammett based Nora Charles in *The Thin Man* on her, and that helped set the popular archetype. Hellman is the literary version of the tough, wisecracking career girls often played by Katharine Hepburn or Carole Lombard, who could compete with men and still be feminine and attractive. Both Jane Fonda, who plays Hellman, and Vanessa Redgrave, who plays Julia, would be drawn to a property that could be not only propaganda for the women's movement but also propaganda for leftwing causes. . . .

For writers who care about what is done to their work, the experience of selling screen rights can be painful. And when you're selling not just the rights to your material but, basically, the rights to your personality, the risks are that much greater. Hellman has been lucky. She is essentially a teller of tales, and Fred Zinnemann, a Hollywood veteran whose strong narrative sense has come through in such films as *The Nun's Story, From Here to*

Eternity, and *Member of the Wedding,* is the ideal director for *Julia.* Although the material sometimes verges on being a little too literary and a little too respectable, Zinnemann makes *Julia* work on its most simple level, as a political thriller, and he gets us involved in the human dimensions of the characters. . . .

The important thing about Hellman as a writer is that you always feel she is telling the truth as she sees it. She is fiercely loyal to the people she cares about, but she doesn't cover up for them, any more than she covers up for herself; you feel she respects them enough to know that the truth can't hurt them. She's still a precocious, temperamental girl who keeps digging away at family secrets, trying to get to the heart of something. And she is not afraid of letting you know what has stayed with her, and how her feelings or her way of seeing has changed. Hellman can be spectacularly wrongheaded, as she was in *Scoundrel Time,* still failing to see, after all these years, that the evils of McCarthyism do not vindicate the follies of the Hollywood Left. It is possible to disagree with her politics and still admire her for behaving with dignity while others were behaving badly—though maybe it would have been better if she had stuck to her earlier resolution, that the only way of dealing with that chapter of her life was to shut up about it.

Jane Fonda has an affinity with the side of Hellman that is passionate, impatient, and stubborn, and she catches it with exciting conviction. This is a highly charged performance; Fonda doesn't grovel or try to turn Lilly into a lovable eccentric. Yet playing a living person whose looks and mannerisms are familiar is much trickier than ordinary acting. One never forgets that one is not watching Hellman, but there are moments when Fonda catches an aspect of her that produces a shock of recognition. If anything, this performance is too uncompromising. Fonda emphazies the bad temper that Hellman writes about, but misses the humorous side that saves the temper from being offensive. In the movie, when Lilly is rude to people, she's really a bit of a monster. . .

Even though she has a starring, title role, Redgrave has precious little screen time, but she is so mesmerizingly radiant, hobbling to a German railway café on crutches, that the whole movie seems steeped in her magic spirit.

Although Lilly slaps a man for suggesting that her relationship with Julia is lesbian, the movie doesn't miss the sexual dimension of the bond between two women who have been close since girlhood. But for the most part, *Julia* avoids the pitfalls of radical feminist agitprop that one might have feared, and even if you're uncomfortable about having sisterhood sold, this movie gets to you. Force of personality in this case gets us over some bad spots in the material; we're willing to overlook it if at times Lilly and Julia are a little too righteous and a little too prescient. . . .

There is a moment in the film, when Lilly and Dash are talking about the difference between sable coats and what really matters, when we're reminded of something else. Some months ago Hellman appeared in a full-page ad in *The New Yorker* draped in a fur coat, with the caption: "What Becomes a Legend Most?" On one level, that ad was appalling. Yet, on another level, there was something magnificently defiant about that face, as deeply grooved as W. H. Auden's, staring out at the world from an ostentatious shell. You could almost hear her cackling, after too many drinks, "Well, why the hell not?"

The question the ad failed to raise explicitly was: "How does a writer become a legend?" Great writing isn't enough to do the trick, though it doesn't necessarily hurt. Beyond that, it takes force of personality and the knack of turning one's own life into a romantic saga. At the end of *Julia*, we see Lilly frozen in time, confronting her past, catching the echoes and glimpses of Dash and Julia that will stay with her for the rest of her life. This is the Hellman who is familiar to readers of *Pentimento*—the fighting old dame of American letters who is still sifting memories, still yelling at old friends and lovers and stubborn maiden aunts, all long dead.

The current notion that gossip is an art form strikes me as nonsense, but what does seem true is that, possibly through the impact of TV, we have become more used to observing the connection between the work and the personality of a writer. Lillian Hellman has the rare gift of dramatizing this connection on the page. Writing about her own life, she has become a literary version of the ideal talk-show guest. Like the turtle that rose from the dead, she has become an icon of survival with honor. It is this emergence of the writer as star personality that the movie celebrates.

Epilogue to Anger   Robert Brustein*

Even in passing, Lillian Hellman engendered controversy—people disputed her age at the time of death. A well-respected playwright and Hollywood screenwriter whose confrontation with the House Un-American Activities Committee in the 1950s was legendary, she survived the penury of the blacklist to establish herself, late in life, in a new career, as the author of a beautifully written series of impressionistic memoirs. This brought renewed fame, wealth, and the respect of the literary community, besides making her a model for independent women everywhere. It also, inevitably, made her the focus of renewed contention. A former friend, Diana Trilling, angered by Hellman's rash imputations regarding her own and her husband Lionel's relation to McCarthyism, wrote a rebuttal in a memoir of her own. Its rejection by the publisher they shared inspired new accusations (denied by Hellman) that she had blocked the book. Others accused her of distortion

*Reprinted from the *New Republic*, 13 and 20 August 1984, 23–25, by permission of the author and the journal.

and misrepresentation. And on the Dick Cavett show, Mary McCarthy delivered her scathing judgment that Lillian had never written a truthful word in her life, including "and" and "the." This brought a libel suit in response.

Previously characterized by enemies as a fellow traveler who continued to embrace Stalinism long after most other American intellectuals had abandoned it, Lillian was now being called a liar and a bully. Herself a victim of blacklisting, she was now thought to be engaged in muffling the free expression of others, leading some to say that she embraced the First Amendment only in her own defense. It was a miserable epilogue to what should have been a respected old age. Although she continued to be an inspiration to the radical young and gifted women (Marsha Norman was among those who testified to Lillian's seminal influence on her playwriting), she was embroiled at the end in bitter quarrels and troublesome litigation with dozens of people, many of them former friends.

Much as they saddened those who loved her, these broils, I believe, are what kept her alive. Stricken first by blindness, and then—chain-smoking to the end—by emphysema, heart attacks, paralysis, a stroke, and the loss of her dearest friend and close companion Hannah Weinstein, Lillian Hellman was dying for over four years, fighting death with mounting rage and determination. Her friends watched her grow frailer and feebler from month to month, fearing that each would be her last; yet every June she returned to Martha's Vineyard after a winter of illness to hold a joint birthday party with John Hersey and Kingman Brewster, even though she had to be carried into the house, placed in a chair, and fed her food. Two years ago her pacemaker popped out of her chest—by this time her skin had become like papier-mâché—but before it could be replaced she had to have carotid arteries operated on in her throat. She was now anorexic and nearly died from malnutrition, a bedridden Job imprisoned inside a broken bag of bones; yet a day before the operation she insisted on putting on some makeup, leaving the hospital, and cooking two geese for a friend's dinner in Boston.

She hated death; she defied it, and she kept it at bay through blind fury. I had an image of her blood congealing, and then set coursing through her veins again by means of her reaction to some new outrage, real or invented. She quarreled with everyone, often over the most trivial issue—she broke with Bill Styron for an entire summer in a dispute over the proper way to cook a ham. She even had a quarrel with her "adopted son," Peter Feibleman, the mildest of men, whom she had known and loved for forty-three years. In a touching graveside eulogy, Feibleman reported the opinions of her nurse: "This lady is half-paralyzed; she's legally blind; she's having rage attacks that are a result of strokes; she has no way of stopping. She says things to people she doesn't necessarily mean and then she regrets them. She cries at night; she can't help that. She can't eat. She can't sleep. She can't walk. . . . I think, frankly, she's dying" (to which Lillian added, when asked how she was feeling, "Not good, Peter. . . . This is the worst case of writer's block I ever had").

But the rages which the nurse attributed to her physical condition, her closest male friend, John Hersey, interpreted as "a rage of the mind against all kinds of injustice—against human injustice and the unfairness of death." Before the onset of pain and illness, her anger was more focused; after, it became a free-floating, cloud-swollen tempest that rained on friend and foe alike.

But throughout her life, even near the end, she remained the most hospitable of women, the most gracious of friends. An inspired cook, though she barely tasted her own dishes, she loved to see her guests well fed (another birthday party had been scheduled and postponed just days before she died). It was this almost maternal preoccupation with nourishment which attracted you regardless of political differences or momentary conflicts; and, anyway, her opinions were really irrelevant to her friendship, except as a pretext to start a fight. (The conservative columnist Joseph Alsop was one of her oldest comrades.) For this reason, I guess, I never took Lillian's politics very seriously, and was always amazed when people, particularly American intellectuals still waging fifty-year-old wars, treated her as a dangerous political thinker.

Lillian's opinions were a channel for her feisty, sharp, satiric nature; I think she was more interested in personalities than issues. Lillian liked nothing better than to fish, and, while sitting in the boat with her line on the bottom waiting for a fluke to bite or a rock bass, to gossip about the frailties of acquaintances. She responded to warmth and thoughtfulness with the gratitude of a childless woman who invested all her emotions in friends, but she went straight to someone's weaknesses with the eye of a peregrine falcon pouncing on a sparrow. What her enemies saw were the envenomed talons, not the warm heart. "Forgive me," she would always say, before discharging an eloquent fusillade of contradiction concerning some innocent remark by one of her guests. But I think she truly wanted forgiveness for whatever wounds her opinionated nature inflicted.

As a playwright, Lillian wrote eight original dramas and four adaptations, before abandoning the stage in the early '60s. Although none are of the first rank, at least three, I believe, have a permanent place in American drama: *Toys in the Attic, The Autumn Garden,* and of course *The Little Foxes.* Skillfully constructed and nailed together with strong scenes, crisp dialogue, and powerful characters, Lillian's theater was fashioned largely under the influence of Ibsen, an unvarnished tribute to contemporary social realism. Like Ibsen, she believed the drama to have a function beyond mere entertainment—that it could be a vehicle for social commentary, psychological insight, and, above all, sharp incisions into the diseased body of a corrupted society. Later in her playwriting career, Lillian made a conscientious effort to loosen up her style—hitherto as carefully arranged as her impeccable coiffure—by employing the more indirect, apparently plotless techniques of Chekhov. But she never wavered in her conviction that theater could be a force for change in what she considered an unethical, unjust, essentially venal world.

Lillian's major theatrical subject was money, how it is made, how it changes lives, what people will do to acquire it. Money, in fact, is usually an additional shadow character in her plays, often the most important one. It can function symbolically, but it also has a tangible, concrete, almost organic nature—in *Toys in the Attic,* money is stroked as if it were a domestic animal. Lillian sometimes seemed to divide the world according to how people's loyalties and values were affected by money (though she loved money herself and usually maintained a sneaking admiration for her villains); this led critics to accuse her of being a melodramatist. It is true that her plays, in the tradition of melodrama, often seem to be confrontations between good and evil, paralleling the passionate friendships and bitter enmities of her life. Her capacity for friendship, in fact, was probably the force that originally drew her to the stage, the most collective of all the arts, just as her quarrels and disappointments eventually repelled her from it. Fiercely loyal herself, she could not abide disloyalty in others. And it may be that her life, with its strong alliances, combative courage, and abrupt domestic scenes, will eventually be considered her greatest theater.

She had died on the downside of her reputation, feeling herself under siege in a society where recognition and respect are always being tossed about by the winds of fashion. "Dear Lillian," said John Hersey at her funeral in a hillside cemetery in Chilmark, "you are a finished woman, now." The bitterness was quenched, the physical pain, the mental anguish, over. Her capacity for anger, about which almost everyone spoke, had hurt herself and others at the end, but it had been a more accurate weapon once, at times a fresh and liberating force. "Jonathan Swift has sailed into his rest," wrote W. B. Yeats about another irascible literary figure, "Savage indignation there / Cannot lacerate his breast." One wishes the same peace for Lillian Hellman, but many of us will surely miss that reckless heart, that wild, cantankerous tongue.

INDEX

Feibleman, Peter, 261–62: *Lilly: Reminiscences of Lillian Hellman*, 9–10

Felheim, Marvin, *The Autumn Garden:* Mechanics and Dialectics, 49–53

feminism, 91–92, 96, 98, 107–8, 259; *see also* Hellman and feminism; women characters

Fifth Amendment, 211–12

Finnish resistance, 92, 151, 223

Fitzgerald, F. Scott, 87, 177

flashback, 66, 67

Fleischer, Leonard and Doris: "The Dramatic Adaptations of Lillian Hellman," 5, 55–64

Fonda, Jane, 253, 254–55, 257, 258, 259

Fortas, Abe, 135, 212

Franco, Francisco, 92, 164; *see also* fascism; Spanish Civil War

Frankfurter, Justice Felix, 146

Fremont-Smith, Eliot, 17

French, Philip, 18

Freud, Sigmund, and Freudianism, 13, 191, 192, 193, 207, 208

Fry, Christopher, 5, 63n6, 64–71

Gandhi, Mahatma, 80

Gardiner, Muriel, 190–92, 193, 196, 205, 207; *Code Name "Mary"*, 191, 196, 205, 206, 208

Gassner, John, 8, 13

Gellhorn, Martha: "Close Encounters of the Apocryphal Kind," 16, 17, 175–90, 196, 199, 206

Genet, Jean, 246

Gide, André, 243

Glazer, Nathan, 17, 165

Goddard, Paulette, 238

Goldwater, Senator Barry, 142

Goldwyn, Samuel, 229, 249

Goleman, Daniel, 210

Goodman, Walter, 18

Gornick, Vivian, 17, 18

gossip, 2, 5

Gray, Paul, 17

Great Depression, 90

Greene, Graham, 10

Grossman, Anita Susan, 18

Group Theater, 91

Gulag Archipelago, 153, 160

Gussow, Mel, 12

HCUA. See HUAC

H. D., 192–93, 208; *Bid Me to Live*, 208; *Tribute to Freud*, 193

HUAC, 14–15, 117–18, 124, 134–36, 137, 139–42, 144–47, 150, 163, 167–68, 171, 172–74, 198, 209–10, 211–13, 235, 237, 247, 250; *see also* McCarthy, Joseph

Hammett, Dashiell, 18, 19, 79, 116–17, 122, 126, 129, 131, 132–33, 134, 137, 144, 145, 156, 157, 158, 171, 172, 173, 174, 177, 199–200, 225, 226, 228, 229, 230–31, 236, 238, 239–40, 242, 243–44, 246–47, 250, 257, 258; *The Maltese Falcon*, 242; *The Thin Man*, 174, 200, 208, 238, 239, 244, 258; *see also* Hellman and Hammett

Hammond, Percy, 10

Hardwick, Elizabeth, 12, 245

Harriman, Margaret Case, 202; "Miss Lily of New Orleans," 19, 219–29

Harris, Julie, 65

Hayes, Richard, 13

Heidegger, Martin, 204

Heilman, Robert, 14

Heisenberg's principle of indeterminacy, 123, 128n12

"Helen," 133

HELLMAN, Lillian: and accidents, 200–201, 205, 210; anger of, 210–11, 213, 257, 260–63; as autobiographer, 14–18, 115–39, 194–214; childhood of, 221–22; and comedy, 6–7; and communism, 9, 14–15, 90, 93–94, 141, 143–44, 151–65; 209–13, 223; "coolness" of, 116, 126, 128n14, 129, 200–202; and critics, 8–18; as director, 2; and evil, 5–7, 11; femininity of, 116–20, 202; and feminism, 3, 15, 91–92, 99; and films, 9; geographical sense of, 202, 205, 219–20, 249; and Hammett, 18, 19, 116, 126, 132–33, 134, 144, 158, 173, 230–31, 236, 238, 242–44, 250, 255–56; life of, 219–30; marriage of, 116, 224; and melodrama, 3–4, 7, 11; and men, 116–17, 118, 228; and moral commitment, 7–8, 10, 11, 14, 250; persona of, 18–21, 219–63; as political dramatist, 90–112, 241; rebelliousness of, 248; and sentimentality, 5–6, 246; and sex, 119–20, 248; in Spain, 181–89, 200–201; and theater, 1, 2–14, 234, 240–41, 244–46, 263; theatrical tricks of, 3–4; and the well-made play, 3, 5, 9, 10, 13, 14; as woman playwright, 2–3, 219; as writer, 117, 226–27, 233–34, 236, 240, 244, 245–46, 259

WORKS: AUTOBIOGRAPHY AND MEMOIR
Maybe, 15, 18, 115, 118–22, 124–27, 130–39, 197, 214

for Measure, 78; *Merchant of Venice,* 74, 81
Shaw, George Bernard, 13, 33
Shepard, Sam, 9, 109
Sherrill, Robert, 17
Shostakovich, Dmitri, 143
Shumlin, Herman, 223, 224, 225, 228
Sidgwick, Henry: "Classification of Duties—Veracity," 211
Simon, John, 17
Skouras, Spyros, 140
Slotkin, Richard: *Regeneration through Violence,* 169
Smith Act, 156, 159
social Darwinism, 98, 100, 105–6
socialism. *See* communism; Marxism
Socialist Worker's Party, 144, 173
Solzhenitsyn, Alexander, 170
Sophocles, 12. *Oedipus,* 40
southern aristocracy, 96, 98–100, 105–6
Soviet army, 1
Spacks, Patricia Meyer, 17, 80, 115–16; *The Female Imagination,* 139
Spanish Civil War, 1, 177, 181–89
Spanish Earth, The, 21n9, 92, 176–77, 180
Spectator, 10
Spender, Stephen, 193, 194, 196, 208–9; *Journals,* 206–7
Spengemann, William, 128
Spivak, Gayatri Chakravorty, 204
Stalin, Joseph and Stalinism, 94, 95, 154, 159–60, 163, 164–65, 209, 211, 261; *see also* communism; Hellman and communism; Marxism
Stander, Lionel, 145
Stein, Gertrude, 238; *Autobiography of Alice B. Toklas,* 139, 196, 199
Steiner, Herbert, 191–92
Strindberg, August, 11
Styron, William, 261
suicide, 34
suspense, 98–99
Szogyi, Alex, 14

TLS, 17
Taylor, Alexander, 11
Taylor, Elizabeth, 12
Taylor, John Russell: *The Rise and Fall of the Well-Made Play,* 31
Terkel, Studs, 171
Terry, Megan, 109
Theroux, Paul, 17
These Three, 21n9

Thompson, Dorothy, 220–21; *Another Sun,* 221
Three, 15, 17, 134, 136, 194, 197, 203, 210–11, 213
Time, 11, 14–15, 141–42
Tischler, Nancy M., 14
Toklas, Alice B., 238; *What Is Remembered,* 214
Towers, Robert, 18
Toys in the Attic, 4, 5, 7, 13, 35, 37, 38, 41, 43–49, 87–89, 93, 95, 97, 262, 263
translation, problem of, 64–65
Triesch, Manfred: *The Lillian Hellman Collection at the University of Texas,* 8
Trilling, Diana, 165, 196–97, 260; *We Must March My Darlings,* 18, 170–72
Trilling, Lionel, 163, 170, 174
Trotsky, Leon, 144
Truman, Harry, 161, 171
"Turtle," 132–33, 134, 257–58
Twentieth Century Fox, 140

Unfinished Woman, An, 2, 8, 14, 15, 16, 17, 18, 79, 115, 117, 119, 121, 122, 129–31, 176, 179, 180, 183, 184, 185, 186, 187, 188–89, 193, 198–202, 204, 205, 208, 250, 255
United Front, 93

van Itallie, Jean-Claude, 109
victim-victimizer syndrome, 74, 76
Vietnam War, 167, 169, 172
villains, 94–95, 96; *see also* evil
Vultures, The (Becque), 48

Wagner Act, 229
Wagner-Martin, Linda: "Lillian Hellman: Autobiography and Truth," 15–16, 128–39
Wallace, Henry, 143, 157–58, 168, 175
Warren, Frank: *Liberals and Communism,* 210
Washington Post, 17
Watch on the Rhine, 3, 7, 12, 34–35, 36, 37, 38, 39–40, 41, 56, 92–94, 146, 174, 205, 207, 220, 226, 241
Watergate, 169, 172
Watts, Richard, Jr., 11
Weeks, Edward, 17
Weinstein, Hannah, 261
"well-made" play, 3, 5, 10, 11, 40, 41, 48, 50, 51, 102; *see also* Hellman and the well-made play

CONTRIBUTORS

This list includes contributors for whom information is currently available.

TIMOTHY DOW ADAMS, associate professor of English at West Virginia University, is associate editor of *A/B: Autobiography Studies*. He is the author of *Telling Lies: Lying in Modern American Autobiography*, scheduled for publication in 1990 by the University of North Carolina Press. His essays on Austen, Melville, Hawthorne, Wright, and others have appeared in *ESQ, Critique, Prose Studies, Mosaic, Biography*, and elsewhere.

JACOB H. ADLER is professor of English at Purdue University. His work on Hellman includes "The Rose and the Fox: Notes on the Southern Drama," in *South: Modern Southern Literature in the Cultural Setting*, ed. Louis D. Rubin, Jr., and Robert D. Jacobs (1961); *Lillian Hellman* (1969); "Modern Southern Drama," in *The History of Southern Literature*, ed. Louis D. Rubin, Jr., et al. (1985); and "Lillian Hellman," in *Fifty Southern Writers since 1900*, ed. Joseph M. Flora and Robert Bain (1987).

MARY LYNN BROE is Louise R. Noun Professor of Women's Studies and English at Grinnell College. She is the author of *Protean Poetic: The Poetry of Sylvia Plath* (1980), editor of *Silence and Power: A Revaluation of Djuna Barnes* (1989), coeditor with Angela Ingram of *Women's Writing in Exile* (1989), and coauthor of *Cold Comfort: Selected Letters of Djuna Barnes* (forthcoming from Random House).

PAMELA S. BROMBERG is associate professor of English and chair of that department at Simmons College. Her recent publications include essays on Drabble, Atwood, and Blake.

ROBERT BRUSTEIN is artistic director and founder of the American Repertory Theatre and director of the Loeb Drama Center at Harvard University, where he is professor of English. He is the drama critic of the *New Republic* and the author of seven books, including *The Theatre of Revolt* (1964), *Critical Moments* (1980), *Making Scenes* (1981), and *Who Needs Theatre* (1987). His essays have appeared in *Harper's*, the *Atlantic*, the *New York Times*, the *Partisan Review*, the *New York Review of Books*, and elsewhere.

ALEXANDER COCKBURN is an editor and journalist who has contributed essays to the *Nation*, the *Atlantic*, the *New York Review of Books*, the *Village Voice*, and other journals. He is coauthor of *Smoke: Another Jimmy Carter Adventure* (1978) and editor of *Political Ecology* (1979) and other books.

MARK W. ESTRIN is professor of English and director of the Film Studies Program at Rhode Island College. His books include *Lillian Hell-*

man: Plays, Films, Memoirs (1980) and *Conversations with Eugene O'Neill,* which he is editing for the University Press of Mississippi. His essays on Hellman, Pinter, Rabe, Lowell, Hitchcock, and others have appeared in *Modern Drama, Literature/Film Quarterly, The Journal of Narrative Technique, Contemporary Dramatists, The International Dictionary of Films and Filmmakers,* and elsewhere.

RICHARD A. FALK is Milbank Professor of International Law and Practice at Princeton University. His extensive writings include *Law, Morality, and War in the Contemporary World* (1963), *The Status of Law in International Society* (1970), *This Endangered Planet* (1971), *A Global Approach to National Policy* (1975), and *Reviving the World Court* (1986).

DORIS ZAMES FLEISCHER teaches humanities at New Jersey Institute of Technology. She holds a doctorate in English and American literature from New York University.

LEONARD FLEISCHER, manager of contributions at Exxon Corporation, is a member of the board of the Foundation of the Dramatists Guild. His essays and reviews have appeared in *Contemporary Dramatists, Saturday Review, Midstream,* and elsewhere. He holds a doctorate in English and American literature from New York University and has taught dramatic literature at several universities. He is a member of the Nominating Committee for Broadway's Tony Awards.

MARTHA GELLHORN is the author of numerous novels, short stories, and essay collections, including *The Face of War* (1959; rpt. 1988), based on her coverage of World War II and wars in Spain, Finland, and China during her years as war correspondent for *Collier's Weekly.* Her novels, several recently reprinted in Penguin editions, include *A Stricken Field* (1940; rpt. 1986) and *Liana* (1944; rpt. 1987). Her most recent collection of essays is *The View from the Ground* (1988).

MARGARET CASE HARRIMAN wrote numerous profiles for the *New Yorker,* fourteen of which were collected in *Take Them Up Tenderly* (1944). Her other books include *The Vicious Circle: The Story of the Algonquin Round Table* (1951) and *Blessed Are the Debonair* (1956). She died in 1966.

JOHN HERSEY is the author of many books of fiction and nonfiction and has written essays and short stories for such journals as the *New Yorker,* the *Atlantic,* and *Harper's.* His books include the Pulitzer Prize–winning *A Bell for Adano* (1944), *Hiroshima* (1946), *The War Lover* (1959), *The Writer's Craft* (1974), *The President* (1975), and *The Call* (1985).

SIDNEY HOOK is senior research fellow at the Hoover Institution and professor of philosophy emeritus at New York University. His extensive writings include *The Metaphysics of Pragmatism* (1927), *From Hegel to Marx* (1936), *Marx and the Marxists* (1955), *Pragmatism and the Tragic Sense of*

Life (1974), *Revolution, Reform and Social Justice* (1975), and the autobiography *Out of Step: An Unquiet Life in the 20th Century* (1987).

PAULINE KAEL, since 1968 the movie critic at the *New Yorker,* is the author of numerous essays and books on film, including *I Lost It at the Movies* (1965); *Kiss Kiss Bang Bang* (1968); *Deeper into Movies,* for which she won a National Book Award in Arts and Letters (1973); *Reeling* (1976); *State of the Art* (1985); and *Hooked* (1989).

ALFRED KAZIN is distinguished professor of English emeritus at the City University of New York Graduate Center. His extensive writings include *On Native Grounds* (1942), *A Walker in the City* (1951), *Starting Out in the Thirties* (1965), *New York Jew* (1978), *An American Procession* (1984), and *A Writer's America: Landscape in Literature* (1988).

MURRAY KEMPTON is a journalist and columnist for *Newsday* whose essays have appeared in a wide variety of periodicals. His books include *Part of Our Time* (1955) and the National Book Award–winning *The Briar Patch* (1973).

MARTIN KNELMAN is film critic and entertainment columnist for *Toronto Life* and a contributing editor at *Saturday Night.* His books include *A Stratford Tempest* (1982) and *Home Movies: Tales from the Canadian Film World* (1987).

HENRY W. KNEPLER is professor of English at Illinois Institute of Technology. He is coauthor of *A Range of Writing* (1959) and *What Is the Play?* (1967) and author of *The Gilded Stage* (1968) and *Man about Paris* (1970).

LINDA WAGNER-MARTIN is Hanes Professor of English at the University of North Carolina, Chapel Hill. Her recent books include *Sylvia Plath: A Biography* (1987) and *Critical Essays on Anne Sexton* (1989), one of several volumes she has edited for G. K. Hall's Critical Essays on American Literature series.

TIMOTHY J. WILES is associate professor of English at Indiana University. He has published articles on O'Neill, Buchner, Gombrowicz, and Witkiewicz and is the author of *The Theater Event: Modern Theories of Performance* (1980). He is currently completing a book on contemporary American playwrights.